Optimization Modeling
with Spreadsheets

Optimization Modeling with Spreadsheets

Second Edition

Kenneth R. Baker

Tuck School of Business, Dartmouth College, Hanover, NH

A JOHN WILEY & SONS, INC. PUBLICATION

Published by John Wiley & Sons, Inc., Hoboken, New Jersey
Published simultaneously in Canada

For general information on our other products and services or for technical support, please contact our Customer Care Department within the United States at (800) 762-2974, outside the United States at (317) 572-3993 or fax (317) 572-4002.

Wiley also publishes its books in variety of electronic formats. Some content that appears in print may not be available in electronic formats. For more information about Wiley products, visit our web site at www.wiley.com.

Library of Congress Cataloging-in-Publication Data:

Baker, Kenneth R., 1943-
   Optimization modeling with spreadsheets/Kenneth R. Baker. — 2nd ed.
      p. cm.
   Includes bibliographical references and index.
   ISBN 978-0-470-92863-9 (cloth)
  1. Mathematical optimization.   2.   Managerial economics–Mathematical models.
3. Electronic spreadsheets.   4.   Programming (Mathematics).   I.   Title.
   HB143.7.B35 2011
   005.54--dc22

                                                                2010036840
Printed in the United States

10   9   8   7   6   5   4   3   2

Table of Contents

6. Integer Programming: Binary Choice Models   **211**

7. Integer Programming: Logical Constraints   **251**

8. Nonlinear Programming   **297**

9. Heuristic Solutions with the Evolutionary Solver   337

Appendices

1. Optimization Software and Supplemental Files   375

2. Graphical Methods in Linear Programming   377

Preface

This is an introductory textbook on optimization—that is, on mathematical programming—intended for undergraduates and graduate students in management or engineering. The principal coverage includes linear programming, nonlinear programming, integer programming, and heuristic programming; and the emphasis is on model building using Excel and Solver.

The emphasis on model building (rather than algorithms) is one of the features that makes this book distinctive. Most textbooks devote more space to algorithmic details than to formulation principles. These days, however, it is not necessary to know a great deal about algorithms in order to apply optimization tools, especially when relying on the spreadsheet as a solution platform.

The emphasis on spreadsheets is another feature that makes this book distinctive. Few textbooks devoted to optimization pay much attention to spreadsheet implementation of optimization principles, and most books that emphasize model building ignore spreadsheets entirely. Thus, someone looking for a spreadsheet-based treatment would otherwise have to use a textbook that was designed for some other purpose, like a survey of management science topics, rather than one devoted to optimization.

WHY MODEL BUILDING?

The model building emphasis is an attempt to be realistic about what business and engineering students need most when learning about optimization. At an introductory level, the most practical and motivating theme is the wide applicability of optimization tools. To apply optimization effectively, the student needs more than a brief exposure to a series of numerical examples, which is the way that most mathematical programming books treat applications. With a systematic modeling emphasis, the student can begin to see the basic structures that appear in optimization models and as a result, develop an appreciation for potential applications well beyond the examples presented in the text.

Formulating optimization models is both an art and a science, and this book pays attention to both. The art can be refined with practice, especially supervised practice, just the way a student would learn sculpture or painting. The science is reflected in the structure that organizes the topics in this book. For example, there are several distinct problem types that lend themselves to linear programming formulations, and it makes sense to study these types systematically. In that spirit, the book builds a library of templates against which new problems can be compared. Analogous structures are developed for the presentation of other topics as well.

WHY SPREADSHEETS?

Now that optimization tools have been made available with spreadsheets (i.e., with Excel), every spreadsheet user is potentially a practitioner of optimization techniques. No longer do practitioners of optimization constitute an elite, highly trained group of quantitative specialists who are well versed in computer software, or their former professor's own code. Now, anyone who builds a spreadsheet model can call on optimization techniques, and can do so without the need to learn about specialized software. The basic optimization tool, in the form of Excel's Standard Solver, is now as readily available as the spellchecker. So why not raise modeling ability up to the level of software access? Let's not pretend that most users of optimization tools will be inclined to shop around for matrix generators and industrial-strength "solvers" if they want to produce numbers. More likely, they will be drawn to Excel.

Students using this book can take advantage of an even more powerful software package called Risk Solver Platform (RSP) that was developed by the creators of Excel's built-in Standard Solver. The educational version of RSP is available at no cost (see Appendix 1), and it introduces students to the capabilities of a sophisticated optimization package. Although this book is not organized as a user's manual, it nevertheless provides most of the information the student needs to become a sophisticated user of RSP.

WHAT'S SPECIAL?

Mathematical programming techniques have been invented and applied for more than half a century, so by now they represent a relatively mature area of applied mathematics. There is not much new that can be said in an introductory textbook regarding the underlying concepts. The innovations in this book can be found instead in the delivery and elaboration of certain topics, making them accessible and understandable to the novice. The most distinctive of these features are as follows.

- The major topics are not illustrated merely with a series of numerical examples. Instead, the chapters introduce a classification for the problem types. An early example is the organization of basic linear programming models in Chapter 2 along the lines of allocation, covering, and blending models. This classification strategy, which extends throughout the book, helps the student to see beyond the particular examples to the breadth of possible applications.

- Network models are a special case of linear programming models. If they are singled out for special treatment at all in optimization books, they are defined by a strict requirement for mass balance. Here, in Chapter 3, network models are presented in a broader framework, which allows for a more general form of mass balance, thereby extending the reader's capability for recognizing and analyzing network problems.

- Interest has been growing in Data Envelopment Analysis (DEA), a special kind of linear programming application. Although some books illustrate DEA with a single example, this book provides a systematic introduction to the topic by providing a patient, comprehensive treatment in Chapter 5.

- Analysis of an optimization problem does not end when the computer displays the numbers in an optimal solution. Finding a solution must be followed with a meaningful interpretation of the results, especially if the optimization model was built to serve a client. An important framework for interpreting linear programming solutions is the identification of patterns, which is discussed in detail in Chapter 4.

- The topic of heuristic programming has evolved somewhat outside the field of optimization. Although a variety of specialized heuristic approaches have been developed, generic software has seldom been available. Now, however, the advent of the evolutionary solver in Solver and RSP brings heuristic programming alongside linear and nonlinear programming as a generic software tool for pursuing optimal decisions. The evolutionary solver is covered in Chapter 9.

- The topic of stochastic programming has been of interest to researchers for quite a while but promises to become a factor in applications now that the latest versions of RSP contain such capabilities as the solution of stochastic programs with recourse. Appendix 4 provides an introduction to this topic area and a glimpse of how to use RSP to solve problems of this type.

Beyond these specific innovations, as this book goes to print, there is no optimization textbook exclusively devoted to model building rather than algorithms that relies on the spreadsheet platform. The reliance on spreadsheets and on a model-building emphasis is the most effective way to bring optimization capability to the many users of Excel.

THE AUDIENCE

This book is aimed at management students and secondarily engineering students. In business curricula, a course focused on optimization is viable in two situations. If there is no required introduction to Management Science at all, then the treatment of Management Science at the elective level is probably best done with specialized courses on deterministic and probabilistic models. This book is an ideal text for a first course dedicated to deterministic models. If instead there is a required introduction to Management Science, chances are that the coverage of optimization glides by so quickly that even the motivated student is left wanting more detail, more concepts and more practice. This book is also well suited to a second-level course that delves specifically into mathematical programming applications.

In engineering curricula, it is still typical to find a full course on optimization, usually as the first course on (deterministic) modeling. Even in this setting, though, traditional textbooks tend to leave it to the student to seek out spreadsheet approaches to the topic, while covering the theory and perhaps encouraging students to write code for algorithms. This book will capture the energies of students by covering what they would be spending most of their time doing in the real world—building and solving optimization problems on spreadsheets.

This book has been developed around the syllabi of two courses at Dartmouth College that have been delivered for several years. One course is a second-year elective for MBA students who have had a brief, previous exposure to optimization during a required core course that surveyed other analytic topics. A second course is a required course for Engineering Management students in a graduate program at the interface between business and engineering. These students have had no formal exposure to spreadsheet modeling, although some may previously have taken a survey course in Operations Research. Thus, the book is appropriate for students who are about to study optimization with only a brief, or even nonexistent exposure to the subject.

ACKNOWLEDGEMENTS

I can trace the roots of this book to my collaboration with Steve Powell in teaching and writing. Using spreadsheets to teach optimization is part of a broader activity in which Steve has been an active and inspiring leader. Were it not for his professional companionship, this book would not have been undertaken. Other authors have been successful in creating spreadsheet-based approaches to familiar topics in Management Science, yet there was much for me to learn about writing effective text material. For their suggestions and guidance, I particularly thank my reviewers on the first edition, Jiu Ding, A. Thomas Mason, James G. Morris, James Pratt, Paul Savory, and Wilbert E. Wilhelm. In addition, Rich Metters, Clay Whybark, Alan Neebe, and Kusum Ailawadi graciously supported my adaptations of their original case material and extended their support to the second edition. Two department chairs, Ron Askin and Asoo Vakharia, generously hosted my short stays in their departments during the development of the first edition. Scott Webster class-tested the first versions of the book and provided a careful and patient accuracy check while suggesting several improvements. Curt Hinrichs, my original editor, orchestrated the initial cycles of review, refinement, and improvement that led to the publication of the first edition. Another very helpful influence has been the feedback from my students at the Tuck School and the Thayer School. Rather than list their names here, I've acknowledged them indirectly throughout the book.

The main technical change in the second edition is the use of Risk Solver Platform, and I am indebted to Dan Fylstra and Edwin Straver at Frontline Systems for being responsive to my queries as they focused on the introduction of an excellent new product. As the second edition comes to fruition, I wish to thank my current editor, Susanne Steitz-Filler, for providing the opportunity to refine and update my work and ultimately to reach out to a new and broader audience.

Chapter 1

Introduction to Spreadsheet Models for Optimization

This is a book about optimization with an emphasis on building models and using spreadsheets. Each facet of this theme—models, spreadsheets, and optimization—has a role in defining the emphasis of our coverage.

A *model* is a simplified representation of a situation or problem. Models attempt to capture the essential features of a complicated situation so that it can be studied and understood more completely. In the worlds of business, engineering, and science, models aim to improve our understanding of practical situations. Models can be built with tangible materials, or words, or mathematical symbols and expressions. A *mathematical model* is a model that is constructed—and also analyzed—using mathematics. In this book, we focus on mathematical models. Moreover, we work with *decision models*, or models that contain representations of decisions. The term also refers to models that support decision-making activities.

A *spreadsheet* is a row-and-column layout of text, numerical data, and logical information. The spreadsheet version of a model contains the model's elements, linked together by specific logical information. Electronic spreadsheets, like those built using Microsoft Excel®, have become familiar tools in the business, engineering, and scientific worlds. Spreadsheets are relatively easy to understand, and people often rely on spreadsheets to communicate their analyses. In this book, we focus on the use of spreadsheets to represent and analyze mathematical models.

This text is written for an audience that already has some familiarity with Excel. Our coverage assumes a level of facility with Excel comparable to a beginner's level. Someone who has used other people's spreadsheets and built simple spreadsheets for some purpose—either personal or organizational—has probably developed this skill level. Box 1.1 describes the Excel skill level assumed. Readers without this level of background are encouraged to first work through some introductory materials, such as the books by McFedries (1) and Reding and Wermers (2).

Optimization is the process of finding the best values of the variables for a particular criterion or, in our context, the best decisions for a particular measure of performance. The elements of an optimization problem are a set of decisions, a criterion, and

BOX 1.1 *Excel Skills Assumed as Background for this Book*

Navigating in workbooks, worksheets, and windows.
Using the cursor to select cells, rows, columns, and noncontiguous cell ranges.
Entering text and data; copying and pasting; filling down or across.
Formatting cells (number display, alignment, font, border, and protection).
Editing cells (using the formula bar and cell-edit capability [F2]).
Entering formulas and using the function wizard.
Using relative and absolute addresses.
Using range names.
Creating charts and graphs.

perhaps a set of required conditions, or *constraints*, that the decisions must satisfy. These elements lend themselves to description in a mathematical model. The term optimization sometimes refers specifically to a procedure that is implemented by software. However, in this book, we expand that perspective to include the model-building process as well as the process of finding the best decisions.

Not all mathematical models are optimization models. Some models merely describe the logical relationship between inputs and outputs. Optimization models are a special kind of model in which the purpose is to find the best value of a particular output measure and the choices that produce it. Optimization problems abound in the real world, and if we're at all ambitious or curious, we often find ourselves seeking solutions to those problems. Business firms are very interested in optimization because making good decisions helps a firm run efficiently, perform profitably, and compete effectively. In this book, we focus on optimization problems expressed in the form of spreadsheet models and solved using a spreadsheet-based approach.

1.1. ELEMENTS OF A MODEL

To restate our premise, we are interested in mathematical models. Specifically, we are interested in two forms—algebraic and spreadsheet models. In the former, we use algebraic notation to represent elements and relationships, and in the latter, we use spreadsheet entries and structure. For example, in an algebraic statement, we might use the variable x to represent a quantitative decision, and we might use some function $f(x)$ to represent the measure of performance that results from choosing decision x. Then we might adopt the letter z to represent a criterion for decision making and construct the equation $z = f(x)$ to guide the choice of a decision. Algebra is the basic language of analysis largely because it is precise and compact.

As an introductory modeling example, let's consider the price decision in the scenario of Example 1.1.

EXAMPLE 1.1   *Price, Demand, and Profit*

Our firm's production department has carried out a cost accounting study and found that the unit cost for one of its main products is $40. Meanwhile, the marketing department has estimated the relationship between price and sales volume (the so called *demand curve* for the product) as follows:

$$y = 800 - 5x \tag{1.1}$$

where y represents quarterly demand and x represents the selling price per unit. We wish to determine a selling price for this product, given the information available.   ■

In Example 1.1, the decision is the unit price, and the consequence of that decision is the level of demand. The demand curve in Equation 1.1 expresses the relationship of demand and price in algebraic terms. Another equation expresses the calculation of profit contribution, by multiplying the demand y by the unit profit contribution $(x - 40)$ on each item

$$z = (x - 40)y \tag{1.2}$$

where z represents our product's quarterly profit contribution.

We can substitute Equation 1.1 into 1.2 if we want to write z algebraically as a function of x alone. As a result, we can express the profit contribution as

$$z = 1000x - 5x^2 - 32,000 \tag{1.3}$$

This step embodies the algebraic principle that simplification is always desirable. Here, simplification reduces the number of variables in the expression for profit contribution. Simplification, however, is not necessarily a virtue when we use a spreadsheet model.

Example 1.1, simple as it is, has some important features. First, our model contains three numerical inputs: 40 (the unit cost), −5 (the marginal effect of price on demand) and 800 (the maximum demand). Numerical inputs such as these are called *parameters*. In some models, parameters correspond to raw data, but in many cases, parameters are summaries drawn from a more primitive data set. They may also be estimates made by a knowledgeable party, forecasts derived from statistical analyses, or predictions chosen to reflect a future scenario.

Our model also contains a decision—an unknown quantity yet to be determined. In traditional algebraic formulations, unknowns are represented as variables. Quantitative representations of decisions are therefore called *decision variables*. The decision variable in our model is the unit price x.

Our model contains the equation that relates demand to price. We can think of this relationship as part of the model's logic. In that role, the demand curve prescribes a relationship between two variables—price and demand—that must always hold. Thus, in our model, the only admissible values of x and y are those that satisfy Equation 1.1.

Finally, our model contains a calculation of quarterly profit contribution, which is the performance measure of interest and a quantity that we wish to maximize. This output variable measures the consequence of selecting any particular price decision in the model. In optimization models, we are concerned with maximizing or minimizing some measure of performance, expressed as a mathematical function, and we refer to it as the *objective function*, or simply the *objective*.

1.2. SPREADSHEET MODELS

Algebra is an established language that works well for describing problems, but not always for obtaining solutions. Algebraic solutions tend to occur in formulas, not numbers, but numbers most often represent decisions in the practical world. By contrast, spreadsheets represent a practical language—one that works very effectively with numbers. Like algebraic models, spreadsheets can be precise and compact, but there are also complications that are unique to spreadsheets. For example, there is a difference between form and content in a spreadsheet. Two spreadsheets may look the same in terms of layout and the numbers displayed on a computer screen, but the underlying formulas in corresponding cells could differ. Because the information behind the display can be different even when two spreadsheets have the same on-screen appearance, we can't always tell the logical content from the form of the display. Another complication is the lack of a single, well accepted way to build a spreadsheet representation of a given model. In an optimization model, we want to represent decision variables, an objective function, and constraints. However, that still leaves a lot of flexibility in choosing how the logic of a particular model is incorporated into a spreadsheet. Such flexibility would ordinarily be advantageous if the only use of a spreadsheet were to help individuals solve problems. However, spreadsheets are perhaps even more important as vehicles for communication. When we use spreadsheets in this role, flexibility can sometimes lead to confusion and disrupt the intended communication.

We will try to mitigate these complications with some design guidelines. For example, it is helpful to create separate modules in the spreadsheet for decision variables, objective function, and constraints. To the extent that we follow such guidelines, we may lose some flexibility in building a spreadsheet model. Moving the design process toward standardization will, however, make the content of a spreadsheet more understandable from its form, so differences between form and content become less problematic.

With optimization, a spreadsheet model contains the analysis that ultimately provides decision support. For this reason, the spreadsheet model should be intelligible to its users, not just to its developer. On some occasions, a spreadsheet might come into routine use in an organization, even when the developer moves on. New analysts may inherit the responsibilities associated with the model, so it is vital that they, too, understand how the spreadsheet works. For that matter, the decision maker may also move on. For the organization to retain the learning that has taken place, successive decision makers must also understand the spreadsheet. In yet another scenario, the analyst develops a model for one-time use but then discovers a need to reuse it several months later in a different context. In such a situation, it's important that the analyst understands the original model, lest the passage of time obscure its purpose and logic. In all of these cases, the spreadsheet model fills a significant communications need. Thus, it is important to keep the role of communication in mind while developing a spreadsheet.

A spreadsheet version of our pricing model might look like the one in Figure 1.1. This spreadsheet contains a cell (C9) that holds the unit price, a cell (C12) that holds the level of demand, and a cell (C15) that holds the total profit contribution. Actually, cell C12 holds Equation 1.1 in the form of the Excel formula =C4+C5*C9. Similarly, cell C15 holds Equation 1.2 with the formula =(C9−C6)*C12. In cell C9, the unit price is initially set to $80. For this choice, demand is 400. The quarterly profit contribution is $16,000.

In a spreadsheet model, there is usually no premium on being concise, as there is when we use algebra. In fact, when conciseness begins to interfere with a model's transparency, it becomes undesirable. Thus, in Figure 1.1, the model retains the demand equation and displays the demand quantity explicitly; we have not tried to incorporate Equation 1.3. This form allows a user to see how price influences profit contribution through demand because all of these quantities are explicit. Furthermore, it is straightforward to trace the connection between the three input parameters and the calculation of profit contribution.

To summarize, our model consists of three parameters and a decision variable, together with some intermediate calculations, all leading to an objective function that we want to maximize. In algebraic terms, the model consists of Equations 1.1 and 1.2, with the prescription that we want to maximize Equation 1.2. In spreadsheet terms, the model consists of the spreadsheet in Figure 1.1, with the prescription that we want to maximize the value in cell C15.

	A	B	C	
1	Price, Demand, and Profit			
2				
3	Inputs			
4		Max. demand	800	
5		Slope	−5	
6		Unit cost	40	
7				
8	Decision			
9		Price	$ 80	
10				
11	Calculation			
12		Demand	400	
13				
14	Outcome			
15		Profit	$ 16,000	
16				

Figure 1.1. Spreadsheet model for determining price.

The spreadsheet is organized into four modules: Inputs, Decision, Calculation, and Outcome, separating different kinds of information. In spreadsheet models, it is a good idea to separate input data from decisions and decisions from outcome measures. Intermediate calculations that do not lead directly to the outcome measure should also be kept separate.

In the spreadsheet model, cell borders and shading draw attention to the decision (cell C9) and the objective (cell C15) as the two most important elements of the optimization model. No matter how complicated a spreadsheet model may become, we want the decisions and the objective to be located easily by someone who looks at the display.

In the spreadsheet of Figure 1.1, the input parameters appear explicitly. It would not be difficult to skip the Inputs section entirely and express the demand function in cell C12 with the formula $=800-5*C9$, or to express the profit contribution in cell C15 with the formula $=(C9-40)*C12$. This approach, however, places the numerical parameters in formulas, so a user would not see them at all when looking at the spreadsheet. Good practice calls for displaying parameters explicitly in the spreadsheet, as we have done in Figure 1.1, rather than burying them in formulas.

The basic version of our model, shown in Figure 1.1, is ready for optimization. But let's look at an alternative, shown in Figure 1.2. This version contains the four modules, and the numerical inputs are explicit but placed differently than in Figure 1.1. The main difference is that demand is treated as a decision variable, and the demand curve is expressed as an explicit constraint. Specifically, this form of the model treats both price and demand as variables in cells C9:C10, as if the two choices could be made arbitrarily. However, the Constraints module describes a relationship between the two variables in the form of Equation 1.1, which can

	A	B	C	D	E
1	**Price, Demand, and Profit**				
2					
3	**Inputs**				
4		Max. demand	800		
5		Slope	−5		
6		Cost	40		
7					
8	**Decisions**				
9		Price	$ 80		
10		Demand	250		
11					
12	**Constraints**				
13		Demand	650	=	800
14					
15	**Outcomes**				
16		Profit	$ 10,000		
17					

Model1   Model2

Figure 1.2. Alternative spreadsheet model for determining price.

equivalently be expressed as

$$y + 5x = 800 \qquad (1.4)$$

We can meet this constraint by forcing cell C13 to equal cell E13, a condition that does not yet hold in Figure 1.2. Cell C13 contains the formula on the left-hand side of Equation 1.4, and cell E13 contains a reference to the parameter 800. The equals sign between them, in cell D13, signifies the nature of the constraint relationship to someone who is looking at the spreadsheet and trying to understand its logic. Equation 1.4 collects all the terms involving decision variables on the left-hand side (in cell C13) and places the constant term on the right-hand side (in cell E13). This is a standard form for expressing a constraint in a spreadsheet model. The spreadsheet itself displays, but does not actually enforce, this constraint. The enforcement task is left to the optimization software. Once the constraint is met, the corresponding decisions are called *feasible*.

This is a good place to include a reminder about the software that accompanies this book. The software contains important files and programs. In terms of files, the book's website[1] contains all of the spreadsheets shown in the figures. Figures 1.1 and 1.2, for example, can be found in the file that contains the spreadsheets for Chapter 1. Those files should be loaded, or else built from scratch, before continuing with the text. As we proceed through the chapters, the reader is welcome to load each file that appears in a figure, for hands-on examination.

1.3. A HIERARCHY FOR ANALYSIS

Before we proceed, some background on the development of models in organizations may be useful. Think about the person who builds a model as an *analyst*, someone who provides support to a decision maker or *client*. (In some cases, the analyst and the client are the same.) The development, testing, and application of a model constitute support for the decision maker—a service to the client. The application phase of this process includes some standard stages of model use.

When a model is built as an aid to decision making, the first stage often involves building a prototype, or a series of prototypes, leading to a model that the analyst and the client accept as a usable decision-support tool. That model provides quantitative analysis of a base-case scenario. In Example 1.1, suppose we set a tentative price of $80. This price might be called a *base case*, in the sense that it represents a tentative decision. As we have seen, this price leads to demand of 400 and profit contribution of $16,000.

After establishing a base case, it is usually appropriate to investigate the answers to a number of "what-if" questions. We ask, what if we change a numerical input or a decision in the model—what impact would that change have? Suppose, for example, that the marginal effect of price on demand (the slope of the demand curve) were -4 instead of -5. What difference would this make? Retracing our algebraic steps, or

---

[1]The URL for the book's website is http://mba.tuck.dartmouth.edu/opt/

revising the spreadsheet in Figure 1.1, we can determine that the profit contribution would be $19,200.

Systematic investigations of this kind are called *sensitivity analyses*. They explore how sensitive the results and conclusions are to changes in assumptions. Typically, we start by varying one assumption at a time and tracing the impact. Then we might try varying two or more assumptions, but such probing can quickly become difficult to follow. Therefore, most sensitivity analyses are performed one assumption at a time. Sometimes, it is useful to explore the what-if question in reverse. That is, we might ask, for the result to attain a given outcome level, what would the numerical input have to be? For example, starting with the base-case model, we might ask, what price would generate a profit contribution of $17,000? We can answer this question algebraically, by setting $z = 17,000$ in Equation 1.3 and solving for x, or, with the spreadsheet model, we can invoke Excel's Goal Seek tool to discover that the price would have to be about $86.

Sensitivity analyses are helpful in determining the robustness of the results and any risks that might be present. They can also reveal how to achieve improvement from better choices in decision making. However, locating improvements this way is something of a trial-and-error process, and trial-and-error probing is inefficient. Faster and more reliable ways of locating improvements are available. Moreover, with trial-and-error approaches, we seldom know how far improvements can potentially reach, so a best outcome could exist that we never detect.

From this perspective, optimization can be viewed as a sophisticated form of sensitivity analysis that seeks the best values for the decisions and the best value for the performance measure. Optimization takes us beyond mere improvement; we look for the very best outcome in our model, the maximum possible benefit or the minimum possible cost. If we have constraints in our model, then optimization also tells us which of those conditions ultimately limit what we want to accomplish. Optimization can also reveal what we might gain if we can find a way to overcome those constraints and proceed beyond the limitations they impose.

1.4. OPTIMIZATION SOFTWARE

Optimization procedures find the best values of the decision variables in a given model. In the case of Excel, the optimization software is known as *Solver*, which is a standard tool available on the Data ribbon. (The generic term *solver* often refers to optimization software, whether or not it is implemented in a spreadsheet.) Optimization tools have been available on computers for several decades, prior to the widespread use of electronic spreadsheets. Before spreadsheets became popular, optimization was available as stand-alone software; it relied on an algebraic approach, but it was often accessible only by technical experts. Decision makers and even their analysts had to rely on those experts to build and solve optimization models. Spreadsheets, if they were used at all, were limited to small examples. Now, however, the spreadsheet allows decision makers to develop their own models, without having to learn specialized software, and to find optimal solutions for those models using Solver. Two trends account for the popularity of spreadsheet optimization. First, familiarity with spreadsheets has become almost ubiquitous, at least in the business world. The spreadsheet has come to represent a common language for analysis. Second, the software packages available for spreadsheet-based optimization now include some of the most powerful tools available. The spreadsheet platform need not be an impediment to solving practical optimization problems.

Spreadsheet-based optimization has several advantages. The spreadsheet allows model inputs to be documented clearly and systematically. Moreover, if it is necessary to convert raw data into other forms for the purposes of setting up a model, the required calculations can be performed and documented conveniently in the same spreadsheet, or at least on another sheet in the same workbook. This allows integration between raw data and model data. Without this integration, errors or omissions are more likely, and maintenance becomes more difficult. Another advantage is algorithmic flexibility: The spreadsheet has the ability to call on several different optimization procedures, but the process of preparing the model is mostly the same no matter which procedure is applied. Finally, spreadsheet models have a certain amount of intrinsic credibility because spreadsheets are now so widely used for other purposes. Although spreadsheets can contain errors (and often do), there is at least some comfort in knowing that logic and discipline must be applied in the building of a spreadsheet.

Table 1.1 summarizes and compares the advantages of spreadsheet and algebraic (3,4) software approaches to optimization problems. The main advantage of algebraic approaches is the efficiency with which models can be specified. With spreadsheets, the elements of a model are represented explicitly. Thus, if the model requires a thousand variables, then the model builder must designate a thousand cells to hold their respective values. Algebraic codes use a different method. If a model contains a thousand variables, the code might refer to $x(k)$, with a specification that k may take on values from 1 to 1000, but $x(k)$ need not be represented explicitly for each of the thousand values.

A second advantage of algebraic approaches is the fact that they can sometimes be tailored to a particular application. For example, the very large crew-scheduling applications used by airlines exhibit a special structure. To exploit this structure in the solution procedure, algebraic codes are sometimes enhanced with specialized subroutines that add solution efficiencies when solving a crew-scheduling problem.

A disadvantage of using spreadsheets is that they are not always transparent. As noted earlier, the analyst has a lot of flexibility in the layout and organization of a spreadsheet, but this flexibility, taken too far, may detract from effective communication. In this book, we try to promote better communication by suggesting

Table 1.1. Advantages of Spreadsheet and Algebraic Solution Approaches

Spreadsheet approaches	Algebraic approaches
Several algorithms available in one place	Large problem sizes accommodated
Integration of raw data and model data	Concise model specification
Flexibility in layout and design	Standardized model description
Ease of communication with nonspecialists	Enhancements possible for special cases
Intrinsic credibility	

standard forms for particular types of models. By using some standardization, we make it easier to understand and debug someone else's model. Algebraic codes usually have very detailed specifications for model format, so once we're familiar with the specifications, we should be able to read and understand anyone else's model.

In brief, commercially available algebraic solvers represent an alternative to spreadsheet-based optimization. In this book, our focus on a spreadsheet approach allows the novice to learn basic concepts of mathematical programming, practice building optimization models, obtain solutions readily, and interpret and apply the results of the analysis. All these skills can be developed in the accessible world of spreadsheets. Moreover, these skills provide a solid foundation for using algebraic solvers at some later date, when and if the situation demands it.

1.5. USING SOLVER

Purchasers of this book may download a powerful software package called *Risk Solver Platform (RSP)* that was developed by the same team that created Excel's Solver and that accommodates all Excel Solver models. (Before continuing with the text, the reader should install the software by following the guidelines and instructions in Appendix 1.) RSP is an integrated software package that includes more than just optimization capabilities, but this book focuses on optimization. Hence, the installation instructions recommend setting this software to operate in *Premium Solver Platform mode*, which exposes all of the optimization features, but hides other features such as Monte Carlo simulation and decision trees. Once the software is installed, a new Risk Solver Platform tab appears in Excel, with its own ribbon of commands. Under Premium Solver Platform mode, a Premium Solver Platform tab appears instead. In addition, the Add-Ins tab contains a Premium Solver choice which displays a Solver Parameters dialog that closely resembles the standard Excel Solver but uses the more powerful optimization capabilities of RSP. For our purposes, these tabs contain the equivalent optimization capabilities, and we may refer to either one.

In the remainder of this book, we assume the use of RSP, but we refer to it simply as Solver. The book covers its four main optimization procedures:

- The nonlinear solver
- The linear solver
- The integer solver
- The evolutionary solver

As in all matters involving software, the user should be aware of the copyright privileges and restrictions that apply to the use of RSP.

In order to illustrate the use of Solver, we return to Example 1.1. The optimization problem is to find a price that maximizes quarterly profit contribution. An algebraic statement of the problem is

$$\text{Maximize} \quad z = (x - 40)y \quad \text{(objective)}$$
$$\text{subject to} \quad y + 5x = 800 \quad \text{(constraint)}$$

This form of the model corresponds to Figure 1.2, which contains two decision variables (x and y, or price and demand) and one constraint on the decision variables. The spreadsheet model in Figure 1.2 is ready for optimization.

To start, we select the Risk Solver Platform tab and click on the Model icon (on the left side of its ribbon). This step opens the *task pane* on the right-hand side of the Excel window. The task pane contains four tabs: Model, Platform, Engine, and Output. Initially, the Model tab displays a window listing several components of the software, including Optimization. In Figure 1.3, we have expanded the Optimization entry on the Model tab. As we specify the elements of our model, they are recorded in the folder icons of this window. At the top of the model tab five icons appear:

- Green "plus" sign, to *Add* model specifications
- Red "delete" sign, to *Remove* specifications
- Orange paired sheets with small blue arrows, to *Refresh* the display after changes
- Green checked sheet, to *Analyze* the model
- Green triangle, to *Solve* the specified optimization problem.

To specify the model we first select the decision cells (C9:C10) and then on the drop-down menu of the *Add* icon, select Add Variable. The range $\$C\$9:\$C\$10$ immediately appears in the Model window, in the folder for Normal Variables. (Another way

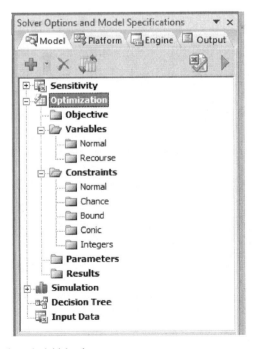

Figure 1.3. Model tab on the initial task pane.

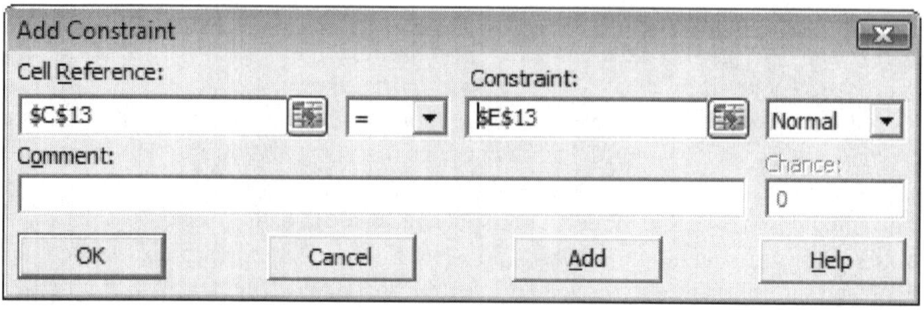

Figure 1.4. Add Constraint window.

to accomplish this step without using the drop-down menu is to highlight the Normal Variables folder icon and simply click the *Add* icon.)

Next, we select the objective cell (C16) and on the drop-down menu of the *Add* icon, select Add Objective. The cell address $C$16 immediately appears in the Model window, in the folder for Objective. By default, the specification assumes that the objective is to maximize this value. (We can implement this step by highlighting the Objective folder and simply clicking the *Add* icon.)

Next, we select the left-hand side of the constraint (C13) and on the drop-down menu of the *Add* icon, select Add Constraint. (Alternatively, we can highlight the Normal Constraints folder icon and click the *Add* icon.) The Add Constraint window appears, with the cell address $C$13 in the Cell Reference box, as shown in Figure 1.4. On the drop-down menu to its right, we select " = " and enter E13 in the Constraint box (or, with the cursor in the box, select cell E13).

When specifying constraints, one of our design guidelines for Solver models is to reference a cell containing a *formula* in the Cell Reference box and to reference a cell containing a *number* in the Constraint box. The use of cell references keeps the key parameters visible on the spreadsheet, rather than in the less accessible windows of Solver's interface. The principle at work here is to communicate as much as possible about the model using the spreadsheet itself. Ideally, another person would not have to examine the task pane to understand the model. (Although Solver permits us to enter numerical values directly into the Constraint box, this form is less effective for communication and complicates sensitivity analysis. It would be reasonable only in special cases where the model structure is obvious from the spreadsheet and where we expect to perform no sensitivity analyses for the corresponding parameter.)

Finally, we press OK and observe that the task pane displays the model's specification, as shown in Figure 1.5. In summary, our model specification is the following:

Objective: C16 (maximize)

Variables: C9:C10

Constraint: C13 = E13

This model is simple enough that we need not address the information on the Platform tab. (However, it is generally a good idea to set the Nonsmooth Model

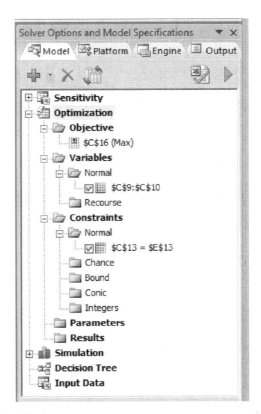

Figure 1.5. Model specification.

Transformation option to *Never*.) At the top of the Engine tab, we observe the default selection of the Standard GRG Nonlinear Engine, which we refer to as the *nonlinear solver*. (To ensure this selection, we uncheck the box for Automatically Select Engine.) This solution algorithm is appropriate for our optimization problem, and we do not need to address most of the other information on the tab. However, one of the options is important.

Although we may guess that the optimal price is a positive quantity, the model as specified permits the price decision to be negative. Such an outcome would not make sense in this problem, so it may be a good idea to limit the model to nonnegative prices. In fact, virtually all of the models in this book involve decision variables that make practical sense only when they are nonnegative, so we will impose this restriction routinely. On the Engine tab of the task pane, we find the *Assume Non-Negative option* in the General group and change it to True, using the drop-down menu on the right-hand side, as shown in Figure 1.6.

Finally, we proceed to the Output tab (or return to the Model tab) and click the *Solve* icon. Solver searches for the optimal price and ultimately places it in the price cell. In this case, the optimal price is $100, and the corresponding quarterly profit contribution is $18,000 as shown in Figure 1.7.

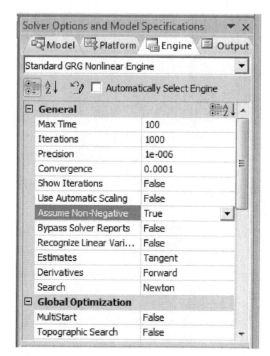

Figure 1.6. Setting the Assume Non-Negative option.

	A	B	C	D	E
1	**Price, Demand, and Profit**				
2					
3	**Inputs**				
4		Max. demand	800		
5		Slope	−5		
6		Cost	40		
7					
8	**Decisions**				
9		Price	$ 100		
10		Demand	300		
11					
12	**Constraints**				
13		Demand	800	=	800
14					
15	**Outcomes**				
16		Profit	$ 18,000		
17					

Model1   Model2

Figure 1.7. Optimal solution for Example 1.1.

Meanwhile, the Output tab's window displays the solution log for the optimiz-ation run. (The detail in this log is controlled by the Log Level option on the Platform tab, but the default setting of *Normal* is usually adequate.) The most impor-tant part of the log is the Solver Results message, which in this case states:

```
Solver found a solution. All
constraints and optimality conditions
are satisfied.
```

This *optimality message*, which is repeated at the very bottom of the task pane, tells us that no problems arose during the optimization and Solver was able to find an optimal solution. The profit-maximizing price is $100, yielding an optimal profit of $18,000. No other price can achieve more than this level. Thus, if we are confident that the demand curve continues to hold, the profit-maximizing decision would be to set price at $100.

We have used Example 1.1 to introduce Solver and its interface. The task pane contains many user-selected options that are not a concern in this problem. In later chapters, we cover many of these settings and discuss when they become relevant. We also discuss the variations that can occur in optimization runs. For example, depending on the initial values of the decision variables, the nonlinear solver may gen-erate the following result message in the solution log:

```
Solver has converged to the current
solution. All constraints are satisfied.
```

This *convergence message* indicates that Solver has not been able to confirm optim-ality. Usually, this condition occurs because of numerical issues in the solution algor-ithm, and the resolution is to rerun Solver from the point where convergence occurred. Normally, one or two iterations are sufficient to produce the optimality message. We discuss Solver's result messages in more detail later.

With Solver, we can minimize an objective function instead of maximizing it. We return to the specification in the window of the Model tab of the task pane and double-click on the entry in the Objective folder. The Change Objective window appears, as shown in Figure 1.8, and we can select the button for Min rather than Max. (A third option allows us to specify a target value and find a set of variables

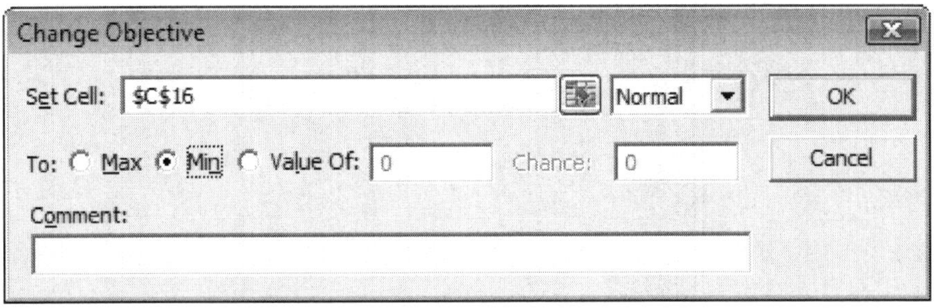

Figure 1.8. Selecting minimization of an objective.

BOX 1.2	*Excel Mini-Lesson: Using Range Names with Solver*

Excel offers the opportunity to refer to a cell range using a custom name. The range name can be entered in the Name Box (located just above the heading for column A) after selecting the desired range of cells. A one-cell range can be named in the same manner.

To illustrate the effect of using named ranges, suppose we return to the model of Figure 1.2 and name the following cells:

Cells	Name
C9:C10	Decisions
C13	Formula
E13	Constant
C16	Profit

Then the task pane window describes the model with range names instead of cell references, as shown in Figure 1.9. When a new user examines the model, this form is likely to be more meaningful than the use of literal cell references because the range names provide both description and documentation. Thus, range names are valuable for situations in which communicating the model to other audiences is an important consideration. When Solver is applied in an organizational setting, the use of range names is normally desirable. In the remainder of this book, however, we will continue to rely on cell references because they relate the information in the task pane directly to the contents of the spreadsheet display.

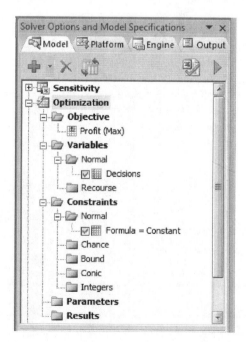

Figure 1.9. Model specification with range names.

that achieves the target value. This is not an optimization tool, and we will not pursue this particular capability.)

When an optimization model contains several decision variables, we can enter them one at a time, creating a list of Normal Variables in the task pane, each with its own checked box. More conveniently, we can arrange the spreadsheet so that all the variables appear in adjacent cells, as in Figure 1.2, and reference their cell range with just one entry in the Normal Variables folder. Because most optimization problems have several decision variables, we save time by placing them in adjacent cells. This layout also makes the information in the task pane easier to interpret when someone else is trying to audit our work, or if we are reviewing it after not having seen it for a long time. However, exceptions to this design guideline sometimes occur. Certain applications lead us to use nonadjacent locations for convenience in laying out the decision variable cells.

SUMMARY

Many types of applications invite the use of Excel's Solver. In one sense, that is what this book is about—the problem types that Solver can handle and the use of Solver to obtain solutions. Thus, the book builds skill and confidence with spreadsheet applications because Solver is a spreadsheet tool. Actually, as mentioned earlier, Solver is a collection of procedures. Therefore, this book describes a variety of applications that can be addressed with spreadsheet capabilities.

In another sense, this book is about the problem types that Solver can handle, but the information on how to run Solver is incidental. The transcendent theme is the building of optimization models. If Solver wasn't around to produce solutions, then some other software would perform the computational task. The more basic skill is creating the model in the first place and recognizing its potential role in decision support.

Thus far, we have introduced six design guidelines for spreadsheet optimization models.

- Separate inputs from decisions and decisions from outputs.
- Create distinct modules for decision variables, objective function, and constraints.
- Display parameters explicitly on the spreadsheet, rather than in formulas.
- Enter parameters in the spreadsheet, rather than in the Add Constraints window.
- Place decision variables in adjacent cells.
- Highlight important cells, such as the decision variables and the objective.

Subsequent chapters introduce additional features of good spreadsheet design. This is not a claim that each example spreadsheet is the only possible way of designing a model, or even that it's the best way. A model should be easy to recognize, debug, use routinely, and pass on to others. A key feature of a good spreadsheet model is its ability to communicate clearly.

Chapters 2–5 deal with the linear solver, introducing many features of optimization analysis in the process. Chapters 6 and 7 deal with models that can be solved with the integer solver, and Chapter 8 deals with the nonlinear solver. The evolutionary solver, which is introduced in Chapter 9, is not properly an optimization procedure in the same sense as the others, but it applies in situations where the other solvers might fail. Each chapter is filled with illustrative examples and followed by a set of practice exercises. If readers work through the examples and the exercises they will develop a firm grasp on how to solve practical optimization problems using spreadsheets.

EXERCISES

1.1. Determining an Optimal Price   A firm's Marketing Department has estimated the demand curve of a product as $y = 1100 - 7x$, where y represents demand and x represents the unit selling price (in dollars) for the relevant decision period. The unit cost is known to be $24. What price maximizes net income from sales of the product?

1.2. Pricing in Two Markets   Global Products, Inc. has been making an electronic appliance for the domestic market. Demand for the appliance is price sensitive, and the demand curve is known to follow the linear function $D = 4000 - 5P$, where D represents annual demand and P represents selling price in the home currency, which is the Frank (F). The cost of manufacturing the appliance is 100F.

   For the coming year, Global is planning to sell the same product in a foreign market, where the currency is the Marc (M). From surveys, the demand curve in the foreign country is estimated to follow a different linear function, $D = 2000 - 2P$, where the price is denominated in Marcs.

   All production will be carried out at Global's domestic plant, with the expectation that the unit cost will remain unchanged. The exchange rate is 1.5 M/F, and Global plans to offer an equivalent price in both markets.

   (a) If Global were to operate exclusively in its domestic market, what would be its profit-maximizing price and its annual profit?

   (b) When Global sells in both markets at one equivalent price, what is its profit-maximizing price and its annual profit?

1.3. Locating a Distribution Center   Northeast Parts Supply is a wholesale distributor of components for printers, fax machines, scanners, and related equipment. Northeast stocks expensive spare parts, which dealers prefer not to hold, and offers same-day delivery on any order. The firm now serves eight dealers in the New England area and wishes to locate its distribution facility at a central point. In particular, its dealers have each been assigned a location on an x–y grid, and Northeast would like to find the best location for the distribution facility.

   The eight dealers and their grid locations are shown in the following table:

Dealer	1	2	3	4	5	6	7	8
x-location	25	82	10	27	93	14	68	147
y-location	32	36	71	58	68	163	149	192

   (a) Determine the location that minimizes the sum of the distances from the distribution facility to the dealers.

   (b) Determine the location that minimizes the maximum distance from the distribution facility to any of the dealers.

1.4. Collecting Credit Card Debt   A bank offers a credit card that can be used in various locations. The bank's analysts believe that the percentage P of accounts receivable collected by t months after credit is issued increases at a decreasing rate. Historical data suggest the following function:

$$P = 0.9[1 - \exp(-0.6t)]$$

The average credit issued in any one month is $125 million, and historical experience suggests that for new credit issued in any month, collection efforts cost $1 million per month.

(a) Determine the number of months that collection efforts should be continued if the objective is to maximize the net collections (dollars collected minus collection costs). Allow for fractional months.

(b) Under the optimal policy in **(a)**, what percentage of accounts receivable should be collected?

1.5. Allocating Plant Output   A firm owns five manufacturing plants that are responsible for the quarterly production of an industrial solvent. The production process exhibits diseconomies of scale. At plant p, the cost of making x thousand pounds of the solvent is approximated by the quadratic function $f(x) = (1/c_p)x^2$. The parameters c_p are plant dependent, as shown in the table.

p	1	2	3	4	5
c_p	3	6	4	8	5

The quarterly volume requirement is 50,000 pounds.

How should production be allocated among the five plants in order to minimize the total cost of meeting the volume requirement?

1.6. Determining Production Lot Sizes   Four products are routed through a machining center that is notorious for its delays. Each product has had stable demand for some time, so that average weekly demand is predictable over a 3–6 month time frame. However, in the short run, demand fluctuates a great deal, and the load at the machining center varies considerably. The production control system dictates the lot size for each of the products. These quantities are shown, along with other relevant information, in the following table.

Product no.	Demand (weekly)	Setup (hours)	Run time (hours/1000)	Lot size
1	100	3	30	100
2	500	15	45	500
3	50	6	75	100
4	250	24	150	1500

With the current lot sizes, the machining center is running at a utilization of about 76%, but long lead times, sometimes over 2 weeks, have discouraged production planners from increasing its load. (A week contains 120 productive hours.) In the past, lead times spiraled out of control when utilization grew to around 80%.

A lead time model for this problem has been constructed on a spreadsheet.[2] The model permits the user to select lot sizes and thereby influence the average lead time through the bottleneck work center. The lead time prediction is based on advanced modeling techniques, but the details of the model are not of primary importance.

What is the shortest possible lead time, and what lot sizes achieve this value?

---

[2]The lead time model is available in the DataSets workbook, at the book's website (http://mba.tuck. dartmouth.edu/opt/).

1.7. Resolving a Construction Dilemma   A library building is about to undergo some reno-
vations that will improve its structural integrity. As part of the process, a number of steel
beams will be carried through the existing bookcases from a broad, open area around
the entry point. The central aisle between the bookcases is 10 feet wide, while the side
aisles (which run perpendicular to the central aisle) are 6 feet wide. The renovation will
require that steel beams be carried through the stacks, down the main aisle and turning
into the smaller aisles.

What is the longest steel beam that can be carried horizontally through this space to a
construction point along the outer walls?

1.8. Selecting the Number of Warehouses   The customers of a particular company are
located throughout an area comprised of S square miles, and they are serviced from k
warehouses. On average, the distance in miles between a warehouse and a customer
is given by the formula $(S/k)^{0.5}$. The annual capital cost of building a warehouse is
$40,000 and the annual operating cost of running a warehouse is $60,000. Annual shipping
costs average $1 per mile per customer.

Suppose that the current market size is 250,000 customers, spread out over an area of
500 square miles. What is the optimal number of warehouses for the firm to operate?

REFERENCES

1. McFedries, P. *Excel 2010 Simplified*. John Wiley and Sons, 2010.
2. Reding, E. and L. Wermers. *Microsoft Office Excel 2010: Illustrated Introductory*. Cengage Learning, 2011.
3. Schrage, L. *Optimization Modeling with LINGO*. Lindo Systems Inc., 2008.
4. Fourer, R., D.M. Gay, and B.W. Kernighan. *AMPL: A Modeling Language for Mathematical Programming (Second Edition)*. Cengage Learning, 2003.

Chapter 2

Linear Programming: Allocation, Covering, and Blending Models

The linear programming model is a very rich context for examining business decisions. A large variety of applications has been reported in the 50 years or so that computers have been available for this type of decision support. Our first task in this chapter is to describe the features of linearity in optimization models. We then begin our survey of linear programming models. Appendix 2 provides a graphical perspective on linear programming. This material may help with an understanding of the linear programming model, but it is not essential for proceeding with spreadsheet-based approaches.

The term *linear* refers to properties of the objective function and the constraints. A linear function exhibits proportionality, additivity, and divisibility. *Proportionality* means that the contribution from any given decision variable to the objective grows in proportion to its value. When a decision variable doubles, then its contribution to the objective also doubles. *Additivity* means that the contribution from one decision is added to (or sometimes subtracted from) the contributions of other decisions. In an additive function, we can separate the contributions that come from each decision variable. *Divisibility* means that a fractional decision variable is meaningful. When a decision variable involves a fraction, we can still interpret its significance for managerial purposes.

The algebra of model building leads us to models that are either linear or nonlinear. Problems in *linear programming* are built from linear relationships, whereas *nonlinear programming* includes other mathematical relationships. Together, these two categories comprise *mathematical programming* problems. Linear methods tend to be more efficient than nonlinear methods, and linear models allow for deeper interpretations. Moreover, it is often a reasonable first step, in many applications, to assume that a linear relationship holds. For those reasons, we devote special attention to the case of linear programming.

Optimization Modeling with Spreadsheets, Second Edition. Kenneth R. Baker
© 2011 John Wiley & Sons, Inc. Published 2011 by John Wiley & Sons, Inc.

In the course of this chapter, we begin to see how different situations lend themselves to basic linear programming representation. Although it might be an oversimplification to say that only a few linear programming model "types" exist, it is still helpful to think in terms of a small number of basic structures when learning how to build linear programming models. This chapter presents three different types, classified as *allocation*, *covering*, and *blending models*. The next chapter covers another very important type, the *network model*. Most linear programming applications are actually combinations of these four types, but seeing the building blocks separately helps to clarify the key modeling concepts. Chapter 5 is devoted to linear programming models for *data envelopment analysis (DEA)*, where the model is essentially an allocation problem, but the significance and application setting is specialized. Before embarking on a tour of model types, however, we start with some preliminary concepts regarding all models we will encounter in the linear programming chapters.

2.1. LINEAR MODELS

Linearity is an important technical consideration in building models for Solver. When working with a linear model, we can call on the linear solver to find optimal solutions. Although Solver contains other procedures, as we mentioned in the previous chapter, the linear solver is the most reliable. As we will see later, it also offers us the deepest technical insights into sensitivity analysis. However, to harness the linear solver, our model must adhere to the requirements of proportionality, additivity, and divisibility.

Linearity is also an important practical consideration in building models. Many modeling applications involve linear relationships. Ultimately, however, linearity is a feature of the model, not necessarily an intrinsic feature of the motivating problem. Therefore, if we use a linear model, it should provide an adequate representation of the problem at hand. In any particular application, the users of a linear model must be satisfied that proportionality, additivity, and divisibility are reasonable assumptions. Even when practical situations involve nonlinear relationships, they may be approximately linear in the region where realistic decisions are likely to lie.

Algebraically, a linear function is easy to recognize. Variables in a linear function have an exponent of 1 and are never multiplied or divided by each other. Recall the demand curve and the profit contribution from Example 1.1:

$$y = 800 - 5x \tag{2.1}$$

$$z = (x - 40)y \tag{2.2}$$

Equation 2.1 is a linear function of x, but Equation 2.2 is nonlinear because it contains the product of x and y. We could of course substitute for y and rewrite the profit function, leading to the following equation:

$$z = 1000x - 5x^2 - 32,000 \tag{2.3}$$

In Equation 2.3, there is no product of variables in the profit contribution, but the function contains the variable x with an exponent of 2, another indication of nonlinearity.

Thus, our pricing model is nonlinear. Special functions, such as $\log(x)$, $\text{abs}(x)$, and $\exp(x)$ are also nonlinear.

Managerially, we can recognize linear behavior by asking questions about proportionality, additivity, and divisibility. For example, suppose we write the total cost of transporting quantities of wheat (w) and corn (c) as $z = 3w + 2c$. To test whether this function is a good representation, we might ask the following questions.

- When we transport an additional unit of wheat, does the total cost rise by same amount, no matter what the level of wheat? (Proportionality)
- When we transport an additional unit of corn, is the increase in total cost affected by the level of wheat? (Additivity)
- Are we permitted to transport a fractional quantity of wheat or corn? (Divisibility)

If the answers are affirmative, we have some evidence that the transportation cost can be represented as a linear function.

When an algebraic model contains several decision variables, we may give them letter names, such as x, y, and z, as in our pricing example. Alternatively, we may number the variables and refer to them as x_1, x_2, x_3, etc. When there are n decision variables, we can write a linear objective function as follows:

$$z = c_1 x_1 + c_2 x_2 + \cdots + c_n x_n$$

where z represents the value of the objective function and the cs are a set of given parameters called *objective function coefficients*. In this expression, the xs appear with exponents of 1 (so that the objective function exhibits proportionality), appear in

BOX 2.1   *Excel Mini-lesson: The SUMPRODUCT Function*

The SUMPRODUCT function computes a quantity sometimes called an *inner product* or a *scalar product*. First, we pair elements from two arrays; then we sum their pairwise products. (The function can be applied to more than two arrays in Excel, but our primary concern in optimization models is the case of two arrays.) The basic form of the function is the following:

SUMPRODUCT(*Array1*, *Array2*)

- *Array1* references a rectangular array; in this instance, normally a row.
- *Array2* references a rectangular array with the same dimensions as *Array1*.

For example, if the two arrays contain {1, 3, 5} and {2, 4, 6}, then the SUMPRODUCT function returns the value $(2 \times 1) + (4 \times 3) + (6 \times 5) = 44$. The arrays must have the same dimensions—that is, one array must have the same number of rows and columns as the other. If the number of cells in each array is the same but the dimensions differ, then the SUMPRODUCT function displays #VALUE! to indicate an error.

separate terms (so that the objective function exhibits additivity), and are not restricted to integers (so that the objective function exhibits divisibility). In a spreadsheet, we could calculate z with the SUMPRODUCT function, which adds the pairwise products of corresponding numbers in two lists of the same length. Thus, in a spreadsheet, we can recognize a linear function if it consists of a sum of pairwise products, where one element of each product is a parameter and the other is a decision variable.

2.1.1. Linear Constraints

Constraints appear in three varieties in optimization models: less-than (LT) constraints, greater-than (GT) constraints, and equal-to (EQ) constraints. Each constraint involves a relationship between a left-hand side (LHS) and a right-hand side (RHS). By convention, the RHS is a number (usually, a parameter), and the LHS is a function of the decision variables. The forms of the three varieties are:

$$\text{LHS} \leq \text{RHS} \quad \text{(LT constraint)}$$
$$\text{LHS} \geq \text{RHS} \quad \text{(GT constraint)}$$
$$\text{LHS} = \text{RHS} \quad \text{(EQ constraint)}$$

We use LT constraints to represent capacities or ceilings, GT constraints to represent commitments or thresholds, and EQ constraints to represent material balance or consistency among related variables. Box 2.2 lists some common examples of these kinds of constraints. For an example of consistency in an EQ constraint, think about a cash-planning application involving a requirement that end-of-month cash (E) must equal start-of-month cash (S) plus collections (C) minus disbursements (D).

BOX 2.2   *Examples of Constraints*

Less-than Constraints
> Number of pounds of steel consumed ≤ number of pounds available
> Number of customers serviced ≤ service capacity
> Thousands of televisions sold ≤ market demand (in thousands)

Greater-than Constraints
> Number of cartons delivered ≥ number of cartons ordered
> Number of nurses scheduled ≥ number of nurses required on duty
> Weighted sum of returns ≥ return threshold

Equal-to Constraints
> Total circuit boards purchased from all vendors = circuit boards available
> Cables fabricated + cables purchased = cables in stock
> Initial inventory + production − final inventory = shipments

In symbols, this relationship translates into the following algebraic expression:

$$E = S + C - D$$

In a typical application, disbursement levels play the role of given parameters and the other quantities are variables. For that reason, start-of-month cash plus collections minus end-of-month cash would become the LHS of an EQ constraint, and disbursements would become the RHS. Algebraically, we could simply rewrite the above expression as follows:

$$S + C - E = D$$

In linear programs, the LHS of each constraint must be a linear function. In other words, the LHS can be represented by a SUMPRODUCT function. In most cases, we actually use the SUMPRODUCT formula in the spreadsheet model. In special cases where the parameters in the formula are all 1s, we may substitute the SUM formula for greater transparency.

2.1.2. Formulation

Every linear programming model contains decision variables, an objective function, and a set of constraints. Before setting up a spreadsheet for optimization, a first step in building the model is to identify these elements, at least in words if not in symbols. Box 2.3 summarizes the questions we should ask ourselves in order to structure the model.

To guide us toward decision variables, we ask ourselves, "What must be decided?" The answer to that question should direct us to a choice of decision variables, and we should be especially precise about the units we are working in. Common examples of decision variables include quantities to buy, quantities to

| BOX 2.3 | *Questions that Help Translate a Problem into an Optimization Model* |

Decision variables
    Ask, *What must be decided?*

Objective function
    Ask, *What measure will we use to compare sets of decision variables?*

Constraints
    Ask, *What restrictions limit our choice of decision variables?*

deploy, quantities to produce, or quantities to deliver. Whatever the decision variables are, once we know their numerical values, we should have a resolution to the problem, though not necessarily the best resolution.

To guide us toward an objective function, we ask ourselves, "What measure will we use to compare sets of decision variables?" It is as if two consultants have come to us with their recommendations on what action to take (what levels of the decision variables to use), and we must choose which action we prefer. For this purpose, we need a yardstick—some measuring function that tells us which action is better. That function will be a mathematical expression involving the decision variables, and it will normally be obvious whether we wish to maximize or minimize it. Maximization criteria usually focus on such measures as profit, revenue, return, or efficiency. Minimization criteria usually focus on cost, time, distance, capacity, or investment. In the model, only one measure can play the role of the objective function.

To guide us toward constraints, we ask ourselves, "What restrictions limit our choice of decision variables?" We are typically not free to choose any set of decisions we like; intrinsic limitations in the problem have to be respected. For example, we might look for capacities that provide upper limits on certain activities and give rise to LT constraints. Alternatively, there may be commitments that place thresholds on other activities, in the form of GT constraints. Sometimes, we wish to specify equations, or EQ constraints, that ensure consistency among a set of variables. Once we have identified the constraints in a problem, we say that any set of decision variables consistent with all the constraints is a *feasible solution*. That is, a feasible solution represents a course of action that does not violate any of the constraints. Among feasible solutions, we want to find the best one.

It is usually a good idea to identify decision variables, objective function, and constraints in words first, and then translate them into algebraic symbols. The algebraic step is useful when we practice the formulation of optimization models because it helps us to be precise at an early modeling stage. In addition, an algebraic formulation can usually be translated into a spreadsheet model directly, although we may wish to make adjustments for the spreadsheet environment. As indicated in Chapter 1, it is desirable to create as much transparency as possible in the spreadsheet version of a model, therefore, our approach will be to construct an algebraic formulation as a prelude to creating the spreadsheet model.

2.1.3. Layout

We follow a disciplined approach to building linear programming models on a spreadsheet by imposing some standardization on spreadsheet layout. The developers of Solver provided model builders with considerable flexibility in designing a spreadsheet for optimization. However, even those developers recognized the virtues of some standardization, and their user's manual conveys a sense that taking full advantage of the software's flexibility is not always consistent with best practice. We adopt many of their suggestions about spreadsheet design.

The first element of our structure is *modularity*. We should try to reserve separate portions of the worksheet for decision variables, objective function, and constraints. We may also want to devote an additional module to raw data, especially in large problems. In our basic models, we should try to place all decision variables in adjacent cells of the spreadsheet (with color or border highlighting). Most often, we can display the variables in a single row, although in some cases the use of a rectangular array is more convenient. The objective function should be a single cell (also highlighted), containing a SUMPRODUCT formula, although in some cases an alternative may be preferable. Finally, we should arrange our constraints so that we can visually compare the LHS's and RHS's of each constraint, relying on a SUMPRODUCT formula to express the LHS, or in some cases, a SUM formula. For the most part, our models can literally reflect *left* and *right* in the layout, although sometimes other forms also make sense.

The reliance on the SUMPRODUCT function is a conscious design strategy. As mentioned earlier, the SUMPRODUCT function is intimately related to linearity. By using this function, we can see structural similarities in many apparently different linear programs, and the recognition of this similarity is key to our understanding. Moreover, by taking this approach, we can build recognizable models in a standard format for virtually any linear programming problem (although other approaches may be better for certain circumstances). In addition, the SUMPRODUCT function has technical significance. Solver is designed to exploit the use of this function, mainly in setting up the problem quickly for internal calculations. This becomes an advantage in large models, so it makes sense to learn the habit while practicing on smaller models.

With the partial standardization implied by these "best practice" guidelines, we may be restricting the creative instinct somewhat, but we gain in several important respects.

- *We enhance our ability to communicate with others.* A standardized structure provides a common language for describing linear programs and reinforces our understanding about how such models are shaped. This is especially true when spreadsheet models are being shown to technical experts.

- *We improve our ability to diagnose errors while building the model.* A standardized structure has certain recognizable features that help us detect modeling errors or simple typos. In a spreadsheet context, we often exploit the ability to copy a small number of cell formulas to several other locations, so we can avoid some common errors by entering part of the standard structure carefully and then copying it appropriately.

- *We make it relatively easy to "scale up" the model.* That is, we may want to expand a model by adding variables or constraints, allowing us to move from a prototype to a practical scale or from a "toy" problem to an "industrial strength" version. The standard structure adapts readily when we wish to expand a model this way.

- *We avoid some interpretation problems when we perform sensitivity analysis.* A standardized structure ensures that Solver will treat the spreadsheet information in a dependable fashion. Otherwise, sensitivity analyses may become ambiguous or confusing.

2.1.4. Results

Just as there are three important modules in our spreadsheet (decision variables, objective function, and constraints), there are three kinds of information to examine in the optimization results.

- The optimal values of the decision variables indicate the best course of action for the model.
- The optimal value of the objective function specifies the best level of performance in the model.
- The status of the constraints reveals which factors in the model truly prevent the achievement of even better levels of performance.

In particular, a LT or GT constraint in which the LHS equals the RHS is called a *tight* or a *binding* constraint. Prior to solving the model, each constraint is a *potential* limitation on the set of decisions, but the optimization of the model identifies which constraints are *actual* limitations. These are the physical, economic, or administrative conditions in the problem that actively restrict the ultimate performance level.

We can think of the solution to a linear program as providing what we might call both tactical and strategic information. *Tactical information* means that the optimal solution prescribes the best possible set of decisions under the given conditions. Thus, if the model represents an actual situation, its optimal decisions represent a plan to implement. *Strategic information* means that the optimal solution identifies which conditions prevent the achievement of better levels of performance. In particular, the model's binding constraints indicate the factors that restrict the objective function. If we don't have to implement a course of action immediately, we can explore the possibility of altering one or more of those constraints in a way that improves the objective. Thus, if the model represents a situation with given parametric conditions, and we want to improve the level of performance, we can examine the possibility of changing the "givens."

Whether we have tactical information or strategic information in mind, we must still recognize that the optimization process finds a solution to the model, not necessarily to the actual problem. The distinction between model and problem derives from the fact that the model is, by its very nature, a simplification. Any features of the problem that were assumed away or ignored must be addressed once we have a solution to the model. For example, a major assumption in linear programs is that all of the model's parameters are known with certainty. Frequently, however, we find that we have to work with uncertain estimates of model parameters. In that situation, it is important to examine the sensitivity of the model's results to alternative assumptions about the values of the parameters.

2.2. ALLOCATION MODELS

We now proceed with our tour of the basic linear programming types. The *allocation problem* calls for maximizing an objective (usually profit-related) subject to LT constraints on capacity. In the traditional economic paradigm, several activities compete for limited resources, and we seek the best allocation of resources among the competing activities. Consider the example of Brown Furniture Company.

EXAMPLE 2.1   *Brown Furniture Company*

Brown Furniture Company makes three kinds of office furniture: chairs, desks, and tables. Each product requires skilled labor in the parts fabrication department, unskilled labor in the assembly department, machining on some key pieces of equipment, and some wood as raw material. At current prices, the unit profit contribution for each product is known, and the company can sell everything that it manufactures. The size of the workforce has been established, so the number of skilled and unskilled labor hours are known. The time available on the relevant equipment has also been determined, and a known quantity of wood can be obtained each month under a contract with a wood supplier. Managers at Brown Furniture would like to maximize their profit contribution for the month by choosing production quantities for the chairs, desks, and tables. The data shown below summarize the parameters of the problem.

	Requirements per unit			
	Chairs	Desks	Tables	Resources available
Fabrication (hr)	4	6	2	2000 hr
Assembly (hr)	3	8	6	2000 hr
Machining (hr)	9	6	4	1440 hr
Wood (sq. ft)	30	40	25	9600 sq. ft
Profit per unit	$16	$20	$14	

■

The data in Example 2.1 would likely come from several sources. The number of labor hours available might be a parameter supplied by the Human Resources Department. The labor required for each product more likely comes from the Production Department, and the contract quantity for wood might come from Procurement. Unit profit contributions can be calculated from information on selling prices and unit costs, which could come from the Marketing and Accounting Departments. In short, the kind of data needed for optimization analysis can often be found in various parts of an organization, and the process of data gathering requires communication with several functions of the firm. Although we won't discuss the details of data sources for most of the other examples in this book, the point is a general one. Data needed for optimization are seldom found in just one place. More typically, we have to pursue an interfunctional network of contacts to obtain the data we need for modeling.

To build a model for this problem, we follow the outline of Box 2.3. To determine decision variables, we ask, "What must be decided?" The answer is the product mix, so we define decision variables as the numbers of chairs, desks, and tables. For the purposes of notation, we can use C, D, and T to represent the number of chairs, the number of desks and the number of tables, respectively.

Next, we ask, "What measure will we use to compare sets of decision variables?" If two people in the organization were to advocate two different production plans, we would respond by calculating the total profit contribution for each one and choosing the larger value. To calculate profit contribution, we add the profit from chairs, the profit from desks, and the profit from tables. Thus, an algebraic expression for total profit becomes:

$$\text{Profit} = 16C + 20D + 14T$$

To identify the model's constraints, we ask, "What restrictions limit our choice of decision variables?" This scenario describes four resource capacities. In words, a production capacity constraint might state that the resources *consumed* in a production plan must be less than or equal to the resources *available*. Laying out those words in the form of an inequality, we can write:

Fabrication hours consumed $\leq$ Fabrication hours available

where we chose to place "hours available" on the RHS because it is represented by a parameter of the model (2000 hours, in this case). Converting the inequality to symbols, we can then write:

Fabrication hours consumed $= 4C + 6D + 2T$

≤ 2000 (Fabrication hours available)

Similar constraints must hold for the assembly hours, machining time, and wood supply:

Assembly hours consumed $= 3C + 8D + 6T \leq 2000$ (Assembly hours available)

Machining time consumed $= 9C + 6D + 4T \leq 1440$ (Machining time available)

Wood consumed $= 30C + 40D + 25T \leq 9600$ (Wood available)

We now have four constraints that describe the restrictions limiting our choice of decision variables C, D, and T. The entire model, stated in algebraic terms, reads as follows:

$$\text{Maximize } z = 16C + 20D + 14T$$

subject to

$$4C + 6D + 2T \leq 2000$$
$$3C + 8D + 6T \leq 2000$$
$$9C + 6D + 4T \leq 1440$$
$$30C + 40D + 25T \leq 9600$$

▲	A	B	C	D	E	F	G
1	Allocation: Basic Model						
2							
3	Decision Variables						
4			C	D	T		
5	Production plan		50	75	100		
6							
7	Objective Function				*Total*		
8	Profit		16	20	14	3700	
9							
10	Constraints				*LHS*		*RHS*
11	Fabrication		4	6	2	850	<=	2000
12	Assembly		3	8	6	1350	<=	2000
13	Machining		9	6	4	1300	<=	1440
14	Wood		30	40	25	7000	<=	9600
15							
	◄ ◄ ► ►►	Allocation	◄				►

Figure 2.1. Model for the Brown Furniture example.

This algebraic statement reflects a standard format for linear programs. Each variable corresponds to a column and each constraint corresponds to a row, with the objective function appearing as a special row at the top of the model. This layout is suitable for spreadsheet display as well.

A spreadsheet model for the allocation problem appears in Figure 2.1. Three modules appear in the spreadsheet, including a highlighted row for the decision variables, a highlighted single cell for the objective function value, and a set of constraint relationships in which the RHS values are highlighted. The cells containing the symbol <= have no function in the operation of the spreadsheet; they are intended as a visual aid to the user, helping to convey the information in the constraints. We place them between the LHS value of the constraint (a formula) and the RHS value (a parameter).

Figure 2.2 shows the formulas in this model. Aside from labels, the model consists of only two kinds of cells: those containing numbers and those containing a SUMPRODUCT formula. This is our standard form for a linear program in a spreadsheet.

Figure 2.1 contains an arbitrary set of values for the decision variables (50 chairs, 75 desks, and 100 tables). We could try different sets of three values in order to see whether we could come up with a good allocation by trial and error. Such an attempt might also be a useful debugging step, to reassure ourselves that the model is complete. For example, suppose we start by fixing the number of desks and tables at zero and varying the number of chairs. For Fabrication capacity, chairs consume 4 hours each and 2000 hours are available; so we could put $2000/4 = 500$ chairs into the plan (i.e., into cell B5), and the result would be feasible for the first constraint. However, we can see immediately—by comparing the LHS and RHS values—that this number requires more machining time than we have available. Therefore, we

◢	A	B	C	D	E	F	G
1	Allocation: Basic Model						
2							
3	Decision Variables						
4			C	D	T		
5	Production plan	50	75	100			
6							
7	Objective Function				Total		
8		Profit	16	20	14	=SUMPRODUCT($B$5:$D$5,B8:D8)		
9							
10	Constraints				LHS		RHS
11		Fabrication	4	6	2	=SUMPRODUCT($B$5:$D$5,B11:D11)	<=	2000
12		Assembly	3	8	6	=SUMPRODUCT($B$5:$D$5,B12:D12)	<=	2000
13		Machining	9	6	4	=SUMPRODUCT($B$5:$D$5,B13:D13)	<=	1440
14		Wood	30	40	25	=SUMPRODUCT($B$5:$D$5,B14:D14)	<=	9600
15							

◄ ◄ ► ►   Allocation   Allocation (2)   ◄

Figure 2.2. Formulas in the Brown Furniture model.

can reduce the number of chairs to 160 (just enough to consume all of the machining hours) and verify that sufficient quantities of the other resources are available to support this volume. Thus, we obtain a feasible plan and a profit contribution of $2560. If we rely on desks alone, instead of tables, we run into limits imposed by both machining capacity and wood supply, resulting in profits of $4800. If we rely solely on tables, we run into limits imposed by assembly capacity, leading to profits of $4666. Next, we might try some plans containing two of the three products, or perhaps all three. Such experiments help us to confirm that the model is working properly and give us a feel for the profit figures that might be achievable.

After verifying the model in this fashion, we proceed to the optimization procedure on the Risk Solver Platform tab, clicking the Model icon on the ribbon to make the task pane visible. We then take the following steps.

- Select cells B5:D5, then choose Add Variables from the drop-down menu on the *Add* icon.
- Select cell E8, then choose Add Objective from the drop-down menu on the *Add* icon.
- Select cells E11:E14, then choose Add Constraint from the drop-down menu on the *Add* icon.
- Fill in the Add Constraint window requiring that the range E11:E14 must be less than or equal to G11:G14 (see Figure 2.3). Then press OK.

At this stage the window on the Model tab displays the full specification, as shown in Figure 2.4.

Next, we go to the Engine tab (see Figure 2.5) and take two steps.

- Select the Standard LP/Quadratic Engine from the drop-down menu. This step specifies the use of the linear solver.
- In the main window, set the option for Assume Non-Negative to True.

Add Constraint   ☒

Cell Reference: Constraint:

$E$11:$E$14   ▦   <= ▾ $G$11:$G$14   ▦   Normal ▾

Comment: Chance:

                                                            0

  OK   Cancel   Add   Help

Figure 2.3. Specifying the constraints.

The first of these steps specifies the use of the linear solver. The second makes it unnecessary to add explicit constraints forcing the variables to be greater than or equal to zero.

We are now ready for the optimization run, which we can invoke by clicking on the green triangle icon on either the Model tab or the Output tab. First, however, we might want to think about some hypotheses. For example, do we expect that the optimal solution will call for all three products? Will it consume all of the available hours? What order of magnitude should we expect for the optimal profit? This step helps us build a better intuition for the problem or perhaps discover an error.

Figure 2.4. Specification for the Brown Furniture model.

Figure 2.5. Specifications on the Engine tab.

If no technical problems occur after we initiate the optimization run, Solver produces the following result message in the solution log on the Output tab:

```
Solver found a solution. All
constraints and optimality conditions
are satisfied.
```

We recognize this as the optimality message, which we encountered in Chapter 1. At this point the optimal solution is displayed on the spreadsheet.

The linear solver implements a version of the algorithm known as the *simplex method*. Although it is not necessary to be acquainted with the simplex method in order to apply linear programming or to appreciate its significance, some exposure to the algorithm may be useful. Appendix 3 provides an algebraic description of the simplex method.

Figure 2.6 displays the optimal solution to our model for the example.

- The optimal plan contains no chairs, 160 desks, and 120 tables.
- The maximum profit contribution is $4880.
- The binding constraints are assembly capacity and machining capacity.

These are the three key pieces of information provided in the solution. Evidently, the profit margin on chairs is not sufficiently attractive for us to devote scarce resources to their production. But even by relying on desks and tables, Brown Furniture can maximize its profit contribution for the month. (We examine the solution in more detail later on.)

Recall the distinction made earlier between tactical and strategic information in the linear program's solution. Faced with implementing a production plan for next month at Brown Furniture, we could pursue the tactical solution, producing no chairs, 160 desks, and 120 tables. However, the tactical solution is the optimal solution

	A	B	C	D	E	F	G
1	Allocation: Basic Model						
2							
3	Decision Variables						
4			C	D	T		
5	Production plan		0	160	120		
6							
7	Objective Function				Total		
8	Profit		16	20	14	4880	
9							
10	Constraints				LHS		RHS
11	Fabrication		4	6	2	1200	<=	2000
12	Assembly		3	8	6	2000	<=	2000
13	Machining		9	6	4	1440	<=	1440
14	Wood		30	40	25	9400	<=	9600
15							

Allocation / Allocation (2) / Allocation (3)

Figure 2.6. Optimal solution to the Brown Furniture model.

for the *model*. Perhaps it is not the optimal solution for the actual *problem* facing Brown Furniture. For example, a relevant marketing consideration might have been omitted from the model. Perhaps our marketing department is reluctant to bring a limited product line to the marketplace—that is, by producing no chairs at all. Even if the optimization of a short-term objective calls for a limited product line, long-term risks may arise if some customers conclude that Brown Furniture cannot make chairs. Thus, the optimal solution of the model may turn out to be only the first step in a discussion of how to reflect long-term marketing needs in short-term planning processes. Possibly, this discussion will lead to revisions in the model, and the optimal solution will be revisited.

On the other hand, if there were time to adjust the resources available at Brown Furniture and we were interested in the strategic implications of the solution, we would want to explore the possibility of acquiring more assembly capacity or machining capacity because those are the binding constraints. We know that additional fabrication capacity or wood supply would not provide any benefit, given current conditions, because we can achieve optimal profits without fully consuming either of those resources. Overcoming the limited supply of assembly capacity and machining capacity is the key to achieving higher profits.

2.2.1. The Product Mix Problem

The *product mix problem* is a variation of the basic allocation model. It follows the structure of the allocation model by prescribing the maximization of profit contribution subject to LT constraints. Typically, the decision variables correspond to quantities of various products to include in a company's product mix. The constraints are usually of two types: capacity constraints on production resources and demand constraints on potential sales. In Example 2.1, suppose that the company markets its chairs, tables, and desks through a distributor who also provides monthly forecasts of demands. Next month's forecasts are:

	Chairs	Desks	Tables
Demand	300	120	144

With this information, we can extend the basic allocation model to include three demand constraints as well. The full model takes the following algebraic form.

$$\text{Maximize } z = 16C + 20D + 14T$$
subject to
$$
\begin{aligned}
4C + 6D + 2T &\le 2000 \\
3C + 8D + 6T &\le 2000 \\
9C + 6D + 4T &\le 1440 \\
30C + 40D + 25T &\le 9600 \\
C &\le 300 \\
D &\le 120 \\
T &\le 144
\end{aligned}
$$

The spreadsheet version of this model simply adds three rows to the model in Figure 2.6. Most easily, the LHS formula can be copied from the wood supply constraint (cell E14) into cells E15:E17 after the new coefficients have been added, as shown in Figure 2.7.

We must then update the model specification so that all seven constraints are included. To make this adjustment most simply, we can select the range E15:E17 and add the corresponding constraints via the Add Constraint window. The updated representation in the window of the Model tab lists two sets of constraints, as shown in Figure 2.8. Although it may not be necessary in every case, it is a good habit to click the *Refresh* icon after adding or deleting variables or constraints, so we do that here.

Alternatively, to update the allocation model, we can double-click on the icon for the existing Normal constraints, which opens the Change Constraint window. This time, we can edit the Cell Reference box and the Constraint box so that the ranges include all seven of the constraints. Then, the window on the Model tab displays only one set of constraints. Again, it is a good habit to click *Refresh*.

A new optimization run then reveals that the optimal product mix becomes 16 chairs, 120 desks, and 144 tables, as shown in Figure 2.9. The optimal profit contribution in the product mix model is $4672. This amount is less than the optimal profit in the original allocation model. Not surprisingly, the imposition of demand ceilings leads to a reduction in the optimal profit. In fact, looking back at Figure 2.7, we

⊿	A	B	C	D	E	F	G
1	**Allocation: Product Mix**						
2							
3	**Decision Variables**						
4			C	D	T		
5	Production plan		0	160	120		
6							
7	**Objective Function**				*Total*		
8	Profit	16	20	14	4880		
9							
10	**Constraints**				*LHS*		*RHS*
11	Fabrication	4	6	2	1200	<=	2000
12	Assembly	3	8	6	2000	<=	2000
13	Machining	9	6	4	1440	<=	1440
14	Wood	30	40	25	9400	<=	9600
15	Chair ceiling	1			0	<=	300
16	Desk ceiling		1		160	<=	120
17	Table ceiling			1	120	<=	144
18							

Figure 2.7. Product mix model.

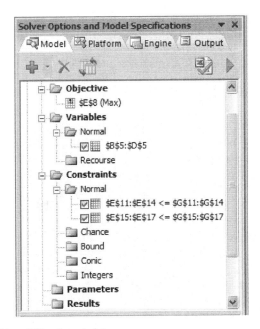

Figure 2.8. Specifying additional constraints.

▲	A	B	C	D	E	F	G	
1	**Allocation: Product Mix**							
2								
3	**Decision Variables**							
4			C	D	T			
5	Production plan	16	120	144				
6								
7	**Objective Function**				*Total*			
8	Profit	16	20	14	4672			
9								
10	**Constraints**				*LHS*		*RHS*	
11	Fabrication	4	6	2	1072	<=	2000	
12	Assembly	3	8	6	1872	<=	2000	
13	Machining	9	6	4	1440	<=	1440	
14	Wood	30	40	25	8880	<=	9600	
15	Chair ceiling	1			16	<=	300	
16	Desk ceiling		1		120	<=	120	
17	Table ceiling			1	144	<=	144	
18								

Mix   Mix (2)

Figure 2.9. Optimal Solution to the product mix model.

can see immediately that the product mix of 160 desks and 120 tables does not meet all of the demand ceiling constraints. This outcome illustrates the intuitive principle that the addition of constraints to a model cannot improve the optimal objective function—it will be the same or worse when constraints are added.

Three binding constraints occur in the product mix model: the demand ceiling for desks, the demand ceiling for tables, and machining capacity. None of the other constraints is binding.

In general, the product mix model involves different types of capacity and perhaps different types of demand. For example, in our scenario, the different types of capacity are labor, equipment, and material inputs for production. Alternatively, the labor might be broken down into regular-time and overtime hours, or the material could come from "make" versus "buy" sources (i.e., from in-house fabrication and assembly or from an outside subcontractor). Similarly, demand could be specified by geographical region or by time period, the latter for a multiperiod formulation. In the multiperiod case, it is usually helpful to keep track of inventory levels, partly because inventories affect costs but also because inventory can be considered yet another source of product, just like regular-time capacity or subcontracted production. One common variation of the basic product mix model is to include GT constraints on potential sales of certain products. A minimum demand quantity might reflect a contractual commitment or represent a sales level that management wishes to meet under any circumstances. Such demand thresholds may or may not be part of the model; the distinctive features of the product mix model are capacity constraints on productive resources and demand constraints on market requirements.

2.3. COVERING MODELS

The *covering problem* calls for minimizing an objective (usually cost related) subject to GT constraints on required coverage. Whereas the allocation model *divides* resources and assigns them to competing activities, the covering model *combines* resources and coordinates activities. Consider the example of Herrick Foods Company.

EXAMPLE 2.2 *Herrick Foods Company*

Herrick Foods Company wishes to introduce packaged trail mix as a new product. The ingredients for the trail mix are seeds, raisins, flakes, and two kinds of nuts. Each ingredient contains a certain amount of vitamins, minerals, protein, and calories; and the Marketing Department has specified the product be designed so that a certain minimum nutritional profile is met. The decision problem is to minimize the product cost and determine the product composition—that is, by choosing the amount of each ingredient in the mix. The data shown below summarize the parameters of the problem.

	Grams per pound					Nutritional requirement
	Seeds	Raisins	Flakes	Pecans	Walnuts	
Vitamins	10	20	10	30	20	16
Minerals	5	7	4	9	2	10
Protein	1	4	10	2	1	15
Calories	500	450	160	300	500	600
Cost/pound	$4	$5	$3	$7	$6	

■

To determine the decision variables, we again ask, "What must be decided?" The answer is we need to determine the amount of each ingredient to put in a package of trail mix. For the purposes of notation, we can use S, R, F, P, and W to represent the number of pounds of each ingredient in a package.

Next, we ask, "What measure will we use to compare sets of decision variables?" This should be the total cost of a package, and our interest lies in the lowest possible total cost. To calculate the total cost of a particular composition, we sum the costs of each ingredient in the package

$$\text{Cost} = 4S + 5R + 3F + 7P + 6W$$

To identify the model's constraints, we ask, "What restrictions limit our choice of decision variables?" In this scenario, the main limitation is the requirement to meet the specified nutritional profile. Each dimension of this profile gives rise to a separate constraint. An example of such a constraint states, in words, that the number of grams of vitamins *provided* in the package must be greater than or equal to the number of grams *required* by the specified profile. Laying out those words in the format of an inequality, we can write

$$\text{Grams of vitamins provided} \geq \text{Grams of vitamins required}$$

where we chose to place "grams required" on the RHS because it is represented by a parameter of the model (16 grams, in this case). Converting the inequality to symbols, we can then write

$$\text{Vitamin content} = 10S + 20R + 10F + 30P + 20W \geq 16 \text{ (Vitamin floor)}$$

Similar constraints must hold for mineral protein, and calorie content. The entire model, stated in algebraic terms, reads as follows.

$$\text{Minimize } z = 4S + \quad 5R + \quad 3F + \quad 7P + \quad 6W$$
$$\text{subject to}$$
$$10S + \quad 20R + \quad 10F + \quad 30P + \quad 20W \geq 16$$
$$5S + \quad 7R + \quad 4F + \quad 9P + \quad 2W \geq 10$$
$$1S + \quad 4R + \quad 10F + \quad 2P + \quad 1W \geq 15$$
$$500S + 450R + 160F + 300P + 500W \geq 600$$

In this basic scenario, no other constraints arise, although we could imagine that there could also be limited quantities of the ingredients available, expressed as LT constraints, or a weight requirement for the package, expressed as an EQ constraint.

A spreadsheet model for the basic scenario appears in Figure 2.10. Again, we see the three modules: a highlighted row for decision variables, a highlighted single cell for the objective function value, and a set of constraint relationships with highlighted RHS's. If we were to display the formulas for this model, we would again see that the only formula in the worksheet is the SUMPRODUCT formula.

Once we have persuaded ourselves that the model is valid, we proceed to the Model tab in the task pane and enter the following information

Objective:	G8 (minimize)
Variables:	B5:F5
Constraints:	G11:G14 $\geq$ I11:I14

As in the allocation model, we move to the Engine tab, specify the linear solver, and invoke the option for nonnegative variables.

After contemplating some hypotheses about the problem (e.g., will the solution require all five ingredients?) we run Solver and find the result message in the solution log. The optimal solution is reproduced in Figure 2.11. It calls for 0.48 lb of seeds, 0.33 lb of raisins, and 1.32 lb of flakes, with no nuts at all. Evidently, nuts are prohibitively expensive, given the nature of the required nutritional profile and the other

Figure 2.10. Model for Herrick Foods example.

ingredients available. The optimal mix achieves all of the nutritional requirements at a minimum cost of $7.54. The tight constraints in this solution are the requirements for minerals, protein, and calories.

Herrick Foods might decide that trail mix without nuts is not an appealing product. This concern illustrates another situation where the solution to the model may not represent a solution to the practical problem. In building the model, we have not considered the implication of a product without nuts. Alerted to this possibility, we may wish to revisit the model and make sure that some nuts appear in the optimal mix. One way to do so is to require a minimum of 0.15 lb of both pecans and walnuts

Figure 2.11. Optimal solution for the Herrick Foods model.

	A	B	C	D	E	F	G	H	I
1	Covering: Trail Mix								
2									
3	Decision Variables								
4		S	R	F	P	W			
5	Amounts	0.47733	0.33413	1.31862	0	0			
6		0.15	0.15	0.15	0.15	0.15			
7	Objective Function						Total		
8	Cost	4	5	3	7	6	$ 7.54		
9									
10	Constraints						LHS		RHS
11	Vitamins	10	20	10	30	20	24.642	>=	16
12	Minerals	5	7	4	9	2	10	>=	10
13	Protein	1	4	10	2	1	15	>=	15
14	Calories	500	450	160	300	500	600	>=	600
15									

Covering / Covering (2) / Covering (3)

Figure 2.12. Herrick Foods model with additional constraints.

in the mix. In Figure 2.12, we show an amended model that requires at least 0.15 lb of every ingredient.

The value of 0.15 appears just below the corresponding decision variable, and in the Model tab of the task pane, we add the constraint that the range B5:F5 must be greater than or equal to the range B6:F6. After this update, we revise the model specification as follows

Objective:	G8 (minimize)
Variables:	B5:F5
Constraints:	B5:F5 ≥ B6:F6
	G11:G14 ≥ I11:I14

The requirement that a particular decision variable must be greater than or equal to a given value is called a *lower bound constraint*. Here, the first set of constraints is formulated as a range of lower bound constraints. Similarly, a requirement that a particular decision variable must be less than or equal to a given value would be called an *upper bound constraint*. (We could have used such constraints in the product mix model, but in Figure 2.9 we posed them in the standard SUMPRODUCT style, so that they resembled the other constraints in the model.)

After including the lower bound constraints, running Solver again produces the optimal solution shown in Figure 2.13. By using linear programming and acknowledging a requirement to include all five ingredients in the ultimate mixture, Herrick Foods has identified the desired composition of its trail mix product.

Imposing lower bounds on the original Herrick Foods model leads to an optimal solution that contains all five of the ingredients. We might have expected that nuts would appear exactly at their lower limit because without the lower bound constraints, the optimization left nuts completely out of the solution. Thus, when we added the lower bound, there was no incentive to include nuts at any level greater than the

Figure 2.13. Optimal solution to the modified Herrick Foods model.

lower bound. The optimal cost is also higher in the amended model than in the original, at $8.33. This result again reflects the intuitive principle that adding constraints to a model cannot improve the objective function—it will be the same or worse when constraints are added.

The trail mix example is a simplified version of a classic covering problem known as the *diet problem*. This problem arises, for example, in the determination of weekly menus for large institutional populations, such as those in nursing homes, prisons, and summer camps. The purpose of the model is to determine meal selection for each of the 21 meals served each week to everyone in a large group. The variables may represent quantities of various food groups (meats, vegetables, fruits, etc.), and weekly nutritional requirements reflect limits on the totals of weekly requirements for fat, calories, protein, carbohydrates, and so on. A common phenomenon, akin to the results of our first trail mix model, is that cost minimization drives the solution toward a limited number of meals. Campers may not find a steady diet of tofu appealing, even if that is the model's optimal solution. Subtle differences between the problem and the model become clearer once a solution is obtained. For that reason, a more detailed and complicated set of constraints must often be added to the diet model in order to generate an appetizing weekly menu.

2.3.1. The Staff-Scheduling Problem

Many service industries face the problem of scheduling their workforce to meet fluctuating staffing requirements. Nurses, telephone operators, toll collectors, and bus drivers operate in this type of environment—providing service over a period that extends beyond the normal 8 hr working day and possibly continuing around the clock. Many companies restrict themselves to full-time workers and they meet fluctuating requirements of this sort by assigning staff to overlapping work shifts. As an example, consider the daily staffing problem at Acme Communications.

EXAMPLE 2.3   *Acme Communications*

Acme Communications operates a regional call center where the workday is broken down into six 4-hour shifts, and each operator works two consecutive shifts. The table below describes staff requirements on each shift.

Shift number	#1	#2	#3	#4	#5	#6
Time period	2 am–6 am	6 am–10 am	10 am–2 pm	2 pm–6 pm	6 pm–10 pm	10 pm–2 am
Requirement	10	20	45	40	50	12

The call center's manager wishes to assign operators to the six available starting times so that the staffing requirements are covered in each period and the total workforce size is as small as possible.   ■

For Acme's problem, the decision variables are the number of operators assigned to each of the six starting times. For example, let x_1 represent the number assigned to begin work on shift #1. These operators work during shifts #1 and #2, from 2 am to 10 am. Similarly, x_2 represents the number assigned to work during shifts #2 and #3, from 6 am to 2 pm. With this notation, the number of operators working during shift #2 must equal $x_1 + x_2$. By a similar logic, the number of operators working during shift #3 must equal $x_2 + x_3$, and so on. Finally, the number working during shift #1 must equal $x_6 + x_1$ because the requirements repeat in 24-hour cycles. An algebraic statement of the problem is shown below.

$$\text{Minimize } z = x_1 + x_2 + x_3 + x_4 + x_5 + x_6$$
$$\text{subject to}$$
$$x_1 \qquad\qquad\qquad + x_6 \geq 10$$
$$x_1 + x_2 \qquad\qquad\qquad \geq 20$$
$$x_2 + x_3 \qquad\qquad \geq 45$$
$$x_3 + x_4 \qquad\qquad \geq 40$$
$$x_4 + x_5 \qquad \geq 50$$
$$x_5 + x_6 \geq 12$$

Figure 2.14 shows a spreadsheet model for this problem.

Staffing models of this sort have a distinctive structure. First, because the number of operators working on any given shift is the total assigned to two starting times, two variables appear in each constraint. Thus, in the spreadsheet, there are two 1s on the LHS of each constraint row. Second, because operators work two consecutive

	A	B	C	D	E	F	G	H	I	J
1	**Covering: Staff Scheduling**									
2										
3	**Decision Variables**	Starting time								
4		2am	6am	10am	2pm	6pm	10pm			
5	Staff	10	43	2	38	12	0			
6										
7	**Objective Function**							*Total*		
8	number	1	1	1	1	1	1	105		
9										
10	**Constraints**							*LHS*		*RHS*
11	2am-6am	1	0	0	0	0	1	10	>=	10
12	6am-10am	1	1	0	0	0	0	53	>=	20
13	10am-2pm	0	1	1	0	0	0	45	>=	45
14	2pm-6pm	0	0	1	1	0	0	40	>=	40
15	6pm-10pm	0	0	0	1	1	0	50	>=	50
16	10pm-2am	0	0	0	0	1	1	12	>=	12
17										

Staff1

Figure 2.14. Staffing model.

shifts, two consecutive 1s appear in the columns corresponding to variables. (In the case of x_6, shifts #6 and #1 are consecutive.) The model specification is as follows

Objective:	H8 (minimize)
Variables:	B5:G5
Constraints:	H11:H16 $\geq$ J11:J16

Figure 2.14 displays an optimal solution, which achieves a total workforce of 105 by assigning various numbers of operators to five starting times, with no one starting work at 10 pm.

In general, we can structure the staff-scheduling model around the shift definition. Time periods correspond to rows in the model and alternative shift assignments correspond to columns. For a problem in which the assignments correspond to days, we can imagine seven constraints (each one representing a daily staffing requirement) and seven assignments (each one corresponding to a different start of a 5-day work stretch). In the constraints module, the column of coefficients under a given shift assignment shows the profile of the work shift. In Figure 2.14, those coefficients are two consecutive 1s, reflecting the fact that each assignment comprises two consecutive 4-hour time periods. In a more detailed version with 2-hour time periods, we can imagine four consecutive 1s. In an hourly version, we can imagine eight consecutive 1s. In most applications, however, when the time periods are this detailed, provisions are usually made for meal breaks as well. As an example, imagine a service facility that operates over a 12-hour span from 6 am to 6 pm. Shifts begin on the hour and contain 8 hours of work with an hour break in the middle. In this case, the columns of the model would appear as follows:

Start:	6 am	7 am	8 am	9 am		
	1	0	0	0	6−7	requirements
	1	1	0	0	7−8	requirements
	1	1	1	0	8−9	requirements
	1	1	1	1	9−10	requirements
	0	1	1	1	10−11	requirements
	1	0	1	1	11−12	requirements
	1	1	0	1	12−1	requirements
	1	1	1	0	1−2	requirements
	1	1	1	1	2−3	requirements
	0	1	1	1	3−4	requirements
	0	0	1	1	4−5	requirements
	0	0	0	1	5−6	requirements

For the particular set of hourly staff requirements shown in Figure 2.15, the optimal staff size is 57.

⊿	A	B	C	D	E	F	G	H	I	
1	Staff Scheduling for 12 hour coverage									
2										
3	Decisions									
4		starts	6	7	8	9				
5			15	17	7	18				
6	Objective									
7		size	1	1	1	1	57			
8										
9	Constraints									
10		6am	1	0	0	0	15	>=	10	
11		7am	1	1	0	0	32	>=	15	
12		8am	1	1	1	0	39	>=	36	
13		9am	1	1	1	1	57	>=	38	
14		10am	0	1	1	1	42	>=	42	
15		11am	1	0	1	1	40	>=	40	
16		noon	1	1	0	1	50	>=	44	
17		1pm	1	1	1	0	39	>=	39	
18		2pm	1	1	1	1	57	>=	36	
19		3pm	0	1	1	1	42	>=	30	
20		4pm	0	0	1	1	25	>=	22	
21		5pm	0	0	0	1	18	>=	18	
22										
	⊮ ◀ ▶ ⊯	Staff1	Staff2							

Figure 2.15. Hourly Staffing model.

However, if work rules allow the lunch break to occur after as few as three hours of work or as many as five hours of work, then 12 full-time shift assignments are available, rather than four. The shift start times would remain the same, but the column profiles would take the following form.

Start:	6	6	6	7	7	7	8	8	8	9	9	9
	1	1	1	0	0	0	0	0	0	0	0	0
	1	1	1	1	1	1	0	0	0	0	0	0
	1	1	1	1	1	1	1	1	1	0	0	0
	0	1	1	1	1	1	1	1	1	1	1	1
	1	0	1	0	1	1	1	1	1	1	1	1
	1	1	0	1	0	1	0	1	1	1	1	1
	1	1	1	1	1	0	1	0	1	0	1	1
	1	1	1	1	1	1	1	1	0	1	0	1
	1	1	1	1	1	1	1	1	1	1	1	0
	0	0	0	1	1	1	1	1	1	1	1	1
	0	0	0	0	0	0	1	1	1	1	1	1
	0	0	0	0	0	0	0	0	0	1	1	1

With these rules in place, the optimal staff size drops to 54. The example illustrates how an "optimal" solution can disguise possible inefficiency until we view the problem from a broader perspective. The solution in the four-shift model of Figure 2.15 is optimal for the situation it describes, but the rigidity of the rules governing shift patterns leads to inefficiency. When these rules become more flexible, then a more efficient solution is attainable. In contrast to the effect of additional *constraints*, additional *flexibility* can improve the objective function. Nevertheless, a good deal of overstaffing occurs in either model. We might have to look beyond the optimization model to avoid some of this remaining inefficiency. For example, if we can create incentives that shift customer demands from one period to another, we can influence the size of the optimal staff.

One variation of the staff-scheduling problem combines full and part-time shifts. We can imagine full-time shifts as columns in which the 1s delineate an eight-hour workday, whereas the part-time shifts might be columns containing a smaller number of 1s. Such models usually have an objective function that measures the cost of the workforce rather than its size, to reflect salary differences between full- and part-time workers. In all these variations, however, the essential structure of the model represents a covering problem by minimizing workforce cost or workforce size subject to a systematic set of GT constraints for time-dependent staffing requirements.

2.4. BLENDING MODELS

Blending relationships are very common in linear programming applications, yet they remain difficult for beginners to identify in problem descriptions and to implement in spreadsheet models. Because of this difficulty, we begin with a special case—the representation of proportions. As an example, let's return to the product mix version of Example 2.1. In Figure 2.9 the optimal product mix consisted of 16 chairs, 120 desks, and 144 tables. Suppose that this outcome is unacceptable because of the imbalance in volumes. For more balance, the Marketing Department might require that each product must make up at least 20% of the units sold.

When we describe outcomes in terms of a proportion, and when we place a floor (or ceiling) on the proportion, we are using a special type of blending constraint. In our example, a direct statement of the requirement for chairs is the following

$$\frac{C}{C + D + T} \geq 0.2$$

This GT constraint has a parameter on the RHS and all the decision variables on the LHS, as is usually the case. Although this is a valid constraint, it is not in *linear* form because the quantities C, D, and T appear in both the numerator and denominator of the fraction. (The ratio divides decision variables by decision variables.) However, we can convert the nonlinear inequality to a linear one with a bit of algebra. First, multiply both sides of the inequality by $(C + D + T)$, yielding

$$C \geq 0.2(C + D + T)$$

Next, collect terms involving the decision variables on the LHS, so that we get

$$0.8C - 0.2D - 0.2T \geq 0$$

This form conveys the same requirement as the original fractional constraint, and we recognize it immediately as a linear form. The coefficients on the LHS turn out to be either the complement of the 20 percent floor $(1 - 0.2)$ or the floor itself (but with a minus sign). In a similar fashion, the requirement that the other products must respect the floor leads to the following two constraints

$$0.8D - 0.2C - 0.2T \geq 0$$
$$0.8T - 0.2C - 0.2D \geq 0$$

Appending these three constraints to the product mix model gives rise to the linear program described in Figure 2.16. In the figure, we show the spreadsheet after the model has been optimized. Before the constraints were added, the optimal mix generated profits of $4672. With the 20 percent floor imposed, we expect optimal profits to drop. As shown in Figure 2.16, the new optimal mix becomes 48 chairs, 120 desks, and 72 tables. Thus, swapping chairs for tables in the product mix, we can achieve the best possible level of profit, achieving a total of $4176. As we might have expected, chairs make up exactly 20 percent of the optimal output in this solution, while desks and tables each account for more than 20 percent.

Whenever we encounter a constraint in the form of a lower limit or an upper limit on a proportion, we can follow similar steps.

	A	B	C	D	E	F	G
1	Allocation: Product Mix with Additional Requirements						
2							
3	Decision Variables						
4			C	D	T		
5	Production plan	48	120	72			
6							
7	Objective Function				Total		
8	Profit	16	20	14	4176		
9							
10	Constraints				LHS		RHS
11	Fabrication	4	6	2	1056	<=	2000
12	Assembly	3	8	6	1536	<=	2000
13	Machining	9	6	4	1440	<=	1440
14	Wood	30	40	25	8040	<=	9600
15	Chair ceiling	1			48	<=	300
16	Desk ceiling		1		120	<=	120
17	Table ceiling			1	72	<=	144
18	Chair proportion	0.8	-0.2	-0.2	5.329E-15	>=	0
19	Desk proportion	-0.2	0.8	-0.2	72	>=	0
20	Table proportion	-0.2	-0.2	0.8	24	>=	0
21							

Figure 2.16. Modified product mix model.

- Write the fraction that expresses the constrained proportion.
- Write the inequality implied by the lower limit or upper limit.
- Multiply through by the denominator and collect terms.

The result should be a linear inequality, ready to incorporate in the model.

In general, the *blending problem* involves mixing materials that have different individual properties and describing the properties of the blend with weighted averages. We might be familiar with the phenomenon of mixing from spending time in a chemistry laboratory mixing fluids with different concentrations of a particular substance, but the concept extends beyond laboratory work. Consider the example of Keogh Coffee Roasters.

EXAMPLE 2.4 *Keogh Coffee Roasters*

Keogh Coffee Roasters blends three types of coffee beans (Brazilian, Colombian, and Peruvian) into ground coffee that is sold at retail. Each kind of bean has a distinctive aroma and taste, and the company has a chief taster who can rate the fragrance of the aroma and the strength of the taste on a scale of 1 to 100. The features of the beans are tabulated below.

Bean	Aroma Rating	Strength Rating	Cost per Pound
Brazilian	75	15	$0.50
Colombian	60	20	$0.60
Peruvian	85	18	$0.70

Keogh would like to create a blend that has an aroma rating of at least 78 and a strength rating of at least 16. However, its supplies of the various beans are limited. The available quantities are 1500 lb of Brazilian, 1200 lb of Colombian, and 2000 lb of Peruvian beans, all delivered under a previously arranged purchase agreement. Keogh wants to make 4000 lb of the blend at the lowest possible cost. ∎

For a little background on blending arithmetic, suppose that we blend Brazilian and Peruvian beans in equal quantities of 25 lb each. Then we should expect the blend to have an aroma rating of 80, just halfway between the two pure ratings of 75 and 85. Mathematically, we take the weighted average of the two ratings

$$\text{Aroma rating} = \frac{75(25) + 85(25)}{25 + 25} = \frac{4000}{50} = 80$$

Now suppose that we blend the beans in amounts B, C, and P. The blend has an aroma rating calculated by a weighted average of the three ratings

$$\text{Aroma rating} = \frac{75B + 60C + 85P}{B + C + P}$$

To impose a constraint that requires the aroma rating to be at least 78, we write

$$\frac{75B + 60C + 85P}{B + C + P} \geq 78$$

Once again, this constraint is nonlinear, by virtue of having decision variables in the denominator of the fraction. However, as shown above, we can convert the requirement into a linear constraint. First, multiply both sides of the inequality by $(B + C + P)$, yielding

$$75B + 60C + 85P \geq 78(B + C + P)$$

Next, collect terms involving the decision variables on the left-hand side, to obtain

$$-3B - 18C + 7P \geq 0$$

This form conveys the same requirement as the original fractional constraint, but in linear form. The coefficients on the left-hand side turn out to be just the differences between the individual aroma ratings (75, 60, 85) and the requirement of 78, with signs indicating whether the individual rating is above or below the target. In a similar fashion, a requirement that the strength of the blend must be at least 16 leads to the constraint

$$-1B + 4C + 2P \geq 0$$

In general, the natural way to describe a blending requirement uses fractions, but in that form, blending requirements are nonlinear. We prefer to convert these requirements to linear constraints because with a linear model we can harness the full power of the linear solver. As we shall see later, the nonlinear solver has more limitations than the linear solver.

Now, with an idea of how to restate the blending requirements, we return to Example 2.4. In addition to the blending constraints, we need a constraint that generates a 4000-lb blend, along with three constraints that limit the supplies of the different beans. The algebraic problem statement is as follows.

$$\text{Maximize } z = 0.50B + 0.60C + 0.70P$$

subject to

$$
\begin{aligned}
-3B - 18C + 7P &\geq 0 \\
-1B + 4C + 2P &\geq 0 \\
B + C + P &\geq 4000 \\
B &\leq 1500 \\
C &\leq 1200 \\
P &\leq 2000
\end{aligned}
$$

Figure 2.17 shows the spreadsheet for our model, which contains a GT constraint and three LT constraints, in addition to the two blending constraints. In a sense, the

	A	B	C	D	E	F	G
1	**Blending: Coffee beans**						
2							
3	**Decision Variables**						
4		B	C	P			
5	Inputs	1500	520	1980			
6							
7	**Objective Function**				*Total*		
8	Cost	0.50	0.60	0.70	2448		
9							
10	**Blending Data**				*Actual*		*Target*
11	Aroma	75	60	85	78.00		78
12	Strength	15	20	18	17.14		16
13							
14	**Constraints**				*LHS*		*RHS*
15	Blend aroma	-3	-18	7	0	>=	0
16	Blend strength	-1	4	2	4540	>=	0
17	Output	1	1	1	4000	>=	4000
18	B-supply	1	0	0	1500	<=	1500
19	C-supply	0	1	0	520	<=	1200
20	P-supply	0	0	1	1980	<=	2000
21							

Figure 2.17. Keogh Coffee Roasters model.

model has what we might think of as covering and allocation constraints, in addition to blending constraints. The Blending Data module, in rows 10–12, is not strictly part of the optimization model. We'll come back to this part of the worksheet later. Each constraint in rows 15–20 is expressed in our standard form: a SUMPRODUCT formula on the LHS and a parameter on the RHS. This model contains three LT constraints and three GT constraints. It is helpful to keep constraints of the same type in adjacent locations on the worksheet, for convenience in entering the constraint information in the task pane. In this case, with only two entries in the Add Constraint window, we can specify all six inequalities.

The output constraint is formulated as an inequality. Although Keogh Coffee Roasters wishes to produce 4000 lb, our model allows the production of a larger quantity if this will reduce costs. (Our intuition probably tells us that we should be able to minimize costs with a 4000-lb blend, but we would accept a solution that reduced costs while producing more than 4000 lb: we could simply throw away the excess.) In many situations, it is a good idea to use the weaker form of the constraint, giving the model some "additional rope" and avoiding EQ constraints. In other words, we should build the model with some latitude in satisfying the constraints of the decision problem whenever possible. The solution will either confirm our intuition (as this one does) or else teach us a lesson about the limitations of our intuition.

The model specification is the following

Objective:	E8 (minimize)
Variables:	B5:D5
Constraints:	E15:E17 ≥ G15:G17
	E18:E20 ≤ G18:G20

The linear solver produces an optimal blend of 1500 lb of Brazilian, 520 lb of Colombian and 1980 lb of Peruvian beans, for a total cost of $2448, as shown in the figure. By using linear programming, Keogh Coffee Roasters can optimize the cost of its blend while meeting its taste and aroma requirements. Of the two blending constraints, only the first (aroma) constraint is binding in this solution; the optimal blend actually has better-than-required strength. The output constraint is also binding (consistent with our intuitive expectation), as is the limit on Brazilian supply.

In Figure 2.19, we calculate the actual aroma and taste ratings in cells E11:E12, using the weighted-average ratio formula directly. For example, the calculation in cell E11 uses the formula =SUMPRODUCT($B$5:$D$5,B11:D11)/E17. Thus, whereas the first constraint of the model is binding (LHS and RHS of row 15 both equal to zero), the aroma calculation in the Blending Data module shows that the weighted average equals the requirement of 78 exactly. Although the second constraint shows that the strength requirement is not binding, the comparison of LHS (4540) with RHS (zero) is not as helpful as a means of interpreting the slack in the constraint. However, cell E12 shows that the optimal blend's strength is 17.14, which we can easily compare to the requirement of 16.

Blending problems arise whenever weighted averages characterize the properties of a composite product. In our example, we treated taste and aroma as if they were numerically objective measures, for the purposes of illustration. However, it is not difficult to enumerate some applications where the parameters are "harder" numbers and blending concerns are relevant.

- Gasoline is a blend, and the octane rating of gasoline is a weighted average of its constituents. The inputs into a gasoline blend have different octane ratings as a function of their crude oil source and their previous processing steps. The classification of gasoline blends as regular, premium, or super premium is usually based on a minimum octane rating in each category. The principle of weighted average blending applies as well to other fluids, such as the viscosity of lubricants, the sugar content of fruit juice or the fat content of ice cream.

- Chemical compounds other than fluids often have such constituents as nickel, copper, sulfur, potassium, and the like. These constituents may have functional benefits, or they may be considered impurities. In either event, different compounds have different percentage compositions of these elements, and compositions blend according to weighted averages when elements are mixed together. The principle of weighted averages applies to metal in alloys, pollutants in emissions, or active ingredients in medications.

- Investment portfolios consist of discrete assets, such as stocks and bonds. Each asset in the portfolio has its own financial characteristics, but properties of the overall portfolio dictate admissible investment strategies. The principle of weighted averages applies to maturities of bonds, rates of return on stocks, and riskiness ratings of assets.

2.5. MODELING ERRORS IN LINEAR PROGRAMMING

We have presented our examples as if they were built by knowledgeable analysts, with each step implemented correctly and all errors avoided. However, someone new to the experience of building optimization models seldom makes it through all of the steps without some kind of difficulty. Even experts run into problems, especially when they are working on complex models. It is probably unrealistic to expect that the process of building and analyzing a model can be carried out without encountering some sort of difficulty along the way. To be effective in modeling, we have to know how to deal with errors when they occur.

2.5.1. Exceptions

Given a linear programming model, Solver always finds an optimal solution, provided one exists. The first kind of modeling error is formulating a model that does not have an optimal solution. Two exceptions can cause difficulties: infeasible constraints and an unbounded objective function.

A model contains *infeasible constraints* if no set of decision variables can satisfy all constraints simultaneously. For example, in the product mix example of

Figure 2.9, suppose we had signed a contract promising that 200 chairs would be delivered to a single large customer, as part of the product mix. Adding the requirement $C \geq 200$ to the other constraints of the model creates an inconsistency. (The implied machining requirement would be 1800 hours, which exceeds the capacity available.) Presented with a set of inconsistent constraints, Solver detects the inconsistency and delivers the following result message in the solution log as well as at the bottom of the task pane:

```
Solver could not find a feasible
solution.
```

Whenever this message appears, there must have been an inconsistency in the set of constraints.

For the model builder, the task is to locate the inconsistency when confronted with the infeasibility message. There are potentially two levels to this task: (1) finding the offending constraint or constraints, and (2) identifying the source of the inconsistency. Sometimes, the offending constraint can be discovered by "eyeballing" the model—scanning for visual clues to the location of an error. For example, a parameter could be entered incorrectly. (Perhaps the chair contract calls for only 20 units, but 200 has been entered inadvertently.) Alternatively, a constraint could be entered backward, as a LT constraint when it should have been a GT constraint. However, the more standard way to search for an inconsistency is to remove constraints from the model, one at a time, and to rerun Solver each time. (In large problems, it might make more sense to remove several constraints at a time.) If the model remains infeasible, restore the constraint and try removing a different one. If the model reaches an optimal solution, then we know that something about the constraint we removed was a partial cause of the infeasibility.

Identifying the source of an inconsistency refers to the part of the task that lies at the interface between model and problem. If the inconsistency resulted from a typo, then it is a simple matter to repair it. However, a more subtle difficulty arises when the formulation contains too many constraints. This result can occur if, during the modeling process, there was a thorough attempt to include all the considerations mentioned by various parties. Isolated desires and secondary considerations could wind up being expressed as model constraints, contributing to a logical conflict. In these situations, it makes sense to eliminate some of the constraints, so that the model is at least feasible. Thereafter, various additional considerations can be revisited, to see whether they can be accommodated without causing infeasibility.

The second kind of modeling error occurs when there is no limit to the objective function in the direction of optimization. An *unbounded objective function* occurs if, with a set of feasible decisions, the objective can grow infinitely positive in a maximization problem or infinitely negative in a minimization problem. The most common cause of an unbounded objective is failure to invoke the Assume Non-Negative option. For example, in the trail mix example of Figure 2.11, suppose we had forgotten to set the option to True. Then it would be mathematically possible to make the objective function as negative as we wish by taking negative quantities for some of the ingredients. Consider the mix corresponding to $R = 115$, $P = -40$, and $W = -50$.

This combination satisfies all four constraints, with a total cost of −$5.00. Mathematically, this mix could be expanded in the same proportion, with all constraints met and the total cost becoming as negative as we like. Presented with conditions that permit an objective function to expand infinitely in the direction of optimization, Solver detects the unbounded possibilities and delivers the following result message in the solution log as well as at the bottom of the task pane:

```
The objective (Set Cell) values do
not converge.
```

The reference to "Set Cell" provides consistency with older versions of the software, which did not use the term "objective."

For the model builder, the task is to locate the cause of an unbounded objective function. The problem could lie in the objective function or in the constraints. A simple typo in an objective function cell could induce unbounded possibilities. However, unboundedness can also occur when a constraint is omitted from the model, allowing decision variables to reach values never intended by the model builder. Whereas locating the cause of infeasibility directs attention to the constraints, it is more difficult to know where to look for the cause of unboundedness.

2.5.2. Debugging

Even a model that contains feasible constraints and a bounded objective function can be logically flawed. Beyond its ability to detect infeasible and unbounded formulations, Solver has no automatic means of detecting logical errors. That responsibility lies with the model builder. However, a few techniques that are helpful to spreadsheet users can augment the capabilities in Solver.

- *Set all decision variables to zero.* A good first step is to enter zero for each of the decision variables and confirm that the objective function and constraints behave as expected. Then, make one variable at a time positive. Taking successive values for a variable equal to 1, 10, and 100 can show whether the scaling properties of the model seem valid.
- *Display formulas.* By simultaneously pressing the Control and tilde (∼) keys, we can look at all the formulas in the spreadsheet window. As in Figure 2.2, we look for the SUMPRODUCT formulas in the cells corresponding to the objective function and the LHS of each constraint. No other formulas are necessary, although in the next chapter we shall look at some cases where an alternative form is convenient. Pressing the Control and tilde keys simultaneously once more restores the display.
- *Invoke Formula Auditing.* The Formula Auditing tools appear on the Formulas tab. In Figure 2.18, we have selected, one at a time, each of the constraint formulas and selected the Trace Precedents icon for each one. The resulting logical map exhibits a systematic structure that helps validate the formulas. An

⊿	A	B	C	D	E	F	G	
1	**Allocation: Product Mix**							
2								
3	**Decision Variables**							
4			C	D	T			
5	Production plan		50	75	100			
6								
7	**Objective Function**				*Total*			
8	Profit	16	20	14	3700			
9								
10	**Constraints**				*LHS*		*RHS*	
11	Fabrication	4	6	2	850	<=	2000	
12	Assembly	3	8	6	1350	<=	2000	
13	Machining	9	6	4	1300	<=	1440	
14	Wood	30	40	25	7000	<=	9600	
15	Chair ceiling	1			50	<=	300	
16	Desk ceiling		1		75	<=	120	
17	Table ceiling			1	100	<=	144	
18								

Mix

Figure 2.18. Formula Auditing with the trace precedence command.

asymmetric set of precedence arrows might suggest where a logical error can be found.

- *Invoke the Cell Edit function.* Selecting a formula cell and pressing the function key F2 can implement a similar kind of validation. The Cell Edit function displays a color-coded interpretation of the formula, highlighting its constituent cells. In linear programming models, this kind of verification might catch a formula in which the range was entered or pasted incorrectly.

- *Use the Change Constraint option.* Another way to verify that ranges are correctly entered involves the Change Constraint window. In the Model tab, double-click the icon for a particular constraint entry. Then the LHS's of the selected constraints are highlighted in the model when the Change Constraint window appears. This step can sometimes detect an error in specifying the location of a constraint, especially in complicated models where constraints might be arranged separately, at different locations on the worksheet.

2.5.3. Logic

In Chapter 1, we pointed out the distinction between the convergence message and the optimality message in finding an optimal solution with the nonlinear solver. When we use the linear solver, that distinction does not arise. If we formulate a model that is feasible and bounded and if we use the linear solver, then the optimality message appears every time; we do not need to rerun Solver.

SUMMARY

This chapter has introduced three classes of linear programming models: allocation, covering, and blending. To some extent, these elementary models allow us to discuss the basic scenarios that lend themselves to linear programming models, so allocation, covering, and blending models might well be taken as the "ABC" of model building with linear programming. Allocation, covering and blending models are also important as building blocks for more complex models because many practical applications are combinations of these structures.

Linearity in both the objective function and constraints is the key structural assumption in linear programming. In the process of building a linear programming model, it is desirable to revisit the requirements of proportionality, additivity, and divisibility, to confirm that their properties apply. Another less prominent assumption is the presumption of certainty in the elements of a linear programming model. Most of the time, linear programs are applied in situations where uncertainty can be suppressed without undermining the value of the model. Nevertheless, advanced forms of linear programming extend to situations where the uncertainty cannot be avoided. Appendix 4 introduces Stochastic Programming, to suggest how linear programming can be adapted to problems containing uncertainty.

Classification of linear programming models provides some immediate benefits. When we are trying to understand someone else's model, our ability to classify may help us appreciate either the overall structure of a model or some of its major parts. Also, when we are trying to develop a model from scratch, we can accelerate the process if we can classify the model or at least one portion of it. Model building requires that we recognize situations that lend themselves to representation in a model. Familiarity with the elementary scenarios that go with allocation, covering, and blending helps us to recognize structure in an actual situation. Finally, when we are debugging our own model, classification allows us to compare what we have built with the standard template. That comparison helps us to detect mistakes we may have made in constraint coefficients and constants or perhaps even in objective function coefficients. Also included in this chapter were a number of suggestions for debugging that apply throughout the remainder of the book.

The classification of linear programs is not as precise as, say, biological classification. As we saw, a linear program can combine types. Although we will encounter additional classes of models in the next three chapters, we will not attempt to classify every possible linear program. Instead, the purpose is to appreciate the kinds of situations that lend themselves well to linear programming. Then, when we encounter similar situations in the world around us, we'll be able to think about those situations in terms of a corresponding linear programming structure. Armed with knowledge of these building blocks, we can analyze new situations by recognizing familiar structures within them, thus identifying some of the important elements (variables and constraints) of the eventual model.

EXERCISES

2.1. Brown Furniture Revisited   Revisit the Brown Furniture allocation example of this chapter. As plans are being made for a new quarter, a revised set of figures on resource availabilities is compiled. The new resource limits are as follows.

Fabrication hours	2000
Assembly hours	1800
Machining hours	1600
Wood supply	9400

The other data, on profit contributions and resource consumptions, all remain unchanged.

(a) What are the optimal production quantities of chairs, desks and tables?

(b) What is the maximum profit contribution?

(c) Which constraints are binding in the optimal solution?

2.2. Allocating Ingredients The Pizza Man is a local shop that plans to make all of its sales this Saturday from its sidewalk tables during the town's holiday parade. On this occasion, the shop's owners know that customers will buy by the slice and any kind of pizza offered will sell. The Pizza Man offers plain, meat, vegetable, and supreme pizzas. Each variety has its own requirement for sauce, cheese, dough, and toppings (in ounces, as shown in the table), and each has its own selling price.

	Plain	Meat	Vegetable	Supreme	Available
Dough	5	5	5	5	200
Sauce	3	3	3	3	90
Cheese	4	3	3	4	120
Meat	0	3	0	2	75
Vegetables	0	0	3	2	40
Price	$8	$10	$12	$15	

The Pizza Man expects to use its entire stock of ingredients and wishes to maximize revenue from its sales.

(a) What mix of pizzas should be made? (Assume that fractions can be sold.)

(b) What is the maximum sales revenue?

(c) Which ingredients are economically scarce (limit profits)?

2.3. Workforce Scheduling The Operations Manager at the Metropolis National Bank has a staffing problem. Demand for clerical staff varies throughout the day, but 24-hour coverage is necessary because the bank handles a number of international transactions. A recent study has shown how many clerical workers are needed each hour in the course of the day, as shown below. (Hour 1 is from midnight to 1 am.)

Hour	1	2	3	4	5	6	7	8	9	10	11	12
Staff	4	3	2	2	3	5	6	6	9	10	10	10

Hour	13	14	15	16	17	18	19	20	21	22	23	24
Staff	12	12	8	6	7	7	7	6	5	4	4	4

Under current labor policies, clerical workers may be assigned to any one of six shifts, some of which overlap. The shifts and salary costs are as follows.

Shift	Daily cost
2 am–10 am	$160
6 am–2 pm	$145
10 am–6 pm	$148
2 pm–10 pm	$154
6 pm–2 am	$156
10 pm–6 am	$160

(a) Provide the operations manager with a schedule that will deploy enough staff to meet the hourly requirements at the minimum daily total cost.

(b) In the optimal schedule, how many hours are overstaffed?

2.4. Selecting a Portfolio A portfolio manager has developed a list of six investment alternatives for a multiyear horizon. These are: Treasury bills, Common stock, Corporate bonds, Real estate, Growth funds, and Savings and Loans. These investments and their various financial factors are described below. In the table, the length represents the estimated number of years required for the annual rate of return to be realized. The annual rate of return is the expected rate over the multiyear horizon. The risk coefficient is a subjective estimate representing the manager's appraisal of the relative safety of each alternative, on a scale of 10. The growth potential is also a subjective estimate of the potential increase in value over the horizon.

	Portfolio data					
Alternative	TB	CS	CB	RE	GF	SL
Length	4	7	8	6	10	5
Annual return (%)	6	15	12	24	18	9
Risk coefficient	1	5	4	8	6	3
Growth potential (%)	0	18	10	32	20	7

The manager wishes to maximize the annual rate of return on a $3 million portfolio, subject to the following restrictions.

The weighted average length should not exceed 7 years.

The weighted average risk coefficient should not exceed five.

The weighted average growth potential should be at least 10 percent.

The investment in real estate should be no more than twice the investment in stocks and bonds (i.e. in CS, CB, and GF) combined.

(a) What is the optimal return (as a percentage) and the optimal allocation of investment funds?

(b) What is the marginal rate of return? In other words, what would be the return on the next dollar invested, if there were one more dollar in the portfolio?

(c) For additional investment beyond the original $3 million, how will the optimal allocation change?

2.5. Oil Blending   An oil company produces three brands of oil: Regular, Multigrade, and Supreme. Each brand of oil is composed of one or more of four crude stocks, each having a different lubrication index. The relevant data concerning the crude stocks are as follows.

Crude stock	Lubrication index	Cost ($/barrel)	Supply per day (barrels)
1	20	7.10	1000
2	40	8.50	1100
3	30	7.70	1200
4	55	9.00	1100

Each brand of oil must meet a minimum standard for a lubrication index, and each brand thus sells at a different price. The relevant data concerning the three brands of oil are as follows.

Brand	Minimum lubrication index	Selling price ($/barrel)	Daily demand (barrels)
Regular	25	8.50	2000
Multigrade	35	9.00	1500
Supreme	50	10.00	750

Determine an optimal output plan for a single day, assuming that production can be either sold or else stored at negligible cost.

The daily demand figures are subject to alternative interpretations. Investigate the following:

(a) The daily demands represent potential sales. In other words, the model should contain demand ceilings (upper limits). What is the optimal profit?

(b) The daily demands are strict obligations. In other words, the model should contain demand constraints that are met precisely. What is the optimal profit?

(c) The daily demands represent minimum sales commitments, but all output can be sold. In other words, the model should permit production to exceed the daily commitments. What is the optimal profit?

2.6. Coffee Blending and Sales   Hill-O-Beans Coffee Company blends four component beans into three final blends of coffee: one is sold to luxury hotels, another to restaurants, and the third to supermarkets for store-label brands. The company has four reliable bean supplies: Argentine Abundo, Peruvian Colmado, Brazilian Maximo, and Chilean Saboro. The table below summarizes the very precise recipes for the final coffee blends, the cost and availability information for the four components, and the wholesale price per pound of the final blends. The percentages indicate the fraction of each component to be used in each blend.

Component (pounds)	Hotel	Rest	Market	Cost per pound	Max. weekly availability
Abundo	20%	35%	10%	$0.60	40,000
Colmado	40%	15%	35%	$0.80	25,000
Maximo	15%	20%	40%	$0.55	20,000
Saboro	25%	30%	15%	$0.70	45,000
Wholesale price per pound	$1.25	$1.50	$1.40		

The processor's plant can handle no more than 100,000 lb per week, and Hill-O-Beans would like to operate at capacity, if possible. Selling the final blends is not a problem, although the Marketing Department requires minimum production levels of 10,000, 25,000, and 30,000 lb, respectively, for the hotel, restaurant and market blends.

(a) To maximize weekly profit, how many pounds of each component should be purchased?

(b) How would the optimal profit change if there were a 1000-lb increase in the availability of Abundo beans? Colmado? Maximo? Saboro?

2.7. Production Planning for Components Rummel Electronics produces two PC cards, a modem and a network adapter. Demand for these two products exceeds the amount that the firm can make, but there are no plans to increase production capacity in the short run. Instead, the firm plans to use subcontracting.

The two main stages of production are fabrication and assembly, and either step can be subcontracted for either type of card. However, the company policy is not to subcontract both steps for either product. (That is, if modem cards are fabricated by a subcontractor, then they must be assembled in house.) Components made by subcontractors must pass through the shipping and receiving departments, just like components made internally. At present, the firm has 5200 hours available in fabrication, 3600 in assembly and 3200 in shipping/inspection. The production requirements, in hours per unit, are given in the following table:

Product/mode	Fabrication	Assembly	Shipping
Modem, made entirely in-house	0.35	0.16	0.08
Network, made entirely in-house	0.47	0.15	0.12
Modem, fabricated by sub	–	0.18	0.10
Network, fabricated by sub	–	0.16	0.15
Modem, assembled by sub	0.35	–	0.09
Network, assembled by sub	0.47	–	0.14

The direct material costs for the modem cards are $3.25 for manufacturing and $0.50 for assembly; for network cards, the costs are $6.10 and $0.50. Subcontracting the manufacturing operation costs $5.35 for modem cards and $8.50 for network cards. Subcontracting the assembly operation costs $1.50 for either product. Modem cards sell for $20, and network cards sell for $28. The firm's policy, for each product, is that at most 40% of the units produced can have subcontracted fabrication, and at most 70% of the units can have subcontracted assembly.

(a) Determine the production and subcontracting schedule that maximizes profits. How many units of each product should be sold, in the optimal plan? What total volume should the subcontractor handle?

(b) Which department capacities limit the manufacturing volume? If 100 hours of over-time could be scheduled, which department(s) should be allocated the overtime? Explain.

2.8. Production Planning for Automobiles   The Auto Company of America (ACA) pro-duces four types of cars: subcompact, compact, intermediate, and luxury. ACA also pro-duces trucks and vans. Vendor capacities limit total production capacity to at most 1,200,000 vehicles per year. Subcompacts and compacts are built together in a facility with a total annual capacity of 620,000 cars. Intermediate and luxury cars are produced in another facility with capacity of 400,000; and the truck/van facility has a capacity of 275,000. ACA's marketing strategy requires that subcompacts and compacts must con-stitute at least half of the product mix for the four car types. Profit margins, market poten-tial, and fuel efficiencies are summarized below.

Type	Profit margin ($/vehicle)	Potential sales (in 000s)	Fuel efficiency (MPG)
Subcompact	150	600	40
Compact	225	400	34
Intermediate	250	300	15
Luxury	500	225	12
Truck	400	325	20
Van	200	100	25

The Corporate Average Fuel Efficiency (CAFE) standards require an average fleet fuel efficiency of at least 27 MPG. ACA would like to use a linear programming model to understand the implications of government and corporate policies on its production plans.

(a) What is the optimal annual profit for ACA?

(b) How much would annual profit drop if the fuel efficiency requirement were raised to 28 MPG?

2.9. Production Planning with Environmental Constraints   You are the Operations Manager of Lovejoy Chemicals, Inc., which produces five products in a common production facility that will be subject to proposed Environmental Protection Agency (EPA) limits on particulate emissions. For each product, Lovejoy's sales poten-tials (demand levels that Lovejoy can capture) are expected to remain relatively flat for at least the next five years. Relevant data for each product are as follows (note: T denotes tons).

Product	Sales potential (T/year)	Variable costs ($/T)	Revenues ($/T)	Particulate emissions (T/T produced)
A	2000	700	1000	0.0010
B	1600	600	800	0.0025
C	1000	1000	1500	0.0300
D	1000	1600	2000	0.0400
E	600	1300	1700	0.0250

Your production facility rotates through the product line because it is capable of producing only one product at a time. The production rates differ for the various products due to processing needs. It takes 0.3 hours to make one ton of A, 0.5 hours for B, and one hour each to make a ton of C, D, or E. The facility can be operated up to 4000 hours each year.

The EPA is proposing a "bubble policy" for your industry. In this form of regulation, imagine that a bubble encloses the manufacturing facility, and only total particulates that escape the bubble are regulated. This sort of policy replaces historical attempts by the EPA to micromanage emissions within a firm, and it allows Lovejoy to make any changes it wishes, provided the total particulate emissions from its facility are kept below certain limits. The current proposal is to phase-in strict particulate emissions limits over the next five years. These limits on total particulate emissions are shown in the table below.

Year	1	2	3	4	5
Allowable emissions (T/year)	unlimited	80	60	40	20

One strategy for satisfying these regulations is to adjust the product mix, cutting back on production of some products if necessary. Lovejoy wishes to explore this strategy before contemplating the addition of new equipment.

(a) Determine the maximum profit Lovejoy can achieve from its product line in the coming year (Year 1).

(b) By solving a series of models corresponding to the imposition and tightening of the emissions limit in future years, determine Lovejoy's maximum profits in each of Years 2–5.

(c) Consider the emissions limit that applies in Year 4. Determine how much Lovejoy should be willing to pay at that time to be allowed emissions of one extra ton of particulates above the limit.

2.10. Cargo Loading You are in charge of loading cargo ships for International Cargo Company (ICC) at a major East Coast port. You have been asked to prepare a loading plan for an ICC freight ship bound for Africa. An agricultural commodities dealer would like to transport the following products aboard this ship.

Commodity	Tons available	Volume per ton (cu. ft)	Profit per ton ($)
1	4000	40	70
2	3000	25	50
3	2000	60	60
4	1000	50	80

You can elect to load any and/or all of the available commodities. However, the ship has three cargo holds with the following capacity restrictions.

Cargo hold	Weight capacity (tons)	Volume capacity (cu. ft)
Forward	3000	100,000
Center	5000	150,000
Rear	2000	120,000

More than one type of commodity can be placed in the same cargo hold. However, because of balance considerations, the weight in the forward cargo hold must be within 10 percent of the weight in the rear cargo hold, and the center cargo hold must be between 40 percent and 60 percent of the total weight on board.

(a) What is the maximum profit and the loading plan that achieves it? What is the optimal total weight to be loaded? What is the optimal total volume to be loaded?

(b) Suppose each one of the cargo holds could be expanded. Which holds and which forms of expansion (weight or volume) would allow ICC to increase its profits on this trip, and what is the marginal value of each form of expansion?

2.11. Computer Center Staffing   You are the Director of the Computer Center for Gaillard College and responsible for scheduling the staffing of the center. It is open from 8 am until midnight. You have monitored the usage of the center at various times of the day and determined that the following numbers of computer consultants are required.

Time of day	Minimum number of consultants required to be on duty
8 am–noon	4
Noon–4 pm	8
4 am–8 pm	10
8 am–midnight	6

Two types of computer consultants can be hired: full-time and part-time. The full-time consultants work for eight consecutive hours in any of the following shifts: morning (8 am–4 pm), afternoon (noon–8 pm), and evening (4 pm–midnight). Full-time consultants are paid $14 per hour.

Part-time consultants can be hired to work any of the four shifts listed in the table. Part-time consultants are paid $12 per hour. An additional requirement is that during every time period, at least one full-time consultant must be on duty for every part-time consultant on duty.

(a) Determine a minimum-cost staffing plan for the center. In your solution, how many consultants will be paid to work full time and how many will be paid to work part time? What is the minimum cost?

(b) After thinking about this problem for a while, you have decided to recognize meal breaks explicitly in the scheduling of full-time consultants. In particular, full-time consultants are entitled to a one-hour lunch break during their eight-hour shift. In addition, employment rules specify that the lunch break can start after three hours of work or after four hours of work, but those are the only alternatives. Part-time consultants do not receive a meal break. Under these conditions, find a minimum-cost staffing plan. What is the minimum cost?

2.12. Make or Buy   A sudden increase in the demand for smoke detectors has left Acme Alarms with insufficient capacity to meet demand. The company has seen monthly demand from its retailers for its electronic and battery operated detectors rise to 20,000 and 10,000, respectively, and Acme wishes to continue meeting demand. Acme's production process involves three departments: Fabrication, Assembly, and Shipping. The relevant quantitative data on production and prices are summarized below.

Department	Monthly hours available	Hours/unit (electronic)	Hours/unit (battery)
Fabrication	2000	0.15	0.10
Assembly	4200	0.20	0.20
Shipping	2500	0.10	0.15
Variable cost/unit		$18.80	$16.00
Retail price		$29.50	$28.00

The company also has the option to obtain additional units from a subcontractor, who has offered to supply up to 20,000 units per month in any combination of electronic and battery operated models, at a charge of $21.50 per unit. For this price, the subcontractor will test and ship its models directly to the retailers without using Acme's production process.

(a) What is the maximum profit and the corresponding make/buy levels? (This is a planning model, and fractional decisions are acceptable.)

(b) Trace the effects of increasing Fabrication capacity by 10 percent. How will the optimal make/buy mix change? How will the optimal profit change?

2.13. Leasing Warehouse Space   Cox Cable Company needs to lease warehouse storage space for five months at the start of the year. It knows how much space will be required in each month, and it can purchase a variety of lease contracts to meet these needs. For example, it can purchase one-month leases in each month from January to May. It can also purchase two-month leases in January through April, three-month leases in January through March, four-month leases in January and February, or a five-month lease in January. In total, there are 15 possible leases it could use. It must decide which leases to purchase, and how many square feet to purchase on each lease.

Since the space requirements differ month-to-month, it may be economical to lease only the amount needed each month on a month-by-month basis. On the other hand, the monthly cost for leasing space for additional months is much less than for the first month, so it may be desirable to lease the maximum amount needed for the entire five months. Another option is the intermediate approach of changing the total amount of space leased (by adding a new lease and/or having an old lease expire) at least once but not every month. Two or more leases for different terms can begin at the same time.

The space requirements (in square feet) and the leasing costs (in dollars per thousand square feet) are given in the tables below.

Month	Space requirements	Lease length	Lease cost
Jan	15,000	1 month	$280
Feb	10,000	2 months	450
Mar	20,000	3 months	600
April	5000	4 months	730
May	25,000	5 months	820

The task is to find a leasing schedule that provides the necessary amounts of space at the minimum cost.

(a) Determine the optimal leasing schedule and the optimal total cost.

(b) Trace the effects of increasing the space required for January. How will the leasing schedule change? How will the total cost change?

2.14. **Production Planning** The Kim Camera Company produces four different camera models, known as C1–C4. Each model can be made by two different methods. The manual method requires work in the Fabrication, Assembly, and Test departments, while the automated method combines the Assembly and Test operations in one department. The first table below describes the price and cost features of the camera models, along with marketing information on the range of possible sales in the coming month. Because model C1 is delivered to one large retailer under a long-term contract, a threshold demand quantity of 1500 units must be met. For the other models, there is flexibility in how much demand to meet, up to a ceiling that represents maximum possible sales.

	C1	C2	C3	C4
Price	125	175	200	135
Manual cost	110	160	155	125
Auto cost	100	112	150	90
Manual margin	15	15	45	10
Auto margin	25	63	50	45
Sales max.	3000	2500	2000	3200
Sales min.	1500	0	0	0

The next table provides data on the various departments at the firm, consisting of the time per camera required in each department and the number of hours available in each department during the month.

	C1	C2	C3	C4	Hours
Manual fab.	3	5	4	4	16,000
Manual asy.	8	12	10	9	30,000
Manual test	2	3	5	2	15,000
Auto fab.	5	6	7	4	24,000
Auto asy/test	4	5	8	5	20,000

(a) What production plan will maximize profit for Kim Camera?

(b) How would the solution in (a) change if there were no threshold requirement for Camera C1?

2.15. Make/Buy Planning   The CammTex Fabric Mill is in the process of deciding on a production schedule. It wishes to know how to weave the various fabrics it will produce during the coming quarter. The sales department has confirmed orders for each of the 15 fabrics that are produced by CammTex. These quarterly demands are given in the table below. Also tabulated is the variable cost for each fabric. The mill operates continuously during the quarter: 13 weeks, 7 days a week, and 24 hours a day.

CammTex uses two types of looms: dobbie and regular. Dobbie looms can make all fabrics, and they are the only looms that can weave certain fabrics such as plaids. The production rate for each fabric on each type of loom is also given in the table. (If the production rate is zero, the fabric cannot be woven on that type of loom.) CammTex has 90 regular looms and 15 dobbie looms.

Fabrics woven at CammTex proceed to the finishing department in the mill and are then sold. Any fabrics not woven in the mill because of limited capacity are subcontracted to an outside producer and sold at the selling price. The cost of purchasing from the subcontractor is also given in the table.

Fabric	Demand (yd)	Dobbie (yd/hr)	Regular (yd/hr)	Mill cost ($/yd)	Sub. cost ($/yd)
1	16,500	4.653	0.00	0.6573	0.80
2	52,000	4.653	0.00	0.555	0.70
3	45,000	4.653	0.00	0.655	0.85
4	22,000	4.653	0.00	0.5542	0.70
5	76,500	5.194	5.313	0.6097	0.75
6	110,000	3.767	3.809	0.6153	0.75
7	122,000	4.055	4.185	0.6477	0.80
8	62,000	5.208	5.232	0.488	0.60
9	7500	5.208	5.232	0.5029	0.70
10	69,000	5.208	5.232	0.4351	0.60
11	70,000	3.652	3.733	0.6417	0.80
12	82,000	4.007	4.185	0.5675	0.75
13	10,000	4.291	4.439	0.4952	0.65
14	380,000	5.208	5.232	0.3128	0.45
15	62,000	4.004	4.185	0.5029	0.70

(a) What is minimum total cost of production and purchasing for CammTex?

(b) Which fabrics should be made at the mill and which should be purchased? For those made at the mill, which loom types should be assigned to their production?

2.16. Production Scheduling   The Seaboch Tire Company produces four lines of tires: the Economy, the Glass-belted, the Snow and the Radial tire. The problem it faces is to schedule two shifts of production during the last quarter of the calendar year. The production process primarily involves the use of vulcanization, fabrication, and plastometer equipment, but the limiting resource is the availability of the vulcanization machines. The four tires require different amounts of time at vulcanization, as tabulated below.

Tire	Econ.	Glass	Snow	Radial
Hours/tire	4.5	5.0	5.5	6.0

A sales forecast is available, breaking down predicted sales (in thousands) by tire type and by month.

Sales	Oct	Nov	Dec
Econ.	8	7	6
Glass	18	16	18
Snow	4	15	15
Radial	6	5	8

In addition, the number of hours of vulcanizing time (in thousands), for each shift and for each month, is also known.

	Oct	Oct	Nov	Nov	Dec	Dec
Shift	1	2	1	2	1	2
Hours	110	100	130	120	120	115

The labor cost of operating the vulcanizing machines is $10 per hour during the first shift and $12 per hour during the second shift. The other relevant cost is storage: It costs $4 per month for storage and handling at the warehouse, regardless of tire type. This cost is incurred if there is not enough labor capacity to meet demand in the month when it occurs.

(a) What production plan will minimize cost and meet demand at Seaboch Tire?

(b) How would the solution in (a) change if sales for each tire in December were 10 percent higher?

Case: JetGreen*

JetGreen flies three airplanes, using a "hub and spoke" flight schedule between Houston and three cities, Chicago, Miami, and Phoenix. These three cities are the "spokes" connected by the Houston "hub." Once each day, the three airplanes fly from the spoke cities to Houston.

*Adapted from case material written by Professor Rob Shumsky of Dartmouth College.

EXHIBIT 2.1   *Price for Each Passenger Route*

		Houston	Chicago	Miami	Phoenix
				Destination	
Origin	Houston	–	$197	$110	$125
	Chicago	$190	–	$282	$195
	Miami	$108	$292	–	$238
	Phoenix	$110	$192	$230	–

They arrive nearly simultaneously at Houston, then connecting passengers change aircraft during a one-hour layover, and the three airplanes return to their starting cities. One set of six flights (3 inbound to Houston and 3 outbound) is called a *bank*. A bank can serve passengers flying on 12 different *routes*: three inbound direct routes (Chicago or Miami or Phoenix into Houston), three outbound direct routes (Houston to Chicago or Miami or Phoenix), and six routes requiring two flights each (Chicago–Miami, Chicago–Phoenix, Miami–Phoenix, Miami–Chicago, Phoenix–Chicago, and Phoenix–Miami).

JetGreen charges a regular price for a one-way ticket on each route. Exhibit 2.1 shows the regular prices. Following a well-established policy, JetGreen offers a discount to senior travelers. The ticket price for a senior traveler is 90 percent of the regular price, rounded down to the next smaller integer number of dollars. (For example, on the Houston-Phoenix route, the senior ticket price is $112.) The marginal cost of flying a passenger on each route is virtually zero.

Each of JetGreen's three airplanes contains 260 seats. Exhibit 2.2 shows demand for the routes in a bank at the regular price, and Exhibit 2.3 shows the demand from seniors (at the discounted price). These figures apply to the times at which JetGreen flies, and they show that passenger demand exceeds airplane capacity on every flight segment. For example, on the flight from Miami to the Houston hub, the total regular demand is the sum of demands for three passenger routes, (Miami to Houston or Chicago or Phoenix), totaling $72 + 105 + 68 = 245$ passengers (from the third row of Exhibit 2.2). For seniors, the comparable figure is $6 + 15 + 8 = 29$, and the total is $245 + 29 = 274$. Because only 260 passengers can travel on the Miami–Houston flight, at least 14 passengers represent lost demand.

When the total demand for a particular flight is larger than the available capacity, an airline can decide whether to accept or reject an offer to buy a ticket for a particular route. Controlling

EXHIBIT 2.2   *Regular Demand During One Bank*

		Houston	Chicago	Miami	Phoenix
				Destination	
Origin	Houston	–	123	80	110
	Chicago	130	–	98	88
	Miami	72	105	–	68
	Phoenix	115	90	66	–

EXHIBIT 2.3   *Senior Demand During One Bank*

		Houston	Destination		
			Chicago	Miami	Phoenix
	Houston	–	12	7	10
Origin	Chicago	15	–	10	13
	Miami	6	15	–	8
	Phoenix	12	8	5	–

sales in this way to maximize revenue is called *revenue management*. For example, JetGreen may decide to sell large numbers of tickets for the Miami–Houston and Miami–Chicago routes, but might severely restrict sales of the Miami–Phoenix tickets. Given the data above, JetGreen might sell tickets to 78 Miami–Houston passengers, 120 Miami–Chicago passengers, and only 62 Miami–Phoenix passengers, thus filling all 260 seats on the Miami–Houston flight. All 14 lost demands would then come from the Miami–Phoenix route.

Assuming that the various demands in Exhibits 2.2 and 2.3 are known, JetGreen wants to determine the number of tickets it should sell to regular and senior passengers on each route.

Chapter 3

Linear Programming: Network Models

In the previous chapter, we examined allocation, covering, and blending models—three basic structures frequently encountered in linear programming applications. A fourth common structure is the *network model*, and we devote a separate chapter to it because of its distinctive nature. The network model describes configurations of flow in a connected system, where the flow might involve material, people, funds, and so on. These configurations are conveniently described with flow diagrams, which help in the development of valid spreadsheet models. The possibility of doing some of the model building with a diagram makes network models a special category of linear programs.

The flow diagram is a modeling tool in its own right, and we can use it as a visual aid or an auditing device. Used as a visual aid, the flow diagram is an accessory, providing a picture of the problem structure to assist us in our main task, which is developing the spreadsheet representation of the linear program. In this role, the flow diagram is a preliminary step; it helps us build the spreadsheet model, and once we've done that, we may no longer need the diagram. Alternatively, used as an auditing device, the flow diagram allows us to translate a network picture directly into an algebraic formulation and vice versa. This approach integrates the flow diagram with the spreadsheet model. In this role, the diagram allows us to develop a model on two fronts simultaneously, and we can use the diagram to check for errors and omissions as we build the spreadsheet model.

In terms of the optimization software, no new features are needed to deal with network models. Therefore, the software features covered in the previous chapter are sufficient for this chapter as well.

We first study three types of special network problems that illustrate the use of flow diagrams as visual aids. The distinguishing feature of *special network models* is an inherent From/To flow pattern that lends itself to the row and column format of the spreadsheet. We then move on to *general network problems* involving other flow patterns, where we illustrate how to integrate the flow diagram with the development of a spreadsheet. As we will see, the distinguishing feature of network models is

Optimization Modeling with Spreadsheets, *Second Edition*. Kenneth R. Baker
© 2011 John Wiley & Sons, Inc. Published 2011 by John Wiley & Sons, Inc.

71

a basic conservation law governing patterns of flow. This feature allows us to identify the key constraints needed for the model. In the course of this chapter, we encounter several applications of the conservation law, and we pay particular attention to the use of flow diagrams in modeling.

3.1. THE TRANSPORTATION MODEL

A central feature of physical supply chains is the movement of product from one or more source locations to a set of destinations where demand occurs. The cost of moving units of product, together with the cost of making the product, accounts for most of the cost of getting products to market. Small wonder, then, that a great deal of attention is paid to controlling the costs that occur in supply chains. The building block for performing this type of analysis is the transportation model. Consider the example of Goodwin Manufacturing.

EXAMPLE 3.1   *The Goodwin Manufacturing Company*

The Goodwin Manufacturing Company is planning next week's shipments from its three manufacturing plants to its four distribution warehouses and is seeking a minimum-cost shipping schedule. Each plant has a potential capacity, expressed in cartons of product, and each warehouse has a demand requirement for the week that must be met. There are 12 possible shipment routes, and for every plant–warehouse combination, the unit shipping cost is known. The following table provides the given information.

(From) plant	(To) Warehouse				
	Atlanta	Boston	Chicago	Denver	Capacity
Minneapolis	$0.60	$0.56	$0.22	$0.40	10,000
Pittsburgh	0.36	0.30	0.28	0.58	15,000
Tucson	0.65	0.68	0.55	0.42	15,000
Requirement	8000	10,000	12,000	9000	

■

Figure 3.1 displays a flow diagram showing the possible routes. In the diagram, the letters on the left designate the manufacturing plants, which supply the product. The letters on the right stand for the warehouses, where the demands occur. In this case, all supply–demand pairs represent potential shipping routes.

Network terminology refers to flow along *arcs* or arrows in the diagram. Each arc connects two *nodes* or circles, and the direction of the corresponding arrow indicates the direction of flow. This flow incurs a cost: the unit cost of flow from any plant to any warehouse is given in Example 3.1. The flows along each of the 12 possible routes constitute the decision variables in the model. Although the diagram does not contain labels for the arcs, it would be natural to use the notation *MA* for the quantity shipped

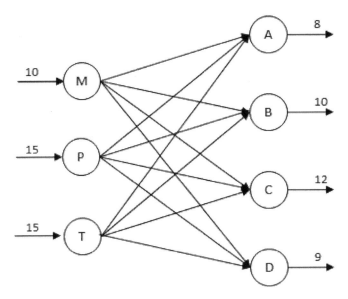

Figure 3.1. Flow diagram for Example 3.1.

on the route from Minneapolis to Atlanta, *MB* for the quantity shipped on the route from Minneapolis to Boston, and so on.

This is an instance of the classical *transportation problem*, which is described by a set of sources and their supplies, a set of destinations and their demands, and the unit cost associated with each source–destination pair. In Example 3.1, the supplies are plant capacities—figures that would be provided by the production or manufacturing function. The demands are customer orders, typically marketing forecasts of near-term requirements, although they could be firm orders in environments where delivery lead times are relatively long. Unit costs are actual costs incurred internally, and they would be estimated from historical data in logistics records. If some of the potential routes had not been in use, the cost on those routes would have to be estimated by knowledgeable people in the distribution or transportation functions. Alternatively, the unit costs could arise as prices set by third parties who take responsibility for transportation of physical goods. In such cases, unit costs would be based on published rates for delivery by truck, rail or air.

Figure 3.2 displays a spreadsheet model for the example. Notice the distinctive From/To structure in the table describing the parameters of the problem. This structure lends itself readily to a row-and-column format, which is the essence of spreadsheet layout. Here, we adopt a convention that associates sources with rows and destinations with columns. In other words, flow moves conceptually in the spreadsheet *from* rows *to* columns. Because of this structure, it is helpful to depart from the standard linear programming layout used in Chapter 2 and to adopt a special format for this type of model. In particular, we can construct a spreadsheet model in rows and columns to mirror the table of parameters given in Example 3.1. In the Parameters

	A	B	C	D	E	F	G	
1	Network: Transportation Problem							
2								
3	Parameters							
4			Atl	Bos	Chi	Den	Capacity	
5		Minn	0.60	0.56	0.22	0.40	10,000	
6		Pitt	0.36	0.30	0.28	0.58	15,000	
7		Tucs	0.65	0.68	0.55	0.42	15,000	
8		Requirement	8,000	10,000	12,000	9,000		
9								
10	Decisions							
11			Atl	Bos	Chi	Den	Sent	
12		Minn	-	-	10,000	-	10,000	
13		Pitt	5,000	10,000	-	-	15,000	
14		Tucs	3,000	-	2,000	9,000	14,000	
15		Received	8,000	10,000	12,000	9,000	39,000	
16								
17	Objective							
18		Total Cost	13,830					
19								

Figure 3.2. Spreadsheet model for Example 3.1.

module of the spreadsheet, we see all of the given information, displayed in an array. In the Decisions module, the decision variables (shaded for highlighting) appear in an array of the same size. At the right of each row is the "Sent" quantity, which is simply the sum of the flows along the row. Below each column of the array is the "Received" quantity, which is the sum in the column. The objective function, which is expressed as a SUMPRODUCT in cell C18, is the total transportation cost for the system. It is the SUMPRODUCT of the two ranges, C5:F7 and C12:F14, that hold the unit cost parameters and the shipment decisions. In algebraic form, the objective function can be expressed as

$$\text{Total cost} = z = 0.60MA + 0.56MB + 0.22MC + \cdots + 0.55TC + 0.42TD$$

The transportation model has two kinds of constraints: LT supply constraints and GT demand constraints. For the Minneapolis plant, the amount shipped from Minneapolis must be no greater than the Minneapolis capacity. In symbols, we can write the capacity constraint as

$$MA + MB + MC + MD \leq 10{,}000$$

For Pittsburgh and Tucson, we have similar constraints:

$$PA + PB + PC + PD \leq 15{,}000$$
$$TA + TB + TC + TD \leq 15{,}000$$

Given the spreadsheet layout, these three constraints constitute a set of LT constraints that say Sent ≤ Capacity, or G12:G14 must be less than or equal to G5:G7. The LHS

	A	B	C	D	E	F	G
1	Network: Transportation						
2							
3	Parameters						
4			Atl	Bos	Chi	Den	Capacity
5		Minn	0.6	0.56	0.22	0.4	10000
6		Pitt	0.36	0.3	0.28	0.58	15000
7		Tucs	0.65	0.68	0.55	0.42	15000
8		Requirement	8000	10000	12000	9000	
9							
10	Decisions						
11			Atl	Bos	Chi	Den	Sent
12		Minn	0	0	10000	0	=SUM(C12:F12)
13		Pitt	5000	10000	0	0	=SUM(C13:F13)
14		Tucs	3000	0	2000	9000	=SUM(C14:F14)
15		Received	=SUM(C12:C14)	=SUM(D12:D14)	=SUM(E12:E14)	=SUM(F12:F14)	=SUM(G12:G14)
16							
17	Objective						
18		Total Cost	=SUMPRODUCT(C5:F7,C12:F14)				
19							

◄ ◄ ► ►   Transport

Figure 3.3. Formulas in the spreadsheet for Example 3.1.

of these constraints simply adds the outbound shipment quantities from a given location. For that reason, we don't really need to use the SUMPRODUCT formula in the worksheet; we can use the simpler SUM formula. Thus, as the display of formulas in Figure 3.3 demonstrates, the spreadsheet model uses both the SUMPRODUCT and SUM functions.

For the Atlanta warehouse, the demand constraint requires that the amount received at Atlanta (from all sources) must be at least as large as the Atlanta demand. As we saw in Chapter 2, it is good practice to use the inequality form of this type of constraint, even though our intuition may tell us that there is no reason to ship more to Atlanta than is demanded. In symbols, this constraint reads

$$MA + PA + TA \geq 8000$$

Similarly, for the other three warehouses, the constraints become

$$MB + PB + TB \geq 10{,}000$$
$$MC + PC + TC \geq 12{,}000$$
$$MD + PD + TD \geq 9000$$

In the spreadsheet, these four constraints constitute a set of GT constraints that say Received ≥ Demand, or C15:F15 must be greater than or equal to C8:F8. Again, the left-hand sides of these constraints can easily be expressed using the SUM formula. In the Model tab of the task pane, we specify the model as follows.

Objective:	C18 (minimize)
Variables:	C12:F14
Constraints:	G12:G14 ≤ G5:G7
	C15:F15 ≥ C8:F8

As usual for linear programs, we select the Standard LP/Quadratic Engine from the drop-down menu on the Engine tab and set the Assume Non-Negative option to True. This will be standard operating procedure when we are solving linear programs, so we won't mention it specifically from now on, unless there is an exception.

The optimal solution, shown in Figure 3.2, achieves the minimum cost of $13,830. All demand constraints in this solution are binding, even though we permitted the model to send more than the requirement to each warehouse. This result makes intuitive sense because shipping more than is required to any warehouse would merely incur excess cost. Once we understand why there is no incentive to exceed demand, we can anticipate that there will be some excess capacity in the solution. This follows from the fact that total capacity comes to 40,000 cartons, while total shipment volume comes to only 39,000, as confirmed in cell G15. In particular, capacity constraints are binding at Pittsburgh and Minneapolis, but an excess capacity of 1000 cartons remains at Tucson.

The solution, shown on the original network in Figure 3.4, may be surprising to someone who has not previously seen the transportation model. Although there are 12 possible shipment routes in the model, the optimal solution uses only six. The flexibility in having three possible sources for meeting each demand is not fully utilized. After a little further thought, this pattern makes sense because many of the unused routes are expensive. Nonetheless, the solution uses the *TA* route, on which the unit cost is $0.65, and avoids the *PC* route, where the unit cost is $0.28. Such choices might be unexpected, but they reflect the systems view that an optimization model can take.

As in other linear programming solutions, the transportation model provides both tactical and strategic information. If Goodwin Manufacturing had to implement a distribution plan immediately, then the plan shown in Figure 3.2 would be the cost-minimizing plan that its management seeks, representing the tactical interpretation of the model. However, if there is time to explore some changes in the given information, as strategic initiatives, then to reduce total transportation cost, we should explore ways of lowering one of the demand requirements or ways of adding capacity to Minneapolis

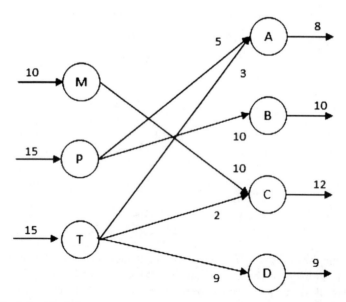

Figure 3.4. Optimal flows for Example 3.1.

or Pittsburgh because these actions loosen the binding constraints. At the margin, adding capacity at Tucson will not help in reducing total cost. Thus, by using linear programming to solve its transportation problem, Goodwin Manufacturing can determine the cheapest way to meet customer demands in the short run. It can identify some economically attractive strategic initiatives as well.

Example 3.1, which contains three sources and four destinations, shows how to build a suitable spreadsheet for the transportation problem. It is straightforward to adapt the spreadsheet design to any number of sources and any number of destinations. Again, the key formulation step is to display cost parameters and shipment quantities as separate arrays.

3.2. THE ASSIGNMENT MODEL

An important special case of the transportation problem has all capacities and all requirements equal to one. Moreover, the number of sources and the number of destinations are the same. This special case is known as the *assignment problem*. The one-to-one matching structure of an assignment is a practical problem. In addition, it arises as a portion of a more complicated model, as we shall see later. For the most part, we can set up and solve this special case in the same way that we dealt with the transportation problem. Consider the example of the Europa Auto Company.

EXAMPLE 3.2 ***Europa Auto Company***

Europa Auto Company is an automaker with six manufacturing plants and six vehicles to produce this year. The firm has learned that it makes sense to produce each vehicle at a unique plant, even though some of the plants are older and less efficient than others. For each possible assignment of a vehicle to a plant, the firm has estimated the annual cost (in millions of dollars) of implementing the assignment. The cost data take the form shown in the following table, which identifies the products by number. The automaker's objective is to minimize the total cost of the assignment.

	Product					
Plant	Compact 1	Coupe 2	Sedan 3	SUV 4	Truck 5	Van 6
Akron	80	56	43	62	46	58
Buffalo	94	50	88	64	63	52
Columbus	94	46	50	40	55	73
Detroit	98	79	71	65	91	59
Evansville	61	59	89	98	45	52
Flint	77	49	65	95	72	91

■

We can think of an *assignment* as a selection of six numbers from the cost table, one from each row and one from each column. (Because the number of products is the same as the number of plants, we can think of either assigning plants to products or assigning products to plants.) The total cost associated with such an assignment is the sum of the numbers selected. This is merely another way of saying that the problem is a special transportation problem in which the row "capacities" are each one and the column "requirements" are also one. As such, we can construct a flow diagram to represent the decision problem in much the same way as in the transportation model of Figure 3.1. The diagram for the automaker example is shown in Figure 3.5, where each of the 36 arcs in the diagram represents part of a potential assignment.

To construct the assignment model algebraically, we define our decision variables as the possible plant–product combinations, $A1, A2, \ldots, F6$. Our objective function (denoted z) is the total cost of an assignment, which can be expressed as the sum of 36 products. Each term in this sum is an assignment cost multiplied by a decision variable.

$$\text{Total cost} = z = 80A1 + 56A2 + 43A3 + \cdots + 72F5 + 91F6$$

There are 12 constraints, 6 for the plants and 6 for the products. The row (plant) constraints are as follows.

$$A1 + A2 + A3 + A4 + A5 + A6 \leq 1$$
$$B1 + B2 + B3 + B4 + B5 + B6 \leq 1$$
$$C1 + C2 + C3 + C4 + C5 + C6 \leq 1$$

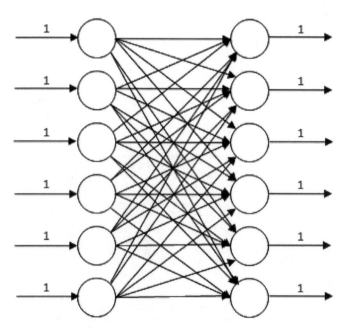

Figure 3.5. Flow diagram for Example 3.2.

$$D1 + D2 + D3 + D4 + D5 + D6 \leq 1$$
$$E1 + E2 + E3 + E4 + E5 + E6 \leq 1$$
$$F1 + F2 + F3 + F4 + F5 + F6 \leq 1$$

These constraints could also be written as equations. Meanwhile, the column (product) constraints are as follows.

$$A1 + B1 + C1 + D1 + E1 + F1 \geq 1$$
$$A2 + B2 + C2 + D2 + E2 + F2 \geq 1$$
$$A3 + B3 + C3 + D3 + E3 + F3 \geq 1$$
$$A4 + B4 + C4 + D4 + E4 + F4 \geq 1$$
$$A5 + B5 + C5 + D5 + E5 + F5 \geq 1$$
$$A6 + B6 + C6 + D6 + E6 + F6 \geq 1$$

Again, these constraints could be written as equations without affecting the problem's solution.

Alternatively, for a more compact algebraic representation, we can use x_{ij} to represent the assignment decisions. Specifically, $x_{ij} = 1$ if vehicle j is made at plant i. In addition, we let c_{ij} denote the cost of assigning plant i to vehicle j. The index i corresponds to a row number and the index j corresponds to a column number. Then, we can express the objective function—the system-wide cost of the assignment—as the following sum

$$z = \sum_i \sum_j c_{ij} x_{ij}$$

The constraints become

$$\sum_j x_{ij} \leq 1, \quad \text{for each plant } i$$

$$\sum_i x_{ij} \geq 1, \quad \text{for each vehicle } j$$

Because the assignment model is a special case of the transportation model with total capacity equal to total demand, we can be sure that the capacity and demand constraints will be binding. (This compact form of the problem statement will be useful to us in later chapters.)

The assignment problem is to minimize z subject to the 12 constraints on the variables. In neither of these formulations are there explicit considerations that would help us avoid fractional values for the decision variables. Although our problem statements allow the decision variables to be fractional, their optimal values will always be either zero or one, as we shall discuss later.

Figure 3.6 shows a spreadsheet model for the assignment problem. It resembles the spreadsheet for the transportation model introduced in Figure 3.2. The upper table contains a 6 × 6 array of assignment costs. The decisions are shown in the lower 6 × 6 table and highlighted. To the right of each row is the row sum and below

	A	B	C	D	E	F	G	H	I	J
1	**Network: Assignment Model**									
2										
3	**Parameters (Costs)**		Com	Coupe	Sedan	SUV	Truck	Van		
4			1	2	3	4	5	6		
5		A	80	56	43	62	46	58		
6		B	94	50	88	64	63	52		
7		C	94	46	50	40	55	73		
8		D	98	79	71	65	91	59		
9		E	61	59	89	98	45	52		
10		F	77	49	65	95	72	91		
11										
12										
13	**Decisions (Assignments)**									
14			1	2	3	4	5	6	*Assigned*	
15		A	0	0	1	0	0	0	1	
16		B	0	1	0	0	0	0	1	
17		C	0	0	0	1	0	0	1	
18		D	0	0	0	0	0	1	1	
19		E	0	0	0	0	1	0	1	
20		F	1	0	0	0	0	0	1	
21		*Assigned*	1	1	1	1	1	1		
22										
23	**Objective (Total Cost)**									
24		314								
25										

Assign

Figure 3.6. Spreadsheet model for Example 3.2.

each of the columns is the column sum. As in the transportation model (Figure 3.2), these cells use the SUM formula. Finally, in cell B24, we highlight the value of the objective function, or total cost, which is computed as the SUMPRODUCT of the cost array and the decision array.

Conceptually, there are capacities of one for each plant and requirements of one for each product, in analogy to the transportation model. Rather than include these parameters on the spreadsheet itself, they are entered as RHS constants in the constraints. Normally, it is not good practice to enter RHS constants in the task pane, because we prefer to show parameters of the model on the spreadsheet itself, where we might want to explore some what-if questions. However, we make an exception here because the right-hand sides will not change: values of one represent the essence of the assignment problem. The specification of the model is as follows.

Objective: B24 (minimize)
Variables: C15:H20
Constraints: I15:I20 $\leq$ 1
              C21:H21 $\geq$ 1

The LT constraints assure that at most one product is assigned to each plant, and the GT constraints assure that each plant has at least one product assigned to it. (As mentioned earlier, we could also express all of the constraints as equations.)

Figure 3.6 displays the optimal solution, which achieves a minimum total cost of $314 million. This optimum is achieved by assigning the Sedan to Plant A, the Coupe to B, the SUV to C, the Van to D, the Truck to E, and the Compact to F. By solving this linear programming problem, Europa can find an economic assignment of vehicle models to plants, thus potentially saving millions of dollars over *ad hoc* assignment methods.

The assignment problem often arises when people must be assigned to tasks. The model assumes that quantitative scores apply to each person–task combination and the objective is to find a minimum (or maximum) total score. One classic application is the assignment of four swimmers to laps in a medley relay, where each lap corresponds to a different stroke, and each swimmer has a lap time for each stroke. The assignment model has also been used to assign workers to shifts, courses to time slots, airline crews to flights, and purchase contracts to supplier bids. For our purposes in modeling, the assignment problem is simply a practical special case of the transportation problem.

3.3. THE TRANSSHIPMENT MODEL

The assignment problem turned out to be a simplified version of the transportation problem, specialized to unit demands and unit supplies. By contrast, the *transshipment problem* is a complicated version of the transportation problem, containing two stages of flow instead of just one. In Figure 3.1—our diagram for the transportation problem—the system contains two levels (plants and warehouses), and all the flow takes place in one stage, from plants to warehouses. In many logistics systems, however, there are three major levels: plants, distribution centers (DCs), and warehouses; in such systems, the flow often takes place in two stages. Consider the example of DeMont Chemical Company.

EXAMPLE 3.3   *DeMont Chemical Company*

DeMont Chemical Company manufactures fertilizer in three plants, referred to as P1, P2, and P3. The company ships its products from plants to two central DCs, designated D1 and D2, and then from the DCs to five regional warehouses, W1–W5. At the DCs, no demand occurs and no capacity limits exist. Demand is associated with the warehouses, and capacities exist at the plants. The system is described in the following two tables, one for each stage. The units for capacity and demand are pounds of fertilizer, and the unit costs are given per pound.

	(To) DC			Capacity
(From) plant	D1	D2		
P1	$1.36	$1.28		2400
P2	1.28	1.35		2750
P3	1.68	1.55		2500

	(To) warehouse				
(From) DC	W1	W2	W3	W4	W5
D1	$0.60	$0.36	$0.32	$0.44	$0.72
D2	$0.80	$0.56	$0.42	$0.40	$0.55
Requirement	1250	1000	1600	1750	1500

■

Figure 3.7 provides a flow diagram for the system, showing the plants on the left-hand side of the diagram, the warehouses on the right, and the DCs in the center. We can think of this system as composed of two side-by-side transportation problems, one involving the plants and DCs and the other involving the DCs and warehouses. All material flow occurs in two stages; that is, material flows first from a plant to a DC and then from a DC to a warehouse. The DCs are called *transshipment points*, referring to the fact that material arrives at those locations and is then subject to further shipment. The essence of the transshipment structure is the coordination of the two transportation stages.

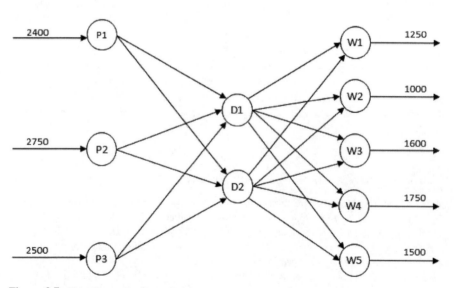

Figure 3.7. Flow diagram for Example 3.3.

	A	B	C	D	E	F	G	H	I
1	Network: Transshipment Problem								
2									
3	Stage 1		*Parameters*				*Decisions*		
4			To						
5		From	D1	D2	Capacity				Sent
6		P1	1.36	1.28	2400		1100	1300	2400
7		P2	1.28	1.35	2750		2750	0	2750
8		P3	1.68	1.55	2500		0	1950	1950
9					Stage cost	9,702.50	3850	3250	
10	Stage 2		*Parameters*				*Decisions*		
11			From						
12		To	D1	D2	Requirement		3850	3250	Received
13		W1	0.60	0.80	1250		1250	0	1250
14		W2	0.36	0.56	1000		1000	0	1000
15		W3	0.32	0.42	1600		1600	0	1600
16		W4	0.44	0.40	1750		0	1750	1750
17		W5	0.72	0.55	1500		0	1500	1500
18					Stage cost	3,147.00			
19	Objective								
20		Total Cost	12,849.50						
21									

Figure 3.8. Spreadsheet model for Example 3.3.

The flow diagram reinforces the fact that the problem involves two side-by-side transportation problems, and we could build a spreadsheet layout showing two stages horizontally on a worksheet, each resembling Figure 3.2 for the transportation model. However, a vertical layout is shown in the worksheet of Figure 3.8. In this layout, the upper portion of the worksheet corresponds to the first stage of plant–DC flow, with costs in the left-hand array and decisions (highlighted) in the right-hand array. Plant capacities appear, just as in the transportation problem, in this portion of the model. Although no requirements appear, Cell F9 contains a SUMPRODUCT formula that accounts for the total transportation cost in the first stage. The lower portion of the sheet corresponds to the second stage of DC–warehouse flow, again with costs in the left-hand array and decisions (highlighted) in the right-hand array. Requirements appear in this segment of the model, and another SUMPRODUCT formula accounts for the total cost of the second stage in cell F18. The total cost for the entire system is the sum of the first stage cost and the second stage cost, as captured in cell C20.

In the upper portion of the model, the sources are represented in rows and the destinations are represented in columns. In the lower portion, this convention is reversed: the sources are represented in columns, and the destinations are represented in rows. Under this "flip flopping" convention, the same columns (in this worksheet, columns C and D for costs, or columns G and H for decisions) correspond to the DCs in both portions of the model. The identification of DCs with unique columns helps to reinforce the need for coordinating the flows in to and out of the DCs. This structure also makes it relatively easy to accommodate an additional DC in the model (by inserting a column in the spreadsheet).

The model specification is as follows

Objective:	C20 (minimize)
Variables:	G6:H8, G13:H17
Constraints:	I6:I8 $\leq$ E6:E8
	I13:I17 $\geq$ E13:E17
	G9:H9 = G12:H12

The formulation contains three LT constraints (one per plant), five GT constraints (one per warehouse), and two EQ constraints (one per DC). The optimal solution in this example is shown in Figure 3.8 with a total cost of \$12,849.50. Thus, DeMont Chemical can take a systems view—and recognize both stages of its supply chain—when it optimizes its distribution costs.

To repeat, the total cost in cell C20 is the sum of the first-stage total cost and the second-stage total cost, and the decision variables appear in two arrays. Three types of constraints are needed in the model: a set of LT constraints for the plant capacities, a set of GT constraints for the warehouse requirements, and a set of EQ constraints balancing the inflows and outflows at the DC locations. Although this last set of constraints could also be expressed in the form of inequalities, the use of equations helps to identify the various constraints by associating a different constraint type (LT, GT, EQ) with each of the three different roles (capacities at the plants, requirements at the warehouses, and transshipment at the DCs). We can also view the EQ constraints as expressing the key *conservation law* of flows in networks: the total quantity flowing out of a node must always be equal to the total quantity flowing in.

To describe the conservation law algebraically, we introduce some notation for the decision variables. Let P2D1 represent the quantity shipped from plant P2 to distribution center D1, and so on. With this notation, we can write the conservation relationship for D1 as follows

$$(\text{Flow Out}) = (\text{Flow In})$$
$$(\text{Flow Out}) - (\text{Flow In}) = 0$$
$$(\text{D1W1} + \text{D1W2} + \text{D1W3} + \text{D1W4} + \text{D1W5}) - (\text{P1D1} + \text{P2D1} + \text{P3D1}) = 0$$

Similarly, for D2, we have

$$(\text{D2W1} + \text{D2W2} + \text{D2W3} + \text{D2W4} + \text{D2W5}) - (\text{P1D2} + \text{P2D2} + \text{P3D2}) = 0$$

Thus, the conservation law takes the form of an equality constraint for particular nodes in the network. This equality constraint is sometimes called a *balance equation*, because it ensures perfect balance between inputs and outputs.

In this approach, we employed the conservation law to help build constraints for the DCs. We did not use the conservation law for the supply and demand nodes. At first glance, it may appear that the conservation law does not necessarily hold at those nodes. For example, if we interpret the input to node P1 as its capacity, we cannot be sure, before solving the optimization problem, whether all of that capacity will be used. Thus, we can't tell whether the total flow out of the node will be equal to the flow in to the node. A similar fact applies to the demand nodes, although as we noted earlier, we can expect the total flow into those nodes to equal the demands when there is an adequate supply in the network as a whole and when minimum cost is the objective. In other words, there is no economic incentive to violate the conservation law at the demand nodes, even though the constraints of the model might permit it. Nevertheless, there is a sense in which the conservation law holds even for the supply and demand nodes. We explore this interpretation in a later section.

3.4. FEATURES OF SPECIAL NETWORK MODELS

The transportation, assignment, and transshipment problems constitute a set of *special network models* in linear programming. They are special in the sense that they all lend themselves easily to the use of a flow diagram, and they all contain a From/To flow structure that suggests a convenient row-and-column layout in a spreadsheet. In particular, we can conveniently display the decision variables as an array in the spreadsheet. When we specify the variables for Solver, we do not enter a row of adjacent cells, which is the standard format. Instead, we enter an array, or in the case of the transshipment model, a pair of arrays. (This feature could obviously be generalized to cases in which we have three or more stages in the model.) With the array format at the heart of the model, the constraints involve limitations on totals across a row or down a column. As a result, the constraints use the SUM formula, rather than the

---

| BOX 3.1 | *Characteristics of Special Network Models* |

Modules

    Data module: capacities, demands, and unit costs.

    Decision module: variables, row sums, and column sums.

    Objective function: total cost of distribution, transportation, or assignment.

Decision variables

    Use array layout reflecting the problem's From/To structure.

    Use an array the same size as the corresponding unit cost array.

Objective function

    Calculate as the SUMPRODUCT(s) of array pairs.

    Minimize total distribution, transportation, or assignment cost.

Constraints

    Sum decision variables along row or column to compute capacity allocated.

    Sum decision variables along row or column to compute demand covered.

    Use LT for capacity, GT for demands to express the most flexible form.

SUMPRODUCT formula that we saw throughout Chapter 2. Box 3.1 summarizes the prominent features of special networks.

One interesting feature of special network models is that an optimal solution always consists of an integer-valued set of decision variables whenever the constraint parameters are integer valued. Recall that the linearity assumption in linear programming allows for divisibility in the values of decision variables. As a result, some or all of the decision variables in an optimal solution may be fractional, and this sometimes makes the result difficult to implement or interpret. However, no such problem arises with special networks; they will always lead to integer-valued solutions as long as the constraint parameters are integers themselves.

Finally, the models of transportation, assignment, and transshipment problems introduced thus far have featured LT constraints for capacities and GT constraints for requirements, along with balance equations in the case of a transshipment model. In the case of the assignment model, its special structure allowed us to use equality constraints from the outset. However, as we shall discover next, it is possible to formulate any of these problems as linear programs built exclusively on balance equations. Although this approach may not seem as intuitive, it does link the flow diagram and the spreadsheet model more closely, as suggested at the beginning of the chapter.

3.5. BUILDING NETWORK MODELS WITH BALANCE EQUATIONS

The transportation model is a special kind of network. As we can readily see in the diagram of Figure 3.1, the nodes can be partitioned into a set of supply locations and a set of demand locations. This partitioning allows us to build a From/To structure suited to the row-and-column format of the spreadsheet. However, we sometimes encounter other network structures that do not lend themselves quite as easily to an array layout for decision variables. For these networks, it may be desirable to formulate the model using the standard linear programming format, with decision variables in a single row and with a SUMPRODUCT function in each of the constraints. In what follows, we provide a glimpse of how to approach network models in such a manner. The distinguishing feature of this approach is the use of balance equations, relying heavily on the information in a flow diagram. To illustrate how this approach works, we return to examples we have already covered. As suggested earlier, the balance equation approach is not the most intuitive way to handle transportation, assignment, and transshipment problems, but it will be useful background when we analyze other network models. By revisiting the transportation, assignment, and transshipment examples (Examples 3.1–3.3) we can explore a new approach while drawing on familiar problems.

The arcs of a network represent possible flow paths, and the quantities flowing along each arc correspond to decision variables in the model. For diagramming purposes, we also represent supply capacities and demand requirements as entering and leaving arcs, respectively, just as in Figure 3.1 or 3.5. Now we take one additional step: we make sure that—for the entire network—the total supply quantity matches the total demand quantity. This feature allows us to write a balance equation for each node in the network.

Balanced totals for supply and demand occur in the assignment example of Figure 3.5. Since the problem comes to us with that feature, we can move from the diagram directly to the balance equations. For node A, the balance equation takes the following form

$$(\text{Flow Out}) - (\text{Flow In}) = 0$$
$$(A1 + A2 + A3 + A4 + A5 + A6) - 1 = 0$$

Similarly, there are 11 other balance equations. The full spreadsheet model, with 36 variables and 12 constraints, is shown in Figure 3.9. The optimal solution produced by Solver achieves the minimum cost of $314 million, which we recognize from Figure 3.6. The set of assignments matches the optimal solution in the earlier formulation as well.

It is not hard to imagine a problem in which total supply and demand are unequal. In fact, our transportation example in Figure 3.1 is just such a case. In this example, total supply is 40,000, while total demand is 39,000. Thus, we might wonder how to deal with problems that come to us with unbalanced totals for supply and demand. Here is how we proceed. We alter the diagram by adding a "dummy" warehouse to capture excess capacity. In our example, the requirement at this fictitious warehouse is 1000, bringing demand and capacity into balance. We then add arcs linking each of the plants to the dummy warehouse, and we assign zero costs to these arcs.

We can think of shipments to the dummy warehouse as shipments to Nowhere. In other words, flows into the dummy warehouse are *virtual* flows that do not actually occur, whereas flows into the first four warehouses correspond to *physical* flows. The virtual flows correspond to unused capacity, which justifies using a cost of zero on these arcs. The complete diagram is shown in Figure 3.10. We see that the original diagram has been augmented so that there are now three capacities and five

	A1	A2	A3	A4	A5	A6	B1	B2	B3	B4	B5	B6	C1	C2	C3	C4	C5	C6	D1	D2	D3	D4	D5	D6	E1	E2	E3	E4	E5	E6	F1	F2	F3	F4	F5	F6		
Decision Variables	0	0	1	0	0	0	0	1	0	0	0	0	0	0	0	0	1	0	0	0	0	0	0	1	0	0	0	0	1	0	1	0	0	0	0	0		
Objective Function	80	56	43	62	46	58	94	50	88	64	63	52	94	46	50	40	55	73	98	79	71	65	91	59	61	59	89	98	45	52	77	49	65	95	72	91	314	
Constraints																																						
Node A	1	1	1	1	1	1	0	0	0	0	0	0	0	0	0	0	0	0	0	0	0	0	0	0	0	0	0	0	0	0	0	0	0	0	0	0	=	1
Node B	0	0	0	0	0	0	1	1	1	1	1	1	0	0	0	0	0	0	0	0	0	0	0	0	0	0	0	0	0	0	0	0	0	0	0	0	=	1
Node C	0	0	0	0	0	0	0	0	0	0	0	0	1	1	1	1	1	1	0	0	0	0	0	0	0	0	0	0	0	0	0	0	0	0	0	0	=	1
Node D	0	0	0	0	0	0	0	0	0	0	0	0	0	0	0	0	0	0	1	1	1	1	1	1	0	0	0	0	0	0	0	0	0	0	0	0	=	1
Node E	0	0	0	0	0	0	0	0	0	0	0	0	0	0	0	0	0	0	0	0	0	0	0	0	1	1	1	1	1	1	0	0	0	0	0	0	=	1
Node F	0	0	0	0	0	0	0	0	0	0	0	0	0	0	0	0	0	0	0	0	0	0	0	0	0	0	0	0	0	0	1	1	1	1	1	1	=	1
Node 1	1	0	0	0	0	0	1	0	0	0	0	0	1	0	0	0	0	0	1	0	0	0	0	0	1	0	0	0	0	0	1	0	0	0	0	0	=	1
Node 2	0	1	0	0	0	0	0	1	0	0	0	0	0	1	0	0	0	0	0	1	0	0	0	0	0	1	0	0	0	0	0	1	0	0	0	0	=	1
Node 3	0	0	1	0	0	0	0	0	1	0	0	0	0	0	1	0	0	0	0	0	1	0	0	0	0	0	1	0	0	0	0	0	1	0	0	0	=	1
Node 4	0	0	0	1	0	0	0	0	0	1	0	0	0	0	0	1	0	0	0	0	0	1	0	0	0	0	0	1	0	0	0	0	0	1	0	0	=	1
Node 5	0	0	0	0	1	0	0	0	0	0	1	0	0	0	0	0	1	0	0	0	0	0	1	0	0	0	0	0	1	0	0	0	0	0	1	0	=	1
Node 6	0	0	0	0	0	1	0	0	0	0	0	1	0	0	0	0	0	1	0	0	0	0	0	1	0	0	0	0	0	1	0	0	0	0	0	1	=	1

Figure 3.9. Standard linear programming format for Example 3.2.

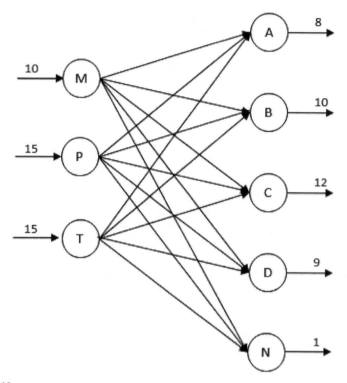

Figure 3.10. Flow diagram for the augmented version of Example 3.1.

requirements, giving rise to eight nodes; and there are 15 routes, corresponding to 15 arcs. However, the net effect has been to recast the original network into an equivalent one containing equal supply and demand quantities. This means that all of the supply available at the plants must ultimately find its way through the network to the warehouses. As a result, there must be a balance equation for every node.

The next step is to translate the diagram into a linear programming model. We again set aside one variable for each arc; thus, we reserve 15 columns for decision variables. There are also eight constraints, one corresponding to each node. The essential requirement for *any* node in the model is a balance equation, that is, an EQ constraint ensuring that total flow into the node matches total flow out of the node, or

$$(\text{Flow Out}) - (\text{Flow In}) = 0$$

For example, at the Minneapolis node, the flow in corresponds to the capacity of 10,000, while the flows out correspond to the arcs (decision variables) *MA*, *MB*, *MC*, *MD*, and *MN*. The balance equation becomes

$$MA + MB + MC + MD + MN - 10,000 = 0$$

or, in standard form, with variables on the left-hand side and constants on the right,

$$MA + MB + MC + MD + MN = 10,000.$$

For the other two plants, we obtain

$$PA + PB + PC + PD + PN = 15{,}000$$
$$TA + TB + TC + TD + TN = 15{,}000$$

For the Atlanta node, the flow in corresponds to the arcs MA, PA, and TA, while the flow out corresponds to the requirement of 8000. The balance equation becomes

$$8000 - MA - PA - TA = 0$$

which we choose to write as

$$-MA - PA - TA = -8000$$

For the other destination nodes, we obtain

$$-MB - PB - TB = -10{,}000$$
$$-MC - PC - TC = -12{,}000$$
$$-MD - PD - TD = -9000$$
$$-MN - PN - TN = -1000$$

Figure 3.11 shows the complete spreadsheet model, in which all constraints are EQ constraints, and the objective function is unchanged from before. Moreover, we can distinguish flows *into* the network as positive right-hand sides (in the first three constraints) from flows *out of* the network, which are negative right-hand sides (in the last five constraints). The model specification is as follows.

Objective:	Q8 (minimize)
Variables:	B6:P6
Constraints:	Q11:Q18 = S11:S18

Figure 3.11. Spreadsheet model for the augmented version of Example 3.1.

When we solve this optimization problem in the usual way, we obtain the same minimum cost we saw previously, $13,830, as shown in Figure 3.11. In this case, the decision variables also match those of Figure 3.2. The optimal solution also contains the decision variable $TN = 1000$, which we interpret as excess capacity of 1000 units at Tucson.

To summarize, we have followed a procedure for translating a network problem into a linear program. This procedure requires a flow diagram, possibly including a dummy node to capture unused capacity. Once we construct such a diagram, we can build the model by following these simple steps.

- Define a variable for each arc.
- Define a constraint for each node.
- Express the balance equation for each node.

In addition, a sign convention for right-hand side constants can provide improved clarity. Under this convention, a balance equation has a positive right-hand side to signal flow into the network and a negative right-hand side to signal flow out of the network.

For distribution problems of this sort, the From/To structure of the situation lends itself most readily to the special network layout shown in Figure 3.2, and that would be the modeling approach of choice. The approach suggested here is more general and would be valuable in situations that are more complicated than transportation, assignment, or transshipment problems. We examine some examples in the next section. Before we proceed, however, here is a perspective on the balance equation model.

The special network models all adhere to the conservation law and the use of balance equations, although it may be necessary to add a dummy node to make sure that all supply capacity is consumed. In the models we built at the outset, the addition of a dummy node and corresponding dummy arcs would have seemed unwieldy or unnecessary. Fortunately, we were able to avoid that step and proceed directly to a convenient formulation that contains inequalities rather than equations. In effect, we were dropping the dummy nodes and arcs from the network. By ignoring those virtual flows, we could change the balance equation for each supply node to a LT inequality. Similarly, we could also change the balance equation for each demand node to a GT inequality, incorporating the additional flexibility suggested in Chapter 2. These simplification steps left us with the network model we saw in Figure 3.2, but with our new perspective, we can interpret it as an adaptation of the balance equation model.

Special purpose solvers have been developed for use on large-scale network problems in industry and academia. Typically, these solvers rely on balance equations and therefore require that formulations contain equality constraints. However, RSP does not presently have the facility to draw on these kinds of solvers. The use of balance equations with Solver may help avoid formulation errors, but it cannot exploit the algorithmic efficiencies that specialized network software packages offer.

3.6. GENERAL NETWORK MODELS WITH YIELDS

In network diagrams for the transportation, assignment, and transshipment models, arcs carry flow from one node to another. Moreover, on every arc, the flow into the destination node is implicitly required to exactly match the flow sent out from the source node. However, we can relax that kind of conservation requirement and extend network models to cases in which flows are subject to yield factors. The yield factors may shrink the amount flowing on an arc, in which cases we speak of a *yield loss*. Alternatively, yield factors may enhance the amount flowing, in which case we speak of a *yield gain*. The next two subsections provide examples.

3.6.1. Models with Yield Losses

Yield loss occurs in manufacturing processes where materials are shaped and trimmed to fit a target design, thus creating material waste. In other settings, quality inspections screen out defective parts. Process yields of these types reduce the amount of material in the main product. Similarly, yield loss may occur in distribution processes, especially with perishable goods. Fluids may partially evaporate during a delivery trip, or vegetables may spoil. The net effect of perishability, as with process yields, is simply a reduction in the amount of a flow that reaches its destination.

EXAMPLE 3.4   *The Goodwin Manufacturing Company Revisited*

The Goodwin Manufacturing Company (of Example 3.1) finds that its product is subject to evaporation in the tanker trucks used for distribution purposes. The average amount of evaporation depends the distance traveled and the average temperature. The following table shows the corresponding yield loss as it has been observed to occur on each of its shipping routes.

(From) plant	(To) warehouse			
	Atlanta	Boston	Chicago	Denver
Minneapolis	0.24	0.19	0.07	0.11
Pittsburgh	0.10	0.05	0.04	0.15
Tucson	0.26	0.41	0.32	0.27

∎

In this scenario, the yield factor tells us what proportion of the material sent along an arc will reach its destination. For the purposes of decision making, we can still measure the amounts sent out along each arc, but we have to adjust those figures to determine how much demand is actually met at each destination. In addition, we cannot know in advance how much material in the aggregate we will ship from the three plants. We know that, after yield losses, we must ship more than the total demand quantity (still 39,000), but we can't tell *how much more* because we don't yet know which shipping routes we'll use. Therefore, if we think of our model containing a demand node for Nowhere, we must now treat the demand at that node as a variable.

For the purposes of illustration, we assume that each plant has a standard capacity of 16,000 units. Our supply constraints resemble those of the balance-equation model of the previous section.

$$MA + MB + MC + MD + MN = 10,000$$
$$PA + PB + PC + PD + PN = 15,000$$
$$TA + TB + TC + TD + TN = 15,000$$

For the Atlanta node, the flow in corresponds to the net amounts on arcs MA, PA, and TA, while the flow out corresponds to the requirement of 8000. The balance equation becomes

$$8000 - 0.76MA - 0.90PA - 0.74TA = 0$$

which we choose to write as

$$-0.76MA - 0.90PA - 0.74TA = -8000$$

For the other destination nodes, we obtain

$$-0.81MB - 0.95PB - 0.31TB = -10,000$$
$$-0.93MC - 0.96PC - 0.68TC = -12,000$$
$$-0.89MD - 0.85PD - 0.73TD = -9000$$
$$-MN - PN - TN - NX = 0$$

In this last constraint, NX measures the total quantity unshipped and does not appear in the objective function. The objective function is the same as the one we used initially.

Figure 3.12 shows the complete spreadsheet model, in which all constraints are EQ constraints, as in the previous section. In particular, the coefficients in rows 16–20 are yield factors, and these values are taken from the parameters in row 10. The model specification is as follows.

Objective:	R8 (minimize)
Variables:	B6:Q6
Constraints:	R13:R20 = T13:T20

When we solve this optimization problem in the usual way, we obtain the minimum cost of $15,498, as shown in Figure 3.12. To achieve this cost, the shipments out of Minneapolis and Pittsburgh exhaust capacity, whereas some excess capacity remains at Tucson. (The solution reflects this pattern because variables MN and PN are zero, but TN is positive.) From the model, we can determine that the total quantity shipped is 44,707, which provides the 39,000 units of demand after accounting for yields.

With yields present in the model, the structure is not as simple as the transportation model, but we can exploit the conservation law to help us develop valid constraints from balance equations.

	A	B	C	D	E	F	G	H	I	J	K	L	M	N	O	P	Q	R	S	T
1	Network: Transportation Problem with Yield Losses																			
2	Balance-Equation Model																			
3																				
4	Decision Variables																			
5		MA	MB	MC	MD	MN	PA	PB	PC	PD	PN	TA	TB	TC	TD	TN	NX			
6		0	0	12,903	3,097	0	5,474	10,526	0	0	0	4,154	0	0	8,553	3,293	3,293			
7	Objective Function																	Total Cost		
8		0.60	0.56	0.22	0.40	0	0.36	0.30	0.28	0.58	0	0.65	0.68	0.55	0.42	0	0	15,498		
9																				
10	Yields	0.76	0.81	0.93	0.89	1	0.90	0.95	0.96	0.85	1	0.74	0.39	0.68	0.73	1	1			
11																				
12	Constraints																	Net flow		Req'd flow
13	Mcap	1	1	1	1	1	0	0	0	0	0	0	0	0	0	0	0	16,000	=	16,000
14	Pcap	0	0	0	0	0	1	1	1	1	1	0	0	0	0	0	0	16,000	=	16,000
15	Tcap	0	0	0	0	0	0	0	0	0	0	1	1	1	1	0	0	16,000	=	16,000
16	Admd	-0.76	0	0	0	0	-0.90	0	0	0	0	-0.74	0	0	0	0	0	-8,000	=	-8,000
17	Bdmd	0	-0.81	0	0	0	0	-0.95	0	0	0	0	-0.39	0	0	0	0	-10,000	=	-10,000
18	Cdmd	0	0	-0.93	0	0	0	0	-0.96	0	0	0	0	-0.68	0	0	0	-12,000	=	-12,000
19	Ddmd	0	0	0	-0.89	0	0	0	0	-0.85	0	0	0	0	-0.73	0	0	-9,000	=	-9,000
20	Ndmd	0	0	0	0	-1	0	0	0	0	-1	0	0	0	0	-1	1	0	=	0
21																				

YieldLoss

Figure 3.12. Spreadsheet model for Example 3.4.

3.6.2. Models with Yield Gains

We look next at flows that expand. Although there are chemicals that exhibit this property, a more familiar application involves money. As money flows through different locations in time, it usually expands. This expansion results from drawing interest or other kinds of investment returns. Consider the familiar problem of investing for college expenses.

EXAMPLE 3.5   *Planning for College*

Two parents want to provide for their daughter's college education with some money they have recently inherited. They would like to set aside part of the inheritance in an account that would cover the needs of their daughter's college education, which begins four years from now. They estimate that first-year college expenses will come to $24,000 and increase $2000 per year during each of the remaining three years of college. The following investments are available.

Investment	Available	Matures	Return at maturity
A	Every year	1 year	6%
B	1, 3, 5, 7	2 years	14%
C	1, 4	3 years	18%
D	1	7 years	65%

The parents would like to determine an investment plan that provides the necessary funds to cover college expenses with the smallest initial investment.   ∎

Investment and funds-flow problems of this sort lend themselves to network modeling. In this type of problem, nodes represent points in time at which funds flow could occur. We can imagine tracking the balance in a bank account, with funds flowing in and out depending on our decisions. In Example 3.5, we include a node for now (time zero), and nodes for the end of years 1 through 7. Tracking time for this purpose, the end of year 3 and the start of year 4 are in effect the same point in time. To construct a typical start-of-year node, we first list the potential inflows and outflows that can occur.

Inflows

Initial investment

Appreciation of investment A from 1 year ago

Appreciation of investment B from 2 years ago

Appreciation of investment C from 3 years ago

Appreciation of investment D from 7 years ago

Outflows

Expense payment for the coming year

Investment in A for the coming year

Investment in B for the coming 2 years

Investment in C for the coming 3 years

Investment in D for the coming 7 years

Not all of these inflows and outflows apply at every point in time, but if we sketch the eight nodes and the flows that do apply, we come up with a diagram such as the

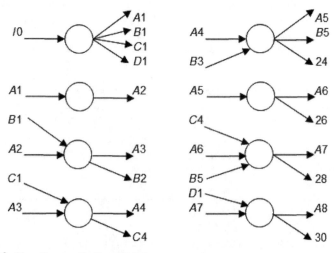

Figure 3.13. Flow diagrams for Example 3.5.

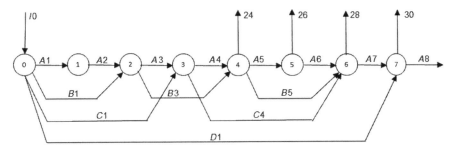

Figure 3.14. Unified flow diagram for Example 3.5.

one shown as Figure 3.13. In this diagram, $A1$ represents the amount allocated to Investment A at time zero, $A2$ represents the amount allocated to Investment A at the start of year 2, and so on. The initial investment in the account is shown as $I0$, and the expense payments are labeled with their numerical values. The diagram shows the different nodes as independent elements, which is all we really need; however, Figure 3.14 shows a tidier diagram in which the nodes are connected in a single flow network.

We do not need the variable $B7$ in the model. A 2-year investment starting in year 7 would extend beyond the 8-year horizon, so this option is omitted. However, the variable $A8$ does appear in the model. We can think of $A8$ as representing the final value in the account. Perhaps it is intuitive that, if we are trying to minimize the initial investment, there is no reason to have money in the account in the end. Still, to verify this intuition, we can include $A8$ in the model, anticipating that we will find $A8 = 0$ in the optimal solution.

The next step is to convert the diagram into a linear programming model. For this purpose, the flows on the diagram become decision variables. Then, each node gives rise to a balance equation, as listed below.

$$
\begin{aligned}
A1 + B1 + C1 + D1 - I0 &= 0 \quad \text{(End of year 0)} \\
A2 - 1.06A1 &= 0 \quad \text{(End of year 1)} \\
A3 + B3 - 1.06A2 - 1.14B1 &= 0 \quad \text{(End of year 2)} \\
A4 + C4 - 1.06A3 - 1.18C1 &= 0 \quad \text{(End of year 3)} \\
A5 + B5 + 24{,}000 - 1.06A4 - 1.14B3 &= 0 \quad \text{(End of year 4)} \\
A6 + 26{,}000 - 1.06A5 &= 0 \quad \text{(End of year 5)} \\
A7 + 28{,}000 - 1.06A6 - 1.14B5 - 1.18C4 &= 0 \quad \text{(End of year 6)} \\
A8 + 30{,}000 - 1.06A7 - 1.65D1 &= 0 \quad \text{(End of year 7)}
\end{aligned}
$$

Figure 3.15 shows these EQ constraints as part of the spreadsheet model. A systematic pattern is formed by the coefficients in the columns of the constraint equations. Each column has two nonzero coefficients: a positive coefficient (of 1), corresponding to the time the investment is made, and a negative coefficient (reflecting

	I0	A1	A2	A3	A4	A5	A6	A7	A8	B1	B3	B5	C1	C4	D1			
Network: Investment Problem							Rates	6%	14%	18%	65%							
Decisions																		
	I0	A1	A2	A3	A4	A5	A6	A7	A8	B1	B3	B5	C1	C4	D1			
	74.422	0.000	0.000	0.000	0.000	24.528	0.000	0.000	0.000	56.240	64.114	24.561	0.000	0.000	18.182			
Objective																		
	74.422																	
Year																		
0	-1	1	0	0	0	0	0	0	0	1	0	0	1	0	1	-0	=	0
1	0	-1.06	1	0	0	0	0	0	0	0	0	0	0	0	0	0	=	0
2	0	0	-1.06	1	0	0	0	0	0	-1.14	1	0	0	0	0	0	=	0
3	0	0	0	-1.06	1	0	0	0	0	0	0	0	-1.18	1	0	-0	=	0
4	0	0	0	0	-1.06	1	0	0	0	0	-1.14	1	0	0	0	-24	=	-24
5	0	0	0	0	0	-1.06	1	0	0	0	0	0	0	0	0	-26	=	-26
6	0	0	0	0	0	0	-1.06	1	0	0	0	-1.14	0	-1.18	0	-28	=	-28
7	0	0	0	0	0	0	0	-1.06	1	0	0	0	0	0	-1.65	-30	=	-30

Invest

Figure 3.15. Spreadsheet model for Example 3.5.

the appreciation rate), corresponding to the time the investment matures. The only exceptions are $I0$ and $A8$, which essentially represent flows into and out of the network. In other funds-flow models, the column coefficients portray the investment-and-return profile on a per-unit basis for each of the variables. Following our sign convention, the right-hand-side constants show the profile of flows in and out of the system over the various time periods. In this case, the constants in the last four constraints are negative, reflecting required outflows from the investment account in the last four years of the plan.

The objective function in this example is simply the initial size of the investment account, represented by the variable $I0$, which we want to minimize. Thus, we can depart from the standard form (which uses the SUMPRODUCT function as an objective) and designate the objective function simply by referencing cell B5. The model specification is as follows.

Objective: B8 (minimize)
Variables: B5:P5
Constraints: Q10:Q17 = S10:S17

When we minimize $I0$, Solver provides the optimal solution shown in Figure 3.15, calling for an initial investment of about $74,422. Compare this with the nominal value of the college expenses, which sum to $108,000. The lower figure for the initial investment testifies to the power of compound interest. In our example, the parents can use linear programming to take advantage of interest rate patterns and minimize the investment they need to make in order to cover the prospective costs of their daughter's college education.

The nature of the optimal solution may not be too surprising. First, the return of 18 percent on the three-year investment is dominated by the return of 6 percent on the one-year investment A, due to compounding. Thus, we should not expect to see any use of the three-year instruments in the optimal solution. The return on the one-year investment is dominated, in turn, by the return on the two-year investment and the

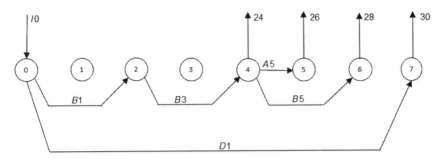

Figure 3.16. Flow diagram with optimal flows for Example 3.5.

return on the seven-year investment. Thus, we should expect to see substantial use of those two instruments. The use of the one-year investment is dictated by timing: Because it is the only investment maturing at the end of year 5, it becomes the vehicle to meet the $26,000 requirement. Prior to that, the solution uses B3 (funded in turn by B1) to cover the first year of expenses and to fund A5. Then B5 covers the third year of expenses, funded by B3. Finally, D1 covers the fourth year of expenses. As expected, the account should be empty at the end of the planning horizon.

The network diagram provides another perspective on this solution structure. In Figure 3.16, we show the network diagram with only the positive flows displayed. The diagram shows clearly that the only vehicle in the optimal solution for meeting

BOX 3.2	*Characteristics of General Network Models for Funds Flow*

Decision variables

    Arcs correspond to sources and uses of funds.

    Make investments; pay off debts owed.

Objective function

    Reference a single variable.

    Minimize initial investment or maximize final value.

Constraints

    Nodes correspond to points in time.

    A balance equation corresponds to each node.

    For investments, the column depicts the pattern of principal and returns.

    For loans, the column depicts the pattern of principal and interest payments.

    RHS constants describe external flows to and from the network.

    Add lower-bound or upper-bound constraints as needed.

the $30,000 requirement at node 7 is the investment in $D1$. Therefore, the size of the initial investment in $D1$ must be $30,000/1.65 = 18,182$. Working backwards, we can also see that the size of $B5$ is dictated by the $28,000 requirement, and $A5$ is dictated by the $26,000 requirement. Once $A5$ and $B5$ are determined, they, together with the $24,000 requirement, dictate the size of $B3$. In turn, $B3$ dictates the size of $B1$. The diagram systematically conveys the detailed pattern in the optimal solution.

Box 3.2 summarizes the important features of network models for funds flow problems. In a multiperiod investment model, flows expand as they travel along arcs. Matter is not conserved as it flows, so we lose the conservation of matter that holds implicitly for flows between nodes in special networks. However, balance equations still apply at each node, in the sense that the total flow out of a node always equals the total flow in. The flows are still denominated in currency wherever they appear in the network. (Money is not converted into product, for example.) By contrast, we look next at a class of network models in which the flows are transformed.

3.7. GENERAL NETWORK MODELS WITH TRANSFORMED FLOWS

Another phenomenon that lends itself to network descriptions is the output of production processes. In this application, a node in the flow diagram represents a process that transforms inputs into outputs. In a transportation network, a node might represent a facility where material is received and ultimately sent out; however, the form of the input flow and the form of the output flow always match. That is, if the input is measured in truckloads, then so is the output. If the input is measured in cartons, then so is the output. The concept holds as well for nodes in a funds-flow network: if the input is measured in dollars, then so is the output. By contrast, production processes alter the material flowing in the system, so outputs may constitute different types of material than the inputs from which they were created. Even with this generalization, network concepts are still applicable. Consider the example of oil refining at Delta Oil Company.

EXAMPLE 3.6   *Delta Oil Company*

A simplified representation of the refining process at Delta Oil Company appears in Figure 3.17. First, the distillation process separates gasoline from other components by heating crude oil under pressure in a distillation tower. The vapors are then collected separately and cooled to produce distillate and other "low-end" by-products. The distillation tower uses five barrels of crude oil to produce three barrels of distillate and two barrels of by-products. Some distillate is blended into gasoline; the rest becomes feedstock for the catalytic cracker.

The catalytic cracking process utilizes high temperatures to break heavy hydrocarbon compounds into lighter compounds. This process produces high quality catalytic gasoline (or catalytic, for short) and other "high-end" by-products. Delta's catalytic cracker requires 2.5 barrels of distillate to produce 1.6 barrels of catalytic and 1 barrel of by-products. (The cracking process creates output volume that exceeds input volume.)

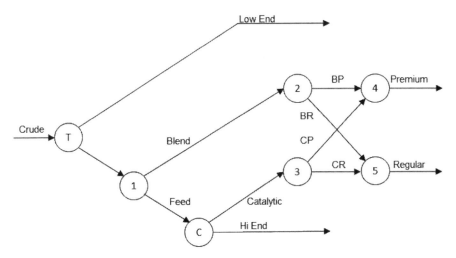

Figure 3.17. Flow diagram for Example 3.6.

Finally, distillate from the distillation tower is blended with catalytic to make regular gasoline and premium gasoline. Premium grade gasoline requires a higher proportion of catalytic in the blend as compared to regular grade gasoline. ∎

We adapt the sketch of production flows and convert it to a standard network flow diagram by labeling each of the arcs in the network, recognizing that these labels will also serve as the names of decision variables in the linear programming model. For convenience, we use some abbreviations, such as *CR*, which represents the amount of catalytic that is combined into regular gasoline. Next, we create node T to represent the tower and node C to represent the cracker. We also add nodes 1, 2, and 3 to represent allocations of flow. At node 1, the distillate must be split into a portion that is directly blended into gasoline and a portion that is used as a feedstock for the cracker. At node 2, the distillate allocated to blending must be split between regular and premium grades of gasoline, and similarly at node 3 for the catalytic produced by the cracker. Finally, nodes 4 and 5 represent the output of the two blending decisions, one for regular and one for premium.

For each node in the diagram, we write a balance equation. Conceptually, however, there is a twist here. Because the nodes represent transformation processes, the input material may differ from the output material, and there may be several input materials and output materials. (In distribution models and yield models, no transformation of material takes place.) We write a balance equation for each output material. For example, the equations for the tower node (T) take the following form.

$$\text{Flows Out} - \text{Flows In} = 0$$

$$Dist - 0.60 \; Crude = 0$$
$$Low - 0.40 \; Crude = 0$$

Thus, this node generates two balance equations, one each for distillate and low-end by-products. Each equation contains one input term, for crude. The coefficients of 0.60 and 0.40 correspond to a fractional split of five barrels into flows of three barrels and two barrels, respectively, for the split between distillate (*Dist*) and low-end by-products (*Low*).

A similar pair of equations applies to the cracker node (C)

$$\text{Flows Out} - \text{Flows In} = 0$$

$$Cat - 0.64\ Feed = 0$$

$$High - 0.40\ Feed = 0$$

The numbered nodes are similar to transshipment nodes in our distribution models, because the inputs and outputs are the same material. At node 1, the distillate must be split into either feedstock (*Feed*) or gasoline blending input (*Blend*). The balance equation becomes

$$Feed + Blend - Dist = 0$$

Nodes 2 and 3 have a similar structure

$$BP + BR - Blend = 0$$
$$CP + CR - Cat = 0$$

Nodes 4 and 5 are also of this type

$$BP + CP - Prem = 0$$
$$BR + CR - Reg = 0$$

The balance equations represent an algebraic description of the flow diagram. Conversely, the flow diagram represents a network representation of the balance equations. The system of balance equations and the network flow diagram are different manifestations of the same model. We can use one form to audit the other in order to check for consistency and eliminate structural errors.

The linear programming model has not been finished. In addition to the network "kernel" for this problem, other types of information are needed, including:

- production capacities for each production process,
- sales potentials for final products,
- blending specifications for gasoline.

The first two of these can be stated in appropriate dimensions, such as barrels per day, whereas the third describes limits on the ratio in which gasoline inputs may be mixed. To illustrate the entire model, suppose the following parametric assumptions apply.

- Tower and cracker capacities: 50,000 and 20,000 barrels/day.
- Sales potential for regular and premium gasoline: 16,000 each.
- Sales potential for by-products: unlimited.

- Blending floor for catalytic in regular gasoline: at least 50 percent catalytic.
- Blending floor for catalytic in premium gasoline: at least 75 percent catalytic.

To complete the model, we need the economic factors that make up the objective function. Suppose the following parametric assumptiosns apply.

- Cost of crude oil: $28 per barrel.
- Cost of operating the tower: $5 per barrel of crude.
- Cost of operating the cracker: $6 per barrel of feedstock.
- Revenue for high-end and low-end by products: $44 and $36 per barrel.
- Revenue for regular and premium gasoline: $50 and $55 per barrel.

Figure 3.18 shows a spreadsheet model for the entire problem. Balance equations form the kernel of the model in rows 12–20. The next pair of constraints, in rows 21–22, contains the blending quality requirements for the grades of gasoline. Finally, the four constraints in rows 23–26 contain the ceilings on production capacities and sales volumes. These could alternatively be incorporated as upper bounds on the variables *Crude*, *Feed*, *Reg*, and *Prem*.

The objective function is made up of revenue from the sales of outputs, the cost of operations, and the cost of input materials. For clarity, we devote a row of the spreadsheet to each of these components of the objective function, recognizing that several of these cells do not apply. In fact, intermediate products such as distillate are not directly

	A	B	C	D	E	F	G	H	I	J	K	L	M	N	O	P	Q
1	**Network: Production Planning Problem**																
2																	
3	**Decisions**	Crude	Dist	Low	Blend	Feed	Cat	High	BR	BP	CR	CP	Reg	Prem			
4	Kbbl.	49.3	29.6	19.7	9.6	20.0	12.8	8.0	8.00	1.60	8.00	4.80	16.0	6.4			
5	**Objective**																
6	price			36				44					50	55			
7	cost	5				6											
8	cost	28															
9	net	-33	0	36	0	-6	0	44	0	0	0	0	50	55	466.400		
10	**Constraints**															LHS	RHS
11																	
12	Tower	-0.60	1	0	0	0	0	0	0	0	0	0	0	0	0.0	=	0
13	Tower capacity	-0.40	0	1	0	0	0	0	0	0	0	0	0	0	0.0	=	0
14	Distillate split	0	-1	0	1	1	0	0	0	0	0	0	0	0	0.0	=	0
15	Cracker	0	0	0	0	-0.64	1	0	0	0	0	0	0	0	0.0	=	0
16	Cracker	0	0	0	0	-0.40	0	1	0	0	0	0	0	0	0.0	=	0
17	Blend split	0	0	0	-1	0	0	0	1	1	0	0	0	0	0.0	=	0
18	Catalytic split	0	0	0	0	0	-1	0	0	0	1	1	0	0	0.0	=	0
19	Reg composition	0	0	0	0	0	0	0	-1	0	-1	0	1	0	0.0	=	0
20	Prem composition	0	0	0	0	0	0	0	0	-1	0	-1	0	1	0.0	=	0
21	Reg quality	0	0	0	0	0	0	0	-0.50	0	0.50	0	0	0	0.0	>=	0
22	Prem quality	0	0	0	0	0	0	0	0	-0.75	0	0.25	0	0	0.0	>=	0
23	Tower capacity	1	0	0	0	0	0	0	0	0	0	0	0	0	49.3	<=	50
24	Cracker capacity	0	0	0	0	1	0	0	0	0	0	0	0	0	20.0	<=	20
25	Reg sales	0	0	0	0	0	0	0	0	0	0	0	1	0	16.0	<=	16
26	Prem sales	0	0	0	0	0	0	0	0	0	0	0	0	1	6.4	<=	16
27																	

Delta

Figure 3.18. Spreadsheet model for Example 3.6.

associated with any costs or revenues at all. The value of the objective function, calculated as a SUMPRODUCT, appears in cell O9. The model specification is
as follows.

Objective:	O9 (maximize)
Variables:	B4:N4
Constraints:	O12:O20 = Q12:Q20
	O21:O22 ≥ Q21:Q22
	O23:O26 ≤ Q23:Q26

Figure 3.18 displays the optimal solution to Delta Oil Company's refining
problem. In brief, the solution achieves a profit contribution of $466,400. It calls
for purchases of 49,333 barrels of crude oil. This quantity leaves the tower with a
small amount of excess capacity, but cracker capacity is fully utilized by the
optimal allocation of distillate. Sales of regular gasoline are limited by market
potential, but this is not the case for premium. Both gasoline products are blended
at their minimum quality requirements, suggesting that catalytic is a scarce resource.
A brief look at the decision variables reveals that there is flow on every arc in the network diagram.

BOX 3.3	*Characteristics of General Network Models for* *Transformation Processes*

Decision variables

   Arcs correspond to materials generated at any stage of the process.

   Define variables as convenient to track costs and revenues.

   Intermediate products appear as arcs, possibly without cost or revenue.

Objective function

   Net revenue or variable cost can be captured as a SUMPRODUCT.

   Maximize net revenue or minimize variable cost in standard form.

Constraints

   Nodes correspond to stages of the process.

   An equation corresponds to each transshipment node.

   At each transformation node, one equation for each output product.

Rest of the model

   Augment the network kernel with capacities and demands.

   Add lower bounds and upper bounds as needed.

Viewed as strategic information, the optimal solution provides useful insights into the determinants of profitability at Delta Oil. Of the two main pieces of process equipment, the cracker is currently the more constraining; however, the tower is not far behind. Capacity may have to be raised in both places for Delta to significantly increase its profits. On the output side, profits are also constrained by demand for regular gasoline. If the marketing department could find additional customers for regular gasoline, this could also lead to increased profits. In short, the strategic implications of the Delta Oil model are typical of product-mix models; however, the construction of the model itself is driven by network-modeling principles.

Returning to the network structure, which lies at the heart of the Delta Oil model, we highlight the key features in Box 3.3.

SUMMARY

This chapter has introduced the network model to accompany allocation, covering, and blending models as one of the four basic linear programming types. The network model is uniquely adapted to the use of network flow diagrams, which can help substantially in constructing and debugging a spreadsheet model.

Among network models, a set of important cases are called special networks. Special network models arise frequently in distribution problems faced by industry. These models also have a structure that leads naturally to a distinctive array-based format for spreadsheet use. The use of arrays reflects the natural From/To structure in the problem itself, which lends itself readily to the row-and-column layout of a spreadsheet. (The array format adds an important case to the standard linear programming format covered in Chapter 2.) Special networks are usually formulated with inequality constraints; although from a more general perspective, these constraints are intuitive simplifications of a set of balance equations.

General network models illustrate the application of balance equations as a means of structuring an optimization problem. The overarching framework for these models is the same standard layout that was emphasized in Chapter 2. Nevertheless, the use of balance equations provides us with a simple recipe for developing a model (or a portion of a model) made up of EQ constraints. These constraints can be formulated directly from an accompanying flow diagram.

EXERCISES

3.1. Distributing a Product   The Nicklaus Razor Blade Company plans to test market a new blade next month. The blades will be stocked in their three warehouses in the following quantities.

Warehouse	A	B	C
Stock (cartons)	50	50	50

Meanwhile, the carton quantities required by the distributors in the four test markets are as follows.

Distributor	D	E	F	G
Requirement	45	15	25	20

The unit costs (in dollars per carton) of shipping the blades from warehouses to distributors are given in the table below.

	D	E	F	G
A	8	10	6	3
B	9	15	8	6
C	5	12	5	7

(a) NRBC wishes to meet the distributor's requirements at the minimum total transportation cost. Find the optimal plan.

(b) Show the network diagram corresponding to the solution in (a). That is, label each of the arcs in the solution and verify that the flows are consistent with the given information.

3.2. Assigning Tasks Suppose a data processing department wishes to assign five programmers to five programming tasks (one programmer to each task). Management has estimated the total number of days each programmer would take if assigned to the different jobs, and these estimates are summarized in the following table.

	Task	1	2	3	4	5
	1	50	25	78	64	60
	2	43	30	70	56	72
Programmer	3	60	28	80	66	68
	4	54	29	75	60	70
	5	45	32	70	62	75

(a) Determine the assignment that minimizes the total programmer days required to complete all five jobs.

(b) Show the network diagram corresponding to the solution in (a). That is, label each of the arcs in the solution and verify that the flows are consistent with the given information.

(c) How would your solution change if programmer 3 could not be assigned to tasks 2 or 4?

3.3. Shipping Grain The Sadeghian Company is in the business of buying and selling grain. An important aspect of the company's business is arranging for the purchased grain to be shipped to customers. If the company can keep freight costs low, its profitability will be improved. Currently, the company has purchased three rail cars of grain at Peoria, seven rail cars at Iowa City, and six rail cars at Lawrence. Fourteen carloads of grain have been sold. The locations and the amount sold at each location are as follows.

Location	Rail car loads
Augusta	2
Gainesville	4
Oxford	3
Columbia	5

All shipments must be routed through either Louisville or Dayton. Shown below are the shipping costs per rail car from the origins to Louisville and Dayton and the costs per rail car to ship from Louisville and Dayton to the destinations.

	Louisville	Dayton
Peoria	1800	1500
Iowa City	1400	1900
Lawrence	1200	1600

	Augusta	Gainesville	Oxford	Columbia
Louisville	4400	3600	3300	3200
Dayton	4200	3500	3100	2700

(a) Determine a shipping schedule that will minimize the freight costs necessary to satisfy demand.

(b) Show the network diagram corresponding to the solution in (a). That is, label each of the arcs in the solution and verify that the flows are consistent with the given information.

3.4. Distributing a Product   The Lincoln Lock Company manufactures a commercial security lock at plants in Atlanta, Louisville, Detroit, and Phoenix. The unit cost of production at each plant is $35.50, $37.50, $37.25, and $36.25, and the annual capacities are 18,000, 15,000, 25,000, and 20,000, respectively. The locks are sold through wholesale distributors in seven locations around the country. The unit shipping cost for each plant–distributor combination is shown in the following table, along with the forecasted demand from each distributor for the coming year.

	Tacoma	San Diego	Dallas	Denver	St Louis	Tampa	Baltimore
Atlanta	2.50	2.75	1.75	2.00	2.10	1.80	1.65
Louisville	1.85	1.90	1.50	1.60	1.00	1.90	1.85
Detroit	2.30	2.25	1.85	1.25	1.50	2.25	2.00
Phoenix	1.90	0.90	1.60	1.75	2.00	2.50	2.65
Demand	5.500	11.500	10.500	9.600	15.400	12.500	6.600

(a) Determine the least costly way of shipping locks from plants to distributors.

(b) Show the network diagram corresponding to the solution in (a). That is, label each of the arcs in the solution and verify that the flows are consistent with the given information.

(c) Suppose that the unit cost at each plant were $10 higher than the original figure. What change in the optimal distribution plan would result? What general conclusions can you draw for transportation models with nonidentical plant-related costs?

3.5. Repositioning Supply The American Rent-a-Car Company has eight outlets in a metropolitan area. American operates under a policy that calls for a specific "target" percentage of all available cars to be located at each outlet at the start of each day. These percentages are summarized in the following table.

Outlet	1	2	3	4	5	6	7	8
Percentage	20	10	20	5	10	20	5	10

For example, if 50 cars are available, 10 should be at outlet 1 at the start of the day. At the end of a day, if the current distribution of cars does not comply with the targets, American employees drive the cars overnight from outlet to outlet so that the new distribution meets the specified targets. The distance between each pair of outlets is given in the following table.

		To outlet						
	1	2	3	4	5	6	7	8
1	–	8	6	7	3	5	4	2
2	8	–	6	5	8	4	6	7
3	6	6	–	8	3	4	7	4
4	7	5	8	–	9	5	3	7
From outlet 5	3	8	3	9	–	5	6	2
6	5	4	4	5	5	–	3	3
7	4	6	7	3	6	3	–	4
8	2	7	4	7	2	3	4	–

At the end of a particular day, American finds that the 100 cars currently available are distributed at the outlets as follows.

Outlet	1	2	3	4	5	6	7	8
Cars	4	14	5	17	22	7	10	21

(a) Given this distribution of cars, find a schedule for minimizing the total distance traveled during the overnight redistribution of the cars.

(b) Show the network diagram corresponding to the solution in (a). That is, label each of the arcs in the solution and verify that the flows are consistent with the given information.

3.6. Designing a Distribution System The Krotzer Company manufactures and distributes meters used to measure electric power consumption. The company started with a small production plant in El Paso and gradually built a customer base throughout Texas. A distribution center was established in Ft Worth, and later, as the business expanded, a second distribution center was established in Santa Fe. The El Paso plant was expanded when the company began marketing its meters in Arizona, California, Nevada, and Utah. With the growth of the West Coast business, the company opened a third distribution center in Las Vegas and just two years ago opened a second production plant in Sacramento.

Manufacturing costs differ between the company's production plants. The cost of each meter produced at the El Paso plant is $10.50. The Sacramento plant uses newer and more efficient equipment, and as a result, its manufacturing costs come to only $10.00 per unit.

The quarterly production capacity is 30,000 meters at the older El Paso plant and 20,000 meters at the Sacramento plant. No shipments are allowed from the Sacramento plant to the Ft. Worth distribution center.

Due to the firm's rapid growth, little attention has been paid to the efficiency of the distribution system, but company management has decided that it is time to address this issue. The cost of shipping a meter from each of the two plants to each of the three distribution centers is shown in the following table.

	Distribution center		
Plant	Ft Worth	Santa Fe	Las Vegas
El Paso	3.20	2.20	4.20
Sacramento	–	3.90	1.20

The company serves nine customer zones from the three distribution centers. The forecast for the number of meters needed in each customer zone for the next quarter is shown in the following table.

Customer zone	Demand (meters)
Dallas	6300
San Antonio	4880
Wichita	2130
Kansas City	1210
Denver	6120
Salt Lake City	4830
Phoenix	2750
Los Angeles	8580
San Diego	4460

The cost per unit of shipping from each distribution center to each customer zone is given in the following table. Note that some distribution centers do not serve certain customer zones because the costs would be prohibitive.

	Customer zone								
DC	Dal	SA	Wich	KC	Den	SLC	Pho	LA	SD
FW	0.30	2.10	3.10	4.40	6.00	–	–	–	–
SF	5.20	5.40	4.50	6.00	2.70	4.70	3.40	3.30	2.70
LV	–	–	–	–	5.40	3.30	2.40	2.10	2.50

In the current distribution system, demand at the Dallas, San Antonio, Wichita, and Kansas City customer zones is satisfied by shipments from the Ft Worth distribution center. In a similar manner, the Denver, Salt Lake City, and Phoenix customer zones are served by the Santa Fe distribution center, and the Los Angeles and San Diego customer zones are served by the Las Vegas distribution center. The El Paso plant supplies the Ft. Worth and Santa Fe distribution centers, while the Sacramento plant supplies the Las Vegas distribution center.

You have been called in to make recommendations for improving the distribution system, and, in particular, to address the following issues.

(a) If the company does not change its current distribution strategy, what will the distribution system cost be for the following quarter?

(b) Suppose that the company is willing to consider dropping the distribution center limitations. In other words, customer zones would not necessarily be assigned to unique distribution centers, and distribution centers would not necessarily be assigned to unique plants. With this added flexibility, by how much could costs be reduced?

(c) In the foreseeable future, the company anticipates moderate growth of about 20 percent in demand. Suppose this growth is met using the current routes and expanding plant capacity as needed. What plant capacities would be required? What would be the total system cost?

(d) Relative to the cost in part (c), how much could both distribution flexibility and plant capacity save in annual expenses? What plant capacities would be required?

3.7. Oil Distribution   Texxon Oil Distributors, Inc., has three active oil wells in a west Texas oil field. Well 1 has a capacity of 93 thousand barrels per day (TBD), Well 2 can produce 88 TBD, and Well 3 can produce 95 TBD. The company has five refineries along the Gulf Coast, all of which have been operating at stable demand levels. In addition, three pump stations have been built to move the oil along the pipelines from the wells to the refineries. Oil can flow from any one of the wells to any of the pump stations, and from any one of the pump stations to any of the refineries, and Texxon is looking for a minimum cost schedule. The refineries' requirements are as follows.

Refinery	R1	R2	R3	R4	R5
Requirement (TBD)	30	57	48	91	48

The company's cost accounting system recognizes charges by the segment of pipeline that is used. These daily costs are given in the tables below, in dollars per thousand barrels.

To		Pump A	Pump B	Pump C
	Well 1	1.52	1.60	1.40
From	Well 2	1.70	1.63	1.55
	Well 3	1.45	1.57	1.30

To		R1	R2	R3	R4	R5
	Pump A	5.15	5.69	6.13	5.63	5.80
From	Pump B	5.12	5.47	6.05	6.12	5.71
	Pump C	5.32	6.16	6.25	6.17	5.87

(a) What is the minimum cost of providing oil to the refineries? Which wells are used to capacity in the optimal schedule?

(b) Show the network diagram corresponding to the solution in (a). That is, label each of the arcs in the solution and verify that the flows are consistent with the given information.

3.8. College Expenses Revisited   Revisit the college expense planning network example of this chapter. Suppose the rates on the four investments A, B, C, and D have dropped to 5, 11, 18, and 55 percent, respectively. Suppose that the estimated yearly costs of college (in thousands) have been revised to 25, 27, 30, and 33.

(a) What is the minimum investment that will cover these expenses?

(b) Show the network diagram corresponding to the solution in (a). That is, label each of the arcs in the solution and verify that the flows are consistent with the given information.

3.9. Cash Planning   A startup investment project needs money to cover its cash flow needs. The cash income and expenditures for the period January through April are as follows.

	Jan.	Feb.	Mar.	Apr.	Total
Cash flow ($000)	−150	−450	500	250	150

At the beginning of May all excess cash will be paid out to investors. There are two ways to finance the project. One is the possibility of taking out a long-term loan at the beginning of January. The interest on this loan is 1 percent per month, payable on the first of the month for the next three months. This loan can be as large as $400,000; the principal is due April 1; and no prepayment is permitted. The alternative is a short-term loan that can be taken out at the beginning of each month. This loan must be paid back at the beginning of the following month with 1.2 percent interest. A maximum of $300,000 may be used for this short-term loan in any month. In addition, investments may be made in a money-market fund at the start of each month. This fund will pay 0.7 percent interest at the beginning of the following month. Assume the following about the timing of cash flows.

• For months in which there is a net cash deficit, sufficient funds must be on hand at the *start* of the month to cover the net outflow.

• For months in which there is a net cash surplus, the net inflow cannot be used until the *end* of the month (i.e., the start of the next month).

(a) What is the maximum amount that can be returned to investors? What is the optimal amount of money to borrow from each of the potential loan sources?

(b) Show the network diagram corresponding to the solution in (a). That is, label each of the arcs in the solution and verify that the flows are consistent with the given information.

(c) Explain the cost of funds for each month in the planning period. That is, if there were a $1000 change in the cash flows for any month, what would be the dollar change in the amount returned to investors?

3.10. Planning Cash   Each Fall, the treasurer of Trefny's department store does financial planning for the next 6 months, September through February. Because of the holiday season Trefny's needs large amounts of cash during October, November, and

December, whereas a large cash inflow is expected after the first of the year when customers pay off their holiday bills. The following table summarizes the predicted net cash flows (in thousands) from "business as usual" operations.

Month	Sep	Oct	Nov	Dec	Jan	Feb
Surplus	$20	–	–	–	30	150
Deficit	–	30	60	90	–	–

The treasurer has three sources of short-term funds to meet the store's needs, although these represent departures from "business as usual." These are as follows.

- *Accounts Receivable Loans.* A local bank will loan Trefny's funds on a month-by-month basis against a pledge on the accounts receivable balance as of the first day of a particular month. The maximum loan is 75 percent of the balance, and the cost of the loan is 1.5 percent per month, assessed on the amount borrowed. The predicted balances (in thousands) under "business as usual" plans are shown below.

Month	Sep	Oct	Nov	Dec	Jan	Feb
Balance	$70	50	70	110	100	50

- *Delayed Payment of Purchases.* All bills for purchases come due on the first of the month, but payments on all or part of these obligations can be delayed by one month. When payments are delayed this way, Trefny's loses the 2 percent discount it normally receives for prompt payment under "business as usual" operations. (Loss of this 2 percent discount is effectively a financing cost.) The predicted payment schedule (in thousands) without the discount is shown below.

Month	Sep	Oct	Nov	Dec	Jan	Feb
Payment	$80	90	100	60	40	50

- *Short-Term Loan.* A bank is willing to loan Trefny's any amount from $40,000 to $100,000 for 6 months, starting September 1. The principal would be paid back at the end of February, and Trefny's would not be permitted to pay off part of the loan, or add to it, during the 6-month period. The cost of the loan is 1 percent per month, payable at the end of each month.

In any month, excess funds can be transferred to Trefny's short-term investment portfolio, where the funds can earn 0.5 percent per month.

(a) Determine a plan for the treasurer that will meet the firm's cash needs at minimum cost. (Assume that all cash flows occur at the beginning of the month.) What is the cost of this plan? Equivalently, what is the maximum amount of funds on hand after February?

(b) Show the network diagram corresponding to the solution in (a). That is, label each of the arcs in the solution and verify that the flows are consistent with the given information.

3.11. Planning a National Economy   The country of Utopia has a newly appointed Minister of International Trade. She has decided that Utopia's welfare can be served best in the upcoming year by maximizing the net dollar value of Utopia's exports (i.e., the dollar value of the exports minus the cost of the materials imported to produce the exports). The following information is relevant to this decision.

- Utopia produces only three products: steel, machinery, and trucks. For the coming year, the minister feels Utopia can sell all it can produce of these three products on the export market at the existing world market prices of $900 per ton of steel, $2500 per machine, and $3000 per truck.
- To produce one ton of steel, it takes 0.05 machines, 0.08 trucks, 0.5 person-years of labor, and imported materials costing $300. Utopia's steel mills have the capacity to produce up to 300,000 tons per year.
- To produce one machine, it takes 0.75 tons of steel, 0.12 trucks, 5 person-years of labor, and imported materials costing $150. Utopia's machinery plants have the capacity to produce up to 50,000 machines per year.
- To produce one truck, it takes 1 ton of steel, 0.1 machine, 3 person-years of labor, and imported materials costing $500. Utopia's truck plants have the capacity to produce up to 550,000 trucks per year.
- The pool of labor in Utopia is equivalent to 1,200,000 person-years.

The minister plans to issue a self-sufficiency edict, declaring that Utopia cannot import steel, machinery, or trucks. She would like to determine the optimal production quantities and optimal export quantities for steel, machinery, and trucks when that edict is in force.

(a) Find the optimal export plan for Utopia's economy, under self-sufficiency.

(b) Show the network diagram corresponding to the solution in (**a**). That is, label each of the arcs in the solution and verify that the flows are consistent with the given information.

(c) Describe, in simple terms that a nontechnical citizen can understand, the solution's message to Utopia for how to manage its economy.

3.12. Retirement Planning   Your uncle has $90,000 that he wishes to invest now in order to use the accumulation for purchasing a retirement annuity in five years. After consulting with his financial advisor, he has been offered four types of fixed-income investments, labeled as investments A, B, C, and D.

Investments A and B are available at the beginning of each of the next five years (call them years 1–5). Each dollar invested in A at the beginning of a year returns $1.20 (a profit of $0.20) two years later, in time for immediate reinvestment. Each dollar invested in B at the beginning of a year returns $1.36 three years later.

Investments C and D will each be available just once in the future. Each dollar invested in C at the beginning of year 2 returns $1.66 at the end of year 5. Each dollar invested in D at the beginning of year 5 returns $1.12 at the end of year 5.

Your uncle is obligated to make a balloon payment on an existing loan in the amount of $24,000 at the end of year 3. He wants to make that payment out of the investment account.

(a) Devise an investment plan for your uncle that maximizes the value of the investment account at the end of five years. How much money will be available for the annuity in five years?

(b) Show the network diagram corresponding to the solution in (**a**). That is, label each of the arcs in the solution and verify that the flows are consistent with the given information.

3.13. Workforce Planning A software company is anticipating increased demand for its products. However, management is concerned about the adequacy of their programmers to meet the increased demand given the history of workforce turnover (5 percent of the programmers leave the company at the end of each month). Rather than hiring new workers, management is contemplating enrolling some or all of their programmers in a month-long intensive training program. After the successful completion of the training program, a programmer would receive an increase in salary and would also sign a contract not to leave the company for at least 6 months. Trained programmers would therefore be immune from normal turnover.

Management believes that successful completion of the program would increase a programmer's productivity by 20 percent and plans to implement a no-layoff policy to encourage participation. However, only 90 percent of the programmers are predicted to complete the training program successfully. Those who enroll in training but do not complete the program successfully will return to the workforce at their pre-training skill level. (For simplicity, assume that they are not candidates for turnover during their training month and that they can enroll in the training program again later.)

The monthly demand for untrained programmers for the next six months is shown in the table below. If trained programmers are available, their higher productivity allows management to satisfy demand with fewer programmers. For example, the demand in January can be satisfied with 100 untrained programmers, or with 82 untrained and 15 trained programmers (since $82 + 1.20 \times 15 = 100$).

Number of untrained programmers required

Month	Jan	Feb	Mar	Apr	May	Jun
Programmers	100	100	115	125	140	150

A programmer cannot be engaged in production and participate in the training program during the same month. At the beginning of January, there are 145 (untrained) programmers on the workforce. Monthly payroll costs to the company are $3000 per untrained programmer (engaged in either production or the training program) and $3300 per trained programmer.

(a) Determine a training schedule for the months of January through June that meets the workforce requirements at minimum cost. What is the optimal cost? (Allow for fractional decisions.)

(b) Show the network diagram corresponding to the solution in (a). That is, label each of the arcs in the solution and verify that the flows are consistent with the given information.

(c) If the company had one less programmer initially (i.e., a workforce of 144), would the cost be higher or lower, and by how much?

(d) If, at the margin, the company could shift demand from June to April (i.e., so that June demand is lower and April demand is higher by the same amount), would the cost be higher or lower, and by how much?

3.14. Workforce Training A department store experiences significant increase in the number of customers toward the end of each calendar year. To accommodate the customers, the store has to make sure there are enough salespeople available. Starting in

July of each year, the store hires new salespeople who have to be trained by the salespeople already working in the store. The training takes one month, and one salesperson can train up to 20 new trainees every month. (The trainers are exclusively committed to training during the month, and are not part of the active sales force.) Experience has shown that one in every 10 trainees fails to complete the training. The estimated monthly demands for salespeople in the second half of the year are shown in the table below. As of July, 150 salespeople are available for sales or training, and personnel records indicate that 3 percent of workforce leave the store at the end of each month. Each trainee is paid $2000 per month, while each sales person is paid $3000 per month, with a $500 monthly premium when they are assigned to training. The store's policy is not to lay off salespeople in the second half of the year.

Month	Salespeople required
July	120
August	135
September	150
October	150
November	170
December	200

(a) Determine a training schedule for the months of July through December that meets the demand requirements at the least cost. What is the optimal hiring plan? (Allow for fractional decisions.) What is the optimal cost?

(b) Show the network diagram corresponding to the solution in (a). That is, label each of the arcs in the solution and verify that the flows are consistent with the given information.

Case: Casey's Famous Roast Beef

Casey's Famous Roast Beef employs mostly high school and college age workers. However, a few employees have been with the company for long time, and owner Casey Carangelo has calculated that he will need the following cash flows to pay his loyal pensioners over the next 14 years. (This year is considered to be year 0.)

Year	01	02	03	04	05	06	07	08	09	10	11	12	13	14
Cash (000s)	8	10	12	14	15	16	17	18	20	22	23	24	25	26

Mr. Carangelo doesn't believe in modern portfolio theory, with its emphasis on diversification. His brief foray into the market during 2008 ended disastrously. The only investments he trusts are US Government bonds. His accountant has recommended three currently available bonds.

	Current price	Annual coupon	Years to maturity	Face value
Bond 1	$980	$50	5	$1000
Bond 2	$970	$55	11	$1000
Bond 3	$990	$60	14	$1000

All bonds will pay their face value when they mature. Their current price is what it costs to buy the bond at the end of this year. Each bond pays its annual coupon (interest, in effect) every December 31, starting next year. At maturity, each bond repays its face value plus the final coupon payment for that year on December 31.

Cash that is carried over from one year to the next (as well as any cash in the portfolio at the start) will be placed in an interest-bearing savings account that currently earns 3 percent per year. Mr Carangelo believes that this rate will remain stable.

Mr Carangelo wants the pension fund, once started, to be self-sustaining over the next fourteen years. In other words, he plans to make a single withdrawal from corporate sources at the start of next year and invest it such that the income from his bonds, plus savings interest, will cover the pension payments each year.

In effect, the following events will happen each December 31, starting next year.

- Mr Carangelo withdraws all the savings account funds, with interest;

- He receives all bond payments;

- He pays required pension benefits;

- He deposits any remaining funds back into the savings account to earn interest over the following year.

Ideally, there should be no money left at the end of the 14-year period.

Mr Carangelo, who knows very little about investments and nothing about linear programming, has asked you to help him figure out how to set up the pension fund.

Case: Hollingsworth Paper Company

The Hollingsworth Paper Company is an integrated manufacturer of paper products for markets throughout the US. Its Container Division produces corrugated cardboard boxes at four plants and sells through six regional distribution centers (DCs). Last year's sales of nearly 60,000 tons accounted for revenues of almost $30 million. Exhibit 3.1 gives a regional breakdown of sales.

Cardboard containers are designed to meet a variety of customer needs. This variety reflects such features as size, shape, thickness, and type of closure. However, the technology is fairly simple and the competitors have the capability to manufacture the same products. To maintain its 10 percent share of the market, Hollingsworth emphasizes its quick and reliable delivery service. The firm has established its DCs to stock most of its standard items close to the major demand locations, but even specialty orders are processed through the DCs just to simplify paperwork.

Because there are several firms in the industry, and because few proprietary advantages exist, the market for cardboard boxes is quite competitive. The prices offered to the customer

EXHIBIT 3.1 *Last Year's Sales by Geographic Region*

Northeast sales (Boston DC)	2600 T	4%
Northeast sales (Philadelphia DC)	9700 T	16%
Southeast sales (Atlanta DC)	15,500 T	26%
Midwest sales (Chicago DC)	10,100 T	17%
Southwest sales (Houston DC)	13,400 T	23%
Far West sales (San Francisco DC)	7500 T	13%
	58,800 T	100%

are virtually the same no matter where the product is made or what its delivery route. This means that the manufacturer absorbs its own freight costs. With price competition as strong as it is, Hollingsworth's freight costs are a critical part of the profit picture.

Production and Distribution Facilities
At present Hollingsworth has four plants with one-shift capacities in the range of 12,000 to 16,000 tons per year. At two of the four plants, production last year fell below one-shift capacity, while in the other two plants a substantial amount of second shift output was necessary. This pattern reflected the concentration of sales in the Midwest and South. Exhibit 3.2 provides details.

The plant located in Nashua, New Hampshire, is Hollingsworth's oldest facility. Its layout and equipment are somewhat outmoded; consequently, its productivity is relatively low. The Portland, Oregon, plant is the company's newest site, with a workforce roughly one half the size of Nashua's. Labor rates are cheapest at Asheville, North Carolina, and most expensive at St Louis, Missouri. Variations in the process and wage rates, together with different utilizations, result in somewhat different costs at each location. An accounting summary of last year's operations revealed that costs per ton varied from a low of $397.61 at Portland to a high of $448.30 at Nashua. Exhibits 3.3–3.5 provide some additional detail on these cost figures.

Patterns of Distribution
Facing a competitive market with tight margins, Hollingsworth has paid particular attention to its freight costs. For a number of years, its policy has been to supply each DC from the nearest plant, thus minimizing the freight component of cost. Exhibit 3.6 lists last year's freight rates.

EXHIBIT 3.2 *Plant Capacities and Production*

Plant	One-shift capacity	Production	% Utilization of one-shift capacity
Nashua, NH	14,000 T	12,300 T	88%
Asheville, NC	12,000 T	15,500 T	129%
St Louis, MO	16,000 T	23,500 T	147%
Portland, OR	12,000 T	7500 T	63%
Total	54,000 T	58,800 T	109%

EXHIBIT 3.3   *Total Costs (per ton)*

Plant	Variable cost	Allocated fixed cost	Total cost
Nashua	$439.80	$8.50	$448.30
Asheville	406.59	10.32	416.91
St Louis	400.41	8.08	408.49
Portland	379.67	17.95	397.61

EXHIBIT 3.4   *Plant Variable Costs (per ton)*

	Materials	Labor	Supervision	Other overhead	Fringe benefits*	Total
Nashua						
1st Shift	$299.20	$104.00	$19.60	$3.40	$13.60	$439.80
2nd Shift	299.20	110.80	20.80	3.40	14.48	448.68
Asheville						
1st Shift	305.20	76.00	13.00	1.20	9.79	405.19
2nd Shift	305.20	81.00	13.60	1.20	10.41	411.41
St Louis						
1st Shift	301.20	74.60	12.40	0.90	9.57	398.67
2nd Shift	301.20	78.80	13.10	0.90	10.11	404.11
Portland						
1st Shift	299.20	61.40	10.10	1.10	7.87	379.67
2nd Shift	299.20	65.00	10.70	1.10	8.33	384.33

*11% of labor and supervision.

Under this company policy, the Nashua plant supplies the Boston and Philadelphia DCs, Asheville supplies the Atlanta DC, St Louis supplies the Chicago and Houston DCs, and Portland supplies the San Francisco DC. This pattern results in very different profits in the various regions, ranging from around $40 per ton in Chicago to a slight loss in Philadelphia. The DC managers, whose annual bonus partly reflects the profits made in their region, have complained about this system for years. Exhibit 3.7 summarizes last year's records.

Expansion Proposals

Over the years Hollingsworth has made investments to improve its productive capacity in several places. As sales in the Midwest grew, the St Louis plant was expanded. New equipment was installed in Asheville to keep pace with sales growth in the South. Based on these experiences, the engineering staff was eventually able to design the new Portland plant, which reduced the cost of meeting demand in the West. Few improvements, however, have been implemented at Nashua. The two-story layout hampers innovation, and the engineers have expressed some

EXHIBIT 3.5   *Plant Fixed Costs*

	Supervision	Fringe benefits*	Other overhead	Depreciation	Total
Nashua					
1st Shift	$60,000	$6600	$8000	$30,000	$104,600
2nd Shift	30,000	3300	2000	–	35,300
Asheville					
1st Shift	60,000	6600	8000	50,000	124,600
2nd Shift	30,000	3300	2000	–	35,300
St Louis					
1st Shift	60,000	6600	8000	80,000	154,600
2nd Shift	30,000	3300	2000	–	35,300
Portland					
1st Shift	60,000	6600	8000	60,000	134,600
2nd Shift	30,000	3300	2000	–	35,300

*11% of labor and supervision.

EXHIBIT 3.6   *Last Year's Transportation Rates per Ton*

	To					
From	Boston	Philadelphia	Atlanta	Chicago	Houston	San Francisco
Nashua	$16.00	$20.00	$64.00	$56.00	$72.00	$104.00
Asheville	52.00	48.00	20.00	56.00	56.00	88.00
St Louis	56.00	52.00	56.00	20.00	32.00	72.00
Portland	112.00	112.00	104.00	64.00	68.00	36.00
Houston	64.00	60.00	48.00	30.00	0.00	76.00

EXHIBIT 3.7   *Last Year's Profits per Ton*

	Selling price	Cost of goods sold	Warehousing selling &* admin. exp.	Freight absorbed	Net profits before taxes
Boston	$500.00	$448.30	$32.00	$16.00	$3.70
Philadelphia	500.00	448.30	32.00	20.00	(0.30)
Atlanta	500.00	416.91	29.00	20.00	34.09
Chicago	500.00	408.49	31.00	20.00	40.51
Houston	500.00	408.49	30.00	32.00	29.51
San Francisco	500.00	397.61	32.00	36.00	34.39

*Includes a 4% sales commission.

EXHIBIT 3.8   *Anticipated Costs for New Facilities*

	Houston	St Louis
Variable Costs per Ton		
Direct materials	$302.40	$301.20
Direct labor	57.00	60.40
Supervision	9.00	10.00
Other overhead*	1.00	1.00
Fixed Operating Costs Per Year		
Supervision	$60,000	$40,000
Other overhead*	8000	8000

*Includes supplies, heat, light, power, insurance.

concern about whether the old building is strong enough to support some of the heavier pieces of machinery now used elsewhere.

As a continuation of these investment initiatives, the Facilities Planning Committee at Hollingsworth has produced two large-scale expansion plans to help meet predicted sales growth over the next 8–10 years. One proposal involves a large addition to the St. Louis plant, while the second proposal involves construction of a new plant in Houston.

The St Louis proposal calls for an expansion of the existing plant sufficient to raise its annual one-shift capacity to 28,000 tons. The cost for the building for this expansion has been estimated at $1.6 million, and there is adequate land at the St Louis site. The equipment investment is estimated to be $1.5 million. The plant expansion would afford Hollingsworth an opportunity to use the latest machinery available.

The Houston proposal calls for building a new plant with annual one-shift capacity of 12,000 tons. Although Hollingsworth already has a DC located in Houston, there would be a need to purchase land for the new plant. The cost of land is estimated at $500,000. The plant itself would cost about $2 million, while the investment in equipment is estimated at $1.5 million, since the technology would be much the same as in the St Louis expansion. Exhibit 3.8 shows additional estimates for the two proposals.

As mentioned earlier, the Facilities Planning Committee anticipates that some kind of expansion will be needed to meet the needs of the market during the next 8–10 years. Over that period, the costs of labor, materials and freight are likely to increase at slightly different rates, but the company controller has commented that the firm's cost structure is not likely to change drastically.

Chapter 4

Sensitivity Analysis in Linear Programs

As described in Chapter 1, sensitivity analysis involves linking results and conclusions to initial assumptions. In a typical spreadsheet model, we might ask what-if questions regarding the choice of decision variables, looking for effects on the performance measure. Eventually, instead of asking how a particular change in the decision variables would affect the performance measure, we might search for the changes in decision variables that have the *best possible* effect on performance. That is the essence of optimization. In Excel, the Data Table tool allows us to conduct such a search, at least for one or two decision variables at a time. An optimization procedure performs this kind of search in a sophisticated manner and can handle several decision variables at a time. Thus, we can think of optimization as an ambitious form of sensitivity analysis with respect to decision variables.

In this chapter, we consider another kind of sensitivity analysis—with respect to parameters. Here, we ask what-if questions regarding the choice of a specific parameter, looking for the effects on the objective function and the effects on the optimal choice of decision variables. Sensitivity analysis has an elaborate and elegant structure in linear programming problems, and we approach it from three different perspectives. First, to underscore the analogy with sensitivity analyses in simpler spreadsheet models, we explore a Solver-based approach that resembles the Data Table tool. Second, we summarize the traditional form of sensitivity analysis, which is also available in Solver. Third, we introduce an interpretation that relies on discovering qualitative patterns in optimal solutions. This pattern-based interpretation enhances and extends the more mechanical sensitivity analyses that the software carries out, and makes it possible to articulate the broader message in optimization analyses.

For the most part, we examine sensitivity analysis with respect to two kinds of parameters in particular—objective function coefficients and constraint constants. The general thrust of sensitivity analysis is to examine how the optimal solution would change if we were to vary one or more of these parameters. However, the flip side of this analysis is to examine when the optimal solution would not change. In other words, an implicit theme in sensitivity analysis, especially for linear

Optimization Modeling with Spreadsheets, *Second Edition*. Kenneth R. Baker
© 2011 John Wiley & Sons, Inc. Published 2011 by John Wiley & Sons, Inc.

programming models, is to discover robust aspects of the optimal solution—features of the solution that do not change at all when one of the parameters changes. As we will see, this theme becomes visible as a kind of "insensitivity analysis" in our three approaches.

Sensitivity analysis is important from a practical perspective. Because we seldom know all of the parameters in a model with perfect accuracy, it makes sense to study how results would differ if there were some differences in the original parameter values. If we find that our results are robust—that is, a change in a parameter causes little or no change in our decisions—then we tend to proceed with some confidence in those decisions. On the other hand, if we find that our results are sensitive to the accuracy of our numerical assumptions, then we might want to go back and try to obtain more accurate information, or we might want to develop alternative plans in case some of our assumptions are not borne out. Thus, tracing the relation between our assumptions and our eventual course of action is an important step in "solving" the problem we face, and sensitivity analyses can often provide us with the critical information we need.

4.1. PARAMETER ANALYSIS IN THE TRANSPORTATION EXAMPLE

In a simple spreadsheet model, we might change a parameter and record the effect on the objective function. In Excel, the Data Table tool automates this kind of analysis for one or two parameters at a time. Risk Solver Platform (RSP) provides a similar tool that allows us to change a parameter, re-run Solver automatically, and record the impact of the parameter's change on the optimal value of the objective function and on the optimal decisions. The output of the tool is the *Parameter Analysis Report*.

As an illustration, we revisit the transportation problem introduced in Chapter 3. In Example 3.1 (Goodwin Manufacturing Company), the model allowed us to find the cost-minimizing distribution schedule in a setting with three plants shipping to four warehouses. We encountered the optimal solution in Figure 3.2, which is reproduced in Figure 4.1. The tight supply constraints are the Minneapolis and Pittsburgh capacities and the optimal total cost in the base case is $13,830.

Suppose that we are using the transportation model as a planning tool and we want to explore a change in the unit cost of shipping from Pittsburgh to Atlanta, which is $0.36 in the base case. We might be negotiating with a trucking company over the charge for shipping, so we want to study a range of alternative values for the *PA* cost. Suppose that, as a first step, we are willing to examine a large range of values, from $0.25 to $0.75. For this purpose we create a cell and enter the formula =PsiOptParam(0.25,0.75). In Figure 4.1, we have reserved column I for sensitivity parameters, and we enter the formula in cell I6. Then, in C6 we reference cell I6. The PsiOptParam function displays the minimum value of its range, so the value $0.25 appears in both cell I6 and cell C6. (To restore the model, we would simply enter the original unit cost of $0.36 in cell C6.)

▲	A	B	C	D	E	F	G	H	I	
1	**Network: Transportation Problem**									
2										
3	Parameters								*Sensitivity*	
4			Atl	Bos	Chi	Den	*Capacity*			
5		Minn	0.60	0.56	0.22	0.40	10,000			
6		Pitt	0.36	0.30	0.28	0.58	15,000		0.25	
7		Tucs	0.65	0.68	0.55	0.42	15,000			
8		*Requirement*	8,000	10,000	12,000	9,000				
9										
10	Decisions									
11			Atl	Bos	Chi	Den	*Sent*			
12		Minn	-	-	10,000	-	10,000			
13		Pitt	5,000	10,000	-	-	15,000			
14		Tucs	3,000	-	2,000	9,000	14,000			
15		*Received*	8,000	10,000	12,000	9,000	39,000			
16										
17	Objective									
18		Total Cost	13,830							
19										

| ◀ ◀ ▶ ▶| Transport | ◀ |

Figure 4.1. Solution for Example 3.1.

Next, we go to the drop-down menu on the Reports icon in the RSP ribbon and select Optimization ▶ Parameter Analysis. The Multiple Optimizations Report, shown in Figure 4.2, appears on the screen. In the Multiple Optimizations Report window, we select the results to track in the upper part of the report and the parameter(s) to vary in the lower part. In particular, we fill out the form by choosing C18 as the objective function cell and C13:F13 as the variables to track. (These four cells represent the optimal shipments from the Pittsburgh plant.) Those selections appear in the upper right-hand window, as shown in Figure 4.3. As a general rule, we prefer to have the objective function listed first, as shown in the figure. In the bottom pair of windows, we select cell I6 as the parameter, so that the form looks like the version shown in Figure 4.3.

Next, we have to specify the number of values between the parameter's lower limit of $0.25 and the upper limit of $0.75. If we specify 11 Major Axis Points, as in Figure 4.3, the step size will be $0.05. (That is, starting at 0.25 and taking steps of 0.05, the eleventh step will be 0.75.) Finally, we click OK on the form. The program inserts a new worksheet in our workbook, labeled Analysis Report, and records the results. Figure 4.4 displays the Parameter Analysis Report, slightly edited for better readability.

The report shows how the optimal total cost changes and how the optimal Pittsburgh shipments change as the unit cost of the *PA* route increases. The first column of the table gives the values of the unit cost under study, from $0.25 to $0.75. The second column gives the corresponding optimal total cost. The four columns C–F, which were selected in Figure 4.3, show the various shipments from

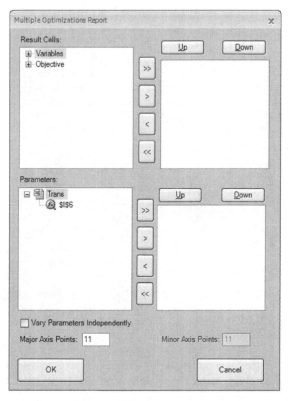

Figure 4.2. Initial Multiple Optimizations Report.

the Pittsburgh plant. Thus, for the range of unit costs ($0.25–$0.75), four distinct profiles appear. For values of $0.30 and $0.35, the base case solution prevails (5000 units to Atlanta and 10,000 units to Boston), but above and below those values the optimal shipping schedule changes.

- At a unit cost of $0.25, the *PA* shipment is 8000 units, and 7000 units are shipped on the *PB* route.
- At unit costs of $0.30 and $0.35, the *PA* shipment is 5000 units, while 10,000 units are shipped on the *PB* route. In effect, there is a shift away from the *PA* route as its cost rises.
- At unit costs of $0.40–$0.65, the *PA* shipment is 3000 units, while 2000 units are shipped on *PC*, as well as 10,000 units on *PB*. Thus, there is a shift away from the *PA* route toward an entirely new route.
- At unit costs of $0.70 and above, the *PA* route is not used at all.

From this information, we can conclude that the optimal shipping schedule is insensitive to changes in the *PA* unit cost, at least between $0.30 and $0.36. Below that interval, the unit cost could become sufficiently attractive that we would want

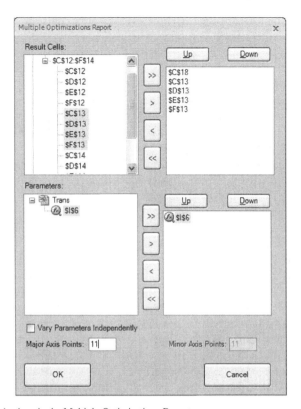

Figure 4.3. Selections in the Multiple Optimizations Report.

	A	B	C	D	E	F
1	Cost	Total	PA	PB	PC	PD
2	$0.25	13,220	8,000	7,000	0	0
3	$0.30	13,530	5,000	10,000	0	0
4	$0.35	13,780	5,000	10,000	0	0
5	$0.40	13,990	3,000	10,000	2,000	0
6	$0.45	14,140	3,000	10,000	2,000	0
7	$0.50	14,290	3,000	10,000	2,000	0
8	$0.55	14,440	3,000	10,000	2,000	0
9	$0.60	14,590	3,000	10,000	2,000	0
10	$0.65	14,740	3,000	10,000	2,000	0
11	$0.70	14,760	0	10,000	4,000	0
12	$0.75	14,760	0	10,000	4,000	0
13						

Analysis Report

Figure 4.4. Parameter Analysis Report for *PA* unit cost.

to shift some shipments to the *PA* route from *PB*. Above that interval, however, the unit cost would become less attractive, and we would eventually want to shift some shipments to the *PC* route. Subsequently, when the profit contribution reaches approximately $0.70, we would prefer not to use the *PA* route at all. Thus, as we face the prospect of negotiating a unit cost for the *PA* route, we can anticipate the impact on Pittsburgh shipments, and on the optimal total cost, from the information in the table.

Because we chose a grid of size $0.05, we don't know the precise cost interval over which the optimal shipping schedule remains unchanged. Since the original unit cost was $0.36, we know that the cost will have to drop to below $0.30 in order to induce a change in the size of the *PA* shipment. We also know that a cost of $0.25 will be sufficient inducement to make a change. The precise cost at which the change occurs must be somewhere between these two values. We can re-run the Parameter Analysis Report with a grid of $0.01 to get a better idea of exactly where the change occurs. One way to do so is to specify new lower and upper limits (such as 0.25 and 0.40) in the PsiOptParam function and change the number of Major Axis Points to 16. Figure 4.5 shows the resulting Parameter Analysis Report.

The refined grid shows that the optimal shipments do not change until the unit cost drops below $0.27 or rises above $0.37. If we wanted to see an even finer grid, we could produce another report with an even smaller step size. However, we can find the precise range of "insensitivity" more directly by other means, as we shall see later.

Two important qualitative patterns are visible in Figure 4.4. First, when an objective function coefficient becomes more attractive, the amount of the corresponding variable in the optimal solution will either increase or stay the same; it cannot drop. (However, the increase need not be gradual: The *PA* shipment jumps from 0 to

	A	B	C	D	E	F	
	Cost	**Total**	**PA**	**PB**	**PC**	**PD**	
1	Cost	Total	PA	PB	PC	PD	
2	$0.25	13,220	8,000	7,000	0	0	
3	$0.26	13,300	8,000	7,000	0	0	
4	$0.27	13,380	5,000	10,000	0	0	
5	$0.28	13,430	5,000	10,000	0	0	
6	$0.29	13,480	5,000	10,000	0	0	
7	$0.30	13,530	5,000	10,000	0	0	
8	$0.31	13,580	5,000	10,000	0	0	
9	$0.32	13,630	5,000	10,000	0	0	
10	$0.33	13,680	5,000	10,000	0	0	
11	$0.34	13,730	5,000	10,000	0	0	
12	$0.35	13,780	5,000	10,000	0	0	
13	$0.36	13,830	5,000	10,000	0	0	
14	$0.37	13,880	5,000	10,000	0	0	
15	$0.38	13,930	3,000	10,000	2,000	0	
16	$0.39	13,960	3,000	10,000	2,000	0	
17	$0.40	13,990	3,000	10,000	2,000	0	
18							

Analysis Report 1

Figure 4.5. Parameter Analysis Report on a refined grid.

3000 to 5000 and to 8000 as we read up the table.) Second, when an objective function coefficient becomes more attractive, the optimal value of the objective function either stays the same or improves. In this example, the total cost remains unchanged when the unit cost of the *PA* route is $0.70 or more; but for $0.65 and below, the total cost decreases as the *PA* cost decreases.

In linear programs, a distinct pattern usually appears in sensitivity tables when we vary a coefficient in the objective function. The optimal values of the decision variables remain constant over some interval of increase or decrease. Beyond this interval, a slightly different set of decision variables becomes positive, and some of the decision variables change abruptly, not gradually. Figure 4.5 illustrates these features even in the limited portion of the optimal schedule that it tracks.

Solver also offers a Parameter Analysis Report for changes in a RHS constant. Suppose that, starting from the base case, we wish to explore a change in the Pittsburgh capacity. (The original figure was 15,000, and at that level, the capacity represents a scarce resource.) To prepare for this analysis, we first have to determine the range of values to study, such as 14,000–24,000. Then we devote a cell in the sensitivity area of the spreadsheet, such as I7, to this parameter. In this cell, we enter the formula =PsiOptParam(14000,24000), and we reference this cell in G13. (To make sure that the analysis varies only this capacity, we set cell C6 back to its original value of $0.36.)

Next, we return to the Reports drop-down menu and ask for an Optimization Parameter Analysis. Using 11 Major Axis Points, we can examine the effect of increasing Pittsburgh capacity from 14,000 to 24,000 in steps of 1000. The report, slightly edited, appears in Figure 4.6. The editing consists of making the titles and format more helpful, but we have manually added column C. The entries in each row of this column represent the incremental change in the optimal objective divided by the change in the RHS constant, from the row above. The formula in cell C3 is =(B2-B3)/(A2-A3), and it has been copied down the column.

	A	B	C	D	E	F	G
1	Capacity	Total	Change	PA	PB	PC	PD
2	14,000	14,120		4,000	10,000	0	0
3	15,000	13,830	-0.29	5,000	10,000	0	0
4	16,000	13,540	-0.29	6,000	10,000	0	0
5	17,000	13,250	-0.29	7,000	10,000	0	0
6	18,000	12,960	-0.29	8,000	10,000	0	0
7	19,000	12,690	-0.27	8,000	10,000	1,000	0
8	20,000	12,420	-0.27	8,000	10,000	2,000	0
9	21,000	12,420	0.00	8,000	10,000	2,000	0
10	22,000	12,420	0.00	8,000	10,000	2,000	0
11	23,000	12,420	0.00	8,000	10,000	2,000	0
12	24,000	12,420	0.00	8,000	10,000	2,000	0
13							

Analysis Report

Figure 4.6. Parameter Analysis Report for Pittsburgh capacity.

The table shows how Pittsburgh shipments and the optimal total cost change as Pittsburgh's capacity varies. The columns correspond to the same outputs that were selected for the previous table, except that the parameter we've varied (Pittsburgh capacity) appears in the first column. The rows correspond to the designated series of input values for this parameter. (For Pittsburgh capacities below 14,000, the optimization problem would be infeasible. At those levels, capacity in the system would be insufficient to meet demand for 39,000 units.) In the table, the following changes appear in the optimal schedule.

- As Pittsburgh's capacity increases above 14,000, total costs drop, and more shipments occur on the *PA* route.
- When Pittsburgh's capacity reaches 18,000, shipments along *PA* level off at 8000. Beyond that capacity level, the solution uses the *PC* route.
- The optimal total cost drops as Pittsburgh's capacity increases to 20,000. Beyond that level, the optimal schedule stabilizes, and total cost remains at $12,420.

Thus, if we can find a way to increase the capacity at Pittsburgh, we should be interested in an increase up to a level of 20,000 from the base-case level of 15,000. By also investigating the cost of increasing capacity, we can quantify the net benefits of expansion. If there are incremental costs associated with expansion to capacities beyond 20,000, such costs are not worth incurring because there is no benefit (i.e., no reduction in total cost) when capacity exceeds that level. With this kind of information, we can determine whether a proposed initiative to expand capacity would make economic sense.

Suppose, for example, that the Pittsburgh warehouse contained some excess space that we could begin to use for just the cost of utilities. Furthermore, suppose this space corresponded to additional capacity of 3000 units and cost $800 to operate. Would it be economically advantageous to use the space? From the Parameter Analysis Report we learn that by adding 3000 units of capacity, and operating with a capacity of 18,000 at Pittsburgh, distribution costs would drop to $12,960, a saving of $870 from the base case. This more than offsets the incremental cost of utilities, making the use of the space economically attractive.

The *marginal value* of additional capacity is defined as the change in the objective function due to a unit increase in the capacity available (in this instance, an increase of one in the value of Pittsburgh's capacity). Starting with the base case, we can calculate this marginal value by changing the capacity from 15,000 to 15,001, re-solving the problem and noting the change in the objective function: Total cost drops to $13,829.71, a decrease of $0.29.

To pursue this last point, we examine the column labeled Change in Figure 4.6. Entries in this column equal the marginal value of Pittsburgh's capacity. For example, the first entry, in cell C3, corresponds to the ratio of the cost change (14,120–13,830) to the capacity change (15,000–14,000), or –0.29. As the table shows, the marginal value starts out at $0.29, drops to $0.27, and eventually levels off at zero. Because the table is built with increments of 1000, we get at least a coarse picture of how the marginal value behaves. To refine this picture, we would have to create a Parameter Analysis Report with increments smaller than 1000.

As Pittsburgh's capacity increases, the marginal value stays level for a while, then drops, stays level at the new value for a while, then drops again. This pattern is an instance of the economic principle known as *diminishing marginal returns*: If someone were to offer us more and more of a scarce resource, its value would eventually decline. In this case, the scarce resource (binding constraint) is Pittsburgh's capacity. Limited capacity at Pittsburgh prevents us from achieving an even lower total cost; that is what makes Pittsburgh's capacity economically scarce.

Starting from the base case—15,000 hours—we should be willing to pay up to $0.29 for each additional unit of capacity at the Pittsburgh plant. This value is also called the *shadow price*. In economic terms, the shadow price is the break-even price at which it would be attractive to acquire more of a scarce resource. In other words, imagine that someone were to offer us additional capacity at Pittsburgh (e.g., if we could lease some automated equipment). We can improve total cost at the margin by acquiring the additional capacity, as long as its price is less than $0.29 per unit. In our example of opening up additional space in the warehouse, the cost of the addition was only $800/3000 = $0.26. This figure is less than the shadow price, indicating that it would be economically attractive to use the space.

Figure 4.6 shows that the marginal value of a scarce resource remains constant in some neighborhood around the base-case value. In this example, the $0.29 shadow price holds for additional capacity up to 18,000 units; then it drops to $0.27. Beyond a capacity of 20,000 units, the shadow price remains at zero. In effect, additional capacity beyond 20,000 units has no incremental value.

A distinct pattern appears in sensitivity tables when we vary the amount of a scarce capacity. The marginal value of capacity remains constant over some interval of increase or decrease. Within this interval, some of the decision variables change linearly with the change in capacity, while other decision variables may stay the same. There is no interval, however, in which all the decision variables remain the same, as is the case when we vary an objective function coefficient. Thus, it is the shadow price—not the set of decision variables—that is insensitive to changes in the amount of a scarce capacity in some interval around the base case. Beyond that range, the story is different. If someone were to continually give us more of a scarce resource, its value would drop and eventually fall to zero. In the case of our transportation example, we can see in Figure 4.6 that the value of additional capacity at Pittsburgh drops to zero at a capacity level of about 21,000.

4.2. PARAMETER ANALYSIS IN THE ALLOCATION EXAMPLE

As a further illustration of the Parameter Analysis Report, let's revisit Example 2.1 of Chapter 2 (Brown Furniture Company) and the model that finds the profit-maximizing product mix among chairs, desks, and tables. We encountered the optimal solution in Figure 2.6, which is reproduced in Figure 4.7. The optimal product mix is made up of

	A	B	C	D	E	F	G	H
1	Allocation: Product Mix							
2								
3	Decision Variables							
4			C	D	T			
5	Production plan	0	160	120				
6								
7	Objective Function				Total			
8	Profit	15	20	14	4880			15
9								
10								
11	Constraints				LHS		RHS	
12	Fabrication	4	6	2	1200	<=	2000	
13	Assembly	3	8	6	2000	<=	2000	
14	Machining	9	6	4	1440	<=	1440	
15	Wood	30	40	25	9400	<=	9600	
16								

Allocation

Figure 4.7. Optimal solution to Example 2.1.

desks and tables, with no chairs; and the tight constraints are assembly and machining hours. The optimal total profit contribution in the base case is $4880.

Suppose that we are using the allocation model as a planning tool and that we wish to explore a change in the price of chairs. This price may still be subject to revision, pending more information about the market, and we want to study the impact of a price change, which translates into a change in the profit contribution of chairs. For the time being, we'll assume that if we vary the price, there will be no effect on the demand potential for chairs. To explore the effect of a price change, we follow the steps introduced in the previous section.

First, we designate a cell for the sensitivity information, in this case cell H8. We enter the formula =PsiOptParam(15,35), anticipating that we'll want to investigate the range of profit contributions from $15 to $35 per unit. We also enter a reference to H8 in cell B8. Next, we go to the drop-down menu for Reports on the RSP tab and select Optimization ▶ Parameter Analysis. In the top portion of the Multiple Optimizations Report window, we select the objective function and variables in the model, placing the objective function cell (E8) at the top of the list. Next, we select H8 as the parameter cell, being careful to select it from the Allocation worksheet if other worksheets appear on the list (because of the fact that they also contain the PsiOptParam function). Then, by selecting 21 Major Axis Points, as shown in Figure 4.8, we can examine the effects on a grid with $1 increments. The report, with some reformatting, is tabulated in Figure 4.9.

The first column of the table gives the values of the parameter (profit contribution for chairs) that we varied. The second column lists the optimal value of the objective function in each case and the third column calculates the rate of change in the objective function per unit change in the parameter. These three columns are, again, the standard part of the report. The last three columns in Figure 4.9 give the optimal values of the three decision variables corresponding to each choice of the input parameter.

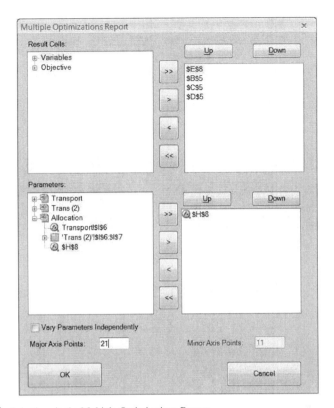

Figure 4.8. Selections in the Multiple Optimizations Report.

The Parameter Analysis Report shows how the optimal profit and the optimal product mix both change as the profit contribution for chairs increases. For the selected range of profit contributions ($15-$35), we see three distinct profiles. For values up to $21, the base case solution prevails, but above $21, the optimal mix changes.

- Chairs stay at zero until the unit profit on chairs rises to $21; then chairs enter the optimal mix at a quantity of about 15.

- When the unit profit reaches $32, the number of chairs in the optimal mix increases to 160. At this stage, and beyond, the optimal product mix is made up entirely of chairs.

- Desks are not affected until the unit profit on chairs rises to $21; then the optimal number of desks drops from 160 to 0.

- Tables stay level at 120 until the unit profit on chairs rises to $21; then the optimal number of tables increases to about 326. When the unit profit on chairs rises to $32, the optimal number of tables drops to 0.

- The optimal total profit remains unchanged until the unit profit on chairs rises to $21; then it increases at a rate that reflects the number of chairs in the product mix.

	A	B	C	D	E
1	$H$8	Profit	Chairs	Desks	Tables
2	15	4880	0	160	120
3	16	4880	0	160	120
4	17	4880	0	160	120
5	18	4880	0	160	120
6	19	4880	0	160	120
7	20	4880	0	160	120
8	21	4880	15.24	0	325.71
9	22	4895	15.24	0	325.71
10	23	4910	15.24	0	325.71
11	24	4926	15.24	0	325.71
12	25	4941	15.24	0	325.71
13	26	4956	15.24	0	325.71
14	27	4971	15.24	0	325.71
15	28	4987	15.24	0	325.71
16	29	5002	15.24	0	325.71
17	30	5017	15.24	0	325.71
18	31	5032	15.24	0	325.71
19	32	5120	160	0	0
20	33	5280	160	0	0
21	34	5440	160	0	0
22	35	5600	160	0	0
23					

Analysis Report

Figure 4.9. Parameter Analysis Report for chair profit contribution.

From this information, we can conclude that the optimal solution is insensitive to changes in the unit profit contribution of chairs, up to about $21. (Because we are operating with a grid of $1, we do not have visibility into what might happen at intermediate values.) Beyond that point, however, the profit on chairs would become sufficiently attractive that we would want to include chairs in the mix. In effect, chairs (and additional tables) substitute for desks when the profit contribution of chairs reaches $21. Subsequently, when the profit contribution reaches $32, additional chairs also substitute for tables. Thus, if we decide to alter the price for chairs, we can anticipate the impact on the optimal product mix from the information in the Parameter Analysis Report.

Again, the table illustrates some general qualitative patterns. First, when we improve the objective function coefficient of one variable, the amount of that variable in the optimal solution will either increase or stay the same; it cannot drop. (The effect on other variables, however, may not follow an obvious direction: The optimal number of tables first increases and then later decreases as the price of chairs rises.) Second, the optimal value of the objective function either stays the same or improves.

Now let's restore the model (by changing B8 back to 16) and consider one of the RHS constants for sensitivity analysis instead of an objective function coefficient. Starting from the base case, suppose we wish to vary the number of machining hours available from 1200 to 2000 in steps of size 50, or equivalently 17 steps. We select cell H9 for sensitivity parameters and enter =PsiOptParam(1200,2000). Then we reference H9 in cell G14, which holds the number of machining hours, and complete the Multiple Optimizations Report, requesting 17 Major Axis Points.

The Parameter Analysis Report (see Figure 4.10) shows how the optimal profit and the optimal decisions both change as the number of machining hours increase. The columns correspond to the same outputs as in the previous table, except for the first column, where the rows correspond to the designated input values for machining capacity. The table reveals the following changes in the optimal product mix.

- Chairs remain out of the product mix until the number of machining hours rises to about 1500. After that, chairs increase with the number of machining hours. At around 1850 machining hours, the number of chairs levels off at about 72.4.

- Desks increase as the number of machining hours rises to about 1450; then desks decrease. At 1850 machining hours, desks drop out of the optimal mix.

- Tables make up the entire product mix until the number of machining hours rises to about 1350. Then the optimal number of tables first decreases, then increases, and eventually levels off at about 297.

- The optimal total profit grows as the number of machining hours rises, eventually leveling off at $5318.

Therefore, as we increase machining capacity above the base-case value of 1440, we have an incentive to alter the product mix. First, the product mix changes by swapping desks for tables (but not necessarily at a ratio of 1 : 1), then by swapping chairs and tables for desks, until the entire product mix becomes devoted to chairs and tables. The qualitative details of the product mix changes are not as important as the fact that the optimal profit contribution increases with the number of machining hours, until leveling off at a capacity of about 1850 hours.

	A $H$9	B Profit	C Change	D Chairs	E Desks	F Tables
1	$H$9	Profit	Change	Chairs	Desks	Tables
2	1200	4200		0	0	300.00
3	1250	4375	3.50	0	0	312.50
4	1300	4550	3.50	0	0	325.00
5	1350	4700	3.00	0	25.0	300.00
6	1400	4800	2.00	0	100.0	200.00
7	1450	4900	2.00	0	175.0	100.00
8	1500	4962	1.24	7.62	170.0	102.86
9	1550	5014	1.05	17.14	145.0	131.43
10	1600	5067	1.05	26.67	120.0	160.00
11	1650	5119	1.05	36.19	95.0	188.57
12	1700	5171	1.05	45.71	70.0	217.14
13	1750	5224	1.05	55.24	45.0	245.71
14	1800	5276	1.05	64.76	20.0	274.29
15	1850	5318	0.84	72.38	0	297.14
16	1900	5318	0	72.38	0	297.14
17	1950	5318	0	72.38	0	297.14
18	2000	5318	0	72.38	0	297.14
19						

Analysis Report 1

Figure 4.10. Parameter Analysis Report for machining hours.

We say "about" 1850 hours because we used a coarse grid in the table, and we cannot observe precisely what machining capacity drives desks completely out of the product mix. If we wanted a more precise value, we would repeat the analysis using a step size less than 50.

The marginal value of additional machining hours is defined as the improvement in the objective function from a unit increase in the number of hours available (i.e., an increase of one in the right-hand side of the machining hours constraint). Starting with the base case, we can calculate this marginal value, or shadow price, by changing the number of machining hours to 1441, re-solving the problem, and tracking the improvement in the objective function. (It grows to $4882, an improvement of $2.)

In Figure 4.10, column C tracks the shadow price over a broader interval, based again on a formula added manually to the table as it was originally generated. Entries in this column represent the change in the optimal objective function value, from the row above, divided by the change in the input parameter. This ratio describes the marginal value of machining hours. As the table shows, the marginal value starts out at $3.50 for a capacity of 1250 machining hours, drops as the number of machining hours increases, and eventually levels off at zero. Actually, the shadow price appears to level off at $2.00 and at $1.05 before it eventually drops to zero. However, because the table is built on increments of 50 hours, we can get only a coarse picture of how this marginal value behaves.

To get a better picture of the marginal value, we can repeat the analysis, using a step size of 25. The Parameter Analysis Report is shown in Figure 4.11. The marginal values are still approximate; however, a clearer picture of the marginal value emerges. As before, the marginal value lies at $3.50 at around 1200 hours; it falls to $2.00 around 1350 hours, to $1.05 around 1475 hours, and finally to zero around 1850 hours. An even smaller step size would be necessary to be more precise about the levels at which the marginal value changes.

In linear programs, a distinct pattern in sensitivity analyses typically arises when we vary the availability of a scarce resource. To repeat, the marginal value of the scarce resource stays constant over some interval of increase or decrease. Within this interval, some of the decision variables change linearly with the change in resource availability, while other decision variables may stay the same. As we acquire more of a scarce resource, its value eventually drops, exhibiting diminishing marginal returns and ultimately falling to zero. In the case of our allocation problem, the value of additional machining hours drops to zero at a capacity level around 1850.

For another perspective on this phenomenon, we can construct a graph of optimal profit as a function of machining capacity. Figure 4.12 shows such a graph, with a distinctive piecewise linear shape. Machining capacity appears on the horizontal axis, and optimal profit appears on the vertical axis. The slope of the line in this graph corresponds to the shadow price for machining capacity. As the graph indicates, the shadow price drops in a piecewise fashion as the capacity increases, eventually stabilizing at zero for capacity levels above 1850. As machining capacity increases beyond this level, the optimal profit levels off at $5318, limited by other constraints in the model.

	A	B	C	D	E	F
1	$H$9	Profit	Change	Chairs	Desks	Tables
2	1200	4200		0	0	300.00
3	1225	4288	3.50	0	0	306.25
4	1250	4375	3.50	0	0	312.50
5	1275	4463	3.50	0	0	318.75
6	1300	4550	3.50	0	0	325.00
7	1325	4638	3.50	0	0	331.25
8	1350	4700	2.50	0	25.00	300.00
9	1375	4750	2.00	0	62.50	250.00
10	1400	4800	2.00	0	100.00	200.00
11	1425	4850	2.00	0	137.50	150.00
12	1450	4900	2.00	0	175.00	100.00
13	1475	4936	1.43	2.86	182.50	88.57
14	1500	4962	1.05	7.62	170.00	102.86
15	1525	4988	1.05	12.38	157.50	117.14
16	1550	5014	1.05	17.14	145.00	131.43
17	1575	5040	1.05	21.90	132.50	145.71
18	1600	5067	1.05	26.67	120.00	160.00
19	1625	5093	1.05	31.43	107.50	174.29
20	1650	5119	1.05	36.19	95.00	188.57
21	1675	5145	1.05	40.95	82.50	202.86
22	1700	5171	1.05	45.71	70.00	217.14
23	1725	5198	1.05	50.48	57.50	231.43
24	1750	5224	1.05	55.24	45.00	245.71
25	1775	5250	1.05	60.00	32.50	260.00
26	1800	5276	1.05	64.76	20.00	274.29
27	1825	5302	1.05	69.52	7.50	288.57
28	1850	5318	0.63	72.38	0	297.14
29	1875	5318	0.00	72.38	0	297.14
30	1900	5318	0.00	72.38	0	297.14
31	1925	5318	0.00	72.38	0	297.14
32	1950	5318	0.00	72.38	0	297.14
33	1975	5318	0.00	72.38	0	297.14
34	2000	5318	0.00	72.38	0	297.14
35						

Analysis Report 2

Figure 4.11. Parameter Analysis Report on a refined grid.

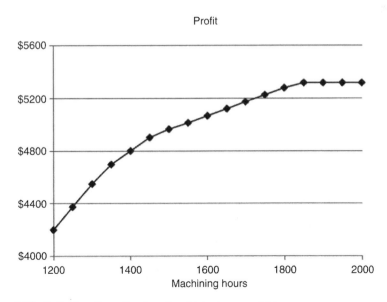

Figure 4.12. Optimal profit as a function of machining hours available.

The Parameter Analysis Report has an option for generating two-way tables in addition to the one-way tables we have examined thus far. For the two-way table, we select two parameters and vary them from minimum to maximum, in a specified step size. In other words, we enter the PsiOptParam function in two places and refer to those functions in two cells of the model. (The ranges and step sizes need not be identical.) The report generated by such a run displays only the values of the optimal objective function.

As an illustration, suppose we want to test the sensitivity of the optimal profit contribution in the allocation example to changes in both the profit contribution of chairs and the profit contribution of desks. Specifically, we vary the unit contribution of chairs from 10 to 60 in steps of 10 and the unit contribution of desks from 15 to 30 in steps of 5. When we ask for a two-way table in the Multiple Optimizations Report window, we check the box for Vary Parameters Independently and then set the Major Axis Points to 6 and Minor Axis Points to 4 (for this illustration), as shown in Figure 4.13. The Parameter Analysis Report is shown in Figure 4.14.

Although two-way tables are available, most sensitivity analyses are carried out for one variable at a time. With a one-at-a-time approach, we can focus on the

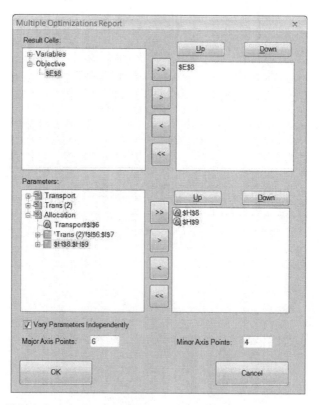

Figure 4.13. Multiple Optimizations Report for a two-way analysis.

	A	B	C	D	E
1	$E$8 : $H$8 by $H$9				
2					
3					
4	$H$8	$H$9			
5		15	20	25	30
6	10	52.5	70.0	104.2	150.0
7	20	52.5	70.0	104.2	150.0
8	30	52.5	70.0	104.2	150.0
9	40	66.7	88.9	111.1	150.0
10	50	83.3	111.1	138.9	166.7
11	60	100.0	133.3	166.7	200.0
12					

Figure 4.14. Parametric Analysis Report for a two-way analysis.

implications of a change in a model parameter for the objective function, decision variables, tightness of constraints, and marginal values. Much of the insight we can gain from formal analysis derives from these kinds of investigations. The two-at-a-time capability is computationally similar, but it does not usually provide as much insight.

4.3. THE SENSITIVITY REPORT AND THE TRANSPORTATION EXAMPLE

As we've seen, the Parameter Analysis Report duplicates for optimization models the main functionality of the Data Table tool for basic spreadsheet models. The report is constructed by repeating the optimization run with different parametric values in the model each time. This transparent logic makes the Parameter Analysis Report a convenient and accessible choice for most of the sensitivity analyses we might want to perform with optimization models. However, Solver provides us with an alternative perspective.

The *Sensitivity Report* is available after an optimization run, once the optimal solution has been found. From the drop-down menu on the Reports icon in the RSP ribbon, we select Optimization ▶ Sensitivity. The Sensitivity Report then appears on a new worksheet, immediately before the model worksheet. The Sensitivity Report has three sections—one each for the objective function, decision variables, and constraints. Figure 4.15 shows the Sensitivity Report for the transportation model in Figure 4.1, after reformatting of some cells.

In the top section, the report records the optimal value of the objective function, as it appears in cell C18. The report also guesses a suitable name for this quantity.[1] In the

---

[1]By default, Solver constructs a name for each cell in this report by looking above it and to its left for text entries in the original spreadsheet.

	A	B	C	D	E	F	G	H	
1	Microsoft Excel 12.0 Sensitivity Report								
2									
3	Objective Cell (Min)								
4		Cell	Name	Final Value					
5		$C$18	Total Cost Atl	13830.00002					
6									
7	Decision Variable Cells								
8				Final	Reduced	Objective	Allowable	Allowable	
9		Cell	Name	Value	Cost	Coefficient	Increase	Decrease	
10		$C$12	Minn Atl	0	0.28	0.60	1E+30	0.28	
11		$D$12	Minn Bos	0	0.30	0.56	1E+30	0.30	
12		$E$12	Minn Chi	10000	0.00	0.22	0.28	1E+30	
13		$F$12	Minn Den	0	0.31	0.40	1E+30	0.31	
14		$C$13	Pitt Atl	5000	0.00	0.36	0.02	0.09	
15		$D$13	Pitt Bos	10000	0.00	0.30	0.09	0.59	
16		$E$13	Pitt Chi	0	0.02	0.28	1E+30	0.02	
17		$F$13	Pitt Den	0	0.45	0.58	1E+30	0.45	
18		$C$14	Tucs Atl	3000	0.00	0.65	0.09	0.02	
19		$D$14	Tucs Bos	0	0.09	0.68	1E+30	0.09	
20		$E$14	Tucs Chi	2000	0.00	0.55	0.02	0.28	
21		$F$14	Tucs Den	9000	0.00	0.42	0.31	0.42	
22									
23	Constraints								
24				Final	Shadow	Constraint	Allowable	Allowable	
25		Cell	Name	Value	Price	R.H. Side	Increase	Decrease	
26		$C$15	Received Atl	8,000	0.65	8000	1000	3000	
27		$D$15	Received Bos	10,000	0.59	10000	1000	3000	
28		$E$15	Received Chi	12,000	0.55	12000	1000	2000	
29		$F$15	Received Den	9,000	0.42	9000	1000	9000	
30		$G$12	Minn Sent	10,000	-0.33	10000	2000	1000	
31		$G$13	Pitt Sent	15,000	-0.29	15000	3000	1000	
32		$G$14	Tucs Sent	14,000	0.00	15000	1E+30	1000	
33									

Figure 4.15. Sensitivity Report for Example 3.1.

second section, the report reproduces the values of the decision variables in the optimal solution (under Final Value) and the values of the coefficients in the objective function (under Objective Coefficient). The Allowable Increase and Allowable Decrease columns show how much we could change any one of the objective function coefficients without altering the optimal decision variables. For example, the objective function coefficient for the *PA* route is $0.36 in the base case, as shown in the first highlighted row of the Sensitivity Report in Figure 4.15. This unit cost could rise to $0.38 without having an impact on the optimal shipping schedule. (This limit is indicated by the allowable increase of 0.02.) In addition, the original value could drop to $0.27 without having an impact on the optimal shipping schedule. (This limit is indicated by the allowable decrease of 0.09.) These increases and decreases from the base case are consistent with the parameter analysis shown in Figure 4.5.

It might be helpful to think about the Sensitivity Report as an "insensitivity report," because it mainly provides information about changes for which some aspect of the base-case solution does not change. Here, for example, the base-case decisions are insensitive to changes in the *PA* unit cost between $0.27 and $0.38. In this interval, the base-case schedule remains optimal. Of course, the optimal total cost will vary with the *PA* unit cost, because some 5000 units are shipped along the *PA* route in the optimal schedule. For example, if the unit cost dropped by $0.04, the optimal schedule would remain unchanged, but the optimal total cost would drop by 5000($0.04) = $200.

The Sensitivity Report is more precise but less flexible than the Parameter Analysis Report. For example, Figure 4.4 provides us with the allowable increase and decrease, but to a precision of only 0.05. We need to search on a smaller grid, as in Figure 4.5, to refine our precision; but even in this more detailed report, we can determine the allowable increase and decrease to a precision of only 0.01. By contrast, the Sensitivity Report provides the values exactly. On the other hand, the Sensitivity Report tells us virtually nothing about what would happen if the *PA* unit cost rose above $0.38, whereas the Parameter Analysis Report can provide a good deal of information.

The entries in the Reduced Cost column of the Sensitivity Report may initially be displayed as a set of zeros for all variables.[2] However, if we display the entries to two decimal places, we see some nonzero values. For decision variables that are not at their upper or lower bounds (and here, the only bound for a variable is zero), the reduced cost is zero. So, for the variable *PA*, which is positive in the optimal shipping schedule, the report shows a reduced cost of zero.

The reduced cost is nonzero if the corresponding decision variable lies at its bound. In this example, that condition means that the route is not used in the optimal schedule. For the *MA* route, the reduced cost is $0.28. The interpretation of this value is as follows. Evidently, the unit cost of the *MA* route is unattractive at its base-case value of $0.60, and we might wonder how much more attractive that unit cost would have to become for the *MA* route to appear in the optimal solution. The answer is given by the reduced cost: The unit cost would have to drop by more than $0.28 before there would be an incentive to ship along the *MA* route. However, we already knew that much, from the Allowable Decrease for the *MA* variable. As this example shows, the Reduced Cost provides information that can be obtained elsewhere, and we need not rely on it.

In the third section, the Sensitivity Report provides the values of the constraint left-hand sides (under Final Value) and the right-hand-side constants (under Constraint RH Side), along with the shadow price for each constraint. Here again, it may be necessary to re-format the column of shadow prices. From the earlier sensitivity analysis for this example, we expect to see a shadow price of $0.29 for Pittsburgh capacity. The Sensitivity Report shows this value as a negative price because it follows a convention of quoting the shadow price as the *increase* in the objective function induced by a unit *increase* in the right-hand side constant. An

---

[2]The format of these cells corresponds to the format of the corresponding decision cell in the original model. Thus, depending on how the model was originally formatted, the figures in this report can be misleading, especially when zeros appear.

increase in the Pittsburgh capacity would allow the optimal total cost to drop, so the shadow price is negative.

The Allowable Increase and Allowable Decrease columns show how much we could change any one of the constraint constants without altering the shadow price. In the case of Pittsburgh capacity (15,000 in the base case), the information in the highlighted row of the report's bottom section indicates that the capacity could increase by 3000 or decrease by 1000 (i.e., it could vary between 14,000 and 18,000) without affecting the shadow price of $0.29. Again, this is an "insensitivity" result, and it is consistent with the information in the Parameter Analysis Report of Figure 4.6. Recall from our earlier discussions, however, that the optimal values of some decision variables change with any increase or decrease in the Pittsburgh capacity.

The Sensitivity Report does not offer information about what occurs outside of the allowable increase and allowable decrease. It is also completely based on one-at-a-time analysis. That is, the presumption is that only one parameter at a time is subject to change. No facility exists in the Sensitivity Report to explore the effects of varying two parameters simultaneously, as in the case of the two-way parameter analysis shown in Figure 4.14.

The sensitivity analysis for right-hand-side constants is omitted for constraints that involve a simple lower or upper bound. That is, if the form of the constraint is *Variable ≤ Ceiling* or *Variable ≥ Floor*, then the Sensitivity Report does not include the constraint. On the other hand, if the same information is incorporated into the model using the standard SUMPRODUCT constraint form (as in the case of the allocation model) or using the SUM constraint form (as in the case of the transportation model) then the Sensitivity Report treats the constraint in its usual fashion and provides ranging analysis.

4.4. THE SENSITIVITY REPORT AND THE ALLOCATION EXAMPLE

As another illustration of the Sensitivity Report, suppose we ask for it after solving Example 2.1, the allocation problem discussed earlier. (Refer to Figure 4.7, but with the original profit coefficient of 16 restored to cell B8.) The Sensitivity Report is shown in Figure 4.16. In the first section, the report shows the optimal value of the objective function (total profit) of $4,880. In the second section, the Sensitivity Report reproduces the optimal solution and tabulates the Allowable Increase and Allowable Decrease for each objective function coefficient. If we ask how much the contribution of chairs ($16 in the base case) could vary without altering the optimal product mix, we can tell from the first Allowable Increase that the contribution could rise by up to $5 or drop by any amount without altering the optimal mix. Thus, a price increase of more than $5 would provide an inducement to include chairs in the product mix. This conclusion could also be drawn from the parameter analysis in Figure 4.7.

Suppose instead that we ask a similar question about desks: How much could the profit contribution for desks ($20 in the base case) change, without altering the

	A	B	C	D	E	F	G	H
1	**Microsoft Excel 12.0 Sensitivity Report**							
2								
3	Objective Cell (Max)							
4		**Cell**	**Name**	**Final Value**				
5		$E$8	Profit Total	4880				
6								
7	Decision Variable Cells							
8				**Final**	**Reduced**	**Objective**	**Allowable**	**Allowable**
9		**Cell**	**Name**	**Value**	**Cost**	**Coefficient**	**Increase**	**Decrease**
10		$B$5	Production plan C	0	-5.00	16	5.00	1E+30
11		$C$5	Production plan D	160	0.00	20	1.00	0.48
12		$D$5	Production plan T	120	0.00	14	0.37	0.67
13								
14	Constraints							
15				**Final**	**Shadow**	**Constraint**	**Allowable**	**Allowable**
16		**Cell**	**Name**	**Value**	**Price**	**R.H. Side**	**Increase**	**Decrease**
17		$E$12	Fabrication LHS	1200	0.00	2000	1E+30	800
18		$E$13	Assembly LHS	2000	1.00	2000	160	80
19		$E$14	Machining LHS	1440	2.00	1440	20	106.67
20		$E$15	Wood LHS	9400	0.00	9600	1E+30	200
21								

Sensitivity Report 2

Figure 4.16. Sensitivity Report for Example 2.1.

optimal solution? From the Sensitivity Report, in the row for desks, we see that the allowable range is from $19.52 to $21.00 (from an Allowable Decrease of about $0.48 to an Allowable Increase of $1.00). Within this interval, the unit profit on desks does not trigger a change in the optimal mix; the best mix remains 160 desks, 120 tables, and no chairs. However, any change outside this range should be examined by re-running the model. Also, if the profit on desks were to increase by $0.75, which lies within the Allowable Increase, the optimal value of the objective function would necessarily change because the 160 desks in the optimal mix would account for a profit increase of $160(\$0.75) = \$120$.

The example involving the profit on desks reinforces the point that the Sensitivity Report cannot "see" beyond the Allowable Increase and Allowable Decrease. The Sensitivity Report tells us nothing about what happens when the profit contribution for desks rises above $21, whereas that information would be available to us from the Parameter Analysis Report, provided we specify a suitable range for the input parameter. Nevertheless, the Sensitivity Report covers all of the decision variables in one report. If we're primarily interested in the allowable increases and decreases around the base case—that is, if we're looking for "insensitivity" information— then the Sensitivity Report is the tool of choice. Had we used the Parameter Analysis Report, we could not have produced information on all three coefficients simultaneously.

In the third section, the Sensitivity Report provides the shadow price for each constraint and the range over which it holds. The Allowable Increase and Allowable Decrease columns show how much we could change any one of the constraint constants without altering any of the shadow prices. For example, we should recognize

Table 4.1. Comparison of the Parameter Analysis and Sensitivity Reports

Parameter Analysis Report	Sensitivity Report
Differences	
Describes user-determined region	Describes "insensitivity" region
Can "see" beyond insensitivity region	Limited to "insensitivity" region
Contains standard and tailored content	Contains standard content
Table grid may need refinements	Allowable increase/decrease are precise
User may require several reports	Information is provided simultaneously
Two-at-a-time analysis is available	One-at-a-time analysis only
Any parameter on the worksheet	Objective coefficients and constraint constants
Similarities	
Report is a new worksheet	Report is a new worksheet
Column names may need revision	Tabulated names may need revision
Entries in report table may need reformatting	Entries in report table may need reformatting

the shadow price on Machining time of $2.00 (from Figure 4.11). However, from the Sensitivity Report, we also know now that this $2.00 value holds up to a capacity of 1460 hours (an allowable increase of 20). Beyond that, there would be a change in the shadow price for machining hours. In fact, there would be a change in the optimal product mix. Once again, we cannot anticipate from Sensitivity Report exactly what that change might look like, whereas the Parameter Analysis Report (Figure 4.11) shows that the expanded machining capacity will make it desirable to add chairs to the product mix.

Thus, the Parameter Analysis Report and the Sensitivity Report provide different capabilities. A comparison of the two approaches is summarized in Table 4.1. Generally, the Parameter Analysis Report is more flexible, whereas the Sensitivity Report is more precise. Although each is suitable for answering particular questions that arise in sensitivity analyses, it would be reasonable to draw on both capabilities to build a comprehensive understanding of the model's solution. One word of warning must be added. The Sensitivity Report can sometimes be confusing if the model itself does not follow a disciplined layout. As described in Chapter 2, we advocate a standardized approach to building linear programming models on spreadsheets. Solver does permit more flexibility in layout and calculation than our guidelines allow, but some users find the Sensitivity Report confusing when running nonstandard model layouts. This problem is less likely to arise with the Parameter Analysis Report.

4.5. DEGENERACY AND ALTERNATIVE OPTIMA

Viewed from the perspective of the Sensitivity Report, each linear programming solution carries with it an allowable range for the objective function coefficients and RHS constants. Within this range, some aspect of the optimal solution remains stable—decision variables in the case of varying objective function coefficients and shadow prices in the case of varying RHS constants. At the end of such a range, the stability no longer persists, and some change sets in. In this section, we examine the endpoints of these ranges as special cases.

First, let's consider the allowable range for a constraint constant. For a particular constraint, there is a corresponding range in which the shadow price holds. At the end of that range, the shadow price is in transition, changing to a different value. At a point of transition, a different shadow price holds in each direction. This condition is referred to as a *degenerate solution*.

Consider our transportation example and its sensitivity report in Figure 4.15. Suppose we are again interested in the analysis of Pittsburgh capacity, originally at 15,000. From the ranging analysis of Figure 4.15, we find that the shadow price of $0.29 holds for capacities of 14,000 to 18,000. At a capacity of 18,000, the shadow price is in transition. We can see from Figure 4.6 that the shadow price is $0.29 below a capacity of 18,000 and $0.27 for capacities above it. Just at 18,000, it would be correct to say that there are two shadow prices, provided that we also explain that the 29-cent shadow price holds for capacity levels below 18,000, and a 27-cent shadow price holds for capacity levels above 18,000. When we take capacity to be exactly 18,000, however, Solver can display only one of these shadow prices. The Sensitivity Report could show the shadow price either as $0.29 but with an allowable increase of zero, or as $0.27 but with an allowable decrease of zero, depending on how the model is expressed on the worksheet.

To recognize a degenerate solution, we look for an entry of zero among the allowable increases and decreases reported in the Constraints section of the Sensitivity Report. This value indicates that a shadow price is at a point of transition. If none of these entries is zero, then the solution is said to be a *nondegenerate solution*, which means that no shadow price lies at a point of transition in the optimal solution. The significance of degeneracy is a warning: It alerts us to be cautious when using shadow prices to help evaluate the economic consequences of altering a constraint constant. We must be mindful that, in a degenerate solution, the shadow price holds in only one direction. If we want to know the value of the shadow price just beyond the point of transition, we can change the corresponding right-hand side by a small amount and then re-run Solver. In our example, we could set Pittsburgh capacity equal to 18,001 and re-optimize. The resulting Sensitivity Report reveals a 27-cent shadow price for the Pittsburgh capacity constraint, along with an Allowable Decrease of one, as shown in the highlighted row of Figure 4.17.

For a complementary result, suppose we have a problem that leads to a nondegenerate solution, and we consider ranging analysis for objective function coefficients. For any particular coefficient, there is a corresponding range in which the optimal values of the decision variables remain unchanged. At the end of that range, more than one optimal solution exists. This condition is referred to as *alternative optima*, or sometimes *multiple optima*.

As an example, consider our original transportation model, as displayed in Figure 4.1. From the ranging analysis of Figure 4.15, we see that the unit cost of the

	A	B	C	D	E	F	G	H
1	Microsoft Excel 12.0 Sensitivity Report							
2								
3	Objective Cell (Min)							
4		Cell	Name	Final Value				
5		$C$18	Total Cost Atl	12959.73				
6								
7	Decision Variable Cells							
8				Final	Reduced	Objective	Allowable	Allowable
9		Cell	Name	Value	Cost	Coefficient	Increase	Decrease
10		$C$12	Minn Atl	0	0.30	0.60	1E+30	0.30
11		$D$12	Minn Bos	0	0.32	0.56	1E+30	0.32
12		$E$12	Minn Chi	10000	0.00	0.22	0.30	1E+30
13		$F$12	Minn Den	0	0.31	0.40	1E+30	0.31
14		$C$13	Pitt Atl	8000	0.00	0.36	0.02	0.63
15		$D$13	Pitt Bos	10000	0.00	0.30	0.11	0.57
16		$E$13	Pitt Chi	1	0.00	0.28	0.27	0.02
17		$F$13	Pitt Den	0	0.43	0.58	1E+30	0.43
18		$C$14	Tucs Atl	0	0.02	0.65	1E+30	0.02
19		$D$14	Tucs Bos	0	0.11	0.68	1E+30	0.11
20		$E$14	Tucs Chi	1999	0.00	0.55	0.02	0.27
21		$F$14	Tucs Den	9000	0.00	0.42	0.31	0.42
22								
23	Constraints							
24				Final	Shadow	Constraint	Allowable	Allowable
25		Cell	Name	Value	Price	R.H. Side	Increase	Decrease
26		$C$15	Received Atl	8,000	0.63	8000	1	1999
27		$D$15	Received Bos	10,000	0.57	10000	1	1999
28		$E$15	Received Chi	12,000	0.55	12000	4001	1999
29		$F$15	Received Den	9,000	0.42	9000	4001	9000
30		$G$12	Minn Sent	10,000	(0.33)	10000	1999	4001
31		$G$13	Pitt Sent	18,001	(0.27)	18001	1999	1
32		$G$14	Tucs Sent	10,999	-	15000	1E+30	4001
33								

Figure 4.17. Sensitivity Report for the near-degenerate case.

PA route can vary from $0.27 to $0.38 without a change in the optimal schedule. At the 38-cent limit of this range, more than one optimal solution exists. To find this solution, we change the unit cost on the PA route to 0.38 and re-run Solver. We find that the optimal total cost is $13,930, as shown in Figure 4.18. In this solution, the shipments from Pittsburgh are 3000 to Atlanta, 10,000 to Boston and 2000 to Chicago, with corresponding adjustments to the Tucson shipments. However, we can verify that the original optimal schedule generates this same total cost. In other words, we have found two different schedules that achieve optimal costs. (In fact, it is possible to show that any weighted average of the two schedules is also optimal; thus, the number of distinct optimal schedules is actually infinite.) Solver is able to display only one of these solutions, depending on how the model is constructed on the spreadsheet.

    To recognize the existence of multiple optima, we look for an entry of zero among the allowable increases and decreases reported in the Decision Variable Cells section of the Sensitivity Report. If there are no zeros, then the optimal solution is a *unique optimum,* and no alternative optima exist. (Strictly speaking, this is true

	A	B	C	D	E	F	G
1	**Network: Transportation Problem**						
2							
3	**Parameters**						
4			Atl	Bos	Chi	Den	*Capacity*
5		Minn	0.60	0.56	0.22	0.40	10,000
6		Pitt	0.38	0.30	0.28	0.58	15,000
7		Tucs	0.65	0.68	0.55	0.42	15,000
8		*Requirement*	8,000	10,000	12,000	9,000	
9							
10	**Decisions**						
11			Atl	Bos	Chi	Den	*Sent*
12		Minn	-	-	10,000	-	10,000
13		Pitt	3,000	10,000	2,000	-	15,000
14		Tucs	5,000	-	-	9,000	14,000
15		*Received*	8,000	10,000	12,000	9,000	39,000
16							
17	**Objective**						
18		Total Cost	13,930				
19							

Transport2

Figure 4.18. Solution with multiple optima.

only for nondegenerate solutions; when the solution is degenerate, these zeros are not necessarily indicators of multiple optima.) Otherwise, the optimal solution displayed on the spreadsheet is one of many alternatives that all achieve the same objective function value. The significance of multiple optima is an opportunity: Knowing that there are alternative ways of reaching the optimal value of the objective function, we might have secondary preferences that we could use as "tiebreakers" in this situation. However, Solver does not have the capability of displaying multiple optima, and it is not always obvious how to generate them on the spreadsheet. In our example, we can at least "trick" Solver into displaying the original optimal schedule for the case of a 38-cent unit cost on the PA route. If we change the unit cost on the PA route to 0.37999 and re-run Solver, we obtain the output we desire. Here, we exploit the fact that this made-up value remains inside the limits of the original ranging analysis (as given in Figure 4.15), but it effectively behaves like the desired parameter of 0.38.

In summary, the Sensitivity Report examines the objective function coefficients and the RHS constants separately in two tables. Taking each parameter independently, and permitting it to vary, the report provides information on its allowable range—the range of values for which the solution remains stable in some way. At the end of these ranges, indicated by the values of the Allowable Increase and Allowable Decrease, special circumstances apply. Box 4.1 summarizes the various conditions that can occur when we start with an optimal solution that is unique and nondegenerate.

BOX 4.1	*Summary of Ranging in Sensitivity Analysis*

Allowable ranges for objective function coefficients

In the range from Allowable Increase to Allowable Decrease

- the values of the decision variables remain the same
- the binding constraints remain binding.

At the boundary of the range

- multiple optima occur
- the decision variables are in transition.

Inside the range (but not on its boundary)

- the optimal set of decision variables is unique.

Allowable ranges for right-hand-side constants

In the range from Allowable Increase to Allowable Decrease

- the shadow prices remain the same
- the zero-valued decision variables remain zero.

At the boundary of the range

- degeneracy occurs
- the shadow price is in transition.

Inside the range (but not on its boundary)

- the shadow prices are unique.

4.6. PATTERNS IN LINEAR PROGRAMMING SOLUTIONS

We often hear that the real take-away from a linear programming model is *insight*, rather than the actual *numbers* in the answer, but where exactly do we find that insight? This section describes one form of insight, which comes from interpreting the qualitative pattern in the solution. Stated another way, the optimal solution tells a "story" about a pattern of economic priorities, and it's the recognition of those priorities that provides useful insight. When we know the pattern, we can explain the solution more convincingly than when we simply transcribe Solver's output. When we know the pattern, we can also anticipate answers to some what-if questions without having to modify the spreadsheet and re-run Solver. In short, the pattern provides a level of understanding that enhances decision making. Therefore, after we optimize a linear programming model, we should always try to describe the qualitative pattern in the optimal solution.

Spotting a pattern involves making observations about both variables and constraints. In the optimal solution, we should ask ourselves, which constraints are binding and which are not? Which variables are positive and which are zero? A *structural scheme* describing the pattern is simply a qualitative statement about binding constraints and positive variables. However, to make that scheme useful, we translate it into a *computational scheme* for the pattern, which ultimately allows us to calculate the precise values of the decision variables in terms of the model's parameters. This computational scheme often allows us to reconstruct the solution in a sequential, step-by-step fashion. To the untrained observer, the computational scheme seems to calculate the quantitative solution directly, without Solver's help. In fact, we are providing only a retrospective interpretation of the solution, and we need to know that solution before we can construct the interpretation. Nevertheless, we are not merely reflecting information in Solver's output; we are looking for an economic imperative at the heart of the situation depicted in the model. When we can find that pattern and communicate it, then we have gained some insight.

The examples in each of the subsections illustrate how to describe a pattern without using numbers. The discussion also introduces two tests that determine whether the pattern has been identified. We'll see how knowledge of the pattern enables us to anticipate the ranges over which shadow prices hold. We'll also see how to anticipate the ranges over which reduced costs hold. In effect, this material amounts to an explanation of information in the Sensitivity Report, although we can go beyond the report. Ultimately, the ability to recognize patterns allows us to appreciate and interpret solutions to linear programs in a comprehensive fashion, but it is a rather different skill than using the Sensitivity Report. The identification of patterns allows us to look beyond the specific quantitative data of a problem and find a general way of thinking about the solution. Unfortunately, there is no recipe for finding patterns—just some guidelines. The lack of a recipe can make the process challenging, even for people who can build linear programming models quite easily. Therefore, our discussion proceeds with a set of examples, each of which illustrates different aspects of working with patterns.

4.6.1. The Transportation Model

Let's return to the transportation example of Figure 4.1. The first thing to notice is that we need to use only six of the available routes in order to optimize costs. As Solver's solution reveals, the *best* routes to use are *MC*, *PA*, *PB*, *TA*, *TC*, and *TD*. Stated another way, the solution tells us that we can ignore the other decision variables.

The solution also tells us that all the demand constraints are binding. This makes intuitive sense because unit costs are positive on all routes, and so there is no incentive to ship more than demand to any destination. A consequence of meeting all demands exactly is that at least one of the supply capacities must be underutilized in the optimal solution because there is a total demand of 39,000 units compared to a total capacity of 40,000. In general, there is no way to anticipate how many sources will be fully utilized and how many will be underutilized, so one useful part of the optimal pattern is the identification of *critical* sources—those that are fully utilized.

The critical sources correspond to binding supply constraints in the model. In the solution, the Minnesota and Pittsburgh plants are at capacity, and Tucson capacity is underutilized. The decision variables associated with Tucson as a source are not determined by the capacity at Tucson; instead, they are determined by other constraints in the model.

In summary, the structural scheme for the pattern is as follows.

- Demands at all five warehouses are binding.
- Capacities at Minnesota and Pittsburgh are binding.
- The desired routes are *MC*, *PA*, *PB*, *TA*, *TC*, and *TD*.

As we shall see, this structural scheme specifies the optimal solution uniquely.

In the optimal schedule, some demands are met entirely from a unique source: Demand at Boston is entirely met from Pittsburgh, and demand at Denver is entirely met from Tucson. In a sense, these are high priority scheduling allocations, and we can think of them as if they are made *first*. There is also a symmetric feature: Supply from Minneapolis all goes to Chicago. Allocating capacity to a unique destination also marks a high priority allocation.

It is tempting to look for a reason why these routes get high priority. At first glance, we might be inclined to think that these are the cheapest routes. For example, Boston's cheapest inbound route is certainly the one from Pittsburgh. However, things get a little more complicated after that. The *TD* route is not the cheapest inbound route for Denver. Luckily, we don't need to have a reason; our task here is merely to interpret the result.

Once we assign the high priority shipments, we can effectively ignore the supply at the Minneapolis plant and the demands at the Boston and Denver warehouses. We then proceed to a second priority level, where we are left with a reduced problem containing two sources and two destinations. Now, the list of best routes tells us that the remaining supply at Pittsburgh must go to Atlanta; therefore, *PA* is a high priority allocation in the reduced problem. Similarly, the remaining demand at Chicago is entirely met from Tucson, so the *TC* route becomes a high priority allocation as well.

Having made the second-priority assignments, we can ignore the supply at Pittsburgh and the demand at Chicago. We are left with a net demand at Atlanta and unallocated supply at Tucson. Thus the last step, at the third priority level, is to meet the remaining demand with a shipment along route *TA*.

In general, the solution of a transportation problem can be described with the following generic computational scheme.

- Identify a high priority demand—one that is met from a unique source—and allocate its entire demand to this route. Then remove that destination from consideration.
- Identify a high priority source—one that supplies a single destination—and allocate its remaining supply to this route. Then remove that source from consideration.

• Repeat the previous two steps using remaining demands and remaining supplies each time until all shipments are accounted for.

The specific steps in the computational scheme for our example are the following.

1. Ship as much as possible on routes *PB*, *TD*, and *MC*.
2. At the second priority level, ship as much as possible on routes *PA* and *TC*.
3. At the third priority level, ship as much as possible on route *TA*.

At each allocation, "as much as possible" is dictated by the minimum of capacity and demand. The following list summarizes computational scheme in priority order.

Route	Priority	Shipment
PB	1	10,000
TD	1	9000
MC	1	10,000
PA	2	5000
TC	2	2000
TA	3	3000

This retrospective calculation of the solution has two important features: It is complete (i.e., it specifies the entire shipment schedule) and it is *unambiguous* (i.e., the calculation leads to just one schedule). Anyone who constructs the solution using these steps will reach the same result.

The structural scheme given earlier characterizes the optimal solution without explicitly using a number. By describing the optimal solution without relying on the specific parameters in the problem, it portrays a qualitative pattern in the solution. Then, by converting that pattern to a computational scheme, we translate the pattern into a list of economic priorities. This list enables us to establish the values of the decision variables one at a time.

This pattern is important because it holds not just for the specific problem that we solved, but also for other problems that are very similar but with some of the parameters slightly altered. For example, suppose that demand at Boston were raised to 10,500. We could verify that the same pattern applies. The revised details of implementing the same pattern are shown in the following list.

Route	Priority	Shipment	Change	Δ Cost
PB	1	10,500	500	150
TD	1	9000	0	0
MC	1	10,000	0	0
PA	2	4500	−500	−180
TC	2	2000	0	0
TA	3	3500	500	325

Summing the cost changes in the last column, we find that an increase of 500 in demand at Boston leads to an increase in total cost of $295. In effect, we have derived the shadow price because the per-unit change in total cost would be $295/500 = $0.59. This value agrees with the shadow price for Boston demand given in the Sensitivity Report (Figure 4.15).

In tracing the changes, we can also anticipate the range over which the shadow price continues to hold. As we add units to the demand at Boston, the pattern induces us to make the same incremental adjustments in shipment quantities we traced in the table above. The pattern of shipments will be preserved, and the list of best routes will remain unaltered, as long as we add no more than 1000 units to the demand at Boston. At that level, the excess capacity in the system disappears, and the pattern no longer holds. In the other direction, as demand at Boston drops, the pattern indicates that we should reduce shipments on *PB* and *TA*, while increasing *PA*. After we have reallocated 3000 units in that way, the allocation on route *TA* disappears. At that point, we have to shift to a new pattern to accommodate a further drop in Boston demand. The limits found here—an increase of 1000 and a decrease of 3000—are precisely the limits on the Sensitivity Report for Boston demand. Thus, using the optimal pattern, we are able to explain the shadow price and its allowable range.

More generally, we can alter the original problem in several ways at once. Suppose demands at Atlanta, Boston, and Chicago are *each* raised by 100 simultaneously. What will the optimal schedule look like? In qualitative terms, we already know from the computational scheme. The qualitative pattern allows us to write down the optimal solution to the revised problem without re-running Solver, but rather by using the priority list and adjusting the shipment quantities for the altered demands. The following table summarizes the calculations.

Route	Priority	Shipment	Change	Δ Cost
PB	1	10,100	100	30
TD	1	9000	0	0
MC	1	10,000	0	0
PA	2	4900	−100	−36
TC	2	2100	100	55
TA	3	3200	200	130

Tracing the cost implications, we find that the 100-unit increases in the three demands combine to increase the optimal total cost by $179. This figure can be obtained by adding the three corresponding shadow prices (and multiplying by the size of the 100-unit increase), but the pattern allows us to take one additional step. We can also determine that the $179 figure holds for an increase (in the combined demand levels) of 1000, which is the level at which the excess supply disappears, or for a decrease of 1500, which is the level at which the shipment along *TA* runs out. Thus, we can find the allowable range for a shadow price corresponding to simultaneous changes in several constraint constants.

4.6.2. The Product Portfolio Model

The product portfolio problem asks which products a firm ought to be making. If contractual constraints force the firm to enter certain markets, then the question is which products to make in quantities beyond the required minimum. Consider Grocery Distributors (GD), a company that distributes 15 different vegetables to grocery stores. GD's vegetables come in standard cardboard cartons that each take up 1.25 cubic feet in the warehouse. The company replenishes its supply of frozen foods at the start of each week and rarely has any inventory remaining at the week's end. An entire week's supply of frozen vegetables arrives each Monday morning at the warehouse, which can hold up to 18,000 cubic feet of product. In addition, GD's supplier extends a line of credit amounting to $30,000. That is, GD is permitted to purchase up to $30,000 worth of product each Monday.

GD can predict sales for each of its 15 products in the coming week. This forecast is expressed in terms of a minimum and maximum anticipated sales quantity. The minimum quantity is based on a contractual agreement that GD has made with a small number of retail grocery chains; the maximum quantity represents an estimate of the sales potential in the upcoming week. The cost and selling price per carton for each product are known. The given information is tabulated as part of Figure 4.19.

GD solves the linear programming model shown in Figure 4.19. The model's objective is maximizing profit for the coming week. Sales for each product are constrained by a minimum and maximum quantity. These are entered as lower and upper bound constraints. In addition, aggregate constraints on purchase expenditures and warehouse space make up the model. The model specification is as follows.

Objective:	R11 (maximize)	
Variables:	C9:Q9	
Constraints:	R14:R15 $\leq$ T14:T15	
Bounds:	C9:Q9 $\geq$ C6:Q6	(lower bounds)
	C9:Q9 $\leq$ C7:Q7	(upper bounds)

Figure 4.19 also displays the solution obtained by running Solver. When we look at the constraints of the problem, we see that the credit limit is binding, but the space

	A	B	C	D	E	F	G	H	I	J	K	L	M	N	O	P	Q	R	S	T
1	General Distributors																			
3	Data	Vegetable	WP	CC	BP	AR	CR	SU	OK	CL	GP	SP	LB	BS	GB	SQ	BR			
4		Cost	2.15	2.20	2.40	4.80	2.60	2.30	2.35	2.85	2.25	2.10	2.80	3.00	2.60	2.50	2.90			
5		Price	2.27	2.48	2.70	5.20	2.92	2.48	2.20	3.13	2.48	2.27	3.13	3.18	2.92	2.70	3.13			
6		Min	300	400	250	0	300	200	150	100	750	400	500	100	500	100	400			
7		Max	1500	2000	900	150	1200	800	600	300	3500	2000	3300	500	3200	500	2500			
9	Decisions	Cartons	300	2000	900	0	1200	200	150	100	750	400	2150	100	3200	100	400			
11	Objective	Profit $	0.12	0.28	0.30	0.40	0.32	0.18	-0.15	0.28	0.23	0.17	0.33	0.18	0.32	0.20	0.23	$3,395.50		
13																		LHS		RHS
14	Constraints	Credit	2.15	2.20	2.40	4.80	2.60	2.30	2.35	2.85	2.25	2.10	2.80	3.00	2.60	2.50	2.90	30,000.00	<=	30,000
15		Space	1.25	1.25	1.25	1.25	1.25	1.25	1.25	1.25	1.25	1.25	1.25	1.25	1.25	1.25	1.25	14,937.50	<=	18,000

Figure 4.19. Optimal solution for GD.

constraint is not. That means space consumption is dictated by other constraints in the problem. When we look at demand constraints, we see that creamed corn, black-eyed peas, carrots, and green beans are purchased at their maximum demands, whereas all other products are purchased at their minimum, except for lima beans. This observation constitutes a first cut at the structural scheme in the optimal solution.

The pattern thus consists of a set of products produced at their minimum levels, another set produced at their maximum levels, and the information that the credit limit is binding. We can translate this pattern into a priority list by treating the products produced at their maximum levels as high priority products. The products produced exactly at their minimum levels are the low priority products. Lima beans are in a unique role. We can think of the solution as assigning the high priority products to their maximum levels and the low priority products to their minimum levels. This brings us to the only remaining positive variable—the lima beans. We assign their quantity so that the credit limit becomes binding.

We can go one step further and recognize from the pattern that we are actually solving a simpler problem than the original: Produce the highest possible value from the 15 products under a tight credit limit. To solve this problem, we can use a common-sense rule: Pursue the products in the order of highest value-to-cost ratio. The only other consideration is satisfying the given minimum quantities. Therefore, we can calculate the solution as follows.

1. Purchase enough of each product to satisfy its minimum quantity.
2. Rank the products from highest to lowest ratio of profit-to-cost.
3. For the highest-ranking product, raise the purchase quantity toward its maximum quantity. Two things can happen: Either we increase the purchase quantity so that the maximum is reached (in which case we go to the next product), or else we use up the credit limit (in which case we stop).

The ranking mechanism prioritizes the products and defines the computational scheme for the pattern. Using these priorities, we essentially partition the set of products into three groups: a set of high priority products, produced at their maximum levels; a set of low priority products, produced at their minimum levels; and a special product, produced at a level between its minimum and its maximum. (The special product is the one we are adding to the purchase plan in our computational scheme when we hit the credit limit.) This procedure is complete and unambiguous, and it describes the optimal solution without explicitly using a number. At first, the pattern was again just a collection of positive decision variables and binding constraints. But we were able to convert that pattern into a prioritized list of allocations—a computational scheme—that established the values of the decision variables one at a time. Table 4.2 summarizes the computational scheme. It ranks the products by profit-to-cost ratio and indicates which products are purchased at either their maximum or minimum quantity.

Actually, Solver's solution merely distinguished the three priority classes; it did not actually reveal the value-to-cost ratio rule explicitly. That insight could come from

Table 4.2. GD's Products, Arranged by Priority

Product	Priority	Quantity	Profit/cost
Creamed corn	1	2000	0.127 (max.)
Black-eyed peas	2	900	0.125 (max.)
Carrots	3	1200	0.123 (max.)
Green beans	3	3200	0.123 (max.)
Lima beans	4	2150	0.118 (spec.)
Green peas	5	750	0.102 (min.)
Cauliflower	6	100	0.098 (min.)
Spinach	7	400	0.081 (min.)
Squash	8	100	0.079 (min.)
Broccoli	9	400	0.079 (min.)
Succotash	10	200	0.078 (min.)
Brussel sprouts	11	100	0.060 (min.)
Whipped potatoes	12	300	0.056 (min.)
Okra	13	150	−0.064 (min.)

reviewing the make-up of the priority classes, or from some outside knowledge about how single-constraint problems are optimized. But this brings up an important point. Usually, Solver does not reveal the economic reason for why a variable is treated as having high priority. In general, it is not always necessary (or even possible) to know *why* an allocation receives high priority—it is important to know only that it does.

As in the transportation example, we can alter the base-case model slightly and follow the consequences for the optimal purchase plan. For example, if we raise the credit limit, the only change at the margin will be the purchase of additional cartons of the medium priority product. Thus, the marginal value of raising the credit limit is equivalent to the incremental profit per dollar of purchase cost for the medium priority product, or $(3.13 - 2.80)/2.80 = 0.1179$. Furthermore, we can easily compute the range over which this shadow price continues to hold. At the margin, we are adding to the 2150 cartons of lima beans, where each carton adds $0.1179 of profit per dollar of cost. As we expand the credit limit, the optimal solution will call for an increasing quantity of lima beans, until it reaches its maximum demand of 3300 cartons. Those extra $(3300 - 2150) = 1150$ cartons consume an extra $2.80 each of an expanded credit limit, thus reaching the maximum demand at an additional $2.80(1150) = \$3220$ of expansion in the credit limit. This is exactly the allowable increase for the credit limit constraint. For completeness, we should also check on the other nonbinding constraint, because we ignored the space constraint in the pattern. The extra 1150 cartons of lima beans consume additional space of $(1.25)1150 = 1437.5$ square feet of space. But this amount can be accommodated by the unused space of 3063 square feet in the original optimal solution. This calculation confirms that lima bean demand reaches its maximum level at the allowable increase of $3220 in the credit limit.

Suppose we increase the amount of a low priority product in the purchase plan. Then, following the optimal pattern (Steps 1–3 above), we would have to purchase less of the medium priority product. Consider the purchase of more squash than the 100-carton minimum. Each additional carton costs $2.50, substituting for about $2.50/2.80 = 0.893$ cartons of lima beans in the credit limit constraint. The net effect on profit is as follows.

- Add a carton of squash (increase profit by $0.20).
- Remove 0.893 cartons of lima beans (decrease profit by $0.2946).
- Therefore, net cost = $0.0946.

Thus, each carton of squash we force into the purchase plan (above the minimum of 100) will reduce profits by 9.46 cents, which corresponds to the reduced cost for squash. Over what range will this figure hold? From the optimal pattern, we see that we can continue to swap squash for lima beans only until the squash rises to its maximum demand of 500 cartons, or until lima beans drop to their minimum demand of 500 or until the excess space is consumed, whichever occurs first. The maximum demand for squash is the tightest of these limits; thus, the reduced cost holds for 400 additional cartons of squash above its minimum demand, a figure that is not directly accessible on the Sensitivity Report.

Comparing the analysis of GD's problem with the transportation problem considered earlier, we see that the optimal pattern, when translated into a computational scheme, is complete and unambiguous in both cases. We can also use the pattern to determine shadow prices on binding constraints and the ranges over which these values continue to hold; similarly, we can use the pattern to derive reduced costs and their ranges as well. A specific feature of GD's model is the focus on one particular bottleneck constraint. This helps us understand the role of a binding constraint when we interpret a pattern; however, many problems have more than one binding constraint.

4.6.3. The Investment Model

Next, let's revisit Example 3.5, the network model for multiperiod investment. The optimal solution is reproduced in Figure 4.20. Because it is a network, all the constraints are binding. Furthermore, six variables are positive in the optimal solution. Therefore, the structural scheme for the pattern is to take every constraint as binding and rely on the following list of variables: $I0$, $A5$, $B1$, $B3$, $B5$, and $D1$. The solution tells us to ignore the other variables.

How can we use the constraints to dictate the values of the nonzero variables? One helpful step is to recreate the network diagram, using just the variables known to be part of the solution. Figure 4.21 shows this version of the network diagram.

	A	B	C	D	E	F	G	H	I	J	K	L	M	N	O	P	Q	R	S
1	Network: Investment Problem						Rates	6%	14%		18%	65%							
2																			
3	Decisions																		
4		I0	A1	A2	A3	A4	A5	A6	A7	A8	B1	B3	B5	C1	C4	D1			
5		74.422	0.000	0.000	0.000	0.000	24.528	0.000	0.000	0.000	56.240	64.114	24.561	0.000	0.000	18.182			
6																			
7	Objective																		
8		74.422																	
9	Year																		
10	0	-1	1	0	0	0	0	0	0	0	1	0	0	1	0	1	0	=	0
11	1	0	-1.06	1	0	0	0	0	0	0	0	0	0	0	0	0	0	=	0
12	2	0	0	-1.06	1	0	0	0	0	0	-1.14	1	0	0	0	0	0	=	0
13	3	0	0	0	-1.06	1	0	0	0	0	0	0	0	-1.18	1	0	0	=	0
14	4	0	0	0	0	-1.06	1	0	0	0	0	-1.14	1	0	0	0	-24	=	-24
15	5	0	0	0	0	0	-1.06	1	0	0	0	0	0	0	0	0	-26	=	-26
16	6	0	0	0	0	0	0	-1.06	1	0	0	0	-1.14	0	-1.18	0	-28	=	-28
17	7	0	0	0	0	0	0	0	-1.06	1	0	0	0	0	0	-1.65	-30	=	-30
18																			

GO   Investment

Figure 4.20. Optimal solution to Example 3.5.

If we think of the cash outflows in the last four years of the model as being met by particular investments, it follows that the last cash flow is met by either $A7$ or $D1$. These are the only investments that mature in year 7, but the structural scheme tells us to ignore $A7$. From Figure 4.21, we can see that the size of $D1$ must exactly cover the required outflow in year 7. Similarly, the candidates to cover the year 6 cash outflow are $A6$, $B5$, and $C4$. Of these, only $B5$ is nonzero, so $B5$ covers the required outflow in year 6. The use of $B5$ also adds to the required outflow in year 4. For the required outflow in year 5, the only nonzero candidate is $A5$, which also adds to the required outflow in year 4. The combined year 4 outflows must be covered by $B3$, which in turn imposes a required outflow in year 2, to be covered by $B1$. Table 4.3 summarizes the calculations, working backward from year 7.

Working down this list, the investment in $D1$ is determined by the requirement in year 7. The size of $B5$ is determined by the requirement in year 6, and similarly, the size of $A5$ is determined by the requirement in year 5. These latter two investments and the given outflow in year 4 together determine the investment in $B3$. (For that reason, we need to know the size of $B5$ and $A5$ before we can calculate the size of

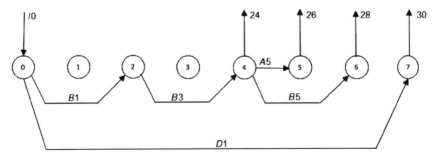

Figure 4.21. Network model corresponding to Figure 4.21.

Table 4.3. Computational Scheme for the Investment Model

Year	Outflow	Met by	Rate	Inflow at year
7	30,000	D1	65%	18,182 at 1
6	28,000	B5	14%	24,561 at 4
5	26,000	A5	6%	24,528 at 4
4	73,089	B3	14%	64,114 at 2
3	0			
2	64,114	B1	14%	56,240 at 1
1	74,422	I0	–	

B3.) The size of B3, in turn, dictates the investment in B1. Finally, the sizes of B1 and D1 determine how much money must be invested initially.

Once again, this description of the solution is complete (specifies the entire invest-ment schedule) and unambiguous (leads to just one schedule). The binding constraints and the positive decision variables, as displayed in Figure 4.21, describe a compu-tational scheme for calculating the values of the decision variables one at a time, as if following a priority list.

As in the other examples, we can obtain shadow prices by incrementing one of the constraint constants and repeating the process. For example, if the last outflow changes to $31,000 then, following the pattern, we know that the only change will be an increase in D1, raising the initial investment. In particular, for an increased outflow of $1000, D1 would have to be augmented by 1000/1.65 (because it returns 65 per-cent) or $606.06. Thus, the shadow price on the last constraint is 0.606, as can be verified by obtaining the Sensitivity Report for the base-case optimization run. To determine the range over which this shadow price holds, we must calculate when some nonbinding constraint becomes tight. For this purpose, the only nonbinding con-straints we need to worry about are the nonnegativity constraints on the variables, because each of the formal constraints in the model is an equality constraint already. The shadow price on the last constraint therefore holds for any increase in the size of the last outflow.

4.6.4. The Allocation Model

In the examples discussed thus far, the pattern led us to a way of determining the vari-ables one at a time, in sequence. After one variable in this sequence was determined, we had enough information to determine the next one, and we could continue until all of the positive variables were determined. Not all solutions lead to this sequential list-ing, however. As an example, let's revisit the allocation model, shown in Figure 4.7.

When we ignore the zero-valued variables and the nonbinding constraints, we are left with a structural scheme consisting of two binding constraints (for assembly and machining capacity) and two positive variables (desks and tables). There is only one way that a product mix of desks and tables can be chosen to precisely consume all assembly and machining capacity. To find that mix, we must solve the following two equations in two unknowns.

$$8D + 6T = 2000$$
$$6D + 4T = 1440$$

The unique solution to the two equations is $D = 160$ and $T = 120$, which is complete and unambiguous for the model. Thus, in this example, we cannot create a priority list for calculating the variables one at a time. Instead, our computational scheme amounts to the solution of a pair of equations, allowing us to compute the values of the two positive variables simultaneously.

Because this is not a difficult system to solve for specific values of D and T, we can also solve it parametrically. Let A and M denote the assembly and machining capacities, respectively. Then the solution is

$$D = (3M - 2A)/2$$
$$T = (3A - 4M)/2$$

This form allows us to evaluate shadow prices easily. For example, if we increase M by a unit amount, D increases by 1.5, T decreases by 2, and the objective function increases by

$$\Delta Profit = 20D + 14T = 20(1.5) + 14(-2) = 30 - 28 = 2$$

We recognize the \$2 shadow price from earlier analysis (Figure 4.16).

We can also use the parametric form to derive the allowable range. Again, suppose we increase M. From the parametric solution, we see that D will increase, but T will drop. The combination also increases the consumption of fabrication hours and wood supply. The pattern will last until T drops to zero, fabrication becomes binding or wood becomes binding, whichever occurs first. It turns out that the first change in the pattern comes from wood. Recall that the wood constraint is

$$40D + 25T \leq 9600$$

Using the parametric solution in our pattern, this expression becomes

$$40(3M - 2A)/2 + 25(3A - 4M)/2 = 10M - 2.5A \leq 9600$$

or, with $A = 2000$

$$10M \leq 14,600$$

Therefore, the pattern holds until $M = 1460$, which corresponds to an allowable increase of 20.

4.6.5. The Refinery Model

To repeat the main idea: When we specify the structural scheme for a pattern in the optimal solution, we focus on the decision variables that are positive and the constraints that are binding. In effect, we ignore zero-valued variables and nonbinding constraints. As a final illustration, we revisit the refinery model of Example 3.6 for

Delta Oil. The optimal solution is reproduced in Figure 4.22. Recall that the dimensions for the variables in this model are thousands of barrels per day.

In the solution, all of the decision variables are positive, so the computational scheme must determine each decision variable. When we look for binding constraints, we find the balance equations, which define relationships among the decision variables, along with four others

- Cracker capacity (at 20,000)
- *Reg* sales (at 16,000)
- *Reg* blend quality (at its floor of 50 percent *Cat*)
- *Prem* blend quality (at its floor of 75 percent *Cat*).

In the computational scheme, these four binding constraints, together with the definitional relationships in the balance equations, dictate the entire optimal solution. We start with the cracker. Because the cracker is at its capacity limit, this means $Feed = 20,000$. Furthermore, the output of the cracker occurs in fixed proportions, so it follows that $Cat = 12,800$ and $High = 8000$.

Next, we can use the fact that regular gasoline sells at its market limit, together with the fact that it is blended at the minimum concentration of catalytic, to deduce that

$$BR = 50\% \text{ of } 16,000 = 8000$$
$$CR = BR = 8000$$

	A	B	C	D	E	F	G	H	I	J	K	L	M	N	O	P	Q
1	Network: Production Planning Problem																
2																	
3	Decisions		Crude	Dist	Low	Blend	Feed	Cat	High	BR	BP	CR	CP	Reg	Prem		
4		Kbbl.	49.3	29.6	19.7	9.6	20.0	12.8	8.0	8.00	1.60	8.00	4.80	16.0	6.4		
5	Objective																
6		price			36				44					50	55		
7		cost	5				6										
8		cost	28														
9		net	-33	0	36	0	-6	0	44	0	0	0	0	50	55	466.400	
10	Constraints															LHS	RHS
11																	
12	Tower	-0.60	1	0	0	0	0	0	0	0	0	0	0	0	0.0 =	0
13	Tower capacity	-0.40	0	1	0	0	0	0	0	0	0	0	0	0	0.0 =	0
14	Distillate split	0	-1	0	1	1	0	0	0	0	0	0	0	0	0.0 =	0
15	Cracker	0	0	0	0	-0.64	1	0	0	0	0	0	0	0	0.0 =	0
16	Cracker	0	0	0	0	-0.40	0	1	0	0	0	0	0	0	0.0 =	0
17	Blend split	0	0	0	-1	0	0	0	1	1	0	0	0	0	0.0 =	0
18	Catalytic split	0	0	0	0	0	-1	0	0	0	1	1	0	0	0.0 =	0
19	Reg composition	0	0	0	0	0	0	0	-1	0	-1	0	1	0	0.0 =	0
20	Prem composition	0	0	0	0	0	0	0	0	-1	0	-1	0	1	0.0 =	0
21	Reg quality	0	0	0	0	0	0	0	-0.50	0	0.50	0	0	0	0.0 >=	0
22	Prem quality	0	0	0	0	0	0	0	0	-0.75	0	0.25	0	0	0.0 >=	0
23	Tower capacity	1	0	0	0	0	0	0	0	0	0	0	0	0	49.3 <=	50
24	Cracker capacity	0	0	0	0	1	0	0	0	0	0	0	0	0	20.0 <=	20
25	Reg sales	0	0	0	0	0	0	0	0	0	0	0	1	0	16.0 <=	16
26	Prem sales	0	0	0	0	0	0	0	0	0	0	0	0	1	6.4 <=	16
27																	

Delta

Figure 4.22. Spreadsheet model for Example 3.6.

Now that we know *Cat* and *CR*, it follows from material balance considerations that $CP = 4800$.

Next, we use the fact that premium gasoline is blended at the minimum concentration of catalytic, to deduce that

$$Prem = 4800/(0.75) = 6400$$

From material balance considerations, we have

$$BP = Prem - CP = 6400 - 4800 = 1600$$

We now know the allocation of the distillate blend, so

$$Blend = BR + BP = 8000 + 1600 = 9600$$
$$Dist = Blend + Feed = 9600 + 20{,}000 = 29{,}600$$

This calculation brings us back to the output of the tower, which we know is 60 percent distillate and 40 percent low-end by-products, yielding one last set of calculations

$$Crude = Dist/0.6 = 29{,}600/0.6 = 49{,}333$$
$$Low = 0.4(Crude) = 19{,}733$$

Thus, the optimal pattern calls for production that fully utilizes cracker capacity and fully exploits sales potential for regular gasoline, while meeting minimum quality levels in the blending of regular and premium gasolines. These qualitative constraints represent the economic drivers that dictate the entire optimal solution.

Table 4.4. Computational Scheme for the Delta Oil Model

Variable	Base case	New case	Change
Feed	20,000	20,000	
Cat	12,800	13,800	1000
High	8000	8000	
BR	8000	8000	
CR	8000	8000	
CP	4800	5800	1000
Prem	6400	7733	1333
BP	1600	1933	333
Blend	9600	9933	333
Dist	29,600	29,933	333
Crude	49,333	49,889	556
Low	19,733	19,956	222

As we pointed out in Chapter 3, catalytic is a scarce resource at Delta Oil. If more catalytic could be produced, Delta would be able to increase its profits. To consider a specific scenario, suppose that a technological alteration of the cracker could produce 1000 more barrels of catalytic without affecting the output of high-end by-products. (In effect, this alteration modifies the original ratio of catalytic output to feedstock input.) The following lists show the implications for the variables in the model. The base-case values come from the calculations illustrated above; the new-case values in Table 4.4 are derived in a similar sequence, starting with the fact that cracker capacity is fully utilized at 20,000 barrels and regular sales are at the 16,000-barrel limit.

The economic implications follow from the objective function. Taking the variables that have nonzero coefficients in the objective function and evaluating the impact of their changed values, we obtain

$$Profit = 55(Prem) + 36(Low) - 33(Crude)$$

or

$$Profit = 55(1333) + 36(222) - 33(556) = 63,000$$

Thus, the alteration in cracker output could produce additional profits of $63,000 if the production plan were adjusted optimally. On a per-unit basis, each barrel of catalytic generated this way would produce $63 of additional profit. This figure provides us with a tangible economic value for catalytic, which is an intermediate product and which presumably has no market. However, if there were a market for catalytic, we know that Delta would want to buy more catalytic at any price below $63 per barrel.

These calculations explain the shadow price on the first cracker constraint, which defines catalytic in the linear programming model. An increase of one on the right-hand side would be equivalent to setting *Cat* equal to one more than 40 percent of the output from the tower. We can interpret this situation as equivalent to obtaining one additional unit of *Cat* from an external source, as if it were freely available outside of our technology. The shadow price tells us how much the objective function would increase, per unit increase in the right-hand-side constant; and in the Constraints section of the Sensitivity Report, we can verify that this value is 63, as shown in Figure 4.23. Thus, our calculation exercise has essentially derived the shadow price. More importantly, we can see how to use the optimal pattern to trace the economic consequences of a technological change in the model.

One additional point is instructive. The $63 shadow price on catalytic has an allowable increase of 1.2. Given the scaling convention in the model, this means that the shadow price holds for an increase of only 1200 barrels of catalytic. To see where this figure comes from, create a third column of figures in Table 4.4, starting with a change in catalytic of 1200. The calculations lead to a *Crude* value of 50,000, meaning that the tower becomes fully utilized. Beyond that level, a new pattern applies.

Cell	Name	Final Value	Shadow Price	Constraint R.H. Side	Allowable Increase	Allowable Decrease
$O$12	Tower LHS	0.0	31.0	0	29.600	0.400
$O$13	Tower LHS	0.0	36.0	0	1E+30	19.733
$O$14	Distillate split LHS	0.0	31.0	0	29.600	0.400
$O$15	Cracker LHS	0.0	63.0	0	1.200	4.800
$O$16	Cracker LHS	0.0	44.0	0	1E+30	8.000
$O$17	Blend split LHS	0.0	31.0	0	9.600	0.400
$O$18	Catalytic split LHS	0.0	63.0	0	1.200	4.800
$O$19	Reg composition LHS	0.0	47.0	0	14.400	1.200
$O$20	Prem composition LHS	0.0	55.0	0	9.600	6.400
$O$21	Reg quality LHS	0.0	-32.0	0	4.800	0.300
$O$22	Prem quality LHS	0.0	-32.0	0	1.200	0.300
$O$23	Tower capacity LHS	49.3	0.0	50	1E+30	0.667
$O$24	Cracker capacity LHS	20.0	20.9	20	0.330	7.500
$O$25	Reg sales LHS	16.0	3.0	16	1.200	14.400
$O$26	Prem sales LHS	6.4	0.0	16	1E+30	9.600

Constraints

| | Delta | SensitivityD |

Figure 4.23. Sensitivity Report (Constraints section) for Example 3.6.

SUMMARY

The primary role of Solver is to find solutions to optimization models. However, some of the most useful information in the model comes from performing sensitivity analysis after the solution has been found. The information available through sensitivity analyses of linear programs is elegant and comprehensive compared to what we find in other optimization techniques. In that sense, the coverage in this chapter represents a kind of benchmark for the information we would like to acquire in conjunction with an optimization analysis.

This chapter covered three approaches to sensitivity analysis: the Parameter Analysis Report, the Sensitivity Report, and the interpretation of optimal patterns. The Sensitivity Report is the most canned approach. It is a well defined report that complements the use of Solver. Most importantly, it automatically reveals shadow prices and allowable ranges.

The Parameter Analysis Report allows the user quite a lot of flexibility, and it provides for linear programs the same kind of capability that Excel's Data Table tool provides for basic spreadsheet models. The effects of modifying a parameter in the model can be traced well beyond the range in the Sensitivity Report, and shadow prices can be computed in Excel whenever we vary a right-hand-side parameter.

The recognition of patterns in linear programming solutions is a way of looking beyond the specific numbers in the result and toward a broader economic imperative. By focusing on positive variables and binding constraints, this interpretation emphasizes the key factors in the model that drive the form of the solution. The ability to detect these factors sharpens our intuition and enhances our ability to implement effective decisions based on the model.

The examples in Section 4.6 illustrate the process of extracting insight from the pattern in a linear programming solution. The first step is to describe a structural scheme for the pattern by examining the optimal decision variables and binding constraints. The more challenging step is to convert this qualitative description into a computational scheme that allows us to "construct" the optimal solution from the given parameters. Ideally, the computational scheme determines the variables one at a time. This scheme can often be interpreted as a list of priorities, and those priorities reveal the economic forces at work.

The pattern that emerges from the economic priorities is essentially a *qualitative* one, in that we can describe it without using specific numbers. However, once we supply the parameters of the constraints, the pattern leads us to the optimal *quantitative* solution. In a sense, it is almost as if Solver first spots the optimal pattern and then says, "Give me the numerical information in your problem." For any specification of the numbers (within certain limits), Solver could then compute the optimal solution by simply following the sequential steps in the pattern's computational scheme. In reality, of course, Solver cannot know the pattern until the solution is determined, because the solution is a critical ingredient in the pattern.

Two diagnostic questions help determine whether we have been successful at extracting a pattern: Is the pattern complete? Is it unambiguous? That is, the pattern must lead us to a full solution of the problem, not just to a partial solution, and it must lead to a unique determination of the variables. As a check on our specification of the pattern, we can derive shadow prices. In each case, the shadow price comes from altering one constraint constant in the original problem. We should be able to trace the incremental changes in the variables, through the various steps in the pattern's computational scheme, and ultimately derive the shadow price for the corresponding constraint. We can also determine marginal values for changing several parameters at a time in much the same way, and we can compute the allowable range over which these marginal values continue to hold.

Unfortunately, it is not always the case that the pattern can be reduced to a list of assignments in priority order. Occasionally, after we identify the positive variables and the binding constraints in the optimal solution, we might be able to say no more than that the pattern comes from solving a system of simultaneous equations determined by those constraints and those variables. Nevertheless, in most cases, as the examples demonstrate, focusing on the pattern can provide added insight beyond the numbers.

Patterns have certain limits, as suggested above. If we think of testing our specification of a pattern by deriving shadow prices, we have to recognize that a shadow price has a limited range over which it holds, as indicated by its allowable increase and allowable decrease. Beyond this range, a different pattern prevails. As we change a constraint constant, the shadow price will eventually change. The same is true of the pattern: Beyond the range in which the shadow price holds, the pattern may change. In the product portfolio example, however, we were able to specify the computational scheme in a general way, so that it holds even when the shadow price changes. In that example, we were able to articulate the pattern at a high enough level of generality that the qualitative "story" continues to hold even for substantial changes in the given data.

EXERCISES

4.1. Transportation Patterns Revisited   Revisit the transportation model of this chapter and the pattern in its optimal solution.

(a) Suppose that Atlanta demand is increased by 100 units. Use the pattern to determine the impact of this increase on the optimal total cost. What is the cost increase per unit increase in demand at Atlanta? For how much of an increase in Atlanta demand will this marginal cost continue to hold? Use the information in the Sensitivity Report to confirm your results.

(b) Repeat part (a) for a decrease of 100 units in Chicago demand.

(c) Repeat part (a) for an increase of 100 units in Minnesota capacity.

4.2. Product Portfolio Revisited   Revisit the product portfolio model of this chapter and the pattern in its optimal solution.

(a) Suppose that the credit limit of $30,000 is tightened. For each thousand-dollar reduction, what is the impact on profit? Use the information in the Sensitivity Report to confirm your results.

(b) Suppose that the minimum requirement for whipped potatoes is raised (above 300 cartons). Using the pattern, determine the impact of this demand increase on the optimal profit. For how much of an increase in demand does this value hold? Where does this information appear on the Sensitivity Report?

4.3. Distributing a Product   The Lincoln Lock Company manufactures a commercial security lock at plants in Atlanta, Louisville, Detroit, and Phoenix. The unit cost of production at each plant is $35.50, $37.50, $37.25, and $36.25, and the annual capacities are 18,000, 15,000, 25,000, and 20,000, respectively. The locks are sold through wholesale distributors in seven locations around the country. The unit shipping cost for each plant–distributor combination is shown in the following table, along with the forecasted demand from each distributor for the coming year.

	Tacoma	San Diego	Dallas	Denver	St Louis	Tampa	Baltimore
Atlanta	2.50	2.75	1.75	2.00	2.10	1.80	1.65
Louisville	1.85	1.90	1.50	1.60	1.00	1.90	1.85
Detroit	2.30	2.25	1.85	1.25	1.50	2.25	2.00
Phoenix	1.90	0.90	1.60	1.75	2.00	2.50	2.65
Demand	5500	11,500	10,500	9600	15,400	12,500	6600

(a) Determine the least costly way of shipping locks from plants to distributors.

(b) List the shadow prices corresponding to each plant's capacity. Which capacity has the largest shadow price? For how large an increase does this value hold?

(c) Describe the qualitative pattern in the solution of part (a).

(d) Use the pattern in (c) to trace the effects of increasing the demands at Tacoma, San Diego and Dallas by 100 simultaneously. How will the shipping schedule change? What will be the change in the optimal total cost?

(e) For how much of a change in demand in part (d) will the pattern persist?

4.4. Make or Buy   A sudden increase in the demand for smoke detectors has left Acme Alarms with insufficient capacity to meet demand. The company has seen monthly demand from its retailers for its electronic and battery-operated detectors rise to 20,000 and 10,000, respectively, and Acme wishes to continue meeting demand. Acme's production process involves three departments: Fabrication, Assembly and Shipping. The relevant quantitative data on production and prices are summarized below.

Department	Monthly hours available	Hours/unit (electronic)	Hours/unit (battery)
Fabrication	2000	0.15	0.10
Assembly	4200	0.20	0.20
Shipping	2500	0.10	0.15
Variable cost/unit		$18.80	$16.00
Retail price		$29.50	$28.00

The company also has the option of obtaining additional units from a subcontractor, who has offered to supply up to 20,000 units per month in any combination of electronic and battery operated models, at a charge of $21.50 per unit. For this price, the subcontractor will test and ship its models directly to the retailers without using Acme's production process.

(a) Determine how the manufacturer should allocate its in-house capacity and how it should utilize the subcontractor. What are the maximum profit and the corresponding make/buy levels? (This is a planning model; fractional decisions are acceptable.)

(b) Investigate the solution for Shipping capacities between 1200 and 2400 hours. Draw a graph showing how the optimal quantities change over this range.

(c) Describe the qualitative pattern in the solution of part (a).

(d) Use the pattern in (c) to trace the effects of increasing the Fabrication capacity by 10%. How will the optimal make/buy mix change? How will the optimal profit change?

(e) For how much of a change in Fabrication capacity will the pattern in (c) persist?

4.5. Selecting an Investment Portfolio   An investment manager wants to determine an optimal portfolio for a wealthy client. The fund has $2.5 million to invest, and its objective is to maximize total dollar return from both growth and dividends over the course of the coming year. The client has researched eight high-tech companies and wants the portfolio to consist of shares in these firms only. Three of the firms (S1–S3) are primarily software companies, three (H1–H3) are primarily hardware companies, and two (C1–C2) are internet consulting companies. The client has stipulated that no more than 40 percent of the investment be allocated to any one of these three sectors. To assure diversification, at least $100,000 must be invested in each of the eight stocks.

The table below gives estimates from the investment company's database relating to these stocks. These estimates include the price per share, the projected annual growth rate in the share price, and the anticipated annual dividend payment per share.

	Stock							
	S1	S2	S3	H1	H2	H3	C1	C2
Price per share	$40	$50	$80	$60	$45	$60	$30	$25
Growth rate	0.05	0.10	0.03	0.04	0.07	0.15	0.22	0.25
Dividend	$2.00	$1.50	$3.50	$3.00	$2.00	$1.00	$1.80	$0.00

You have been asked to develop an initial planning model (i.e., fractional outcomes for the decisions are acceptable).

(a) Determine the maximum return on the portfolio. What is the optimal number of shares to buy for each of the stocks? What is the corresponding dollar amount invested in each stock?

(b) Draw a graph that shows how the optimal dollar return varies with the minimum investment floor for the stocks (currently $100,000). Consider a range up to $300,000.

(c) Describe the qualitative pattern in the solution of part (a).

(d) Use the pattern in (c) to trace the effects of additional investment, beyond the original $2.5 million. How will the portfolio change? What is the marginal rate of return? Confirm this rate in the Sensitivity Report.

(e) For how much of a change in the investment quantity will the pattern in (c) persist?

4.6. College Expenses Revisited   Revisit the college expense planning network example of Chapter 3. Suppose the rates on the four investments A, B, C, and D have dropped to 5, 11, 18, and 55 percent, respectively. Suppose that the estimated yearly costs of college have been revised to 25, 27, 30, and 33.

(a) Determine the minimum investment that will cover college expenses.

(b) Use shadow price information to determine how much the initial investment would have to increase to cover an additional dollar of college expenses in the first year. Repeat for the second, third and fourth years.

(c) Describe the pattern in the optimal solution of part (a).

(d) Use the pattern in (c) to determine the marginal cost (of increased initial investment) that would be incurred to meet additional expenses in the first year of college.

(e) Repeat (d) for the second, third, and fourth years.

4.7. Leasing Warehouse Space   Cox Cable Company needs to lease warehouse storage space for five months at the start of the year. It knows how much space will be required in each month. However, since these space requirements are quite different, it may be economical to lease only the amount needed each month on a month-by-month basis. On the other hand, the monthly cost for leasing space for additional months is much less than for the first month, so it may be desirable to lease the maximum amount needed for the entire five months. Another option is the intermediate approach of changing the total amount of space leased (by adding a new lease and/or having an old lease expire) at least once but not every month. Two or more leases for different terms can begin at the same time.

The space requirements (in square feet) and the leasing costs (in dollars per thousand square feet) are given in the tables below.

Month	Space requirements	Lease length	Lease cost
Jan	15,000	1 month	$280
Feb	10,000	2	450
Mar	20,000	3	600
April	5000	4	730
May	25,000	5	820

The task is to find a leasing schedule that provides the necessary amounts of space at the minimum cost.

(a) Determine the optimal leasing schedule and the optimal total cost.

(b) Consider what happens when the cost of a 5-year lease (currently $820) changes. Construct a graph showing how total cost varies with the cost of a 5-year lease, over the range from $800 to $1000.

(c) Describe the qualitative pattern in the solution of part **(a)**.

(d) Use the pattern in **(c)** to trace the effects of increasing the space required for January. How will the leasing schedule change? How will the total cost change? Confirm this cost in the Sensitivity Report.

(e) For how much of a change in January's requirement will the pattern in **(c)** persist? Confirm this change in the Sensitivity Report.

4.8. Purchasing Components   American Electronics Corporation (AEC) is a leading manufacturer of networked computer systems and associated peripherals. Their product line consists of two families, the Desktop (DK) family and the Workstation (WS) family. Within each family, different models are for sale, as shown in the table of marketing data. In the table below, we find Marketing's estimates of the maximum demand potential in the coming quarter for some of the individual models and for each family. In addition, information is given on minimum demand levels, which represent sales contracts already signed with major distributors.

Model	Min. demand	Max. demand	Selling price
DK-1	–	1800	$3000
DK-2	600	–	2000
DK-3	–	300	1500
DK family		3600	
WS-1	500	–	1500
WS-2	400	–	800
WS family		2500	

AEC is a vertically integrated firm, manufacturing many of its key components in its own factories. Recently, AEC headquarters has learned from its Semiconductor Division that the supply of their new CPU chips is quite limited. In addition, the Memory Division has capacity to produce just a finite number of disk drives, even with a two-shift production schedule, and there is industry-wide rationing of memory chips (which AEC purchases externally). This information, in the form of quarterly supply quantities, along with information on the composition of the various products, is summarized in the table below.

Component	Usage in					Supply limit
	DK-1	DK-2	DK-3	WS-1	WS-2	
CPU chip	1	1	1	1	1	6000
Disk drives	1	2	1	2	1	9000
Memory chips	4	2	2	2	1	12,000

In order to help understand the problem they were facing, planners at AEC have asked you to build a linear programming model. Since AEC is following a program of no layoffs, and since nearly all production costs are fixed, the model should maximize revenue for the coming quarter, subject to supply and demand constraints.

(a) Determine the optimal product mix. What are the maximum revenue and the corresponding mix?

(b) Describe the qualitative pattern in the solution.

(c) Use the pattern in (b) to trace the effects of increasing the Disk Drive Supply capacity by 150. How will the product quantities change? How will the optimal profit change?

(d) For how much of a change in the Disk Drive Supply capacity will the pattern persist?

4.9. Production Planning for Automobiles   The Auto Company of America (ACA) produces four types of cars: subcompact, compact, intermediate and luxury. ACA also produces trucks and vans. Vendor capacities limit total production capacity to at most 1,200,000 vehicles per year. Subcompacts and compacts are built together in a facility with a total annual capacity of 620,000 cars. Intermediate and luxury cars are produced in another facility with capacity of 400,000; and the truck/van facility has a capacity of 275,000. ACA's marketing strategy requires that subcompacts and compacts must constitute at least half of the product mix for the four car types. Profit margins, market potential and fuel efficiencies are summarized below.

Type	Profit margin ($/vehicle)	Market potential (sales in 000s)	Fuel efficiency (MPG)
Subcompact	150	600	40
Compact	225	400	34
Intermediate	250	300	15
Luxury	500	225	12
Truck	400	325	20
Van	200	100	25

Current Corporate Average Fuel Efficiency (CAFE) standards require an average fleet fuel efficiency of at least 27 MPG. ACA would like to use a linear programming model to understand the implications of government and corporate policies on its production plans.

(a) Determine the optimal production plan for ACA. What is the maximum profit and the corresponding mix?

(b) Describe the qualitative pattern in the solution.

(c) Use the pattern in (b) to trace the effects of increasing market potential for all vehicle types by 10 units, simultaneously. How will the product quantities change? How will the optimal profit change?

(d) For how much of a simultaneous change in the demands will the pattern in (b) persist?

(e) Investigate how much annual profit would drop if the fuel efficiency requirement were raised above 27 MPG. Build a table showing the requirement and the optimal profit, with fuel efficiencies of 27 MPG through 32 MPG in steps of 1 MPG.

4.10. Production Planning with Environmental Constraints   You are the Operations Manager of Lovejoy Chemicals, Inc., which produces five products in a common production facility that will be subject to proposed Environmental Protection Agency (EPA) limits on particulate emissions. For each product, Lovejoy's sales potentials (demand levels that Lovejoy can capture) are expected to remain relatively flat for at least the next five years. Relevant data for each product are as follows. (Note: T denotes tons.)

Product	Sales potential (T/year)	Variable costs ($/T)	Revenues ($/T)	Particulate emissions (T/T produced)
A	2000	700	1000	0.0010
B	1600	600	800	0.0025
C	1000	1000	1500	0.0300
D	1000	1600	2000	0.0400
E	600	1300	1700	0.0250

Your production facility rotates through the product line, because it is capable of producing only one product at a time. The production rates differ for the various products due to processing needs. It takes 0.3 hours to make one ton of A, 0.5 hours for B, and one hour each to make a ton of C, D, or E. The facility can be operated up to 4000 hours each year.

The EPA has proposed a "bubble policy" for your industry. In this form of regulation, an imaginary bubble encloses the manufacturing facility and only total particulates that escape the bubble are regulated. This sort of policy replaces historical attempts by the EPA to micromanage emissions within a firm, and it allows Lovejoy to make any changes it wishes, provided the total particulate emissions from its facility are kept below certain limits. The current proposal is to phase-in strict particulate emissions limits over the next five years. These limits on total particulate emissions are shown in the table below.

Year	1	2	3	4	5
Allowable emissions (T/year)	Unlimited	80	60	40	20

One strategy for satisfying these regulations is to adjust the product mix, cutting back on production of some products if necessary. Lovejoy wishes to explore this strategy before contemplating the addition of new equipment.

(a) Determine the maximum profit Lovejoy can achieve from its product line in the coming year (Year 1). For each future year (Years 2–5), as emissions limits are imposed and tightened, what will Lovejoy's profits be?

(b) Describe the qualitative pattern in the solution.

(c) Suppose the EPA were to issue transferable emissions rights to firms in the industry. Use the pattern in (b) to determine how much Lovejoy would be willing to pay in Year 4 to be allowed to emit one extra ton of particulates above the proposed limit.

4.11. Oil Distribution Texxon Oil Distributors, Inc., has three active oil wells in a west Texas oil field. Well 1 has a capacity of 93 thousand barrels per day (TBD), Well 2 can produce 88 TBD and Well 3 can produce 95 TBD. The company has five refineries along the Gulf Coast, all of which have been operating at stable demand levels. In addition, three pump stations have been built to move the oil along the pipelines from the wells to the refineries. Oil can flow from any one of the wells to any of the pump stations, and from any one of the pump stations to any of the refineries, and Texxon is looking for a minimum-cost schedule. The refineries' requirements are as follows.

Refinery	R1	R2	R3	R4	R5
Requirement (TBD)	30	57	48	91	48

The company's cost accounting system recognizes charges by the segment of pipeline that is used. These daily costs are given in the tables below, in dollars per thousand barrels.

	To	Pump A	Pump B	Pump C
	Well 1	1.52	1.60	1.40
From	Well 2	1.70	1.63	1.55
	Well 3	1.45	1.57	1.30

	To	R1	R2	R3	R4	R5
	Pump A	5.15	5.69	6.13	5.63	5.80
From	Pump B	5.12	5.47	6.05	6.12	5.71
	Pump C	5.32	6.16	6.25	6.17	5.87

(a) Determine the least costly way of supplying oil from the wells to the refineries.

(b) Describe the qualitative pattern in the solution.

(c) Use the pattern in (b) to trace the effects of increasing the demands at R1 and R2 by the same quantity simultaneously. How will the shipping schedule change? How will the total cost change?

(d) For how much of a change in demand will the pattern in (b) persist?

4.12. Selecting a Portfolio   A portfolio manager has developed a list of six investment alternatives for a multiyear horizon. These are: Treasury bills, Common stock, Corporate bonds, Real estate, Growth funds, and Savings & Loans. These investments and their various financial factors are described below. In the table, the length represents the estimated number of years required for the annual rate of return to be realized. The annual rate of return is the expected rate over the multiyear horizon. The risk coefficient is a subjective estimate representing the manager's appraisal of the relative safety of each alternative, on a scale of 10. The growth potential is also a subjective estimate of the potential increase in value over the horizon.

	Portfolio data					
Alternative	TB	CS	CB	RE	GF	SL
Length	4	7	8	6	10	5
Annual return (%)	6	15	12	24	18	9
Risk coefficient	1	5	4	8	6	3
Growth potential (%)	0	18	10	32	20	7

The manager wishes to maximize the annual rate of return on a $3 million portfolio, subject to the following restrictions.

The weighted average length should not exceed 7 years.

The weighted average risk coefficient should not exceed 5.

The weighted average growth potential should be at least 10 percent.

The investment in real estate should be no more than twice the investment in stocks and bonds (i.e., in CS, CB, and GF) combined.

(a) What is the optimal return (as a percentage) and the optimal allocation of investment funds?

(b) What is the marginal rate of return, as indicated by the shadow price information in the Sensitivity Report? Confirm this marginal rate by raising the investment amount slightly and re-solving the linear program.

4.13. Coffee Blending and Sales   Hill-O-Beans Coffee Company blends four component beans into three final blends of coffee: One is sold to luxury hotels, another to restaurants, and the third to supermarkets for store-label brands. The company has four reliable bean supplies: Argentine Abundo, Peruvian Colmado, Brazilian Maximo, and Chilean Saboro. The table below summarizes the very precise recipes for the final coffee blends, the cost and availability information for the four components, and the wholesale price per pound of the final blends. The percentages indicate the fraction of each component to be used in each blend.

Component (lb)	Hotel	Rest	Market	Cost per pound	Max weekly availability
Abundo	20%	35%	10%	$0.60	40,000
Colmado	40%	15%	35%	$0.80	25,000
Maximo	15%	20%	40%	$0.55	20,000
Saboro	25%	30%	15%	$0.70	45,000
Wholesale price Per pound	$1.25	$1.50	$1.40		

The processor's plant can handle no more than 100,000 pounds per week, and Hill-O-Beans would like to operate at capacity. There is no problem in selling the final blends, although the Marketing Department requires minimum production levels of 10,000, 25,000, and 30,000 pounds, respectively, for the hotel, restaurant, and market blends.

(a) In order to maximize weekly profit, how many pounds of each component should be purchased?

(b) What is the shadow price (from the Sensitivity Report) on the availability of Maximo beans?

(c) How much (per pound) should Hill-O-Beans be willing to pay for additional pounds of Maximo beans in order to raise total profit?

4.14. Production Planning for Components   Rummel Electronics produces two PC cards, a modem and a network adapter. Demand for these two products exceeds the amount that the firm can make, but there are no plans to increase production capacity in the short run. Instead, the firm plans to use subcontracting.

The two main stages of production are fabrication and assembly, and either step can be subcontracted for either type of card. However, the company policy is not to subcontract both steps for either product. (That is, if modem cards are fabricated by a subcontractor, then they must be assembled in-house.) Components made by subcontractors must pass through the shipping and receiving departments, just like components made internally. At present, the firm has 5200 hours available in fabrication, 3600 in assembly and 3200 in shipping/inspection. The production requirements, in hours per unit, are given in the following table:

Product/mode	Fab.	Asy.	Ship.
Modem, made entirely in-house	0.35	0.16	0.08
Network, made entirely in-house	0.47	0.15	0.12
Modem, fabricated by sub	–	0.18	0.10
Network, fabricated by sub	–	0.16	0.15
Modem, assembled by sub	0.35	–	0.09
Network, assembled by sub	0.47	–	0.14

The direct material costs for the modem cards are $3.25 for manufacturing and $0.50 for assembly; for network cards, the costs are $6.10 and $0.50. Subcontracting the manufacturing operation costs $5.35 for modem cards and $8.50 for network cards. Subcontracting the assembly operation costs $1.50 for either product. Modem cards sell for $20, and network cards sell for $28. The firm's policy, for each product, is that at most 40 percent of the units produced can have subcontracted fabrication, and at most 70 percent of the units can have subcontracted assembly.

(a) Determine the production and subcontracting schedule that will maximize profits. How many units of each product should be sold, in the optimal plan? What volume should the subcontractor handle?

(b) If 100 hours of overtime could be scheduled, which department(s) should be allocated the overtime. (Use the Sensitivity Report to justify your answer.)

4.15. Make/Buy Planning   The CammTex Fabric Mill is in the process of deciding on a production schedule. It wishes to know how to weave the various fabrics it will produce during the coming quarter. The sales department has confirmed orders for each of the 15 fabrics that are produced by CammTex. These quarterly demands are given in the table below. Also tabulated is the variable cost for each fabric. The mill operates continuously during the quarter: 13 weeks, 7 days a week, and 24 hours a day.

There are two types of looms: dobbie and regular. Dobbie looms can make all fabrics, and they are the only looms that can weave certain fabrics such as plaids. The production rate for each fabric on each type of loom is also given in the table. (If the production rate is zero, the fabric cannot be woven on that type of loom.) CammTex has 90 regular looms and 15 dobbie looms.

Fabrics woven at CammTex proceed to the finishing department in the mill and then are sold. Any fabrics that are not woven in the mill because of limited capacity will be subcontracted to an outside producer and sold at the selling price. The cost of purchasing from the subcontractor is also given in the table.

Fabric	Demand (Yd)	Dobbie (Yd/Hr)	Regular (Yd/Hr)	Mill cost ($/Yd)	Sub. cost ($/Yd)
1	16,500	4.653	0.00	0.6573	0.80
2	52,000	4.653	0.00	0.555	0.70
3	45,000	4.653	0.00	0.655	0.85
4	22,000	4.653	0.00	0.5542	0.70
5	76,500	5.194	5.313	0.6097	0.75
6	110,000	3.767	3.809	0.6153	0.75
7	122,000	4.055	4.185	0.6477	0.80
8	62,000	5.208	5.232	0.488	0.60
9	7500	5.208	5.232	0.5029	0.70
10	69,000	5.208	5.232	0.4351	0.60
11	70,000	3.652	3.733	0.6417	0.80
12	82,000	4.007	4.185	0.5675	0.75
13	10,000	4.291	4.439	0.4952	0.65
14	380,000	5.208	5.232	0.3128	0.45
15	62,000	4.004	4.185	0.5029	0.70

(a) What is minimum total cost of production and purchasing for CammTex?

(b) Construct a table showing how the optimal total cost varies with the number of Dobbie looms available, in the range 10–18.

(c) Describe the qualitative pattern in the solution of part (a).

(d) Use the pattern in (c) to trace the effect on the optimal cost of increasing demand for fabric 6 by 100 yards.

(e) Repeat (d) for fabric 5.

(f) Repeat (d) for fabric 4.

4.16. Cash Planning   A startup investment project needs money to cover its cash flow needs. The cash income and expenditures for the period January through April are as follows.

	Jan	Feb	Mar	Apr	Total
Cash flow ($000)	−150	−450	500	250	150

At the beginning of May all excess cash will be paid out to investors. There are two ways to finance the project. One is the possibility of taking out a long-term loan at the beginning of January. The interest on this loan is 1 percent per month, payable on the first of the month for the next three months. This loan can be as large as $400,000; the principal is due April 1; and no prepayment is permitted. The alternative is a short-term loan that can be taken out at the beginning of each month. This loan must be paid back at the beginning of the following month with 1.2 percent interest. A maximum of $300,000 may be used for this short-term loan in any month. In addition, there is the possibility of investing in a money-market fund at the start of each month. This fund will pay 0.7 percent interest at the beginning of the following month.

Assume the following about the timing of cash flows.

- For months in which there is a net cash deficit, there must be sufficient funds on hand at the *start* of the month to cover the net outflow.
- For months in which there is a net cash surplus, the net inflow cannot be used until the *end* of the month (i.e., the start of the next month).

(a) What is the maximum amount that can be returned to investors?

(b) Describe the pattern in the optimal solution.

(c) Use the pattern in **(b)** to derive the cost of funds for each month in the planning period. That is, if there is a $1000 change in the cash flows for any month, what would be the dollar change in the amount returned to investors?

(d) Show how the shadow prices in the Sensitivity Report can be used to confirm the answers in **(c)**.

Case: Cox Cable and Wire Company

Meredith Ceh breathed a sigh of relief. Finally, all the necessary figures seemed to be correctly in place, and her spreadsheet looked complete. She was confident that she could analyze the situation that John Cox had described, but she wondered if there were other concerns she should be addressing in her response.

Mr Cox, president of Cox Cable and Wire Company, and grandson of the company's founder, had asked Meredith to come up with plans to support the preliminary contract he had worked out with Midwest Telephone Company. The contract called for delivery of 340 reels of cable during the summer. He was leaving the next day to negotiate a final contract with Midwest and wanted to be sure he understood all of the implications.

According to Mr Cox, he had been looking for a chance to become a supplier to a large company like Midwest, and this seemed to be the right opportunity. Demand from some of Cox Cable's traditional customers had slackened, and as a result there was excess capacity during the summer. Nevertheless, he wanted to be sure that, from the start, his dealings with Midwest would be profitable, and he had told Meredith that he was looking for a profitability target of at least 25 percent. He also wanted her to confirm that there was sufficient capacity to meet the terms of the contract. He had quickly mentioned a number of other items, but those were secondary to profitability and capacity.

Background

The Cox Cable and Wire Company sold a variety of products for the telecommunications industry. At its Indianapolis plant, the company purchased uncoated wire in standard gauges, assembled it into multiwire cables, and then applied various coatings according to customer specification. The plant essentially made products in two basic families—standard plastic and high quality Teflon. The two coatings came in a variety of colors, but these were changed easily by introducing different dyes into the basic coating liquid.

The production facilities at Indianapolis consisted of two independent process trains (semi-automated production lines), referred to as the General and National trains, after the companies that manufactured them. Both plastic-coated and the Teflon-coated cable could be produced on either process train; however, Teflon coating was a faster process due to curing requirements. Planning at Cox Cable was usually done on an annual and then a quarterly basis. The labor force was determined by analyzing forecast demand for the coming year, although revisions were possible as the year developed. Then, on a quarterly basis, more specific machine schedules were made up. Each quarter the process trains were usually shut down for planned maintenance, but the maintenance schedules were determined at the last minute, after production plans were in place, and they were often postponed when the schedule was tight.

Due to recent expansions, there was not much storage space in the plant. Cable could temporarily be stored in the shipping area for the purposes of loading trucks, but there was no space for cable to be stored for future deliveries. Additional inventory space was available at a nearby public warehouse.

Meredith had become familiar with all of this information during her first week as a summer intern. At the end of the week, she had met with Mr Cox and he had outlined the Midwest contract negotiation.

The Contract

The preliminary contract was straightforward. Midwest had asked for the delivery quantities outlined in Exhibit 4.1. Prices had also been agreed on, although Mr. Cox had said he wouldn't be surprised to find Midwest seeking to raise the Teflon delivery requirements during the final negotiation.

Meredith had gone first to the Production Manager, Jeff Knight, for information about capacity. Jeff had provided her with data on production times (Exhibit 4.2), which he said were pretty reliable, given the company's extensive experience with the two process trains. He also gave her the existing production commitments for the summer months, showing the available capacity given in Exhibit 4.3. Not all of these figures were fixed, he said. Apparently, there was a design for a mechanism that could speed up the General process train. Engineers at Cox Cable planned to install this mechanism in September, adding 80 hours per month to capacity. "We could move up our plans, so that the additional 80 hours would be available to the shop in August," he remarked. "But that would probably run about $900 in overtime expenses, and I'm not sure if it would be worthwhile."

EXHIBIT 4.1	Contract Delivery Schedule and Prices	
Month	Plastic	Teflon
June	50	30
July	100	60
August	50	50
Price	$360	$400

EXHIBIT 4.2	Production Capabilities, in Hours per Reel	
Process train	Plastic	Teflon
General	2.0	1.5
National	2.5	2.0

EXHIBIT 4.3	*Unscheduled Production Hours*	
Month	General	National
June	140	250
July	60	80
August	150	100

EXHIBIT 4.4	*Accounting Data for Production*	
Cost category	General	National
Machine Depr.	$50.00/hr	$40.00/hr
Direct labor	16.00	16.00
Supervisor	8.00	8.00
Production Ohd	12.00	12.00

After putting some of this information into her spreadsheet, Meredith spoke with the plant's Controller, Donna Malone, who had access to most of the necessary cost data. Meredith learned that the material in the cables cost $160 per reel for the plastic-coated cable, and $200 for the Teflon-coated cable. Packaging costs were $40 for either type of cable, and the inventory costs at the public warehouse came to $10 per reel for each month stored. "That's if you can get the space," Donna commented. "It's a good idea to make reservations a few weeks in advance, otherwise we might find they're temporarily out of space." Donna also provided standard accounting data on production costs (Exhibit 4.4). According to Donna, about half of the production overhead consisted of costs that usually varied with labor charges, while the rest was depreciation for equipment other than the two process trains. The machine depreciation charges were broken out separately, as determined at the time the machinery was purchased. For example, the General process train originally cost $500,000 and, for tax purposes, had an expected life of five years, or about 10,000 hours; hence its depreciation rate of $50 per hour.

The Analysis

Meredith was able to consolidate all of the information she collected into a spreadsheet (Exhibit 4.5).[3] Making what she felt were reasonable assumptions about relevant cost factors, she was able to optimize the production plan, and she determined that it should be possible to meet the 25 percent profitability target. Nevertheless, there seemed to be several factors in it that were subject to change—things that had come up in her various conversations, such as maintenance, warehousing, and the possibility of modifying the contract. She expected that Mr Cox would quiz her about all of these factors, and she knew it would be important for her to be prepared for his questions.

---

[3]The spreadsheet can be found at the book's website: www.mba.tuck.dartmouth.edu/opt/.

Chapter 5

Linear Programming: Data Envelopment Analysis

Chapters 2 and 3 examined the basic types of structures that appear in formulations of linear programs—allocation, covering, blending, and network models. Not every application of linear programming can be classified as one of those four types, but most applications resemble one or more of them. In this chapter, we look at a type of linear program that has a special application and a special kind of interpretation. This type is associated with *Data Envelopment Analysis*, or DEA. For classification purposes, the DEA model is essentially an allocation model, but its unique applications make it an important type of model to study in its own right.

As the examples in Chapters 2 and 3 indicated, linear programming is typically used as an *ex ante* tool in planning, that is, as an aid in choosing among alternative possible courses of action. In DEA, linear programming is used as an *ex post* tool, to evaluate performance that has already been observed. Compared to other linear programming applications, DEA is a relative newcomer. The first articles on the methodology began appearing in the mid-1970s, and researchers have been elaborating the theory ever since. As recognition of DEA has spread, the technique has been applied in a variety of settings, such as public schools, courts of law, hospitals, oil and gas production, vehicle maintenance, and banking.

The primary elements in a DEA study are a set of *decision-making units* (DMUs), along with their measured inputs and outputs. The DMUs may be different branches of the same large bank, or different hospitals in the same region or different offices of the same insurance company, but they should be reasonably homogeneous and separately managed. In the ideal case, the DMUs have a well defined set of common inputs and outputs.

The purpose of DEA is to determine which of the DMUs make efficient use of their inputs and which do not. For the inefficient units, the analysis can actually quantify what levels of improved performance should be attainable. In addition, the analysis indicates where an inefficient DMU might look for benchmarking help as it searches for ways to improve.

Optimization Modeling with Spreadsheets, *Second Edition*. Kenneth R. Baker

DEA produces a single, comprehensive measure of performance for each of the DMUs. If the situation were simple, and there were just one input and one output, then we would define performance as the ratio of output to input, and we would likely refer to this ratio as "productivity" or "efficiency." The best ratio among all the DMUs would identify the most efficient DMU, and every other DMU would be rated by comparing its ratio to the best one. As an example, suppose that we have been hired as consultants to the White River Dairy Cooperative.

EXAMPLE 5.1   *The White River Dairy Cooperative*

Five dairy farms make up the White River Dairy Cooperative. The farms are similar in that they all produce just one product—milk. Furthermore, the major resource for the farms is their cows. Last month's activity is summarized in the following table.

	Cows	Milk	Productivity	Efficiency
Farm 1	15	60	4.0	0.80
Farm 2	10	48	4.8	0.96
Farm 3	20	70	3.5	0.70
Farm 4	12	60	5.0	1.00
Farm 5	16	72	4.5	0.90

Using the data in this table, our task is to identify efficient and inefficient dairy farms.   ■

In this example, productivity is calculated as the ratio of milk produced to cows owned, or output divided by input. The efficiency rating in the table is just a normalized measure of the same thing. In other words, the value of 1.00 is assigned to the maximum productivity in the set (for Farm 4), and the remaining values are calculated as the ratio of each farm's productivity to the maximum productivity in the set.

Without access to detailed knowledge about the operation of each farm, we might infer that Farm 4 has achieved its maximum efficiency rating because of factors such as the following.

- Investment in the latest milking equipment (Technology).
- Adherence to a regular maintenance schedule (Procedures).
- Incentives for worker quality and productivity (Management).

Something about these categories of factors is probably lacking at the other farms. For instance, if Farm 1 could employ the same technology, procedures, and management as Farm 4, then we would expect that with 15 cows, it should be able to achieve a milk output of 75. (This target figure is the productivity of the best farm multiplied by the number of cows at Farm 1. This output target can also be computed as the actual output for Farm 1 divided by the efficiency of Farm 1.) Alternatively, we would expect that the same milk output of 60 should be achievable with only 12 cows (obtained by multiplying the input by the efficiency). In any event, the comparative analysis provides two kinds of information for Farm 1: First, its productivity could be as much as 25 percent higher than it actually was, and second, it could probably learn a lot by studying—and even imitating—the operation of Farm 4.

In more practical cases, a DMU is characterized by outputs and inputs. Productivity is still a ratio, usually a weighted sum of the outputs divided by a weighted sum of the inputs. When more than one output exists, we need to use weights in order to value a combination of outputs and quantify them in a single number. The same holds for inputs. When we can quantify the value of outputs and inputs in a single number, then we can take their ratio and compute a productivity measure. We can also normalize that value by comparing it to productivities of other DMUs and scale the results so that the best value is 1. By relying on efficiency, DEA is useful when no single output metric captures performance comprehensively and when some measure of outputs relative to inputs seems appropriate. This makes DEA a valuable tool for situations in which several dimensions of performance are important.

DEA has often been applied in nonprofit industries, characterized by multiple outputs of interest and some ambiguity about the relative importance of those outputs. For example, in comparing the performance of mental health clinics, it might be difficult to place relative values on services for domestic abuse and drug addiction. DEA is well suited to this type of situation because it does not require importance weights for the various outputs (or inputs) to be established beforehand. Instead, as we shall see, it determines the weights in the analysis and allows each DMU to be evaluated in its best possible light.

Even in for-profit industries, a total profit figure may not be adequate for evaluating productivity. In the case of branch banks, which we use for the purposes of illustration, suppose that profit is entirely determined by loan and deposit balances. In the short run, fluctuations in the profit margins for loans or deposits may influence a branch's profits, but short-run profits may not indicate how productive the branch has been at developing and managing loans and deposits. In addition, short-run profits at a particular time may not indicate how well the branch will perform when the market shifts and margins change. Therefore, a gross profit figure may not be the best measure of branch productivity. Instead, DEA combines the loan and deposit balances into a single output measure, considering every possible ratio of profit margins, and chooses the margins that are most favorable to the branch being evaluated. Then, having chosen a favorable set of loan and deposit margins for each branch, the DEA program rates the efficiency of each branch on a scale of 0 to 1.

5.1. A GRAPHICAL PERSPECTIVE ON DEA

To illustrate the use of weighted averages in DEA, we move from the one-input, one-output case of dairy farms to a simplified one-input, two-output case involving branch banks. This time, we illustrate the analysis with a graphical approach.

EXAMPLE 5.2   *Metropolis National Bank*

Metropolis National Bank operates five branches around the city. The branches all offer the same services and rely on identical mixes of labor and capital. As a result, the cost of operation is the same at each branch, although their profiles of loans and deposits differ. The following table summarizes the level of branch performance for the previous quarter.

DMU	Expense	Loans	Deposits	Efficiency
Branch 1	100	10	31	1.00
Branch 2	100	15	25	0.83
Branch 3	100	20	30	1.00
Branch 4	100	23	23	0.92
Branch 5	100	30	20	1.00

In the table, last quarter's inputs are represented by total expenses (in thousands of dollars), which happen to be identical for the branches. The table also provides the levels of activity in loans and deposits, shown separately. Loan and deposit levels are expressed in millions of dollars, averaged over the previous quarter.   ■

As shown in the table, Branches 1, 3, and 5 have the highest efficiency rating of 1; therefore, they are classified as efficient. An efficiency rating of 1 means that we can find a pair of weights on loans and deposits for which the branch would be the most productive branch in the system. For instance, suppose the weights are 3 for loans and 33 for deposits. Then the weighted values of outputs for the branches are as follows.

DMU	Loans	Deposits	Value
Branch 1	10	31	1053
Branch 2	15	25	870
Branch 3	20	30	1050
Branch 4	23	23	828
Branch 5	30	20	750

In this comparison, Branch 1 has the highest value. For the pair of weights (3, 33), Branch 1 is the most productive DMU on the list. On the other hand, if the weights were (12, 10), then Branch 5 would be the most productive. As long as we can find at least one set of weights for which Branch 1 achieves the highest value, then Branch 1 is classified as efficient. Later, we impose some restrictions on the weights chosen.

For Branches 2 and 4, the story is different: No possible weights exist on loans and deposits that would make these branches the most productive. For Branch 2, this is easy to see, because it is "dominated" by Branch 3—that is, Branch 3 performs better on both dimensions than Branch 2. Since the input expenses are the same, whatever weights we choose for loans and deposits, Branch 3 will show a higher total value than Branch 2 and therefore greater productivity. The case of Branch 4, however, is less clear. No other branch dominates Branch 4, yet it is still inefficient because no pair of weights can give Branch 4 the highest output value.

Figure 5.1 displays the output for each branch as a point on a two-dimensional graph. Thus, Branch 1 corresponds to the point (10, 31) in the figure. The points are labeled by branch number.

For any inefficient branch, such as Branch 4, the DEA procedure creates a *Hypothetical Comparison Unit* (HCU) that is built from the features of efficient units. These efficient DMUs are referred to as the *reference set* for the inefficient branch. In the case of Branch 4, the reference set is made up of Branches 3 and 5, and the comparison unit corresponds to the point (25, 25) in Figure 5.2. We can form the comparison unit by adding 0.5 times the profile (inputs and outputs) of Branch 3 and 0.5 times the profile of Branch 5

$$
\begin{array}{rl}
0.5 \text{ (Branch 3 Data)} = 0.5 \ (100 & 20 \quad 30) \\
0.5 \text{ (Branch 5 Data)} = 0.5 \ (100 & 30 \quad 20) \\
\hline
\text{HCU Data} = \quad (100 & 25 \quad 25)
\end{array}
$$

Thus, we obtain a hypothetical branch with an input of 100 and with outputs of 25 (loans) and 25 (deposits). Graphically, the point (25, 25), labeled 4′, lies on the straight line connecting points 3 and 5, as shown in Figure 5.2. Among all the points on the line (i.e., all linear combinations of 3 and 5), 4′ is the only one that contains the same ratio of loans and deposits as that of Branch 4. Thus, we can think of the comparison unit as producing the same product mix, but producing

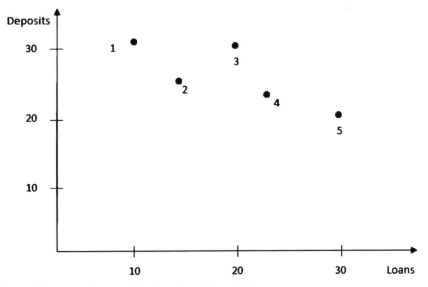

Figure 5.1. Outputs for each of the branches in Example 5.2.

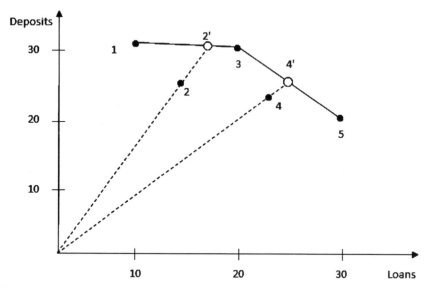

Figure 5.2. Outputs for the HCUs in Example 5.2.

more of it than Branch 4. Consequently, the comparison unit dominates Branch 4, even though there is no actual branch that does.

For Branch 2, the HCU corresponds to the point (18.1, 30.2), labeled 2′ in Figure 5.2. Although we noted that Branch 2 is dominated by Branch 3, this comparison unit does not correspond to point 3 because the output mix for Branch 3 is different from the mix for Branch 2. The hypothetical point 2′, however, has a deposits-to-loans ratio of 25:15, which matches the ratio for Branch 2, but with greater output. Furthermore, the point 2′ lies on the line connecting points 1 and 3, so that Branches 1 and 3 form the reference set for Branch 2.

In the DEA approach, we presume that an inefficient branch can improve its performance by emulating one or more of the efficient branches in its reference set. In the case of Branch 2, that would mean emulating aspects of Branches 1 and 3, the components of its HCU. In the case of Branch 4, that would mean emulating aspects of Branches 3 and 5.

The efficiency measure also has a geometric interpretation in Figure 5.2. The distance from the origin to the point representing Branch 4 is 92 percent of the distance from the origin to 4′. This percentage matches the efficiency of Branch 4. Similarly, the point representing Branch 2 is located 82.8 percent of the way from the origin to 2′.

Under our definition of efficiency, Branch 1 is efficient although it has far less loan activity than Branch 3 and only minimally larger deposits. Similarly, a branch with $1 more in deposits than Branch 1 and no loans at all would also be efficient. That is because we can conceive of a set of weights for loans and deposits that would make such a branch the most productive of all the branches. In particular, if deposits were very profitable for the bank, and loans were not very profitable, then the branch with \$1 more in deposits would have a more valuable total output in terms of profitability. Such a profitability relationship might be very unlikely, but it is still possible. Thus, when we use DEA, we deal with a theoretical notion of efficiency—based on what is conceivable, not what is likely.

Spotting dominance in our example does not require DEA. We can simply scan the data if we want to detect dominance. However, as the number of outputs and inputs increases, a dominance relationship like the one between Branches 2 and 3 becomes less likely. Consequently, direct comparisons do not reveal many inefficient DMUs, and DEA becomes more valuable. Once we proceed beyond two outputs, geometric analyses are difficult or impossible, and we lose the intuition that it provides. For larger problems, we need an algebraic approach. In fact, even with two outputs, the graphical approach is limited. Our branch bank example was simplified because identical inputs existed for all branches. If there were differences in the inputs, then the graphical display of outputs would not convey the full comparison. In general, DEA relies on an algebraic approach, and, as we shall see, on linear programming.

5.2. AN ALGEBRAIC PERSPECTIVE ON DEA

In order to describe a generic DEA model in algebraic terms, we let

$$x_{ik} = i\text{th input quantity for DMU}(k)$$
$$y_{jk} = j\text{th output quantity for DMU}(k)$$

The x- and y-values represent given information. In our branch bank example, for Branch 1 (or $k = 1$), we have

$$x_{11} = 1\text{st input quantity for Branch } 1 = 100$$
$$y_{11} = 1\text{st output quantity for Branch } 1 = 10$$
$$y_{21} = 2\text{nd output quantity for Branch } 1 = 31$$

Next, we define the weights, which play the role of decisions in the model

$$v_i = \text{weight for the } i\text{th input}$$
$$u_j = \text{weight for the } j\text{th output}$$

If there were one output and one input, as in the case of milk and cows, we could measure productivity as y_k/x_k and then normalize this measure to compute efficiency. We would have no need for weights at all. When there are two outputs, as in the example of branch banks, we need weights to calculate an aggregate value for the outputs. In the case of loans and deposits, there could well be actual profit margins, reflecting market prices, that we could use for weights; but in other settings, there may not be a market price for all of the relevant outputs. For that reason, we refer to weights rather than to prices as a means of valuing inputs and outputs. As we shall see, the weights are obtained from the data, that is, they are determined intrinsically.

When there is more than one output, we use Y_k to denote the weighted value of outputs. That is, we let

$$Y_k = u_1 y_{1k} + u_2 y_{2k} + u_3 y_{3k} + \cdots$$

Suppose that in the branch bank example, the weights selected are $u_1 = 0.2$ and $u_2 = 0.3$. Then the output value for Branch 1 is $0.2(10) + 0.3(31) = 11.3$. Similarly, we use X_k to denote the weighted value of the inputs, where

$$X_k = v_1 x_{1k} + v_2 x_{2k} + v_3 x_{3k} + \cdots$$

Suppose that in the branch bank example, we take $v_1 = 0.1$. Then the input value for Branch 1 is $0.1(100) = 10$. For an arbitrary set of nonnegative weights, we can compute productivity as the ratio of the weighted value of outputs to the weighted value of inputs. With the values of u_1, u_2, and v_1 just mentioned, the productivity measure for Branch 1 would be $11.3/10 = 1.13$. With those weights, the best productivity among the five branches is 1.30 for Branch 3. Therefore, the efficiency for Branch 1 would be calculated as $1.13/1.3 = 0.869$. Later, we will constrain the weights so that they normalize the measure of productivity. This means that the highest productivity measure in the comparison is 1. With normalizing weights, we define efficiency as $E_k = Y_k/X_k$, where the capital letters are shorthand for weighted sums.

The performance of a particular DMU is considered efficient if the performance of other DMUs does not provide evidence that one of its inputs or outputs could be improved without worsening some of its other inputs or outputs. In other words, the performance is efficient if it is impossible to construct a HCU that does better.

In our notation, the subscript k refers to the kth DMU. Our approach will be to choose a particular DMU for evaluation and to denote it with the subscript $k = 0$. But this same DMU will still be included among the values of $k > 0$.

Now we can give an outline of the steps in DEA.

- Select a particular DMU to be the focus of the analysis and refer to it as DMU(0).
- Choose (u_j, v_i) so that they maximize the ratio E_0. In other words, choose the weights that are most favorable to the mix of inputs and outputs belonging to DMU(0), but use one set of weights for evaluating all DMUs.
- Normalize the measure of productivity by requiring that $Y_k/X_k \leq 1$ for all DMUs. In other words, the value of the output can never be greater than the value of the input. Since DMU(0) corresponds to one of the DMU(k), the largest value E_0 could achieve is 1.
- If the ratio Y_0/X_0 is equal to 1, then DMU(0) is classified as efficient; that is, we have found a set of weights for which its outputs are at least as valuable as the outputs of any other DMU would be with the same inputs.

- If this ratio is less than 1, then DMU(0) is said to be inefficient; that is, for even the most favorable choice of weights, there will be some other DMU, or weighted combination of DMUs, that achieves higher productivity.

In the next section, we implement these steps using a spreadsheet model.

5.3. A SPREADSHEET MODEL FOR DEA

We can use a standard linear programming format to implement a spreadsheet model for DEA. We begin by entering a table containing the data in the problem. Usually, this table will have columns corresponding to inputs and outputs, and rows corresponding to DMUs. Figure 5.3 shows this layout for the branch bank example. The decision variables are the weights for inputs and outputs. The decision variable cells appear below the table containing the data, in the highlighted cells C12:E12.

First, we fix the weighted value of the inputs, arbitrarily, at $X_0 = 1$. In the spreadsheet, this equation is enforced by requiring that cell F16 must equal H16. Moreover, because of the form of X_0, it is easily expressed as a SUMPRODUCT of input weights

	A	B	C	D	E	F	G	H
1	Data Envelopment Analysis							
2	Branch Bank Example							
3								
4	Data	Branch	Expense	Loans	Deposits			
5		1	100	10	31			
6		2	100	15	25			
7		3	100	20	30			
8		4	100	23	23			
9		5	100	30	20			
10								
11				Analysis for Branch 1				
12	Decisions		0.01	0	0.032258			
13	Objective			10	31	1.000		
14								
15	Constraints							
16		Input value	100	0	0	1	=	1
17		Normalizing 1	-100	10	31	0.00000	<=	0
18		Normalizing 2	-100	15	25	-0.19355	<=	0
19		Normalizing 3	-100	20	30	-0.03226	<=	0
20		Normalizing 4	-100	23	23	-0.25806	<=	0
21		Normalizing 5	-100	30	20	-0.35484	<=	0
22								

Branch1

Figure 5.3. Model for Branch 1 in Example 5.2.

(v_i) and input values (x_{i0}). This equality constraint is just a scaling step; we could set the input value equal to any number we like. Having fixed the weighted input value X_0 in the denominator of Y_0/X_0, it follows that maximizing the ratio E_0 amounts to maximizing Y_0, the weighted value of the outputs. Now, Y_0 can be expressed as a SUMPRODUCT of output weights (u_j) and output values (y_{j0}). The value of Y_0, which plays the role of an objective function, is located in cell F13. Therefore, we have a maximization problem in which the objective function is the weighted output value and the weighted input value is constrained to equal 1.

Next, we adopt the convention that the efficiency of a DMU cannot exceed 1. This convention reflects the sense that "perfect" efficiency is 100 percent, and we saw this convention used earlier in Examples 5.1 and 5.2. This requirement is just a way of ensuring that the value of the output can never be greater than the value of the input. In symbols, we write $Y_k/X_k \leq 1$, for every k representing a DMU, or equivalently, $Y_k - X_k \leq 0$. These *normalizing conditions* become the remaining constraints of the model.

These steps lead to a relatively simple linear programming model. The form of the model can be expressed as follows.

Maximize Y_0

subject to:

$$X_0 = 1 \qquad \text{scaling of the input value (one constraint)}$$
$$-X_k + Y_k \leq 0 \quad \text{efficiency no greater than 1, for each DMU}(k)$$

Figure 5.3 shows the spreadsheet for the analysis, using the standard format for an allocation model. The objective function in this model corresponds to the output value of Branch 1, computed by a SUMPRODUCT formula in cell F13. The equation that fixes the value of inputs appears in row 16, and the normalizing constraints (requiring that output values never exceed input values) can be found in rows 17–21.

The model specification is as follows

Objective:	F13 (maximize)
Variables:	C12:E12
Constraints:	F16 = H16
	F17:F24 $\leq$ H17:H21

When we run Solver, we obtain an objective function of 1.00, as shown in the figure, along with the following weights,

Input	Expense weight (v_1)	0.01
Output	Loans weight (u_1)	0.00
Output	Deposits weight (u_2)	0.032258

With these weights, the input value is $X_0 = 1.0$ and the output value is $Y_0 = 1.0$ for Branch 1, resulting in an efficiency of 100 percent. In the solution, cells F18:F21 all show negative values. This means that the output value is strictly less than the input value for each of the other DMUs. Since the input values are identical in this example, it follows that none of the other DMUs can achieve the productivity of Branch 1 at its most favorable weights (0, 0.032258).

Figure 5.4 shows the analysis for Branch 2. The format is the same as the format for Branch 1, and only two changes occur. First, the objective function now contains data for Branch 2 in row 13. Second, the coefficients for the constraint on input value contain data for Branch 2 in row 16. (In this example, that change does not actually alter row 16, but in other examples, it could.) Otherwise, the parameters of the linear program remain unchanged from the analysis for Branch 1. When we run Solver on this model, we obtain an objective function of 0.828, as shown in the figure, along with the following weights.

Input	Expense weight (v_1)	0.01	
Output	Loans weight (u_1)	0.003125	
Output	Deposits weight (u_2)	0.03125	

With these weights, the input value is $X_0 = 1.0$, and the output value is $Y_0 = 0.828$, resulting in an efficiency of 82.8 percent. In this solution, cells F17 and F19 are

	A	B	C	D	E	F	G	H
1	Data Envelopment Analysis							
2	*Branch Bank Example*							
3								
4	Data	*Branch*	*Expense*	*Loans*	*Deposits*			
5		1	100	10	31			
6		2	100	15	25			
7		3	100	20	30			
8		4	100	23	23			
9		5	100	30	20			
10								
11				Analysis for Branch 2				
12	Decisions		0.01	0.003125	0.03125			
13	Objective			15	25	0.828		
14								
15	Constraints							
16		Input value	100	0	0	1	=	1
17		Normalizing 1	-100	10	31	0.00000	<=	0
18		Normalizing 2	-100	15	25	-0.17188	<=	0
19		Normalizing 3	-100	20	30	0.00000	<=	0
20		Normalizing 4	-100	23	23	-0.20938	<=	0
21		Normalizing 5	-100	30	20	-0.28125	<=	0
22								

Branch1　Branch2

Figure 5.4. Model for Branch 2 in Example 5.2.

zero. This means that the normalizing constraint is binding for Branches 1 and 3. In other words, Branches 1 and 3 have efficiencies of 100 percent, even at the most favorable weights (0.003125, 0.03125) for Branch 2.

We could construct similar spreadsheet models for the analyses of Branches 3, 4, and 5 following the same format. However, much of the content on those worksheets would be identical, so a more efficient approach makes sense. In Figure 5.5, we show a single spreadsheet model that handles the analysis for all five branches. As before, the array in rows 4–9 contains the problem data. Cell F11 contains the branch number for the DMU under analysis. Based on this choice, two adjustments occur in the linear programming model. First, the outputs for the branch being analyzed must be selected for use in the objective function, in cells D13:E13. Second, the inputs for the branch being analyzed must be selected for use in the EQ constraint, in cell C16. These selections are highlighted in bold in Figure 5.5. The INDEX function uses the branch number in cell F11 to draw the objective function coefficients from the data array and reproduce them in cells D13:E13. It also draws the input value from the data array and reproduces it in cell C16. The three cells in bold format change when a different selection appears in cell F11.

	A	B	C	D	E	F	G	H
1	Data Envelopment Analysis							
2	*Branch Bank Example*							
3								
4	Data	*Branch*	*Expense*	*Loans*	*Deposits*			
5		1	100	10	31			
6		2	100	15	25			
7		3	100	20	30			
8		4	100	23	23			
9		5	100	30	20			
10								
11				Analysis for Branch	4			
12	Decisions		0.01	0.02	0.02			
13	Objective			23	23	0.920		
14								
15	Constraints							
16		Input value	**100**	0	0	1	=	1
17		Normalizing 1	-100	10	31	-0.18000	<=	0
18		Normalizing 2	-100	15	25	-0.20000	<=	0
19		Normalizing 3	-100	20	30	0.00000	<=	0
20		Normalizing 4	-100	23	23	-0.08000	<=	0
21		Normalizing 5	-100	30	20	0.00000	<=	0
22								

Branch1 / Branch2 / **Branch4**

Figure 5.5. Model for any branch in Example 5.2.

BOX 5.1   *Excel Mini-Lesson: The INDEX Function*

The INDEX function in Excel finds a value in a rectangular array according to the row number and column number of its location. The basic form of the function, as we use it for DEA models, is the following:

INDEX(*Array,Row,Column*)

- *Array* references a rectangular array.
- *Row* specifies a row number in the array.
- *Column* specifies a column number in the array.

In the example of Figure 5.5, suppose *Array* = C5:E9, *Row* = F11, and *Column* = 2. When cell F11 contains the number 4, the function INDEX(C5:E9,F11,2) would find the element in the fourth row and second column of the array in cells C5:E9. In this case, the function returns the Loans output value for Branch 4, or 23. This calculation would be suitable for cell D13.

    When we work with a one-column array, we can omit the Column argument in the INDEX function. Thus, in the worksheet, we can also use the function INDEX(D$5:D$9,$F$11) for cell D13 and then copy that formula into cell E13.

We want to solve the model in Figure 5.5 several times, once for each DMU. To do so, we vary the contents of cell F11 from 1 to 5. Since each solution requires a reuse of the worksheet, we save the essential results in some other place before switching to a new DMU. In particular, we save the weights and the value of the objective function. Figure 5.6 shows a worksheet containing a summary of the five optimizations for the five-branch example (one from each choice of cell F11 in Figure 5.5). The original data are reproduced in rows 4–9, and the optimal decision variables and efficiencies appear in rows 12–17. This summary can be generated automatically with the parameter analysis capability described in Chapter 4.

    As we can see in Figure 5.6, there are three efficient branches in our example: Branches 1, 3, and 5. Branches 2 and 4 are inefficient, with efficiencies of 82.8 percent and 92 percent, respectively. The numerical results agree with the graphical model. Thus, we have developed a spreadsheet prototype that implements the DEA approach. Later, we build on this set of results and use the spreadsheet model to compute additional information pertinent to the analysis.

    Before proceeding, it is important to note that Example 5.2 remains somewhat specialized. It has only one input dimension, and all the DMUs have identical input levels. The example has only two output dimensions, but by taking the inputs to be identical and by taking the outputs as two dimensional, we can depict the solution graphically, as in Figures 5.1 and 5.2. As mentioned earlier, if the inputs were different for all the DMUs, we would not have been able to convey the analysis graphically. However, the spreadsheet model, in the same form as Figures 5.5 and 5.6, accommodates the more general problem without difficulty.

	A	B	C	D	E	F
1	Data Envelopment Analysis					
2	*Branch Bank Example -- Summary*					
3						
4	Data	*Branch*	*Expense*	*Loans*	*Deposits*	
5		1	100	10	31	
6		2	100	15	25	
7		3	100	20	30	
8		4	100	23	23	
9		5	100	30	20	
10						
11	Results					
12		*Branch*	*Expense*	*Loans*	*Deposits*	*Efficiency*
13		1	0.01	0	0.032258	1.000
14		2	0.01	0.003125	0.03125	0.828
15		3	0.01	0.02	0.02	1.000
16		4	0.01	0.02	0.02	0.920
17		5	0.01	0.033333	0.00	1.000
18						

Summary

Figure 5.6. Summary of the analysis for Example 5.2.

5.4. INDEXING

Quantitative measures of performance are not always absolute figures. Often, it is more meaningful and more convenient to measure performance in relative terms. To create indexed data, we assign the best value on a single input or output dimension an index of 100, and other values are assigned the ratio of their value to the best value. In effect, all performance values are expressed in percentages, relative to the best performance observed.

The use of indexed data does not present difficulties for DEA. In fact, the DEA calculations are, perhaps, more intuitive when based on indexed data because the result tends to be optimal weights of approximately the same order of magnitude, which may not be the case without indexing.

To illustrate how indexing works, we return to Example 5.2. When we scan the loan values for the various branches, the highest output in the comparison comes from Branch 5, with an output of 30. If we treat a level of 30 as the base, we can express the loan values for each of the other branches as a percentage of Branch 5 output. Table 5.1 summarizes the scaled values that result, for both loans and deposits.

Suppose we perform the linear programming analysis using the indexed values instead of the original, raw data. How does the analysis change? Figure 5.7, which

Table 5.1. Scaled Values from Example 5.2

DMU	Loans	Index	Deposits	Index
Branch 1	10	33.3	31	100.0
Branch 2	15	50.0	25	80.6
Branch 3	20	66.7	30	96.8
Branch 4	23	76.7	23	74.2
Branch 5	30	100.0	20	64.5

shows the analysis of Branch 4 using indexed values, conveys the main point. The value of the objective function remains unchanged (at 92 percent in this case), even though the values of the decision variables are different from those in the original model (compare Figure 5.5). This example shows that the efficiency calculation is robust in the sense that it depends only on the relative magnitudes of the output levels, and these can be scaled for convenience without altering the efficiency values produced by the analysis.

Within each of the output dimensions being evaluated, only relative values matter, so it is always possible to use raw data even when the dimensions are quite different. In Example 5.2, the sizes of loans and deposits are of roughly the same magnitude—tens

	A	B	C	D	E	F	G	H
1	**Data Envelopment Analysis**							
2	***Branch Bank Example***							
3								
4	**Indexed Data**	*Branch*	*Expense*	*Loans*	*Deposits*			
5		1	100	33.3	100.0			
6		2	100	50.0	80.6			
7		3	100	66.7	96.8			
8		4	100	76.7	74.2			
9		5	100	100.0	64.5			
10								
11				Analysis for Branch		4		
12	**Decisions**		0.01	0.006	0.0062			
13	**Objective**			**76.667**	**74.194**	0.920		
14								
15	**Constraints**							
16		Input value	**100**	0	0	1	=	1
17		Normalizing 1	-100	33.3	100.0	-0.18000	<=	0
18		Normalizing 2	-100	50.0	80.6	-0.20000	<=	0
19		Normalizing 3	-100	66.7	96.8	0.00000	<=	0
20		Normalizing 4	-100	76.7	74.2	-0.08000	<=	0
21		Normalizing 5	-100	100.0	64.5	0.00000	<=	0
22								

Index

Figure 5.7. Analysis of Branch 4 in Example 5.2, with indexing.

of millions of dollars. Suppose we had used another dimension of performance, calculated as the nondefault rate on commercial and residential mortgages. For this measure, the given data might be proportions no larger than one, but it will not be a problem to mix such data with numbers in the tens of millions, because it is only relative levels, within a performance dimension, that really matter in DEA. As a result, we do not have to worry about scaling the data. Nevertheless, it is sometimes advantageous to use indexing because it leads to some comparability in the weights selected by the optimization model.

5.5. FINDING REFERENCE SETS AND HCUs

We identify an efficient DMU by solving the linear program and finding a value of 1 for the objective function. By contrast, an optimal value less than 1 signifies that the DMU is inefficient. The first main result in DEA is classifying the various DMUs as either efficient or inefficient. For the efficient DMUs, there may not be much more to say. As we shall see later, advanced variations of the analysis can discriminate among the efficient DMUs. Initially, however, these are not analyzed further. Instead, attention focuses on the inefficient DMUs. If we solve a version of the linear program and discover that a DMU is inefficient, the analysis proceeds by identifying the corresponding reference set and describing the associated HCU. In order to carry out this part of the analysis, we can draw on the shadow price information in the Sensitivity Report.

To illustrate how the analysis proceeds, we move next to an example with multiple inputs and multiple outputs. The simplest such case would be a two-input, two-output structure, as in the example of evaluating a chain of nursing homes.

EXAMPLE 5.3   *Hope Valley Health Care Association*

The Hope Valley Health Care Association owns and operates six nursing homes in adjoining states. An evaluation of their efficiency has been undertaken, using two inputs and two outputs. The inputs are staffing labor (measured in average hours per day) and the cost of supplies (in thousands of dollars per day). The outputs are the number of patient-days reimbursed by third-party sources and the number of patient-days reimbursed privately. A summary of performance data is shown in the table below.

DMU	Staff hours per day	Supplies per day	Reimbursed patient days	Privately paid patient days
Facility 1	150	0.2	14,000	3500
Facility 2	400	0.7	14,000	21,000
Facility 3	320	1.2	42,000	10,500
Facility 4	520	2.0	28,000	42,000
Facility 5	350	1.2	19,000	25,000
Facility 6	320	0.7	14,000	15,000

■

A spreadsheet model for the analysis of the six DMUs is shown in Figure 5.8, which displays the specific analysis for Facility 5. In a full set of six optimization runs for this model, we find that the first four units are all efficient, while Facilities 5 and 6 are inefficient. The efficiencies are summarized in cells G6:G11.

Next, we illustrate the further analysis of Facility 5. The first step is to re-run Solver for Facility 5 and obtain the Sensitivity Report, which is shown with some reformatting in Figure 5.9. The information we need can be found in the Constraints section of the Sensitivity Report, in the rows corresponding to the normalizing constraints of the original model, which have right-hand-side constants of zero. The specific values we seek are the shadow prices corresponding to the six normalizing constraints, as highlighted in Figure 5.9.

To proceed, we copy the shadow prices for the normalizing constraints and paste them into column J of the spreadsheet, so that they match up with the corresponding constraint rows, as shown in Figure 5.8. The next step is to identify which shadow prices are positive; the DMUs corresponding to those make up the reference set. In Figure 5.8, we can observe that the shadow prices are positive in normalizing constraints corresponding to Facilities 1, 2, and 4. This means that Facilities 1, 2, and 4 form the reference set for Facility 5. The results are summarized as follows.

DMU	Shadow price	Reference set
Facility 1	0.2000	Yes
Facility 2	0.0805	Yes
Facility 3	0.0000	
Facility 4	0.5383	Yes
Facility 5	0.0000	
Facility 6	0.0000	

Having identified the reference set for Facility 5, we next construct a HCU. In cells C26:F26 we lay out a row resembling the original row of data for Facility 5. The entry in cell C26 is calculated as the SUMPRODUCT of the shadow prices and the six values of the first input (staff hours) from the array of input data. This calculation yields the value 342.125, as shown below. This number represents the staff hours of the HCU.

DMU	Staff hours per day	Shadow price	
Facility 1	150	0.2000	
Facility 2	400	0.0805	
Facility 3	320	0.0000	
Facility 4	520	0.5383	
Facility 5	350	0.0000	
Facility 6	320	0.0000	SUMPRODUCT = 342.125

	A	B	C	D	E	F	G	H	I	J	K
1	**Data Envelopment Analysis**										
2	*Nursing Home Example*										
3											
4	**Data**		*Inputs*		*Outputs*						
5		*DMU*	*Staff Hrs*	*Supplies*	*Reimbursed*	*Private*	*Efficiency*				
6		1	150	0.2	14	3.5	1.0000				
7		2	400	0.7	14	21	1.0000				
8		3	320	1.2	42	10.5	1.0000				
9		4	520	2.0	28	42	1.0000				
10		5	350	1.2	19	25	0.9775				
11		6	320	0.7	14	15	0.8675				
12											
13						Analysis for Facility 5					
14	**Decisions**		0.001099	0.512821	0.011512	0.030351					
15	**Objective**				19	25	0.9775				
16										Shadow	
17	**Constraints**									Prices	
18		Input value	350	1.2	0	0	1.00000	=	1		
19		Normalizing 1	-150	-0.2	14	3.5	0.00000	<=	0	0.2000	
20		Normalizing 2	-400	-0.7	14	21	0.00000	<=	0	0.0805	
21		Normalizing 3	-320	-1.2	42	10.5	-0.16484	<=	0	0.0000	
22		Normalizing 4	-520	-2.0	28	42	0.00000	<=	0	0.5383	
23		Normalizing 5	-350	-1.2	19	25	-0.02250	<=	0	0.0000	
24		Normalizing 6	-320	-0.7	14	15	-0.09419	<=	0	0.0000	
25											
26		HCU for 5	342.125	1.173	19	25					

H ◀ ▶ H   Facilities

Figure 5.8. Analysis for Facility 5 in Example 5.3.

	A	B	C	D	E	F	G	H
1	**Microsoft Excel 14.0 Sensitivity Report**							
2								
3	Objective Cell (Max)							
4	Cell	Name		Final Value				
5	$G$15	Efficiency		0.977498692				
6								
7	Decision Variable Cells							
8				Final	Reduced	Objective	Allowable	Allowable
9	Cell	Name		Value	Cost	Coefficient	Increase	Decrease
10	$C$14	Decisions Staff Hrs		0.00110	0.00	0	18.310	244.940
11	$D$14	Decisions Supplies		0.51282	0.00	0	0.840	0.063
12	$E$14	Decisions Reimbursed		0.01151	0.00	19	2.203	2.333
13	$F$14	Decisions Analysis for Facility		0.03035	0.00	25	3.500	2.598
14								
15	Constraints							
16				Final	Shadow	Constraint	Allowable	Allowable
17	Cell	Name		Value	Price	R.H. Side	Increase	Decrease
18	$G$18	Input value Efficiency		1.00000	0.97750	1	1E+30	1.000
19	$G$19	Normalizing 1 Efficiency		0.00000	0.20000	0	0.055	0.134
20	$G$20	Normalizing 2 Efficiency		0.00000	0.08048	0	0.204	0.123
21	$G$21	Normalizing 3 Efficiency		-0.16484	0.00000	0	1E+30	0.165
22	$G$22	Normalizing 4 Efficiency		0.00000	0.53833	0	0.0418	0.500
23	$G$23	Normalizing 5 Efficiency		-0.02250	0.00000	0	1E+30	0.023
24	$G$24	Normalizing 6 Efficiency		-0.09419	0.00000	0	1E+30	0.094
25								

H ◀ ▶ H   Sensitivity Report

Figure 5.9. Sensitivity report for Facility 5 in Example 5.3.

The specific formula in cell C26 is =SUMPRODUCT($J$19:$J$24,C6:C11). Next, this calculation is copied to cells D26:F26, using absolute addresses for the shadow prices in column J, as shown in Figure 5.8. The resulting numbers provide the description of an HCU for Facility 5.

$$0.2000 \text{ (Facility 1 Data)} = 0.2000 \ (150 \quad 0.20 \quad 14 \quad 3.5)$$
$$0.0805 \text{ (Facility 2 Data)} = 0.0805 \ (400 \quad 0.70 \quad 14 \quad 21.0)$$
$$0.5383 \text{ (Facility 4 Data)} = 0.5383 \ (520 \quad 2.00 \quad 28 \quad 42.0)$$
$$\overline{\text{HCU Data} = \qquad\qquad (342 \quad 1.17 \quad 19 \quad 25.0)}$$

In particular, the outputs of the comparison unit, which are (19, 25), match the outputs of Facility 5 precisely. However, the inputs (342.125, 1.173) are slightly smaller than the inputs of Facility 5. In other words, the comparison unit achieves the same outputs as Facility 5, but with lower input levels. By its construction, the comparison unit has inputs and outputs that are weighted averages of those for the facilities in the reference set. Thus, a weighted combination of Facilities 1, 2, and 4 provides a target for Facility 5 to emulate.

The analysis of Example 5.3 shows how the shadow prices can be used as weighting factors to construct the HCU. In general, the comparison unit has outputs that are at least as large as the outputs of the inefficient unit being analyzed and inputs that are no larger than the inputs of the unit being analyzed. In this case, the actual inputs for Facility 5 are staff hours of 350 and a supply level of 1.2. The analysis suggests that efficient performance, as exemplified by Facilities 1, 2, and 4, would allow Facility 5 to produce the same outputs with inputs of only 342.125 staff hours and a supplies level of 1.173.

How could Facility 5 achieve these efficiencies? DEA does not tell us. It merely suggests that Facilities 1, 2, and 4 would be reasonable benchmarking targets for Facility 5. Then, by studying differences in technology, procedures, and management, Facility 5 might be able to identify and implement changes that could lead it to improved performance.

In Example 5.3, Facilities 1–4 are all efficient, but only Facilities 1, 2, and 4 form the reference set for Facility 5. An exploration of the analysis for Facility 6 leads to a similar conclusion: Its reference set also consists of Facilities 1, 2, and 4. Although Facility 3 is efficient, it does not appear in any reference sets. Evidently, it is not a facility that Facility 5 or 6 should try to emulate. We might guess that this is the case because its output mix is quite different.

5.6. ASSUMPTIONS AND LIMITATIONS OF DEA

Although we have relied on the term "efficient," it would be more appropriate to use the term *relatively* efficient—that is, the productivity of a DMU is evaluated relative to the other units in the set being analyzed. DEA identifies what we might call "best practice" within a given population. However, that does not necessarily mean that the efficient units compete well with DMUs outside the population. Thus, we have to resist the temptation to make inferences beyond the population under study.

As mentioned earlier, DEA works well when there is some ambiguity about the relative value of outputs. No *a priori* price or other judgment about the relative value of the outputs is needed. Because prices are not given, it should not be obvious what output mix would be best. (This applies to inputs as well.) DEA performs its evaluation by assuming weights that are as favorable as possible to the DMU being evaluated. However, DEA may not be very useful in a situation where a distinct hierarchy of strategic goals exists, especially if one goal strongly influences performance.

Some applications of DEA have run into complaints that the output measures may be influenced by factors that managers cannot control. In response, variations of the DEA model have been developed that can accommodate uncontrollable factors. Such a factor can be added by simply including it in the model; there is no need to specify any of its structural relationships or parameters. Thus, a factor that is neither an economic resource nor a product, but is instead an attribute of the environment, can easily be included. An example might be the convenience of a location for a branch bank, which could be treated as an input.

One of the technical criticisms often raised about DEA relates to the use of completely arbitrary weights. In particular, the basic DEA model allows weights of zero on any of the outputs. (Refer to Figure 5.3 as an illustration.) A zero-valued weight in the optimal solution means that the corresponding input or output has been discarded in the evaluation. In other words, it is possible for the analysis to completely avoid a dimension on which the DMU happens to be relatively unproductive. This may sound unfair, especially since the inputs and outputs are usually selected for their strategic importance, but it is consistent with the goal of finding weights that place the DMU in the best possible light. In response, some analysts suggest imposing a lower bound on each of the weights, ensuring that each output dimension receives at least some weight in the overall evaluation. Choosing a suitable lower bound is difficult, however, because of the flexibility available in scaling performance data. (Recall the discussion of indexed values earlier.) A more uniform approach is to impose a lower bound on the product of performance measure and weight. For any input dimension, the product of input value and weight is sometimes called the *virtual input* on that dimension. Similarly, for any output dimension, the product of output value and weight is sometimes called the *virtual output*. The virtual outputs are the components of the efficiency measure, and we can easily require that each component account for at least some minimal portion of the efficiency, such as 10 percent. In the analysis of Branch 1 (see Figure 5.10), we can compute the virtual outputs for each performance dimension in cells D14 and E14. Then, we add constraints forcing these values to be at least 10 percent (as specified in cell F14). With these lower bounds added, it is not possible to place all the weight on just one dimension. As shown in Figure 5.10, the imposition of a 10 percent lower bound for the contribution from each dimension reduces the efficiency rating for Branch 1 to 92.7 percent when the model is optimized. As the example illustrates, when we impose additional requirements, we may turn efficient DMUs into inefficient ones.

A related criticism is that the weight may be positive but still quite small on an output dimension that is known to be strategically important. In this situation, it

	A	B	C	D	E	F	G	H
1	**Data Envelopment Analysis**							
2	*Branch Bank Example*							
3								
4	**Data**	*Branch*	*Expense*	*Loans*	*Deposits*			
5		1	100	10	31			
6		2	100	15	25			
7		3	100	20	30			
8		4	100	23	23			
9		5	100	30	20			
10								
11				Analysis for Branch 1				
12	**Decisions**		0.01	0.01	0.02667			
13	**Objective**			10	31	0.927		
14		Virtual output		0.1	0.82667	10%		
15	**Constraints**							
16		Input value	100	0	0	1	=	1
17		Normalizing 1	-100	10	31	-0.07333	<=	0
18		Normalizing 2	-100	15	25	-0.18333	<=	0
19		Normalizing 3	-100	20	30	0.00000	<=	0
20		Normalizing 4	-100	23	23	-0.15667	<=	0
21		Normalizing 5	-100	30	20	-0.16667	<=	0
22								

Bounds

Figure 5.10. Analysis of Branch 1 with lower bounds.

is possible to add a constraint to the model that will force the virtual output of one important measure to be greater than the virtual output other measures. These kinds of additional constraints may improve the logic, but they sacrifice transparency in the model.

Another technical criticism relates to the fact that a DEA evaluation often produces a number of efficient DMUs, and it would be satisfying to have a tie-breaking mechanism for distinguishing among the efficient units. One way to break ties is to omit the normalizing constraint for the kth DMU when it is the subject of evaluation. When we do so, we tend to get some efficiencies above 1.0, and we are much less likely to get ties in the performance metric. Another response is more complicated but perhaps more equitable. The evaluation of the kth DMU produces a set of optimal weights that are, presumably, as favorable as possible to unit k. Suppose we call these "price set k." When we evaluate DMU k, we compute the value of its outputs under each of the price sets (price set 1, price set 2, etc.). Then we average the output values obtained under the various price sets and rank the DMUs based on their average values over all price sets. The average value on which the DMUs are ranked is called the *cross-efficiency*. This method makes ties less likely but involves more computation.

Although we started with a small one-input/one-output example and then moved on to larger examples, it does not follow that a DEA model should be built with as many inputs and outputs as possible. In fact, there is a good reason to limit the number of variables. A large number of outputs and inputs has a tendency to cause nearly every unit to appear efficient. Therefore, a judicious choice of outputs and inputs retains the power of DEA but tends to limit the number of DMUs that attain the maximum efficiency. The literature recommends an ideal number of DMUs of two or three times the total number of inputs and outputs. In practice, it makes sense to limit consideration to those inputs and outputs that are broadly considered to be of strategic importance to the units being evaluated.

The DEA model accommodates multiple inputs and outputs and makes no assumption about the functional form relating outputs to inputs. In other words, any type of production function is permissible. However, the efficiency measure itself and the construction of a HCU both involve some assumptions. First, the comparison unit is defined by assuming that weighted averages of efficient units are feasible operating possibilities. In other words, there are no major "lumpy" relationships in the production function. Second, the comparison unit is interpreted as the output potential that could be achieved if the unit under consideration were to maintain its mix of inputs and outputs. Here, DEA assumes constant returns to scale. More advanced variations of the DEA model allow for alternative assumptions about returns to scale.

SUMMARY

The DEA model represents a fifth type of linear programming model, along with allocation, covering, blending, and network models covered in Chapters 2 and 3. In a strict sense, the DEA model is a variation on the allocation type, but because its use is so specialized, we have given it separate treatment here.

For the purposes of spreadsheet implementation, the DEA model should be built with the kind of flexibility exemplified by Figure 5.5. That is, the analysis of every DMU can be done in the same worksheet, simply by updating a single cell. A documented analysis is likely to need a separate location to keep a summary of the linear programming results, as illustrated in the worksheet of Figure 5.6. In addition, to identify and analyze the properties of an HCU, we also need to obtain the Sensitivity Report, making use of its shadow price information as shown in Figure 5.8.

The DEA model was introduced in the 1970s, and for many years, it was a topic known mainly to a small group of researchers. Their work extended the theory underlying DEA, made progress enhancing the computational aspects of the analysis, and reported on selected applications. Over a period of many years, corporations and consultants have slowly discovered DEA and begun to use it more frequently. As application catches up with theory, the DEA model promises to find more significant use in the future.

EXERCISES

5.1. **Evaluating Manufacturing Efficiency** You have been asked to measure the relative efficiency of five competing manufacturers of apple juice. Each of the firms in the study controls the process of growing and harvesting apples, producing the juice, and delivering the juice to regional distributors. You have decided that your study should recognize one input, which is the acreage devoted to apple trees, and one output, which is the number of gallons of juice delivered last year, in thousands.

	Acres	Gallons
Firm 1	100	10
Firm 2	110	15
Firm 3	122	20
Firm 4	115	23
Firm 5	96	30

(a) Calculate the productivity for each firm.

(b) Calculate the efficiency of each firm.

(c) Which firm, if any, would you recommend as a benchmarking target for Firm 3?

5.2. **Expanding Manufacturing Efficiency**   Returning to the firms you studied in the previous exercise, you discover that they now make two products—apple juice and apple sauce. The firms still effectively use only one important resource, which is the apples grown in their own orchards, but they have different marketing strategies and hence their product mixes differ. The relevant data are shown in the table below.

	Acres	Juice	Sauce
Firm 1	100	10	31
Firm 2	110	15	25
Firm 3	122	20	30
Firm 4	115	23	23
Firm 5	96	30	20

(a) Perform a DEA evaluation for this set of firms, listing the efficiency for each firm.

(b) For each of the inefficient units, find the reference set and calculate the inputs and outputs for a corresponding HCU.

(c) Compare the results with the analysis of the branch bank example in the chapter. What are the differences in the given data? What are the differences in results?

5.3. **Hope Valley Health Care (Revisited)**   Revisit Example 5.3 and revise the given data set so that all input and output measures are indexed. That is, each value on a particular input or output dimension is assigned its percentage relative to the highest value in the set. Using indexed data, redo the analysis.

(a) Which nursing homes are efficient?

(b) What are the efficiencies of the inefficient nursing homes?

(c) For each of the inefficient units, find the reference set and calculate the indexed inputs and outputs for a corresponding HCU. Then convert these indexed values to the original scale.

5.4. **Evaluating Hospital Efficiency**   DEA has been used to measure the relative efficiency of a group of hospitals. This study involved seven teaching hospitals; data on three input measures and four output measures are provided in Table 5.2.

Table 5.2. Inputs and Outputs for Seven Hospitals

	Input measures		
Hospital	Full-time equivalent nonphysicians	Supply expense ($1000s)	Bed-days available ($1000s)
A	310.0	134.60	116.00
B	278.5	114.30	106.80
C	165.6	131.30	65.52
D	250.0	316.00	94.40
E	206.4	151.20	102.10
F	384.0	217.00	153.70
G	530.1	770.80	215.00

	Output Measures			
Hospital	Patient-days (65 or older) (000s)	Patient days (under 65) (000s)	Nurses trained	Interns trained
A	55.31	49.52	291	47
B	37.64	55.63	156	3
C	32.91	25.77	141	26
D	33.53	41.99	160	21
E	32.48	55.30	157	82
F	48.78	81.92	285	92
G	58.41	119.70	111	89

(a) Perform a DEA evaluation for this set of units, listing the efficiency for each hospital.

(b) Consider the performance of Hospital D. What is the interpretation of the efficiency measure for Hospital D?

(c) Which hospitals would you recommend Hospital D consider emulating to improve its efficiency?

(d) What are the inputs and outputs of the HCU for Hospital D?

5.5. **Evaluating Restaurant Efficiency**   Celia's Tacqueria is a chain of five Mexican restaurants in Florida. A DEA evaluation is being conducted to make comparisons of the different locations. Input measures for the restaurants include weekly hours of operation, full-time equivalent staff, and weekly supply expenses. Output measures of performance include average weekly contribution to profit, market share, and annual growth rate. Data for the input and output measures are shown in Table 5.3.

(a) Perform a DEA evaluation for this set of units, listing the efficiency and the virtual outputs for each of restaurants.

(b) For each of the inefficient units, find the reference set and calculate the inputs and outputs for a corresponding HCU.

5.6. **Evaluating Branch Bank Efficiency**   A large national bank is interested in evaluating the performance of several of its branches. For this purpose, it has collected data for a

Table 5.3. Inputs and Outputs for Five Restaurants

	Input measures		
Restaurant	Hours of operation	FTE staff	Supplies ($)
Jacksonville	96	16	850
Daytona	110	22	1400
Gainesville	100	18	1200
Ocala	125	25	1500
Orlando	120	24	1600

	Output measures		
Restaurant	Weekly profit ($)	% Market share	% Growth rate
Jacksonville	3800	25	8.0
Daytona	4600	32	8.5
Gainesville	4400	35	8.0
Ocala	6500	30	10.0
Orlando	6000	28	9.0

DEA study (Table 5.4). Three inputs have been selected for the study: personnel hours, operating expenses, and floor space. Three outputs have also been selected; these count the number of transactions in different areas of the bank. In particular, transactions are tracked in Deposits and Capital Transfers, Credit Processing, and Foreign Receipts.

(a) Perform a DEA evaluation for the branches, listing the efficiency for each branch.

(b) For each of the inefficient units, find the reference set.

5.7. **Modifying the Efficiency Measure in DEA**   DEA does not distinguish among efficient DMUs because they are assigned efficiencies of 1.0 by the standard procedure. One suggestion for modifying the procedure is the following. For each efficient DMU, repeat the analysis (i.e., solve the linear programming problem) without retaining the DMU being evaluated in the set of constraints. In this form of the model, an efficient DMU may turn out to have efficiency greater than 1.0.

Analyze Exercise 5.4 using this approach, calculating the revised efficiency rating for each of the DMUs.

(a) List the hospitals in order of their revised efficiencies.

(b) For each hospital, compute how much change occurs between the efficiency rating in the standard procedure and the revised efficiency rating.

5.8. **Modifying the Efficiency Measures in DEA**   DEA does not distinguish among efficient DMUs because they are assigned efficiencies of 1.0 by the standard procedure. One suggestion for modifying the procedure is the following. For each efficient DMU, repeat the analysis (i.e., solve the linear programming problem) without retaining the DMU being evaluated in the set of constraints. In this form of the model, an efficient DMU may turn out to have efficiency greater than 1.0.

Table 5.4. Inputs and Outputs for 17 Branch Banks

Branch code	Inputs			Outputs		
	Labor	Expenses	Space	Deposits	Credit	Foreign
1	34515	6543	591	268836	9052	11242
2	49960	11830	550	475144	15697	15967
3	20652	3464	427	133020	3696	6937
4	49024	7603	478	355909	12918	16594
5	36923	8723	830	240679	4759	8087
6	28967	4606	474	211183	3188	5621
7	28452	7425	182	147364	5302	40618
8	45911	8013	790	130161	12070	115022
9	26890	14662	447	156828	15102	1336
10	47376	7576	764	297925	16797	12030
11	57913	12035	875	462603	2698	13232
12	43477	7255	1109	300976	12299	24368
13	49786	10909	405	233178	6248	4701
14	30045	4264	479	110976	8675	19796
15	56579	8895	840	363048	6370	10788
16	43824	12690	801	130219	20417	28133
17	33823	4143	381	146804	47508	21856

Analyze Exercise 5.5 using this approach, calculating the revised efficiency rating for each of the DMUs.

(a) List the restaurants in order of their revised efficiencies.

(b) For each restaurant, compute how much change occurs between the efficiency rating in the standard procedure and the revised efficiency rating.

5.9. DEA Efficiency with an Additional Constraint   Review Exercise 5.4. Add constraints that require virtual outputs of at least 2 percent.

(a) With the additional constraints, calculate the efficiencies of the hospitals. Comparing the original analysis, what patterns do you see?

(b) Repeat the analysis with a minimum of 10 percent on the virtual outputs.

(c) What are the advantages and disadvantages of using the additional constraint?

5.10. DEA Efficiency with an Additional Constraint   Review Exercise 5.5. Add constraints that require virtual outputs of at least 10 percent.

(a) With the additional constraints, calculate the efficiencies of the restaurants. Comparing the original analysis, what patterns do you see?

(b) Repeat the analysis with a minimum of 20 percent on the virtual outputs.

(c) What are the advantages and disadvantages of using the additional constraint?

5.11. DEA Efficiency with Side Constraints   Review Exercise 5.5. After looking at the analysis, your corporate client proposes a refinement. Since the corporation has emphasized market share in other divisions, the following constraint is suggested: the virtual

Table 5.5. Data on 20 Finnish Universities

	Input	Outputs			
ID	Costs	Inheritances	Rebates	Warrants	Collections
1	9.13	7.525	34.114	21.958	3.840
2	13.60	8.301	23.270	35.966	8.632
3	5.76	10.909	13.392	11.527	4.931
4	11.24	16.621	36.817	27.552	9.522
5	15.57	22.809	95.776	23.611	12.266
6	5.65	1.777	0.156	1.314	39.011
7	21.60	15.107	70.958	54.216	10.809
8	8.57	7.919	48.688	14.032	5.923
9	6.01	7.066	36.304	5.445	2.936
10	8.02	8.858	43.610	13.774	4.274
11	9.93	8.999	36.852	20.661	8.151
12	7.90	8.278	45.222	6.191	5.327
13	5.15	6.763	18.704	10.620	3.540
14	6.42	8.984	13.600	12.319	3.752
15	5.94	7.686	25.906	8.242	2.483
16	8.68	7.227	16.965	17.581	6.274
17	4.86	3.356	23.672	4.298	2.482
18	10.33	8.558	30.540	17.770	8.005
19	21.97	12.234	92.020	29.530	14.763
20	9.70	7.674	41.162	13.272	4.503
21	6.34	8.168	16.613	8.264	5.047
22	7.70	7.884	15.749	14.502	3.034
23	5.99	5.666	27.546	5.243	3.410
24	5.20	6.923	12.613	4.298	3.040
25	6.36	7.352	23.510	5.744	4.207
26	8.87	6.456	38.100	9.645	3.093
27	10.71	13.642	23.862	14.631	4.631
28	6.49	7.675	17.972	8.269	2.756
29	15.32	15.341	55.415	16.361	12.530
30	7.00	8.369	14.918	9.883	4.328
31	10.50	9.608	37.910	13.493	5.035
32	10.88	10.648	36.962	14.248	4.844
33	8.52	8.967	24.672	11.841	3.753
34	7.61	6.111	31.734	7.657	2.872
35	10.91	9.778	42.725	12.169	4.657
36	9.72	7.713	5.897	14.600	9.251
37	12.63	11.082	41.586	16.420	5.647
38	11.51	9.066	28.491	16.284	5.962
39	6.22	6.627	14.667	7.703	3.083

(Continued)

Table 5.5. *Continued*

ID	Input Costs	Inheritances	Rebates	Warrants	Collections
40	5.29	3.958	20.416	1.961	1.835
41	8.78	6.558	31.720	8.596	4.831
42	13.50	4.769	26.469	20.877	4.170
43	12.60	6.680	30.280	9.085	19.449
44	8.10	8.103	9.708	8.534	7.502
45	9.67	6.004	19.460	10.708	8.033
46	12.37	11.253	28.500	12.528	6.741
47	9.50	8.674	23.542	8.992	3.664
48	11.47	10.300	15.576	13.740	6.458
49	11.78	12.221	14.325	10.100	5.021
50	12.57	10.432	18.306	16.387	3.924
51	50.26	32.331	150.000	45.099	19.579
52	12.70	9.500	22.391	14.900	5.803
53	13.30	7.530	21.990	14.655	8.324
54	5.60	3.727	12.208	5.388	2.837
55	11.75	5.198	13.280	13.618	7.104
56	8.47	6.149	19.453	6.505	3.300
57	8.36	5.959	17.110	4.655	3.077
58	11.07	7.247	16.338	8.686	6.620
59	10.38	7.761	16.440	6.014	3.313
60	11.83	5.347	12.410	12.238	4.567
61	12.71	6.320	13.632	8.530	5.161
62	11.19	6.578	10.900	3.523	3.456

output for market share should be at least 150 percent of the virtual output from either profit or growth.

(a) With the side constraints added, calculate the efficiencies of the five restaurants.

(b) What are the advantages and disadvantages of using the side constraint?

5.12. **DEA with Cross-Efficiencies**   Review Exercise 5.5. After looking at the analysis, your corporate client proposes yet another refinement to break ties in the efficiency ratings. The evaluation of the kth DMU produces a set of "optimal prices" that are as favorable as possible to unit k. Suppose we call these "set k prices." Now, to evaluate DMU k, compute the value of its efficiency (output value divided by input value) under each of the price sets (set 1 prices through set 5 prices, in this case). Then, average the five efficiency values. This average value is called the cross-efficiency.

(a) Rank the DMUs based on cross-efficiency.

(b) What are the advantages and disadvantages of using the cross-efficiency measure?

5.13. **Evaluating Universities**   A study of Finnish universities is aimed at determining an efficiency ranking. Two inputs are used: the university's annual budget and the selectivity

Table 5.6. Data on 62 Municipal Departments

ID	Input Costs	Outputs Inheritances	Rebates	Warrants	Collections
1	9.13	7.525	34.114	21.958	3.840
2	13.60	8.301	23.270	35.966	8.632
3	5.76	10.909	13.392	11.527	4.931
4	11.24	16.621	36.817	27.552	9.522
5	15.57	22.809	95.776	23.611	12.266
6	5.65	1.777	0.156	1.314	39.011
7	21.60	15.107	70.958	54.216	10.809
8	8.57	7.919	48.688	14.032	5.923
9	6.01	7.066	36.304	5.445	2.936
10	8.02	8.858	43.610	13.774	4.274
11	9.93	8.999	36.852	20.661	8.151
12	7.90	8.278	45.222	6.191	5.327
13	5.15	6.763	18.704	10.620	3.540
14	6.42	8.984	13.600	12.319	3.752
15	5.94	7.686	25.906	8.242	2.483
16	8.68	7.227	16.965	17.581	6.274
17	4.86	3.356	23.672	4.298	2.482
18	10.33	8.558	30.540	17.770	8.005
19	21.97	12.234	92.020	29.530	14.763
20	9.70	7.674	41.162	13.272	4.503
21	6.34	8.168	16.613	8.264	5.047
22	7.70	7.884	15.749	14.502	3.034
23	5.99	5.666	27.546	5.243	3.410
24	5.20	6.923	12.613	4.298	3.040
25	6.36	7.352	23.510	5.744	4.207
26	8.87	6.456	38.100	9.645	3.093
27	10.71	13.642	23.862	14.631	4.631
28	6.49	7.675	17.972	8.269	2.756
29	15.32	15.341	55.415	16.361	12.530
30	7.00	8.369	14.918	9.883	4.328
31	10.50	9.608	37.910	13.493	5.035
32	10.88	10.648	36.962	14.248	4.844
33	8.52	8.967	24.672	11.841	3.753
34	7.61	6.111	31.734	7.657	2.872
35	10.91	9.778	42.725	12.169	4.657
36	9.72	7.713	5.897	14.600	9.251
37	12.63	11.082	41.586	16.420	5.647
38	11.51	9.066	28.491	16.284	5.962
39	6.22	6.627	14.667	7.703	3.083

(*Continued*)

Table 5.6. *Continued*

	Input	Outputs			
ID	Costs	Inheritances	Rebates	Warrants	Collections
40	5.29	3.958	20.416	1.961	1.835
41	8.78	6.558	31.720	8.596	4.831
42	13.50	4.769	26.469	20.877	4.170
43	12.60	6.680	30.280	9.085	19.449
44	8.10	8.103	9.708	8.534	7.502
45	9.67	6.004	19.460	10.708	8.033
46	12.37	11.253	28.500	12.528	6.741
47	9.50	8.674	23.542	8.992	3.664
48	11.47	10.300	15.576	13.740	6.458
49	11.78	12.221	14.325	10.100	5.021
50	12.57	10.432	18.306	16.387	3.924
51	50.26	32.331	150.000	45.099	19.579
52	12.70	9.500	22.391	14.900	5.803
53	13.30	7.530	21.990	14.655	8.324
54	5.60	3.727	12.208	5.388	2.837
55	11.75	5.198	13.280	13.618	7.104
56	8.47	6.149	19.453	6.505	3.300
57	8.36	5.959	17.110	4.655	3.077
58	11.07	7.247	16.338	8.686	6.620
59	10.38	7.761	16.440	6.014	3.313
60	11.83	5.347	12.410	12.238	4.567
61	12.71	6.320	13.632	8.530	5.161
62	11.19	6.578	10.900	3.523	3.456

rating (for which higher is better). Four outputs are used: the number of graduates (receiving their primary degree), the number of advanced graduates (receiving a post-graduate degree), a progress index (measured against a standard rate of progress toward the corresponding degree), and a completion index (measuring the propensity of students to finish their degree requirements). The data are provided in Table 5.5.

(a) Perform a DEA evaluation for the universities, listing the efficiency for each.

(b) How many of the 20 universities are efficient?

5.14. Evaluating Municipal Departments   An effort is underway to evaluate several municipal departments in the UK that collect taxes related to property. One input is used: the annual cost of operating the municipal office. Four outputs are measured, relating to different activities carried out in each of the departments. The data are shown in Table 5.6.

(a) Perform a DEA evaluation for the departments, listing the efficiency for each unit.

(b) How many of the 62 DMUs are efficient?

Case: Branch Performance at Nashville National Bank[1]

In 1993, Ann Maruchek, Chief Operating Officer of Nashville National Bank (NNB), had been at the helm during a heady time of rapid expansion that saw NNB grow from three to ten branches in five years. Unfortunately, that expansion led to some personnel problems. Many of the branch managers began complaining about discrepancies in pay, titles, and resources, and they focused on the branch performance appraisal process. One older branch manager who had received an unfavorable performance review threatened to sue NNB for age discrimination if he was fired.

Determining some measure of bank branch performance was essential. Without some agreed upon performance measure, varied decisions such as branch expansion/closure, managerial promotion, and resource allocation would otherwise be left to the "feel" of senior management. At the time, Ann gave all branch manager performance reviews herself. Being a very "hands-on" type of manager, she felt that she was in an informed position to pass judgment on each branch. She based her judgments on what she felt each branch should have accomplished during the past year, given their location, past performance, and so on, but she had no particular benchmark for this purpose.

During most of the 1980s, when there were only three branches and she knew each manager well, her informal style seemed to work well. With the complexity of a larger branch network combined with the political factions that arose within NNB, it became clear that a more formal approach was necessary. Under her informal evaluation system, many managers felt that the negotiating and presentation skills of branch managers could be a more important factor in their performance appraisals than the actual performance of their branch.

Branch Growth at Nashville National Bank

NNB was founded in 1970 as a largely retail bank serving upper-middle class customers in Nashville. NNB had only three branches within Davidson County when it merged with a failed thrift, Belle Meade S&L, in 1989 and gained three more branches. In 1991, NNB purchased another failing institution, Farmer's Bank, which added one branch. Last year NNB and People's Bank merged, bringing the total branches in the NNB system to 10.

Each of the acquisitions was made because the banks were considered "good buys," rather than for strategic considerations. Outwardly, few changes were made for the new branches. The employees of the purchased bank were kept on at their current pay scale and title. Few procedural changes were implemented to make them conform to NNB's methods. For instance, loan application and review were different from branch to branch. At the extreme, only the former Farmer's Bank branch made agricultural loans.

The major changes NNB made were to the backroom operations. The most significant change was to the computer systems. The disparate systems were integrated to ensure that accounts could be accessed in real time from any branch in the NNB system. This was greatly appreciated by their customers, as many customers preferred to process transactions at a variety of branches in the NNB system, not just the particular branch that opened their account.

The acquired branches catered to different market segments than NNB traditionally embraced. Belle Meade S&L focused on retail banking for the same upper-middle income customers. Farmer's Bank was established to provide both retail and commercial services for agricultural purposes. As agriculture declined in importance in the local economy, the market share

---

[1]This case was written by Professor Richard Metters of Emory University and is used with permission.

of Farmer's commensurately decreased. People's Bank provided retail services to a basically middle class clientele.

Assessing Branch Productivity

Although it is clearly necessary to have some measure of branch performance, there is considerable disagreement in the industry about what should be measured and how to measure it. Several different measurement and reporting techniques are currently used by different banks to evaluate branches. Ann decided to compare the formal branch performance evaluation systems that peer banks use to see whether one would fit at NNB.

Measuring productivity is often a simple matter for many individual jobs, but can become complex for branches with multiple goals. For example, if teller A handles 200 transactions per day whereas teller B handles 250 transactions, teller B is more productive, other things equal. However, if those tellers handle different types of transactions, then the raw data given is no longer sufficient, and the transactions must be weighted according to standard times. If teller A's 200 transactions were judged to require 8 standard hours whereas teller B's 250 transactions required only 7.5 standard hours, then teller A would be considered more productive.

Evaluating branch productivity is more complicated than evaluating individual tellers. There are multiple strategic directives, such as customer satisfaction, profitability, growth of the customer base, and so on, that are all measured differently and cannot easily be combined into a single measure. But even when profitability is the only goal, there are often multiple measures that should be consulted.

For example, assume that profit is derived from only loans and deposits. Due to a lack of match-funding[2] the net interest earned on the loan and deposit portfolios can vary widely. In some years, loans are highly profitable whereas deposits are marginally so, in other years the reverse is true. If measured on profit alone, branches that are very good at generating checking accounts may be viewed as excellent branches one year and poor performers the next—even if they are performing at a sustained level of excellence in generating deposits. Consequently, gross profit may not always be an appropriate performance measure. Because of these difficulties and others, branch effectiveness can be difficult to assess.

Branch Managers Revolt

The problem of evaluating branches was brought to the forefront by a cabal of the former People's Bank managers. It was already known that they had lower ranking than other branch managers, but they had believed that this was due to the merger process and that salaries were relatively equal. When they inadvertently discovered the wide gaps in salaries between branch managers (see Exhibit 5.1) they were furious. They demanded that Ann bring their titles and salaries up to the level of the other managers.

Clay Whybark, President of NNB, was against any pay increases. He believed that the former People's branches were not producing as well as the others and that their managers should be paid accordingly. Realizing that his "feel" was not going to be good enough to placate his branch managers, he instructed Ann to come up with an objective method of determining how well the branches were doing.

---

[2]"Match funding" refers to how a bank funds its loans and deposits of different maturities. As a simplified example, for a bank to loan money for a 30-year mortgage, it can get the money for the loan from the overnight federal funds market or a long-term deposit account. If it funds a long-term loan of 10 percent from a long-term deposit of 5 percent, the loan is match funded and is guaranteed to be profitable. If it funds the long-term loan from the short-term overnight market, there is a danger that the overnight rates may rise substantially over the course of the loan, making the loan unprofitable.

EXHIBIT 5.1		*Branch Manager Salaries*	
Original bank	Branch number	Branch manager title	Branch manager salary
NNB	1	Vice President (V.P.)	$48,000
NNB	2	Vice President	$52,500
NNB	3	Senior V.P.	$65,000
Belle Meade	4	Vice President	$50,000
Belle Meade	5	Senior V.P.	$60,000
Belle Meade	6	Vice President	$46,000
Farmer's	7	Vice President	$52,000
People's	8	Assistant V.P.	$38,000
People's	9	Assistant V.P.	$36,000
People's	10	Assistant V.P.	$34,000

Measuring Branches: Available Techniques

Ann narrowed the choice of alternatives to three commonly used techniques, branch profitability, branch ranking and branch goals, and one emerging technique that has been used only recently: data envelopment analysis.

- *Branch Profitability.* Many banks evaluate branches by fashioning financial statements for each branch. Interest and fee income from accounts is credit to the branch where the accounts originated. This income is netted against interest costs and non-interest expenses to determine a profitability level (see Exhibit 5.2).

- *Ranking Reports.* An alternative is to evaluate branches according to performance in specific areas separately, rather than using a single profitability number.

- *Goal Reports.* Pre-set goals are negotiated with each branch manager in a variety of areas. Performance evaluation is based on the percentage of goal attained. The categories used for goal reporting would be similar to those used in ranking reports.

- *Data Envelopment Analysis (DEA).* Formally, DEA is a linear programming technique for measuring the relative efficiency of facilities where each facility has more than one desired output or needed input. In practical terms, DEA is a measurement tool for businesses that have many different sites performing similar tasks, when a single overall measure, such as profit or ROI, is not sufficient. DEA combines numerous relevant outputs and inputs into a single number that represents productivity, or "efficiency."

The DEA Study

Ann decided to use DEA to evaluate the NNB branch system. She initially used four outputs and three inputs (Exhibit 5.3). The outputs chosen were branch profit, a deposit transaction index, a new account index and an existing account index. Later, at the specific request of the Farmer's branch manager, Ann also included agricultural loan balances as an output.

Branch profitability was obtained from standard accounting reports. From these reports, Ann calculated the average monthly profit for the last three years and used that figure directly. Each of the other measures was a composite of several items. The transaction index multiplied the number of transactions handled at a branch by the standard time required to perform the

EXHIBIT 5.2	*Sample Branch Profitability Statement ($000)*
Interest income from loans*	384.2
Federal funds sold**	0.0
Total interest income	384.2
Interest expense from deposits*	(185.5)
Federal funds purchased**	(23.0)
Total interest expense	(208.5)
Provision for credit losses	(26.5)
Net interest income after Provision for credit losses	149.2
Noninterest income	
Deposit account fees	22.2
Loan fees	12.1
Total noninterest income	32.3
Noninterest expense	
Salaries	(35.0)
Benefits	(7.4)
Occupancy	(4.1)
Other expense	(18.2)
Total noninterest expense	(64.7)
Net income before support expenses	116.8
Specific support expense***	(32.6)
Net income before general expense	84.2
General support expense****	(22.4)
Net income	61.8

*Income/expense from loan and deposit accounts initially opened by branch.

**If more deposits are taken in than loans given out, the excess is sold on the Federal Funds (FF) market. If excessive loans are granted, the money is borrowed from the FF market.

***Expenses of central administration directly related to branch activity.

****Expenses of central administration not directly related to any specific branch (e.g., president's salary).

transaction. For example, handling a routine deposit takes 20 seconds, but writing a cashier's check takes 3 minutes. The branch with the largest amount of standard time was given an index value of 100 and the other branches were indexed accordingly.

Similar procedures were used for new and existing accounts. A certificate of deposit for $10,000 at 5.5 percent interest is far less profitable than a regular savings account with a $10,000 balance at 3.0 percent. Consequently, indices using approximate profitability ratings were used to weight new and existing account activity.

For inputs, Ann used the average monthly personnel and total branch expenses over the past three years. Also, some locations were clearly better than others and branches located in

EXHIBIT 5.3   *Raw Data for the Analysis*

Branch	Personnel expense	Total expense	Location index	Branch profit	Deposit trans. index	New account index	Account balance index	Ag loan bal.
1	39	80	9	95	65	100	90	0
2	37	82	9	70	68	78	77	0
3	41	92	8	108	75	80	100	0
4	42	88	9	63	68	69	73	0
5	54	99	10	115	77	85	98	0
6	37	84	10	85	72	69	90	0
7	45	92	7	12	17	12	34	25
8	65	125	7	45	93	40	52	0
9	73	109	8	39	94	45	58	0
10	79	118	9	50	100	38	65	0

(Handwritten annotations: "Inputs" above Personnel/Total/Location columns; "Outputs" above Branch profit/Deposit trans./New account columns; "Outputs" above Account balance/Ag loan columns.)

209

EXHIBIT 5.4   *Branch Efficiencies and Output Factor Weightings*

Branch	Efficiency	Branch profit	Transaction index	New account	Existing account index	Agricultural loans index
1	1.00	0.00	0.00	1.00	0.00	0.00
2	1.00	0.00	0.76	0.24	0.00	0.00
3	1.00	1.00	0.00	0.00	0.00	0.00
4	0.92	0.00	0.84	0.08	0.00	0.00
5	0.98	0.98	0.00	0.00	0.00	0.00
6	1.00	0.23	0.77	0.00	0.00	0.00
7	1.00	0.00	0.00	0.00	0.00	1.00
8	1.00	0.00	1.00	0.00	0.00	0.00
9	1.00	0.00	1.00	0.00	0.00	0.00
10	0.99	0.03	0.95	0.00	0.00	0.00

Data is not 100% correct

prime spots would reasonably be expected to perform better, so a "location desirability" estimate was included as an input.

According to Ann's calculations, nearly every branch was perfectly efficient and of the three that had less than 100 percent efficiency, the lowest efficiency was 92 percent (see Exhibit 5.4 for a summary). The inescapable conclusion was that the former People's branch managers were right—they were underpaid.

When Ann presented her method and conclusions at the next Executive Operating Committee meeting, she was met with a less than enthusiastic response. When she finished, a stony silence ensued and Ann noticed that Clay was starting down at the desk with his head in his hands.

Aleda Roth, Senior Vice President and head of the check-processing center, was the first to speak. "This is garbage. Clay, give me three days and I'll give you something you can use." When Ann began to protest, Clay interrupted, "Wait a minute, Ann. Let's hear what Aleda has to say."

• Ann applied date without weighting
b don't let DEA assign
weight of zero

Chapter 6

Integer Programming: Binary Choice Models

An *integer programming* model is a linear program with the requirement that some or all of the decision variables must be integers. In principle, we could distinguish between linear and nonlinear programs with integer variables, but the latter are extremely difficult and generally beyond the capability of Solver. We focus on the role of integer variables in what would otherwise be linear programming models. Thus far, we have not paid much explicit attention to whether the decision variables take on integer values. In Chapter 3, we pointed out that in special network models, integer solutions are guaranteed. In other cases, we often encountered integer solutions without explicitly requiring integers, so there seemed to be no need to discuss integrality. In still other cases, we seemed to be content with fractional solutions, especially when the decision variables were scaled. In this chapter, the role of integer values takes center stage.

This chapter first describes how Solver handles integer programs. Next, we explore the basic capital budgeting model as a way of introducing binary variables and developing some intuition for the effects of integer requirements on decision variables. Then, in the remainder of the chapter, we look at models characterized by binary choice. In these optimization models, all decisions are of a yes/no variety. Other uses of binary variables are covered in the next chapter.

Before we discuss how to handle the integer requirement using Solver, we return briefly to the subject of integers in linear programs. Recall that one of the three conditions of linearity is divisibility—that is, the fact that fractional values make sense for decision variables. Consider Example 2.1, the allocation model for chairs, desks, and tables. As it turned out, the optimal solution contained no chairs, 160 desks, and 120 tables, so that the decisions happened to all be integers. Suppose instead that the problem had been posed with only 1800 assembly hours available, rather than the 2000 of the base case. Then the optimal product mix would have been 13.33 chairs, 220 desks, and no tables. Is the fractional number of chairs meaningful?

At first glance, it may seem to make no sense to talk about one-third of a chair in the product mix. Certainly, if we were interested in the tactical implications of the

Optimization Modeling with Spreadsheets, Second Edition. Kenneth R. Baker
© 2011 John Wiley & Sons, Inc. Published 2011 by John Wiley & Sons, Inc.

solution, it would not make sense for us to produce one-third of a chair to help meet demand (or to count on the profit that the fractional chair would generate). However, there are two interpretations of the fraction that do make sense. For one, we should be willing to round off. That is, we might interpret the optimal solution as 13 chairs and 220 desks. This solution would use less capacity than the optimal solution but would clearly be feasible. Another possibility might be to round up the number of chairs to 14, leaving desks at 220. Although this rounded-up solution violates the precise statement of capacity, the violation is on the order of one tenth of a percent in the case of assembly capacity and half a percent in the case of machining capacity. Since we are unlikely to "know" the given information in this problem to a precision of one part in a thousand, we may well accept the rounded-up product mix as an implementable solution.

A second interpretation is also possible. We might want to think of the model as representing a routine weekly planning model that specifies conditions in a typical or average week. In that context, when we encounter a figure like 13.33 in the optimal mix, we could interpret it as a long-run average. That is, the fractional value prescribes a three-week cycle with 13 chairs in weeks 1 and 2, and 14 chairs in week 3. Thus, rounded-off values and planning averages provide us with two interpretations that might allow us to tolerate fractional answers to linear programs when fractions seem impractical in literal terms. In addition, we might be primarily interested in understanding the economic priorities in the optimal solution (as discussed in Chapter 4), and the details of the decision variables might be of secondary importance. Since linear programming models are usually guides to decisions, rather than fully automated substitutes for decision makers, we might well be satisfied with noninteger solutions to most of our linear programs. Still, there are some cases where only integers will suffice. In those cases, the requirement of integer values is crucial, and it influences how we use Solver.

Broadly speaking, there are perhaps three types of integer programming models. The first type is essentially a linear program but with an inflexible requirement that some or all of the variables must be integer. For example, a decision variable might correspond to the number of times in a production schedule that a piece of equipment is shut down for a maintenance check. In this instance, a value such as 2.59 will not suffice; we must have an integer. For this purpose, we designate some variable in the model as an *integer variable*.

The second type is a model in which some of the key decisions are of the yes/no variety. For example, a decision variable might correspond to whether or not we purchase a parcel of land. In this instance, we model our decision with a variable that is allowed to be only zero or one. We refer to such a decision as a *binary choice*, because there are only two alternatives, and we use *binary variables* to represent the decision. Binary variables are integer variables that are limited to the values zero or one. In this chapter, we mainly focus on models involving binary choice.

The third type is a model that contains certain relationships that we might not normally think of as linear. For example, suppose that we are contemplating a plant expansion in which we may add a new manufacturing line to the factory. If we proceed with the expansion, then we can produce a particular component internally. If we don't expand, then we will have to buy the component from an external vendor. In other words, our make/buy alternatives are *contingent* on the decision to expand. Such a contingency is an example of a *logical* or *qualitative constraint*, but we can capture it in a model if we use binary variables to represent the decision to expand and the decision to produce components in house. Other kinds of qualitative constraints can often be represented using binary variables, and in the next chapter we focus on models involving logical constraints.

6.1. USING SOLVER WITH INTEGER REQUIREMENTS

To illustrate how to use Solver for integer programming, let's consider the staffing problem faced by a call center. Daily requirements for staff are usually developed from studies of congestion in the service system. Then an optimization model helps determine how large a staff is needed to cover the staffing requirements.

EXAMPLE 6.1   *Callum Communications*

Callum Communications runs a small call center that operates seven days a week. Callum requires a specified minimum number of employees to be at work each day, to provide the necessary level of customer service. Under union regulations, employees at the call center must all work full-time schedules, which means five consecutive workdays and two days off per week. Furthermore, employees whose regular schedules include a weekend day receive a pay premium. Specifically, employees who work five weekdays are paid $400 per week. Employees who work one of the weekend days are paid $440, and employees who work both of the weekend days are paid $470. The minimum daily requirements for workers are described in the following table.

Day	Sun	Mon	Tue	Wed	Thu	Fri	Sat
Requirement	16	18	18	17	13	8	5

Callum's management wishes to minimize the cost of salaries paid to the workforce while meeting the staffing requirements.   ∎

At the call center, seven different work shifts are possible under union rules. Each shift starts a five-day work period on a particular day. For example, suppose we use *SU* to represent the number of employees who start work on Sunday, *MO* for the number who start work on Monday, and so on. These variables can make sense only if their values are integers. The constraints require that the number of employees assigned to work a given day must be at least as large as the daily minimum. For example, the number working on Thursday ($SU + MO + TU + WE + TH$) must be greater than or equal to 13, and a similar constraint applies for each of the other days of the week. In addition, the total salary cost for a week plays the role of the objective function. The algebraic model, shown below, is a variation on the staff-scheduling model introduced in Chapter 2.

Minimize $z =$ 440SU +400MO +440TU +470WE +470TH +470FR +470SA

subject to

SU				+WE	+TH	+FR	+$SA \geq 16$
SU	+MO				+TH	+FR	+$SA \geq 18$
SU	+MO	+TU				+FR	+$SA \geq 18$
SU	+MO	+TU	+WE				+$SA \geq 17$
SU	+MO	+TU	+WE	+TH			≥ 13
	+MO	+TU	+WE	+TH	+FR		≥ 8
		+TU	+WE	+TH	+FR	+$SA \geq 5$	

Figure 6.1 shows the complete spreadsheet model. It is also a variation of the spreadsheet model for staff scheduling introduced in Chapter 2. When we treat this model as a linear programming problem, the model specification is as follows.

Objective:	I8 (minimize)
Variables:	B5:H5
Constraints:	I11:I17 $\geq$ K11:K17

As shown in Figure 6.1, Solver produces a solution containing some fractions (e.g., 3.667 employees starting on Monday) and a total cost of $8656.67.

	A	B	C	D	E	F	G	H	I	J	K
1	**Staff Scheduling**										
2											
3	**Decision Variables**	Starting day									
4		SU	MO	TU	WE	TH	FR	SA			
5	staff	11	3.667	0	1.667	0	2.667	0.667			
6											
7	**Objective Function**								Total		
8	cost	440	400	440	470	470	470	470	8656.67		
9											
10	**Constraints**								LHS		RHS
11	SU	1	0	0	1	1	1	1	16	>=	16
12	MO	1	1	0	0	1	1	1	18	>=	18
13	TU	1	1	1	0	0	1	1	18	>=	18
14	WE	1	1	1	1	0	0	1	17	>=	17
15	TH	1	1	1	1	1	0	0	16.33333	>=	15
16	FR	0	1	1	1	1	1	0	8	>=	8
17	SA	0	0	1	1	1	1	1	5	>=	5
18											

|◄ ◄ ► ►| Staffing

Figure 6.1. Spreadsheet model for Example 6.1.

Figure 6.2. Declaring integer variables in Example 6.1.

The application of Solver to integer programming models, once they are formulated, is relatively straightforward. Solver treats the requirement that a variable must be integer as an additional constraint. Along with the familiar constraint types $\leq$, $\geq$, and $=$, the drop-down menu in the Add Constraint window also permits *int* and *bin*. The *int* constraint designates a variable to be integer valued, while the *bin* constraint designates a variable to be either 0 or 1 (binary valued). To produce an integer solution in Example 6.1, we add a constraint that designates the decision variables to be integers, as shown in Figure 6.2. The specification of the model in the task pane is shown in Figure 6.3, where we can see the explicit designation of integer variables.

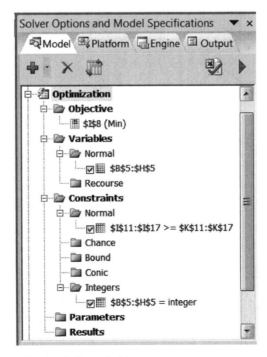

Figure 6.3. Model specification for Example 6.1.

Once we build the model and designate particular variables as integer or binary, the next step is to examine the options in the Integer group of the Engine tab on the task pane. The key option is the Integer Tolerance option, which should normally be set to zero. At some other setting, such as 0.05, Solver is guaranteed to find a solution that is no worse than 5 percent away from the optimum, as measured by the objective function. Clearly, we would prefer to find the very best solution, and this calls for an Integer Tolerance parameter of zero. However, in some large models, a tight Integer Tolerance level may require the solution procedure to take a great deal of time. Therefore, we sometimes keep the level at 0.05 while we are debugging a large model, and we leave it at that level if we find that solution times are prohibitively long otherwise. If Solver can locate a solution at the 0.05 level in a reasonable amount of time, we can experiment further by lowering the parameter toward zero.

With the integer variables designated and the Integer Tolerance option set, Solver produces an optimal solution, shown in Figure 6.4, with a total cost of $8790. On the surface, at least, there is no intuitive reason why we would have anticipated this result based on the solution to the linear program. It is not, for example, a rounded-off version of the optimal solution. Thus, by using the integer programming capability in Solver, Callum can meet its staffing requirements with minimum salary cost.

As suggested by this example, integer programming models look just like linear programming models, except for the fact that certain variables are constrained to be integer valued. The differences occur within Solver, not in the spreadsheet model. Moreover, finding a solution with Solver simply requires the user to take two additional steps beyond the typical procedure for solving linear programs—that is, designating integer variables and setting the Integer Tolerance parameter. When the only role of integers in a model is to avoid fractional values in what otherwise would be a normal linear program, then the formulation principles we covered in

	A	B	C	D	E	F	G	H	I	J	K
1	**Staff Scheduling**										
2											
3	**Decision Variables**	Starting day									
4		SU	MO	TU	WE	TH	FR	SA			
5	staff	11	4	0	2	0	3	0			
6											
7	**Objective Function**								Total		
8	cost	440	400	440	470	470	470	470	8790.00		
9											
10	**Constraints**								LHS		RHS
11	SU	1	0	0	1	1	1	1	16	>=	16
12	MO	1	1	0	0	1	1	1	18	>=	18
13	TU	1	1	1	0	0	1	1	18	>=	18
14	WE	1	1	1	1	0	0	1	17	>=	17
15	TH	1	1	1	1	1	0	0	17	>=	15
16	FR	0	1	1	1	1	1	0	9	>=	8
17	SA	0	0	1	1	1	1	1	5	>=	5
18											

Staffing   Staffing2

Figure 6.4. Optimal integer solution to Example 6.1.

Chapters 2 and 3, along with the *int* constraint, are likely to suffice. That was the case in Example 6.1.

In some cases, such as the call center model, all of the variables are constrained to be integers. This type of model is sometimes called a *pure integer program*. In other cases, certain variables may be integers, but others are allowed to be noninteger. A model containing both kinds of variables is called a *mixed integer program*. Using Solver, the only difference between these two cases is the set of variables designated by the *int* constraint.

At the level of building models for use with Solver, integer programming may seem to be a minor technical extension of what we can already do with linear programming. However, as we explore the formulation of integer programs using binary variables in this chapter and the next, a very different picture emerges. The opportunity to use binary variables provides access to a class of models that is actually very different from linear programming.

The solution algorithm within Solver for handling integer programs is generically known as a *branch and bound procedure*. At the end of this chapter, we take a look at how such a procedure works.

6.2. THE CAPITAL BUDGETING PROBLEM

A binary variable, which takes on the values 0 or 1, can represent a *yes/no decision*—that is, a decision that represents a choice between taking an action and not taking it. We sometimes think in terms of discrete projects, where the decision to undertake the project is represented by the value 1 and the decision to forego the project is represented by the value 0. A classical example arises in conjunction with the *capital budgeting problem*, as illustrated by the Newton Corporation.

EXAMPLE 6.2   *The Newton Corporation*

Division A of the Newton Corporation has been allocated $40 million for capital projects this year. Managers in Division A have examined various possibilities and have proposed five projects for the capital budgeting committee to consider. The projects cover a variety of activities and functional areas, and there is just one of each type. The projects are listed below.

P1 Renovate the production facility for greater efficiency.
P2 License a new technology for use in production.
P3 Expand advertising by naming a stadium.
P4 Purchase land and construct a new headquarters building.
P5 Introduce a new product to complement the current line.

Each project has an estimated net present value (NPV), and each requires a capital expenditure, which must come out of the budget for capital projects. The following table summarizes the possibilities, as they have been provided to the committee, with all figures in millions of dollars.

Project	P1	P2	P3	P4	P5
NPV	2.0	3.6	3.2	1.6	2.8
Expenditure	12	24	20	8	16

The committee would like to maximize the total NPV from projects selected, subject to a $40-million limit on capital expenditures. This $40-million constraint makes it impossible to undertake all five projects; a subset of the five must be selected.   ∎

The problem facing the Newton Corporation can be posed as an allocation model with one constraint, as shown below with objective function and constraint scaled to represent millions of dollars.

$$\text{Maximize } z = 2.0P1 + 3.6P2 + 3.2P3 + 1.6P4 + 2.8P5$$
$$\text{subject to}$$
$$12P1 + 24P2 + 20P3 + 8P4 + 16P5 \leq 40$$

A spreadsheet model for this problem is shown in Figure 6.5. (A feasible, but suboptimal set of choices is displayed.) If we treat the model as if it were a simple linear program, we can specify the problem as follows.

Objective:	G8 (maximize)
Variables:	B5:F5
Constraints:	$G11 \leq I11$

In the discussion that follows, we elaborate on the development and interpretation of the integer programming model as it is derived from the linear programming model. Our purpose is to develop some intuition for binary variables in optimization models, and we won't elaborate in the same way for the other modes we introduce later.

	A	B	C	D	E	F	G	H	I
1	Capital Budgeting Model								
2									
3	Decision Variables								
4	Project no.	P1	P2	P3	P4	P5			
5	Accept?	1	1	0	0	0			
6									
7	Objective Function								
8	NPV	2.0	3.6	3.2	1.6	2.8	5.6		
9									
10	Constraints								Budget
11	Expenditures	12	24	20	8	16	36	<=	40
12									

CapBud

Figure 6.5. Linear program for Example 6.2.

Figure 6.6. Optimal solution to the linear program for Example 6.2.

The optimal NPV in the linear program for Example 6.2 appears to be $8 million, as shown in Figure 6.6, but the solution would require the selection of project P4 five times. However, none of the projects can be implemented more than once. In particular, it is not possible to buy the same parcel of land and build new headquarters five times; obviously, that activity can be done only once.

To prevent any project from being implemented several times, we can require each of the variables to be no greater than 1. If we optimize the model as a linear program, imposing an upper bound of 1 on each of the variables, the maximum NPV comes to just over $7 million, as shown in Figure 6.7, but the optimal mix of projects is P1, P4, P5, and one-fifth of P3. However, none of the projects can be done in a fractional amount. In the case of P3, we cannot pay for a fraction of a stadium name; the project is indivisible and must be either accepted or rejected in its entirety. No part-way adoption of any of the projects is possible. Therefore, we must use binary variables, as all-or-nothing variables, to represent choices.

Figure 6.7. Optimal solution to the linear program for Example 6.2 with ceilings of 1.

Having seen why a purely linear programming approach is unsuitable for the situation at the Newton Corporation, we add the constraint that each variable is binary. The model specification is as follows.

Objective:	G8 (maximize)
Variables:	B5:F5
Constraints:	$G11 \leq I11$
	B5:F5 = binary

The optimal solution achieves a NPV of $6.8 million, achieved by accepting projects P1, P3, and P4, as shown in Figure 6.8. This figure represents the largest value that can be achieved with the five candidate projects from the allocation of a $40 million budget.

The capital budgeting model captures a well known allocation problem, in which each candidate project is either included in the solution once or not at all. Finding solutions can be difficult because of the "lumpy" nature of the projects as they consume resources in the budget constraint. Let's take a closer look at the nature of our solution.

In a problem with one constraint on expenditures, the intuitive approach would be to rank the projects by the ratio of value achieved to capital expenditure required, or in this case, the ratio of NPV to capital expense. If we calculate those ratios, we obtain the following numbers.

Project	P4	P5	P1	P3	P2
NPV	1.6	2.8	2.0	3.2	3.6
Expense	8	16	12	20	24
Ratio	0.200	0.175	0.167	0.160	0.150

	A	B	C	D	E	F	G	H	I
1	Capital Budgeting Model								
2									
3	Decision Variables								
4	Project no.	P1	P2	P3	P4	P5			
5	Accept	1	0	1	1	0			
6									
7	Objective Function								
8	NPV	2.0	3.6	3.2	1.6	2.8	6.8		
9									
10	Constraints								Budget
11	Expenditures	12	24	20	8	16	40	<=	40
12									

H ◀ ▶ H   CapBud CB2 CB3 **CB4**

Figure 6.8. Optimal integer solution for Example 6.2.

In the table, we have ordered the projects with the highest ratio on the left. Therefore, using ratios to represent priorities, the intuitive rule would suggest adopting projects P4, then P5, and then continuing in order until the budget is consumed. If we followed that logic, we would adopt P4 and P5, but their expenditures of $36 million would leave no room in the budget for other projects, and the total NPV would be $4.4 million. However, by judiciously departing from the priority ordering, we can reject P5 and instead adopt P1 and P3, thus achieving a full use of the capital budget and a NPV of $6.8 million. The lumpiness of capital expenses means that we can't adopt fractional projects and follow our intuitive sense of priorities. Instead, we have to account for the implications of each combination of expenditures in terms of the budget remaining when we examine which combinations of projects make sense. The number of combinations is large enough that it becomes tedious to write down all the possibilities. In large problems, that task would be prohibitively time consuming, yet an integer programming model can provide us with optimal solutions readily.

The capital budgeting model illustrates decisions that are of the yes/no variety. In fact, all variables in the capital budgeting model are of this type. In other integer programming models, some of the variables might correspond to yes/no decisions (and thus to binary variables), while other variables resemble the familiar types of decisions that we have seen in other linear programming models.

6.3. SET COVERING

The covering model is one of the basic linear programming model types. As introduced in Chapter 2, the model contains covering decisions corresponding to variables that are assumed to be divisible. However, when the decisions are of the yes/no variety, we have a binary-choice version of the covering model known as the *set-covering problem*. To describe how this model might arise, consider the situation at the Metropolis Police Department.

EXAMPLE 6.3   *Metropolis Police Department*

The police department in the city of Metropolis, has divided the city into 15 patrol sectors so patrol cars can respond quickly to service calls. Until recently, the streets have been patrolled overnight by 15 patrol cars, one in each sector. However, severe budget cuts have forced the city to eliminate some patrols. The chief of police has mandated that each sector should be covered by at least one unit located within the sector or in an adjacent sector.

The simplified map (Figure 6.9) depicts the 15 patrol sectors in the city. Any pair of sectors that share a boundary are considered to be adjacent. (Sectors 4 and 5 are adjacent, but not Sectors 3 and 5.) In addition, Sectors 7 and 14 are not accessible from each other because their boundary is the site of the Goose Pond Dam, while Sectors 9 and 13 are not mutually accessible due to the terrain of Moose Mountain, which is located at their boundary.

Having analyzed the map, the chief wants to know what number of patrol units will be required to provide service to the city's 15 sectors.   ∎

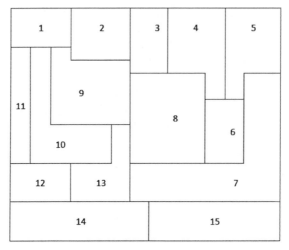

Figure 6.9. Sector map for Example 6.3.

Although the map is the basic source of data for this problem, we can use it to create an *adjacency array* for modeling purposes. This array is shown in Figure 6.10. In the figure, the numbered rows and columns correspond to the various sectors. An entry of 1 appears in row i and column j if sectors i and j are adjacent. (Each sector is considered adjacent to itself.)

A model for minimizing the required number of patrols can be constructed around the adjacency array by defining binary variables as follows.

$$y_j = 1 \quad \text{if a patrol is assigned to sector } j$$
$$y_j = 0 \quad \text{otherwise}$$

Then the objective function—the total number of patrols—can be expressed as the sum of the y_j values. In the model of Figure 6.11, this sum is represented as the SUMPRODUCT of the decision row and a row containing all 1s. To formulate constraints, suppose we focus on row i in the array, which corresponds to sector i. The SUMPRODUCT of this row and the decisions yields the number of patrols that can service county i. In the problem, we require coverage from at least one patrol for every row. In words, our model takes the following form.

Minimize $z =$ the number of patrols

subject to

Patrols servicing sector $i \geq 1$, (for all $i = 1, 2, \ldots, 15$)

In algebraic terms, we can let a_{ij} represent the adjacency data in the array of Figure 6.10. That is, $a_{ij} = 1$ if sectors i and j are adjacent and $a_{ij} = 0$ if not. Then

	1	2	3	4	5	6	7	8	9	10	11	12	13	14	15
1	1	1	0	0	0	0	0	0	1	1	1	0	0	0	0
2	1	1	1	0	0	0	0	0	1	0	0	0	0	0	0
3	0	1	1	1	0	0	0	1	1	0	0	0	0	0	0
4	0	0	1	1	1	1	0	1	0	0	0	0	0	0	0
5	0	0	0	1	1	1	1	0	0	0	0	0	0	0	0
6	0	0	0	1	1	1	1	1	0	0	0	0	0	0	0
7	0	0	0	0	1	1	1	1	0	0	0	0	1	1	1
8	0	0	1	1	0	1	1	1	1	0	0	0	1	0	0
9	1	1	1	0	0	0	0	1	1	1	0	0	1	0	0
10	1	0	0	0	0	0	0	0	1	1	1	1	1	0	0
11	1	0	0	0	0	0	0	0	0	1	1	1	0	0	0
12	0	0	0	0	0	0	0	0	0	1	1	1	1	1	0
13	0	0	0	0	0	0	1	1	1	1	0	1	1	1	0
14	0	0	0	0	0	0	1	0	0	0	0	1	1	1	1
15	0	0	0	0	0	0	1	0	0	0	0	0	0	1	1

Figure 6.10. Adjacency array for Example 6.3.

we can write

$$\text{Minimize } z = \sum y_j$$

subject to

$$\sum_j a_{ij} y_j \geq 1, \quad (\text{for all sectors } i = 1, 2, \ldots, 15)$$

In the spreadsheet of Figure 6.11, we have positioned the constraint information immediately to the right of the data array because the rows of the array give rise to constraints. We then specify the model as follows.

Objective:	R7 (minimize)
Variables:	C5:Q5
Constraints:	R11:R25 $\geq$ T11:T25
	C5:Q5 = binary

Figure 6.11 shows the optimal solution, obtained with the linear solver and an Integer Tolerance of 0, which calls for assigning patrols to Sectors 3, 7, and 10. By using an integer programming model, the police department can provide service to Metropolis while minimizing the number of patrols needed.

The generic set covering problem involves the selection of objects to meet given coverage requirements, where selection is a matter of binary choice. Each column in the constraints of the model (refer to Figure 6.11 as an example) corresponds to an object and the coverage it provides. When the coverage is expressed with 0s and 1s (the constraint coefficients in a column), we can think of the 1s as defining a coverage

		1	2	3	4	5	6	7	8	9	10	11	12	13	14	15				
Set Covering: Deploying Patrols																				
Decisions																				
Sector		1	2	3	4	5	6	7	8	9	10	11	12	13	14	15				
Locate?		0	0	1	0	0	0	1	0	0	1	0	0	0	0	0				
Objective		1	1	1	1	1	1	1	1	1	1	1	1	1	1	1	3		Number of Locations	
Adjacency Data																				
		1	2	3	4	5	6	7	8	9	10	11	12	13	14	15		Constraints		
	1	1	1	0	0	0	0	0	0	1	1	1	0	0	0	0	1	>=	1	cover 1
	2	1	1	1	0	0	0	0	0	1	0	0	0	0	0	0	1	>=	1	cover 2
	3	0	1	1	1	0	0	0	1	1	0	0	0	0	0	0	1	>=	1	cover 3
	4	0	0	1	1	1	1	0	1	0	0	0	0	0	0	0	1	>=	1	cover 4
	5	0	0	0	1	1	1	1	0	0	0	0	0	0	0	0	1	>=	1	cover 5
	6	0	0	0	1	1	1	1	1	0	0	0	0	0	0	0	1	>=	1	cover 6
	7	0	0	0	0	1	1	1	1	0	0	0	1	1	1	1	1	>=	1	cover 7
	8	0	0	1	1	0	1	1	1	1	0	0	1	0	0	0	2	>=	1	cover 8
	9	1	1	1	0	0	0	0	1	1	1	0	0	1	0	0	2	>=	1	cover 9
	10	1	0	0	0	0	0	0	0	1	1	1	1	1	0	0	1	>=	1	cover 10
	11	1	0	0	0	0	0	0	0	0	1	1	1	0	0	0	1	>=	1	cover 11
	12	0	0	0	0	0	0	0	0	0	1	1	1	1	1	0	1	>=	1	cover 12
	13	0	0	0	0	0	0	1	1	1	1	0	1	1	1	0	2	>=	1	cover 13
	14	0	0	0	0	0	0	1	0	0	0	0	1	1	1	1	1	>=	1	cover 14
	15	0	0	0	0	0	0	1	0	0	0	0	0	0	1	1	1	>=	1	cover 15

SetCover

Figure 6.11. Optimal solution for Example 6.3.

set (i.e., the set of rows in which 1s appear). Thus, the selection of objects is equivalent to the selection of sets, and the problem is to choose the minimum number of sets and still provide the required coverage. This interpretation gives rise to the name *set-covering problem.*

6.4. SET PACKING

As we saw in the previous section, the covering model of linear programming leads to an analog in binary-choice programming. In a similar fashion, the allocation model of linear program leads to another analog. This model contains allocation constraints rather than covering constraints; otherwise, it resembles the set-covering model. To describe how this model might arise, consider the expansion problem faced by the Happy Landings Motel Company.

EXAMPLE 6.4   *Happy Landings Motels*

The Happy Landings Motel has been a successful one-of-a-kind business in its original location. Its new owner has decided to replicate the motel at several locations and form a small chain. More expansion will follow if this first phase is a success. The new owner has identified nine potential locations where a motel might be located. However, some of these locations are within 30 miles of each other, and the owner prefers to separate motels in the chain by at least 30 miles to avoid cannibalizing demand. The following information about location conflicts has been obtained from a map.

Potential site	Potential sites within 30 miles
1	2
2	1, 5, 7
3	5, 6, 8, 9
4	6, 7
5	2, 3, 6, 8
6	3, 4, 5, 7
7	2, 4, 6
8	3, 5
9	3

The new owner wants to build motels on as many sites as possible, while adhering to the 30-mile requirement. ∎

Again, the raw data for this problem comes from a map, organized according to the list given in Example 6.4. For modeling purposes, it's convenient to convert this information into a *conflict array*. This array is shown in Figure 6.12, as part of the ultimate model. In the figure, the numbered rows and columns correspond to the various

	A	B	C	D	E	F	G	H	I	J	K	L	M	N
1	Set Packing: Choosing Sites													
2														
3	Decisions													
4	Site		1	2	3	4	5	6	7	8	9			
5	Select?		1	0	0	1	0	0	0	1	0			
6														
7	Objective		1	1	1	1	1	1	1	1	1	3		
8														
9	Adjacency Data		1	2	3	4	5	6	7	8	9			
10		1	1	1								1	<=	1
11		2	1	1			1		1			1	<=	1
12		3			1		1	1		1	1	1	<=	1
13		4				1		1	1			1	<=	1
14		5		1	1		1	1		1		1	<=	1
15		6			1	1	1	1	1			1	<=	1
16		7		1		1		1	1			1	<=	1
17		8			1		1			1		1	<=	1
18		9			1						1	0	<=	1
19														

SetPack

Figure 6.12. Optimal solution for Example 6.4.

motel sites. An entry of 1 appears in row i and column j if sites i and j are within 30 miles of each other.

A model for maximizing the number of nonconflicting motel sites can be constructed around the conflict array by defining binary variables

$$y_j = 1 \quad \text{if a motel is assigned to site } j$$
$$y_j = 0 \quad \text{otherwise}$$

Then the objective function—the total number of motels—can be expressed as the sum of the y_j values. In the model of Figure 6.12, this sum is represented as the SUMPRODUCT of the decision row and a row containing all 1s. To formulate constraints, suppose we focus on row i in the array, which corresponds to site i. The SUMPRODUCT of this row and the decisions yields the number of assigned sites (possibly including site i itself) that conflict with site i. In the problem, we require the number of conflicts to be at most 1, for any site. In words, our model takes the following form.

Maximize $z =$ the number of sites

subject to

Sites in conflict with $i \leq 1$,   (for all $i = 1, 2, \dots, 9$)

In algebraic terms, we can let a_{ij} represent the conflict data in the array of Figure 6.12. That is, $a_{ij} = 1$ if sites i and j are within 30 miles and $a_{ij} = 0$ if not. Then we can write

Maximize $z = \sum y_j$

subject to

$$\sum_j a_{ij} y_j \leq 1, \quad \text{(for all sites } i = 1, 2, \dots, 9)$$

In the spreadsheet of Figure 6.12, we specify the model as follows.

Objective:	L7 (maximize)
Variables:	C5:K5
Constraints:	L10:L18 $\leq$ N10:N18
	C5:K5 $=$ binary

Figure 6.12 shows the optimal solution, obtained with the linear solver and an Integer Tolerance of 0, which calls for choosing sites 1, 4, and 8. By using an integer programming model, the new owner can open as many new motels as the 30-mile limit allows.

The generic version of this problem involves the selection of objects that avoid given conflict possibilities, with selection represented by binary choice. Each column in the constraints of the model (refer to Figure 6.12 as an example) corresponds to an object and the conflicts it generates. When the conflicts are expressed with 0s and 1s (the constraint coefficients in a column), we can think of the 1s as defining a conflict set (i.e., the set of rows in which 1s appear.) Thus, the selection of objects is equivalent to the selection of sets, and the problem is to "pack in" the maximum number of sets without creating conflicts. This interpretation gives rise to the name *set-packing problem*.

6.5. SET PARTITIONING

As another example of a binary choice model, we consider a *matching problem*. The term "matching" refers to identifying pairs—that is, associating one object in a population with exactly one other object. This structure differs from the assignment problem of Chapter 3, which calls for matching an object in one population, such as products, to an object in another population, such as factories. Consider the exam-scheduling problem as it arises at Oxbridge College.

EXAMPLE 6.5   *Oxbridge College*

Oxbridge College faces the problem of devising an exam schedule at the end of every term. By tradition, the exam period lasts four days, and exams are scheduled in the morning of each day. In other words, there are four available exam periods. To create an exam schedule, the college registrar assigns courses to exam days according to the course meeting time. Thus, all courses that meet Monday at 9am are assigned the same exam day. Eight distinct meeting times occur in the college calendar, and the registrar wants to assign two to each of the four exam days. However, when two times are assigned to the same exam day, some students may have a time conflict because they are enrolled in courses that meet at those two times. Special arrangements must then be made for such students. The registrar's office has an information system that can determine, for any pair of class times, how many students are taking courses at both times. With this information, the registrar would like to devise an exam schedule that makes the number of exam conflicts as small as possible because that minimizes the number of cases in which special arrangements have to be made. For the current term, the conflict numbers are displayed in the following table.

Time	T2	T3	T4	T5	T6	T7	T8
T1	20	15	18	14	16	11	8
T2		26	32	29	19	14	18
T3			40	32	29	26	20
T4				35	31	23	26
T5					31	26	27
T6						27	31
T7							26

■

It's not necessary to fill in the entire array because of symmetry: the number of conflicts between T_i and T_j is the same as the number of conflicts between T_j and T_i.

A	Pairs / Conflicts / Variables
Set Partitioning: The Matching Problem	
Pairs	1,2 1,3 1,4 1,5 1,6 1,7 1,8 2,3 2,4 2,5 2,6 2,7 2,8 3,4 3,5 3,6 3,7 3,8 4,5 4,6 4,7 4,8 5,6 5,7 5,8 6,7 6,8 7,8
Conflicts	20 15 18 14 16 11 8 26 32 29 19 14 18 40 32 29 26 20 35 31 23 26 31 26 27 27 31 26
Decision Variables	
	0 0 0 1 0 0 0 0 0 0 1 0 0 0 0 0 0 0 1 0 0 1 0 0 0 0 0 0
Objective Function	
76	Total Number of Conflicts
Constraints	

	Constraint rows
Time 1	1 1 1 1 1 1 1 0 0 0 0 0 0 0 0 0 0 0 0 0 0 0 0 0 0 0 0 0 1 = 1
Time 2	1 0 0 0 0 0 0 1 1 1 1 1 1 0 0 0 0 0 0 0 0 0 0 0 0 0 0 0 1 = 1
Time 3	0 1 0 0 0 0 0 1 0 0 0 0 0 1 1 1 1 1 0 0 0 0 0 0 0 0 0 0 1 = 1
Time 4	0 0 1 0 0 0 0 0 1 0 0 0 0 1 0 0 0 0 1 1 1 1 0 0 0 0 0 0 1 = 1
Time 5	0 0 0 1 0 0 0 0 0 1 0 0 0 0 1 0 0 0 1 0 0 0 1 1 1 0 0 0 1 = 1
Time 6	0 0 0 0 1 0 0 0 0 0 1 0 0 0 0 1 0 0 0 1 0 0 1 0 0 1 1 0 1 = 1
Time 7	0 0 0 0 0 1 0 0 0 0 0 1 0 0 0 0 1 0 0 0 1 0 0 1 0 1 0 1 1 = 1
Time 8	0 0 0 0 0 0 1 0 0 0 0 0 1 0 0 0 0 1 0 0 0 1 0 0 1 0 1 1 1 = 1

Match

Figure 6.13. Spreadsheet model for Example 6.5.

Although it is convenient to present the data in a half-array, it can also be presented in a horizontal layout, as in the standard linear programming format. (See rows 3 and 4 of Figure 6.13.)

The essential decision in this problem is a binary choice for matching. The binary decision variables x_{ij} are defined as follows.

$x_{ij} = 1$ if class time Ti and class time Tj are assigned to the same exam day.

$x_{ij} = 0$ otherwise

Because symmetry allows us to work with just half the conflict array, we need to define the x_{ij} variables only for $i < j$, which comes to 28 pairs. Then we can write the objective function as a SUMPRODUCT in the form $\sum c_{ij}x_{ij}$, where c_{ij} represents the number of conflicts occurring when Ti and Tj are assigned to the same exam day, and where the sum is taken over all 28 potential assignments. Because the quantity c_{ij} contributes to this sum only when $x_{ij} = 1$, the objective function measures the total number of conflicts in the exam schedule. Constraints are needed to make sure that each class time is assigned exactly one match. The algebraic model takes the following form.

Minimize $z = 20x_{12} + 15x_{13} + 18x_{14} + \quad \cdots \quad + 26x_{78}$

subject to

$$x_{12} + x_{13} + x_{14} + x_{15} + x_{16} + x_{17} + x_{18} = 1$$
$$x_{12} + x_{23} + x_{24} + x_{25} + x_{26} + x_{27} + x_{28} = 1$$
$$x_{13} + x_{23} + x_{34} + x_{35} + x_{36} + x_{37} + x_{38} = 1$$
$$x_{14} + x_{24} + x_{34} + x_{45} + x_{46} + x_{47} + x_{48} = 1$$
$$x_{15} + x_{25} + x_{35} + x_{45} + x_{56} + x_{57} + x_{58} = 1$$
$$x_{16} + x_{26} + x_{36} + x_{46} + x_{56} + x_{67} + x_{68} = 1$$
$$x_{17} + x_{27} + x_{37} + x_{47} + x_{57} + x_{67} + x_{78} = 1$$
$$x_{18} + x_{28} + x_{38} + x_{48} + x_{58} + x_{68} + x_{78} = 1$$

Figure 6.13 shows the spreadsheet model. The layout follows the standard linear programming layout introduced in Chapter 2. By transforming the layout of the conflict data from the original half-array into one long row in Figure 6.13, we facilitate the standard layout.

The model specification is the following.

Objective:	A10 (minimize)
Variables:	B7:AC7
Constraints:	AD13:AD20 = 1
	B7:AC7 = binary

After entering this information, we set Integer Tolerance to 0 and run the linear solver. The minimal number of conflicts is 76, as shown in the figure, and the optimal pairings are Time 1 with Time 5, Time 2 with Time 6, Time 3 with Time 8, and Time 4 with Time 7. By using an integer programming model, Oxbridge can thus limit the number of exam conflicts to the minimum possible level.

The binary-choice model in Figure 6.13 resembles the set covering model and the set packing model, except for the constraint type. Again, we can think of columns as sets, and in this case, the 1s in each column identify the pair of objects in the corresponding match. The problem involves choosing a full match—that is, a collection of pairs such that each object appears exactly once in the collection. The "exactly once" requirement means that the sets selected must partition the population of objects into mutually exclusive and exhaustive subsets. For that reason, this problem type is often called a *set-partitioning problem.*

In Example 6.5, the number of class times is exactly equal to twice the number of exam days. More generally, the number of class times could be slightly less than twice the number of exam days, and a similar model could be used. For example, if there were six class times rather than eight, then only two pairings would be needed, and two of the class times would be unpaired. To accommodate this condition, we could state the model constraints as LT inequalities and add a constraint to ensure that at least two pairings took place.

Although Example 6.5 occurs in the setting of scheduling exams, the same kind of matching model can be used to schedule class meetings (or training courses, or conference sessions, etc.) when there are at most two items per time period. Several additional conditions may apply as well, but the basic structure of such problems often corresponds to the matching problem.

6.6. PLAYOFF SCHEDULING

An application area for integer programming that has received increasing attention lately is the scheduling of sports teams in professional leagues. Although basic guidelines exist for the creation of a "balanced" schedule, a good deal of flexibility remains, and several specific considerations come into play in determining an "optimal" schedule. As an example, a relatively new league in Latin America has just begun to examine the possibility of optimized scheduling.

EXAMPLE 6.6   *The Latin American Soccer Association*

Soccer is a popular spectator sport in Latin America, and as the year draws to a close, attention is focused on the Latin American Soccer Association (LASA), which administers the annual league competition. LASA also pays attention to trends in attendance, income from television contracts, and the interactions between soccer games and the broader national culture. One of its activities is drawing up a schedule for the season-ending playoff series.

The LASA league consists of 12 teams which compete against each other during a 24-week regular season. Then, after a one-week break, the playoffs begin. Six teams—three from each division—qualify for the playoffs based on their regular season performance. In the playoffs, each team must play each of the other qualifying teams. After those games have been played, the teams with the best record in each division meet in the championship game.

The playoff games are played on Saturdays, and each team plays every week. Several schedules can be constructed that allow the playoffs to be completed in five weeks, but the LASA Executive Board has determined that some schedules are preferable to others. In particular, they have noticed that attendance is relatively greater when two teams of the same division play each other (reflecting intradivision rivalries) and when games are relatively later in the schedule (reflecting the importance of the later games in determining the ultimate division winners). The Board has concluded that total attendance will be maximized if intra-division games are played as late as possible in the schedule.   ∎

When we examine the LASA problem closely, we can identify two basic constraints: (1) each team must play every other team, and (2) each team plays exactly one game each week. As a consequence, the schedule must require at least five weeks. When we turn to the objective, we observe that each team plays two intradivision rivals. Therefore, at best, the intradivision rivalries can be placed in the last two weeks of the schedule. Normally, it is not too difficult to devise a five-week schedule containing the 15 required games, even with pencil and paper. However, it may not be so easy to determine whether all intradivision rivalries can be placed in the last two (or even three) weeks. That's where an integer programming model can be useful.

To build the model, we rely on a binary-choice variable.

$$x_{jkt} = 1 \quad \text{if teams } j \text{ and } k \text{ meet in week } t \text{ of the schedule}$$
$$\phantom{x_{jkt} = } 0 \quad \text{otherwise}$$

We need to define these x_{jkt} variables for the 15 distinct pairs of teams corresponding to $j < k$, as well as for each of the five weeks. This specification gives us a total of 75 binary variables. Then it is straightforward to write the constraints of the problem. For the one-game-per-week constraint, we write

$$\sum_{\substack{k \neq j}}^{6} x_{jkt} = 1 \quad \text{for each team } j \text{ and week } t \qquad (6.1)$$

For the play-everyone-else constraint, we write

$$\sum_{t=1}^{6} x_{jkt} = 1 \quad \text{for each pair of teams } (j, k) \qquad (6.2)$$

The model contains 30 constraints of type (6.1) and 15 constraints of type (6.2), for a total of 45 constraints.

For the objective function, let's assume we wish to maximize the following expression.

$$\text{Maximize } z = \sum_{t=1}^{5} \sum_{k \neq j}^{6} c_{jkt} x_{jkt}$$

This expression represents a sum containing 75 terms. In selecting the coefficients c_{jkt}, we first need a mechanism that favors intradivision games over the other games. An easy way is to associate a zero coefficient with each pairing of teams from different divisions. Then, for the intradivision games, we need a mechanism that favors later weeks over earlier weeks. For this purpose, we could associate a positive objective function coefficient equal to the week number for each variable. Thus, we define the following coefficients

$c_{jkt} = t$ if intradivision teams j and k meet in week t of the schedule
    0   otherwise

Perhaps the notion of "later week" deserves a closer look. In our assignment of coefficient values, we would permit the model to place two intradivision games in week 4 (making a contribution of 8 to the objective) rather than placing one intradivision game in week 5 (making a contribution of just 5). However, if we do not find that trade-off desirable, we could use an alternative scheme.

The spreadsheet model for the LASA problem is not difficult to build, but we must keep its size in mind: 45 constraints and 75 variables. For reasons of readability, Figure 6.14 shows just the upper left portion of the model. The variables appear in row 15, with rows 13 and 14 containing labels for the variables. Specifically, the pair (j, k) appears in row 13 and the week t appears in row 14. The first set of constraints, corresponding to (6.1) appears in rows 18–47, and the second set, corresponding to (6.2) appears in rows 49–63. Row 48 reproduces the team pair in row 13 for easier reference.

Figure 6.15 shows the entire model. All the constraints are equations with right-hand-side constants equal to 1, so this model takes the form of a set-partitioning problem. The sets of constraints corresponding to (6.1) and (6.2) each have distinctive, repeating clusters of nonzero coefficients, which become visible when we zoom out and display the entire model in one window. By examining the model at this zoom level, we can scan the layout for possible typos or omissions.

The model specification is the following

Objective:	BZ16 (maximize)
Variables:	C15:BY15
Constraints:	BZ18:BZ47 = 1
	BZ49:BZ63 = 1
	C15:BY15 = binary

13	Teams	12	13	14	15	16	23	24	25	26	34	35	36	45	46	56	12	13	14	15	16	23	24	25	26	34	35	36	45	46	56
14	Week	1	1	1	1	1	1	1	1	1	1	1	1	1	1	1	2	2	2	2	2	2	2	2	2	2	2	2	2	2	2
15	Variables	0	0	0	0	1	0	1	0	0	0	1	0	0	0	0	0	0	1	0	0	0	1	1	0	0	0	0	0	0	0
16	Objective	1	1	0	0	0	1	0	0	0	0	0	0	1	1	1	2	2	0	0	0	2	0	0	0	0	0	0	2	2	2
17																															
18	1 game/week per team	1	1	1	1	1																									
19	30	1					1	1	1	1																					
20			1				1				1	1	1																		
21				1				1			1			1	1																
22					1				1			1		1		1															
23						1				1			1		1	1															
24																	1	1	1	1	1										
25																	1					1	1	1	1						
26																		1				1				1	1	1			
27																			1				1			1			1	1	
28																				1				1			1		1		1
29																					1				1			1		1	1

48	Pairs	12	13	14	15	16	23	24	25	26	34	35	36	45	46	56	12	13	14	15	16	23	24	25	26	34	35	36	45	46	56
49	15	1															1														
50			1															1													
51				1															1												
52					1															1											
53						1															1										
54							1															1									
55								1															1								
56									1															1							
57										1															1						
58											1															1					
59												1															1				
60													1															1			
61														1															1		
62															1															1	
63																1															1

Playoffs

Figure 6.14. Portion of the spreadsheet model for Example 6.6.

A solution appears in both Figures 6.14 and 6.15, but the entire schedule is more usefully displayed in a table such as in Table 6.1, with shading to designate intradivision games.

In the optimal schedule, all intradivision games are played in weeks 3–5. Although six intradivision games must be played, they cannot all fit into the final two weeks of the schedule.

The LASA scenario leads to a simple version of the playoff scheduling problem. In actual practice, administrative bodies are concerned about several other features of a schedule. For example, it's common to keep track of home and away games and to restrict a schedule so that no team plays more than two consecutive games at home. In other settings, governing boards keep track of especially "strong" teams and require that no team be scheduled to play two strong teams in successive weeks. Finally, in many countries, soccer games compete with cultural events, so leagues often prohibit games on dates corresponding to local festivals, bicycle races, or

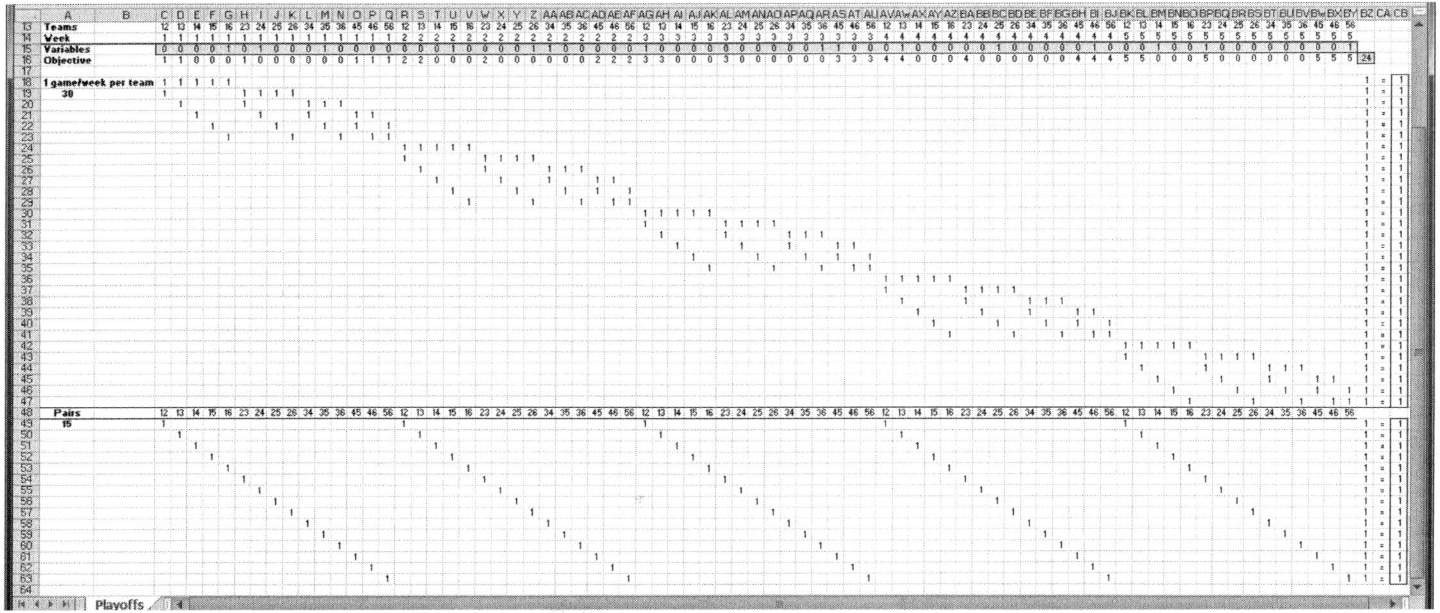

Figure 6.15. Spreadsheet model for Example 6.6.

Table 6.1. Playoff Schedule for LASA

		\	Week			
		1	2	3	4	5
	1	16	15	12	13	14
	2	24	26	21	25	23
Team	3	35	34	36	31	32
	4	42	43	45	46	41
	5	53	51	54	52	56
	6	61	62	63	64	65

religious celebrations. Considerations such as these can be accommodated with integer programming models, but sometimes the scheduling models grow quite large.

6.7. SOLVING A LARGE-SCALE SET PARTITIONING PROBLEM

In this section, we examine a very large type of binary choice problem. It is considered large because it contains a large number of variables, not to mention a large number of feasible possibilities. Although the size of the problem outstrips the normal capabilities of Solver, the set partitioning model provides us with an alternative approach to finding a solution. The scenario at Courier Express gives rise to such a problem.

EXAMPLE 6.7   *Courier Express*

Courier Express serves 12 locations in its region with delivery service from a central transportation hub. Each day, trucks are sent out to several locations, where they deliver and collect packages. Then the trucks return to the hub, where the pickups are sorted and sent on, and where incoming packages are sorted and loaded on trucks in preparation for the next day's work. Each truck leaves the hub, visits some locations, and then returns to headquarters. The dispatching problem is to route the trucks so that some truck visits each location. Distances between locations are known. Courier Express wants to find a dispatching plan that achieves the minimum total distance traveled by its trucks each day.   ∎

The distance data for Example 6.7 can be displayed in an array, as shown in Figure 6.16. In this array, the element appearing in row i and column j is d_{ij}, the distance from location i to location j. Location 1 corresponds to the depot, and locations 2–13 correspond to the pickup and delivery points.

To analyze this problem, we first assume that Courier Express deploys four trucks and that each truck travels to three locations before returning to the depot. For each truck, we want to assign a set of locations and a sequence for those locations. We refer to this assignment as a *segment*. Each segment has a total distance, dictated by the sequence in which the truck visits the locations and returns to the depot. A full solution is made up of four segments, one for each truck. For a group of four segments to be feasible, each location must be visited exactly once.

	1	2	3	4	5	6	7	8	9	10	11	12	13
1	0	70	13	36	37	25	40	74	88	54	40	62	65
2	70	0	99	44	15	83	16	73	61	86	57	45	97
3	13	99	0	16	33	31	60	19	73	61	25	88	57
4	36	44	16	0	66	49	22	15	20	66	66	23	13
5	37	15	33	66	0	27	93	66	99	57	79	79	26
6	25	83	31	49	27	0	14	17	67	48	89	54	94
7	40	16	60	22	93	14	0	54	60	77	71	25	92
8	74	73	19	15	66	17	54	0	88	66	25	42	72
9	88	61	73	20	99	67	60	88	0	21	70	57	93
10	54	86	61	66	57	48	77	66	21	0	49	89	89
11	40	57	25	66	79	89	71	25	70	49	0	42	46
12	62	45	88	23	79	54	25	42	57	89	42	0	96
13	65	97	57	13	26	94	92	72	93	89	46	96	0

Figure 6.16. Distance data for Example 6.7.

Figure 6.17 displays a model for this situation. Columns B–Z correspond to 25 segments. In column B, for example, the truck travels from the depot (city 1) to cities 7, 12, and 9 in order, and then returns to the depot. This route is specified in rows 25–29. Based on that route, the pairwise distances between locations are recorded in rows 31–34 and their total appears in row 36. These 25 segments have been selected randomly.

The remainder of Figure 6.17 shows a set partitioning model in which binary-choice variables indicate whether a segment should be selected. The objective function is the SUMPRODUCT of the binary variables and the total distances in row 36. The constraints in the model require that each location must be selected exactly once. Thus, the model attempts to find the best feasible combination of

A	B	C	D	E	F	G	H	I	J	K	L	M	N	O	P	Q	R	S	T	U	V	W	X	Y	Z	AA	AB	AC
24 Segment No.	1	2	3	4	5	6	7	8	9	10	11	12	13	14	15	16	17	18	19	20	21	22	23	24	25			
25	1	1	1	1	1	1	1	1	1	1	1	1	1	1	1	1	1	1	1	1	1	1	1	1	1			
26	7	10	4	4	6	13	12	5	5	7	11	12	7	5	10	12	8	4	3	11	10	3	4	11	13			
27	12	5	7	5	7	12	2	7	12	13	4	3	13	3	9	13	7	12	11	7	8	6	7	13	13			
28	9	12	6	6	6	3	5	9	10	10	3	10	13	5	5	7	6	3	13	5	11	5	11	2	5			
29	1	1	1	1	1	1	1	1	1	1	1	1	1	1	1	1	1	1	1	1	1	1	1	1	1			
30																												
31 Distances	40	54	36	36	25	65	62	37	37	40	40	62	40	37	54	62	74	36	13	40	54	13	36	40	65			
32	25	57	22	66	14	96	45	93	79	92	66	88	92	33	21	96	54	23	25	71	66	31	22	46	0			
33	57	79	14	27	14	88	15	60	89	89	16	61	0	33	99	92	14	88	46	93	25	27	71	97	26			
34	88	62	25	25	25	13	37	88	54	54	13	54	65	37	37	40	25	13	65	37	40	37	40	70	37			
35																												
36 Total Distance	210	252	97	154	78	262	159	278	259	275	135	265	197	140	211	290	167	160	149	241	185	108	169	253	128			
37																												
38 Selection	0	0	0	0	1	0	0	0	0	1	0	0	0	0	1	0	0	0	0	0	0	0	1	0	0	672		
39 2	0	0	0	0	0	0	1	0	0	0	0	0	0	0	0	0	0	0	0	0	0	0	0	1	0	0	=	1
40 3	0	0	0	0	0	1	0	0	0	0	1	1	0	1	0	0	0	1	1	0	0	1	0	0	0	1	=	1
41 4	0	0	1	1	0	0	0	0	0	0	1	0	0	0	0	0	1	0	0	0	0	1	0	0	0	0	=	1
42 5	0	1	0	1	0	0	1	1	1	0	0	0	1	1	0	0	0	0	1	0	1	0	0	1		2	=	1
43 6	0	0	1	1	0	0	0	0	0	0	0	0	0	1	0	0	0	0	1	0	0	0	0	0		2	=	1
44 7	1	0	1	0	1	0	0	1	0	1	0	0	1	0	0	1	1	0	0	1	0	0	1	0	0	2	=	1
45 8	0	0	0	0	0	0	0	0	0	0	0	0	0	0	1	0	0	0	1	0	0	0	0	0		0	=	1
46 9	1	0	0	0	0	0	0	1	0	0	0	0	0	1	0	0	0	0	0	0	0	0	0	0		1	=	1
47 10	0	1	0	0	0	0	0	0	0	1	1	0	1	0	0	0	1	0	0	0	0	0	0	1	0	2	=	1
48 11	0	0	0	0	0	0	0	0	0	1	0	0	0	0	0	0	0	1	1	1	0	1	1	0		0	=	1
49 12	1	1	0	0	0	1	1	0	1	0	0	1	0	0	0	1	0	1	0	0	0	0	0	0	0	2	=	1
50 13	0	0	0	0	0	1	0	0	0	0	1	0	0	1	0	0	1	0	0	0	0	0	1	1		1	=	1

Analysis

Figure 6.17. Set partitioning model for Example 6.7.

	B	C	D	E	F	G	H	I	J	K	L	M	N	O	P	Q	R	S	T	U	V	W	X	Y	Z	AA	AB	AC
24 Segment No.	1	2	3	4	5	6	7	8	9	10	11	12	13	14	15	16	17	18	19	20	21	22	23	24	25			
25	1	1	1	1	1	1	1	1	1	1	1	1	1	1	1	1	1	1	1	1	1	1	1	1	1			
26	7	10	4	4	6	13	12	5	5	7	11	12	7	5	10	12	8	4	3	11	10	3	4	11	13			
27	12	5	7	5	7	12	2	7	12	13	4	3	13	3	9	13	7	12	11	7	8	6	7	13	13			
28	9	12	6	6	6	3	5	9	10	10	3	10	13	5	5	7	6	3	13	5	11	5	11	2	5			
29	1	1	1	1	1	1	1	1	1	1	1	1	1	1	1	1	1	1	1	1	1	1	1	1	1			
30																												
31 Distances	40	54	36	36	25	65	62	37	37	40	40	62	40	37	54	62	74	36	13	40	54	13	36	40	65			
32	25	57	22	66	14	96	45	93	79	92	66	88	92	33	21	96	54	23	25	71	66	31	22	46	0			
33	57	79	14	27	14	88	15	60	89	89	16	61	0	33	99	92	14	88	46	93	25	27	71	97	26			
34	88	62	25	25	25	13	37	88	54	54	13	54	65	37	37	40	25	13	65	37	40	37	40	70	37			
35																												
36 Total Distance	210	252	97	154	78	262	159	278	259	275	135	265	197	140	211	290	167	160	149	241	185	108	169	253	128			
37																												
38 Selection	0	0	0	0	0	0	0	0	0	0	0	0	0	0	1	0	1	1	0	0	0	0	0	1	0	791		
39 2	0	0	0	0	0	0	1	0	0	0	0	0	0	0	0	0	0	0	0	0	0	0	1	0		1	=	1
40 3	0	0	0	0	0	1	0	0	0	0	1	1	0	1	0	0	0	1	1	0	0	1	0	0		1	=	1
41 4	0	0	1	1	0	0	0	0	0	0	1	0	0	0	0	0	1	0	0	0	1	0	0	0		1	=	1
42 5	0	1	0	1	0	0	1	1	1	0	0	0	0	1	1	0	0	0	1	0	1	0	0	1		1	=	1
43 6	0	0	1	1	1	0	0	0	0	0	0	0	0	0	0	1	0	0	0	1	0	0	0			1	=	1
44 7	1	0	1	0	1	0	0	1	0	1	0	0	1	0	0	1	1	0	0	1	0	0	1	0	0	1	=	1
45 8	0	0	0	0	0	0	0	0	0	0	0	0	0	0	0	1	0	0	1	0	0	0	0			1	=	1
46 9	1	0	0	0	0	0	0	1	0	0	0	0	0	1	0	0	0	0	0	0	0	0	0			1	=	1
47 10	0	1	0	0	0	0	0	0	1	1	0	1	0	0	1	0	0	1	0	0	0	1	0	0		1	=	1
48 11	0	0	0	0	0	0	0	0	0	1	0	0	0	0	0	0	0	1	1	0	1	1	0			1	=	1
49 12	1	1	0	0	0	1	1	0	1	0	0	1	0	0	1	0	1	0	0	0	0	0	0	0		1	=	1
50 13	0	0	0	0	0	1	0	0	0	1	0	0	1	0	0	1	0	0	0	1	0	0	0	1	1	1	=	1

Figure 6.18. Optimal solution for the model.

the 25 segments. (It's possible, however, that no feasible combination can be found.) Although the initial set of decision variables shown in Figure 6.17 is infeasible, a Solver run produces an optimal total distance of 791, as shown in Figure 6.18.

It is unlikely that the solution to the problem shown in Figure 6.18 is truly an optimal solution to the overall problem because it is based on 25 randomly selected segments. However, we can repeat the analysis by generating another set of randomly selected segments and finding another solution. In fact, we can repeat this procedure several times. Figure 6.19 provides a view of the entire model, starting with the distance array in rows 3–15. Rows 19–21 contain a segment generator, which consists of random locations. These selections are determined by the formula =RANDBETWEEN(2,13). We can generate a new set of segments by pressing the F9 key; then we can copy the data in rows 19–21 and paste the values into rows 26–28. The formulas in the spreadsheet find the individual distances between locations by looking up values in the distance array, thus updating the objective function in cell AA38. The coefficients on the left-hand side of the constraints are binary values corresponding to the numbers in the segments of rows 26–28. Thus, as soon as we paste data into rows 26–28, the formulas in the spreadsheet update the set partitioning model. A Solver run finds a new optimal solution.

The revised model gives rise to a solution that may be better or worse than the previous one. However, we can repeat the segment generating procedure several times, saving the best solution encountered. In one set of trials, we repeated the procedure a dozen times and generated a solution with a total distance of 720.

How good is the solution thus obtained? It is difficult to say for sure. However, the repeated solution of a randomly generated subproblem seems to show considerable potential for generating good solutions. In addition, we can strengthen our approach in at least two ways. First, we can expand the model and include more segments. Our 25-segment model gave rise to an integer programming model with 25 variables and 12 constraints. It would not be difficult to solve problems containing 40 or 50 segments, and the sampling mechanism would likely be more effective. (An experiment using 40 segments with about a dozen trials generated a solution with a value of 627.)

Truck Dispatching

	1	2	3	4	5	6	7	8	9	10	11	12	13
1	0	70	13	36	37	25	40	74	88	54	40	62	65
2	70	0	99	44	15	83	16	73	61	86	57	45	97
3	13	99	0	16	33	31	60	19	73	61	25	88	57
4	36	44	16	0	66	49	22	15	20	66	66	23	13
5	37	15	33	66	0	27	93	66	99	57	79	79	26
6	25	83	31	49	27	0	14	17	67	48	89	54	94
7	40	16	60	22	93	14	0	54	60	77	71	25	92
8	74	73	19	15	66	17	54	0	88	66	25	42	72
9	88	61	73	20	99	67	60	88	0	21	70	57	93
10	54	86	61	66	57	48	77	66	21	0	49	89	89
11	40	57	25	66	79	89	71	25	70	49	0	42	46
12	62	45	88	23	79	54	25	42	57	89	42	0	96
13	65	97	57	13	26	94	92	72	93	89	46	96	0

Segment Generator

Segment	1	2	3	4	5	6	7	8	9	10	11	12	13	14	15	16	17	18	19	20	21	22	23	24	25
Generator	3	5	3	10	13	8	6	12	8	13	6	11	12	11	3	8	12	8	9	9	10	13	10	6	
	2	5	4	6	11	7	5	6	5	10	13	4	5	7	11	13	11	13	9	2	8	7	5	4	12
	7	5	11	10	6	4	7	12	12	5	8	10	4	3	5	11	4	11	2	5	8	12	2	13	6

Segment No	1	2	3	4	5	6	7	8	9	10	11	12	13	14	15	16	17	18	19	20	21	22	23	24	25
	1	1	1	1	1	1	1	1	1	1	1	1	1	1	1	1	1	1	1	1	1	1	1	1	1
	8	6	3	9	3	11	5	9	10	10	8	13	12	7	10	8	6	6	13	13	9	5	7	10	13
	9	3	4	4	6	11	4	3	9	12	10	8	8	3	12	9	3	7	12	13	6	9	7	12	12
	13	6	10	3	8	3	9	11	7	11	11	3	2	2	13	10	4	3	10	8	12	8	9	8	8
	1	1	1	1	1	1	1	1	1	1	1	1	1	1	1	1	1	1	1	1	1	1	1	1	1

Distances

74	25	13	88	13	40	37	88	54	54	74	65	62	40	54	74	25	25	65	65	88	37	40	54	65
88	31	16	20	31	0	66	73	21	89	66	72	42	60	89	88	31	14	96	0	67	99	0	89	96
93	31	66	16	17	25	20	25	60	42	49	19	73	99	96	21	16	60	89	72	54	88	60	42	42
65	25	54	13	74	13	88	40	40	40	40	13	70	70	65	54	36	13	54	74	62	74	88	74	74

Total Distance	320	112	149	137	135	78	211	226	175	225	229	169	247	269	304	237	108	112	304	211	271	298	188	259	277

Selection (objective = 767)

Figure 6.19. Improved solution for Example 6.7.

Second, we don't have to limit ourselves to segments containing exactly three locations. By constructing the model with some two-location segments and some four-location segments, we increase our chances of finding an asymmetric combination that might work even better. (Another experiment along these lines generated a solution value of 625.)

In this example, it is important to recognize that a direct attempt to find an optimal solution is likely to be impractical. If we tried to build a set-partitioning model containing all the possible segments, we would be facing the construction of a binary-choice model with hundreds of millions of variables—well beyond the capabilities of Solver. Perhaps we could imagine building a specialized algorithm tailored to the specific problem we want to solve, but that approach has drawbacks, too. We would need specialized code, and there would still be no guarantee that our algorithm would converge in a reasonable amount of time. Relying on randomly-generated segments may well be our best approach to finding at least a good solution.

6.8. THE ALGORITHM FOR SOLVING INTEGER PROGRAMS

We can give a rough outline of the procedure that Solver uses to find solutions to integer programming models, drawing on an example. For this purpose, we revisit

Example 2.1 (Brown Furniture Company), in which the problem is to determine the best allocation of resources to the production of chairs, desks, and tables. Suppose the problem has changed slightly so that there are 1900 available hours of fabrication capacity, 1850 of machining, and 1450 of assembly, along with 9600 square feet of wood. The linear programming problem is as follows.

$$
\begin{array}{lrrrcl}
\text{Maximize } z = & 16C & +20D & +14T & & \\
\text{subject to} & & & & & \\
& 4C & +6D & +2T & \leq & 1900 \\
& 3C & +8D & +6T & \leq & 1850 \\
& 9C & +6D & +4T & \leq & 1450 \\
& 30C & +40D & +25T & \leq & 9600
\end{array}
$$

Now we require all variables in the solution to be integers—that is, we want the number of chairs, desks, and tables to all be integers so that we can interpret the solution literally, as a viable schedule for the month.

When Solver tackles an integer programming problem, its first step is simply to ignore the integer restrictions and treat the problem as a normal linear program. This is called the *relaxed problem*, in the sense that the integer constraints are relaxed. We refer to this linear program as problem P. If we are fortunate, the optimal solution to this problem will contain integer decision variables and we will have solved the integer program. In this example, unfortunately, the optimal solution does not consist of integers, and we obtain

Solution to P

$C = 9.26, \quad D = 227.8, \quad T = 0$

$z^* = 4703.7$

The value of the objective function is at least an *upper bound* on the best value we could attain with integer values. No integer-valued solution could improve on the solution to the relaxed problem, in which the integer constraints do not apply.

Solver recognizes that this solution is infeasible for the integer program and creates two new linear programming problems to solve. The first, which we refer to as P_1, corresponds to the original problem, with the additional constraint $D \leq 227$. The second, referred to as P_2, corresponds to the original problem, with the requirement $D \geq 228$. In other words, we select a noninteger variable in the optimal solution and append one of two constraints: we force this variable to be either no larger than the next lower integer, or no smaller than the next higher integer. We could use an arbitrary rule to select which variable to constrain or a rule with a little more intelligence. Here, we choose the variable that is closest to an integer value.

The better of the solutions to the integer versions of P_1 and P_2 must be the optimal solution to the original problem. The reason is that together the two problems correspond to all feasible choices of integer decision variables, because they exclude only the cases associated with D-values strictly between 227 and 228, none of which is an integer. The implication is that we can forget the original problem for now and concentrate just on the two modified problems that replaced it, P_1 and P_2. If we can solve both of those as integer programs, we will have the solution we seek.

Next, Solver tackles P_1. Intuitively, we might expect the optimal solution to contain D at a value of 227 because it "wants" to be 227.8, but the additional constraint prevents it from being that large. Indeed, that is the case, and we obtain the following result.

$$Solution \ to \ P_1$$
$$C = 9.33, \ D = 227, \ T = 1$$
$$z^* = 4703.3$$

As we might expect, the additional constraint leads to a drop in the optimal objective function. More importantly, we still weren't lucky enough to produce an integer solution because C remains noninteger.

When Solver tackles P_2 (where $D \geq 228$), the optimal solution is as follows

$$Solution \ to \ P_2$$
$$C = 8.67, \ D = 228, \ T = 0$$
$$z^* = 4698.7$$

Having replaced the original problem with two modified problems, the status of our search is shown in Figure 6.20. Here, each (linear programming) problem is represented by a node in the tree diagram. We say that we *branch* from the original problem P to the modified problems P_1 and P_2. This means that we need only examine the two replacement problems and not the original. In a sense, the search has been effective so far because we started with a model that generated two noninteger decision variables, but now we are dealing with models that generate only one noninteger decision variable.

Next, we select P_1 for branching. We recognize that the optimal solution is infeasible for the integer version of P_1 because the value of C is noninteger. Hence, we create two modified versions to solve, one in which we add the constraint $C \leq 9$; the other in which we add the constraint $C \geq 10$. These bounds use the integers on either side of the value of C in the optimal solution to P_1. We refer to these problems as P_{11} (with

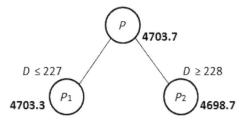

Figure 6.20. First level of branching.

$C \leq 9$) and P_{12} (with $C \geq 10$). Now we can forget P_1. The best among the solutions of P_{11}, P_{12}, and P_2 will be the solution we seek.

When we solve P_{11} we obtain the following result.

Solution to P_{11}

$C = 9,\ D = 227,\ T = 1.17$

$z^* = 4700.3$

The optimal solution is still noninteger, and the objective function has dropped slightly from the value in P_1. When we solve P_{12} we obtain the following result

Solution to P_{12}

$C = 10,\ D = 220,\ T = 10$

$z^* = 4700$

Here, we have been fortunate, and the solution to the linear program contains three integer-valued decision variables. It was not merely good fortune, of course: The systematic choice of additional constraints helped lead us to an integer solution. This solution is a feasible integer solution to the original problem. Now, the status of our search is shown in Figure 6.21. In principle, we could pursue the search from P_{11} or P_2.

Consider the linear program in P_2 and its objective function, which Solver has optimized at 4698.7. The solution of P_2 is still not feasible for the integer program, and the only way we can produce an integer-feasible solution is to impose additional constraints. Thus, the value 4698.7 represents an upper bound on the best solution we could find in this part of the search tree. When we add constraints to P_2, its objective function cannot get better, so it can be no larger than 4698.7. Since we have already found an integer-feasible solution with an objective function value of 4700, there is no reason to look for a feasible solution to P_2 because its objective function value could not be as good as the 4700 we have already found. We say that we have *fathomed* the

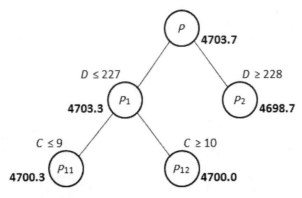

Figure 6.21. Second level of branching.

search tree below P_2, in the sense that we have implicitly evaluated all the branches that might emanate from P_2 and determined from the bound that none of the branches could be as good as the feasible solution we have already encountered.

We turn next to P_{11}. Its bound is 4700.3. Because this value is larger than that of the best integer solution we have found, it is still possible that we could find a better solution by branching from P_{11}. Because the only noninteger decision variable in P_{11} is $T = 1.17$, we branch to P_{111} (adding the constraint $T \leq 1$) and P_{112} (adding the constraint $T \geq 2$), and we obtain the following results.

Solution to P_{111}

$C = 9$, $D = 227$, $T = 1$

$z^* = 4698$

Solution to P_{112}

$C = 9$, $D = 226.4$, $T = 2$

$z^* = 4699.5$

We now have enough information to identify the optimal solution to the original problem. The solution to P_{111} contains integer decision variables, but its objective function is not as large as the integer-feasible solution to P_{12}. In addition, we can fathom P_{112} because its upper bound is 4699.5, also not as large as the integer-feasible solution to P_{12}. The final status of our search is shown in Figure 6.22, where we can see that the solution to P_{12} turns out to be optimal.

For any integer programming problem, Solver begins with the relaxed (linear) problem and finds the optimal solution to the corresponding linear program. If

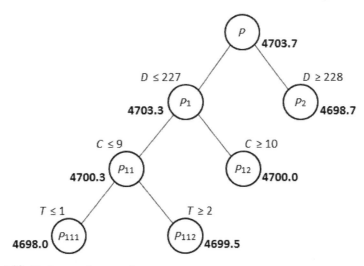

Figure 6.22. Final status of tree search.

all of the variables are integer, the solution to the integer program has been found. If not, x_1 will turn out to be either an integer or a fraction. If it is a fraction, Solver replaces the original problem with two derived problems (P_1 and P_2), each with an additional constraint that forces the solution away from the fractional value in the original. On the other hand, if x_1 is an integer, Solver then examines x_2. Two alternatives may arise, depending on whether x_2 is an integer or a fraction. If it is a fraction, Solver creates two derived problems containing additional constraints that force the solution away from the fractional value of x_2. Otherwise, Solver proceeds to examine x_3, and so on.

At each stage in this procedure, Solver maintains a list of unsolved problems. This list is structured so that the best integer-feasible solution to the problems on the list will be the optimal solution for the original model. One at a time, problems are removed from the list and addressed by solving them as linear programs. Either the solution will be integer-feasible, or the problem will be replaced by two other problems, each containing an additional constraint. This procedure requires the solution of a series of linear programs. The list might get quite long, but the procedure ultimately produces an optimal solution with integer-valued decision variables. The replacement of a problem on the list by two others is called *branching*. This name comes from a tree-like diagram that traces the different problems (as in Figure 6.22).

As we saw, it is possible to curtail the list of problems that have to be solved. Any time we encounter an integer-feasible solution, the branching in that portion of the tree is finished. Elsewhere, branching may lead to an infeasible linear program, which also terminates branching. Otherwise, we can try to use the bounds to fathom certain problems and also terminate the branching. Suppose that, at some stage of solving a maximization problem, the list contains a problem with a value (upper bound) that is worse than the value of the objective function in an integer-feasible solution already encountered. Whenever the bound on a derived problem is worse than the value of a known integer solution, then the derived problem may be removed from the list because its solution could never be optimal. (The mirror image of this statement holds when we are minimizing: in that case, whenever the bound on a derived problem is higher than the value of a known integer solution, then we can remove the derived problem from the list.)

The generic name for the overall procedure Solver uses is *branch and bound*, reflecting the two mechanisms that guide the search. Branching replaces a problem on the list with two problems that are, in some sense, closer to being solved as integer programs. Bounding explores whether a particular problem could just be deleted from the list because it offers no hope of finding an optimum. Nevertheless, the essence of the procedure is to solve a number of linear programs, to replace one problem with two whenever an integer constraint is violated, and to use bounds to remove problems from the list in order to reduce the workload. Because this procedure relies on the solution of many linear programs, it is as reliable a procedure as the linear solver on which it depends. That is, the branch and bound procedure is guaranteed to produce a global optimum.

SUMMARY

The ability to treat variables as integer valued, and in particular, the ability to designate variables as binary, opens up a wide variety of optimization models that can be addressed with Solver. This chapter introduced two broad classes of models that can be handled effectively with Solver. The first type of model is one that resembles a linear program but with the requirement that certain variables must be integer valued. For the purposes of using Solver, this requirement is added to the linear programming model as an additional constraint. The second type of model is one in which certain decisions exhibit an all-or-nothing structure, representing actions that are indivisible. Such decisions are modeled by binary variables, which are simply integer-valued variables no less than zero and no greater than one. Binary variables allow us to model the occurrence of yes/no choices and to exploit Solver, provided that the structure of the model is linear in all other respects.

In this second category, we explored three closely related model structures: set covering, set packing, and set partitioning. In the basic form of these models, the objective function coefficients and the right-hand side constants are 1s, but generalizations are also possible, as illustrated in some of the exercises at the end of this chapter.

In the next chapter, we examine a broader set of integer programming models, based on the ability to represent logical constraints using binary variables. In those models, the logical conditions do not seem linear, but they can be expressed in linear forms with the help of binary variables.

EXERCISES

6.1. Callum Communications (Revisited) Revisit Example 6.1. Suppose that the objective at Callum Communications is to minimize the number of employees, rather than to minimize the total cost.

(a) What is the minimum number of employees needed at the call center?

(b) Does the solution in (a) achieve the minimum salary cost?

6.2. Make or Buy A sudden increase in the demand for smoke detectors has left Acme Alarms with insufficient capacity to meet demand. The company has seen monthly demand from its retailers for its electronic and battery-operated detectors rise to 20,000 and 10,000, respectively, and Acme wishes to continue meeting demand. Acme's production process involves three departments: Fabrication, Assembly, and Shipping. The relevant quantitative data on production and prices are summarized below.

Department	Monthly hours available	Hours/unit (electronic)	Hours/unit (battery)
Fabrication	2000	0.15	0.10
Assembly	4200	0.20	0.20
Shipping	2500	0.10	0.15
Variable cost/unit		$18.80	$16.00
Retail price		$29.50	$28.00

The company also has the option to obtain additional units from a subcontractor, who has offered to supply up to 20,000 units per month in any combination of electronic and battery-operated models, at a charge of $21.50 per unit. For this price, the subcontractor will test and ship its models directly to the retailers without using Acme's production process.

(a) Acme wants an implementable schedule, so all quantities must be integers. What are the maximum profit and the corresponding make/buy levels?

(b) Compare the maximum profit in (a) to the maximum profit achievable without integer constraints. Does the integer solution correspond to the rounded-off values of the noninteger solution? By how much (in percentage terms) do the integer restrictions alter the value of the optimal objective function?

6.3. Selecting an Investment Portfolio   An investment manager wants to determine an optimal portfolio for a wealthy client. The fund has $2.5 million to invest, and its objective is to maximize total dollar return from both growth and dividends over the course of the coming year. The client has researched eight high-tech companies and wants the portfolio to consist of shares in these firms only. Three of the firms (S1–S3) are primarily software companies, three (H1–H3) are primarily hardware companies, and two (C1–C2) are internet consulting companies. The client has stipulated that no more than 40 percent of the investment be allocated to any one of these three sectors. To assure diversification, at least $100,000 must be invested in each of the eight stocks. Moreover, the number of shares invested in any stock must be a multiple of 1000.

The table below gives estimates from the investment company's database relating to these stocks. These estimates include the price per share, the projected annual growth rate in the share price, and the anticipated annual dividend payment per share.

	Stock							
	S1	S2	S3	H1	H2	H3	C1	C2
Price per share	$40	$50	$80	$60	$45	$60	$30	$25
Growth rate	0.05	0.10	0.03	0.04	0.07	0.15	0.22	0.25
Dividend	$2.00	$1.50	$3.50	$3.00	$2.00	$1.00	$1.80	$0.00

(a) Determine the maximum return on the portfolio. What is the optimal number of shares to buy for each of the stocks? What is the corresponding dollar amount invested in each stock?

(b) Compare the solution in which there is no integer restriction on the number of shares invested. By how much (in percentage terms) do the integer restrictions alter the value of the optimal objective function? By how much (in percentage terms) do they alter the optimal investment quantities?

6.4. Production Planning for Components   Rummel Electronics produces two PC cards, a modem and a network adapter. Demand for these two products exceeds the amount that the firm can make, but there are no plans to increase production capacity in the short run. Instead, the firm plans to use subcontracting.

The two main stages of production are fabrication and assembly, and either step can be subcontracted for either type of card. However, the company policy is not to subcontract both steps for either product. (That is, if modem cards are fabricated by a

-house.) Components made by subcontrac-
ing departments, just like components
J hours available in fabrication, 3600 in
The production requirements, in hours per

	Fab.	Ass.	Ship.
e	0.35	0.16	0.08
ouse	0.47	0.15	0.12
ocontractor	–	0.18	0.10
subcontractor	–	0.16	0.15
by subcontractor	0.35	–	0.09
led by subcontractor	0.47	–	0.14

direct material costs for the modem cards are $3.25 for manufacturing and $0.50
mbly; for network cards, the costs are $6.10 and $0.50. Subcontracting the man-
ring operation costs $5.35 for modem cards and $8.50 for network cards.
Subcontracting the assembly operation costs $1.50 for either product. Modem cards
sell for $20, and network cards sell for $28. The firm's policy, for each product, is that
at most 40 percent of the units produced can have subcontracted fabrication, and at
most 70 percent of the units can have subcontracted assembly.

(a) Determine the production and subcontracting schedule that will maximize profits,
given that Rummel Electronics wishes its schedule to contain an integer number of
units produced and subcontracted.

(b) Solve the problem without the integer restrictions. What is the solution? By how
much (in percentage terms) do the restrictions alter the value of the optimal objective
function?

6.5. Catering Logistics Jessica's Catering Service bakes and delivers lasagnas to parties
and group meetings. In a typical week, Jessica has around 40 orders. Each order involves
a specific amount of the required lasagna in pounds. A small group would need about
20 lb, whereas a large group would need almost triple that amount. The following
table shows the different customer orders that have come in this week, grouped into
eight categories by weight.

Job type	1	2	3	4	5	6	7	8
Weight (lbs)	20	25	30	35	40	45	50	55
Number	10	5	4	7	3	9	2	1

Jessica has an inventory of 25 six-lb trays and 18 ten-lb trays. Although she appears to
have enough capacity in her trays, she would like to plan her orders so that the amount
of excess lasagna is kept to a minimum.

How many six-lb trays and ten-lb trays should Jessica use for each of the orders?

6.6. Location of Services The Division of Motor Wyoming (DMV) in Wyoming operates
several offices around the state. Citizens must travel to one of these offices to register a car,

obtain a title, renew an operator's license, and perform a number of other minor activities. However, it is expensive for the DMV to operate a large number of offices, so the DMV has been keeping some offices open only three days per week and closing down other offices entirely in an attempt to reduce expenses. Recently, the suggestion was made to have one mobile DMV office which would operate out of a trailer and appear in a different location each day. The question then became: How much coverage could the mobile design provide? A possible standard was proposed: Locate the mobile office so that at least once a week, residents of the state could go to the DMV in their own county, or in a neighboring county.[1]

Is it possible to locate the mobile office in such a way that for any county, the office will either locate in that county or locate in a neighboring county at least once per (5-day) week? If so, which counties should host the office for a day? If not, what is the minimum number of days required to provide all residents access within their county or a neighboring county?

6.7. Reservation Scheduling   Roth Auto Rentals, a car rental company specializing is SUVs, is making up a schedule for the next weekend's demands. The peak demand period occurs on the weekend, when Roth may not have enough SUVs to meet demand. The customer demands that have been logged in are listed below.

Days	Customers
Fri–Mon	1
Fri–Sat	4
Fri–Sun	5
Sat–Sun	4
Sat–Mon	3
Sun–Sun	2

The rental cost depends on which days the contract covers.

Days	FSSM	FS	FSS	SS	SSM	Sun
Rate	119.95	69.95	99.95	74.95	89.95	39.95

Roth Auto Rentals carries only one type of vehicle and expects to have 10 SUVs available for rental over the weekend.

(a) What is the maximum revenue that can be generated from the list of orders?

(b) In the optimal solution of (a), what percentage of customer demand is satisfied?

(c) In the optimal solution of (a), what percentage of dollar demand is satisfied?

(d) Answer the set of three questions above for fleet sizes of 11–16.

6.8. Scheduling Reservations   Reed's Rent-a-Car is a traditional auto rental company facing the problem of assigning vehicles to weekend demands. However, Reed's distinguishes rentals by car type. Its fleet consists of three compact (C) cars, five mid-size (M) cars and three full-size (F) cars. The customer demands that have been logged in are listed below.

Days	C	M	F
Fri–Mon	0	1	0
Fri–Sat	1	2	1
Fri–Sun	2	2	1
Sat–Sun	1	3	0
Sat–Mon	3	0	0
Sun–Sun	0	1	1

The rental rates depend on how many days the contract covers. Prices for compact cars are shown below. Mid-size cars carry a 10 percent premium, and full-size cars carry a 20 percent premium.

Days	1	2	3	4
Rate	39.95	74.95	99.95	119.95

(a) Assume Reed's were to prohibit a customer who ordered one size from renting another size. What is the maximum revenue that can be generated from the list of orders?

(b) Assume Reed's were to permit a customer to substitute a larger size for any order, but with no change in price. What is the maximum revenue that can be generated from the list of orders?

(c) In the optimal solution of (b), what percentage of dollar demand is satisfied?

6.9. Allocating Components to Assemblies   Bikes.com is a web-based company that sells bicycles on the internet. Its distinctive feature is that it allows customers to customize the design when they order and then to receive quick delivery. Bikes.com gives customers choices for frame size (34, 36, 38), suspension (standard or heavy-duty), and gear speeds (5, 10, 15). As a result, customers can order one of 18 possible combinations (3 × 2 × 3). The company shorthand refers to frame size as Option A (A1 is the 34-inch model, A2 is the 36-inch model, and A3 is the 38-inch model). Similarly, the standard suspension is option B1, and the heavy-duty suspension is B2. The gear speeds are C1 (5), C2 (10), and C3 (15).

Rather than stock 18 different types of bicycles, Bikes.com holds inventories of the major components and then assembles the bikes once a customer order comes in. Orders are taken Mondays through Wednesdays, assemblies are done on Thursdays, and shipments go out on Fridays. Thus, at the close of business on Wednesday, Bikes.com has an inventory of components and a list of orders, and its task is to match components with orders to meet as much demand as possible. The tables below describe customer orders for this week and the inventory status at the end of Wednesday.

Model	1	2	3	4	5	6	7	8	9	10	11	12	13	14	15	16	17	18
A	1	1	1	1	1	1	2	2	2	2	2	2	3	3	3	3	3	3
B	1	1	1	2	2	2	1	1	1	2	2	2	1	1	1	2	2	2
C	1	2	3	1	2	3	1	2	3	1	2	3	1	2	3	1	2	3
Orders	4	5	0	5	1	7	0	4	8	1	2	0	5	6	4	0	1	5

Component	A1	A2	A3	B1	B2	C1	C2	C3
Inventory	12	20	30	20	25	18	16	20

(a) What is the maximum number of customer orders that can be satisfied this week?

(b) Suppose that the profitability varies by model type, as shown in the table below. What is the maximum profit that can be achieved from this week's orders?

Model	1	2	3	4	5	6	7	8	9	10	11	12	13	14	15	16	17	18
Profit	45	55	70	65	75	90	47	57	72	67	77	92	50	60	75	70	80	95

6.10. The Latin American Soccer Association (Revisited) Revisit Example 6.6. Suppose that the Latin American Soccer Association (LASA) decides to create a longer playoff schedule. They want each team to play two games against the teams in its own division and one game against each team in the other division. Construct a playoff schedule that maximizes the number of games played by intra-division rivals toward the end of the season.

(a) How many weeks are required for the entire schedule?

(b) How many variables and constraints appear in the optimization model?

(c) What is an optimal schedule for LASA?

(d) Review your schedule in part (c) and determine whether the same two teams ever meet in successive weeks. Amend the model to prohibit such meetings and construct an optimal schedule.

6.11. Cutting Stock Poly Products sells packaging tape to industrial customers. All tape is sold in 100-foot rolls that are cut in various widths from a master roll, which is 15 inches wide. The product line consists of the following widths: $2''$, $3''$, $5''$, $7''$, and $11''$. These can be cut in different combinations from a 15-inch master roll. For example, one combination might consist of three cuts of $5''$ each. Another combination might consist of two $2''$ cuts and an $11''$ cut. Both of these combinations use the entire 15-inch roll without any waste, but other combinations are also possible. For example, another combination might consist of two $7''$ cuts. This combination creates one inch of waste for every roll cut this way.

Each week, Poly Products collects demands from its customers and distributors and must figure out how to configure the cuts in its master rolls. To do so, the production manager lists all possible combinations of cuts and tries to fit them together so that waste is minimized while demand is met. (In particular, demand must be met exactly, because

Poly Products does not keep inventories of its tape.) This week's demands are shown below.

Size	2″	3″	5″	7″	11″
Demand	20	30	40	50	60

(a) How many combinations can be cut from a 15-inch master roll so that there is less than two inches of waste (i.e., the smallest quantity that can be sold) left on the roll?

(b) Find a set of combinations that meets demand exactly and generates the minimum amount of waste. (Stated another way, the requirement is to meet or exceed demand for each size, but any excess must be counted as waste.) What is the optimal set of combinations and the minimum amount of waste?

Case: Motel Location for Nature's Inn

Nature's Inn operates a motel chain with two types of motels. Under its brand Comfort Express (CE), it offers a relatively inexpensive, spartan motel. Under its Family Suites (FS) brand, it offers a more expensive motel distinguished by various extra features. Both brands are associated with the latest ideas in green building design, attracting a segment of the customer market that is willing to let considerations of sustainability influence its purchasing decisions. Following a successful first round of expansion in the Northeast region, Nature's Inn is planning another round of expansion, this time into the Midwest region.

Working with a real estate consultant, Nature's Inn has identified ten potential sites for the location of new motels. Each site can accommodate either a CE motel or a FS motel (but not both). Using historical data from the Northeast region, the consultant has estimated the net present value (NPV) of the cash flows attainable over the next ten years at each location, with separate figures for CE and FS.

EXHIBIT 6.1   *Proximity Data and Economic Estimates*

Location	Locations within 30 miles	Locations within 40 miles	CE NPV ($ million)	FS NPV ($ million)
1	2	2, 6	10.147	11.899
2	1	1	12.191	11.242
3	4	4	13.359	10.731
4	3	3, 5	9.344	7.519
5	–	4	11.388	14.235
6	9	1, 8, 9	6.935	9.636
7	8, 10	8, 10	12.629	8.687
8	7, 9, 10	6, 7, 9, 10	13.505	10.293
9	6, 8, 10	6, 8, 10	9.344	9.709
10	7, 8, 9	7, 8, 9	8.249	11.461

The consultant has also carried out a survey to explore the extent to which demand might be affected when two motels are located in close proximity. The first finding was that CE customers and FS customers are different segments, for the most part, and little crossover demand occurs. On the other hand, among CE and FS customers, competition occurs when motels are located too close to each other. The data suggest that competition becomes an economic factor for CE motels when they are located within 30 miles of each other and for FS motels within 40 miles of each other. Nature's Inn has therefore decided to respect these distances in their choice of locations: In the Midwest, CE motels will not be located within 30 miles of each other, and FS motels will not be located within 40 miles of each other. The results of the consultant's work are summarized in Exhibit 6.1.

The task for Nature's Inn is now to develop a location plan for its Midwest expansion.

Chapter 7

Integer Programming: Logical Constraints

In the previous chapter, we covered how to solve integer programming problems using Solver. We also introduced the use of binary variables, which represent yes/no decisions, and we saw how binary variables arise naturally in set covering, set packing, and set partitioning. In this chapter, we expand the use of binary variables in connection with relationships we call *logical constraints* that restrict consideration to certain combinations of variables. Normally, we might not immediately think of these restrictions as linear constraints, but we can capture them in linear form with the use of binary variables.

We begin with the illustration of a *counting constraint*. This term refers to a quantitative constraint for counting our decisions, and the use of binary variables makes counting easy. As an example, we revisit the capital budgeting problem which, in its basic form, is a pure integer program containing binary variables and one constraint. We encountered this structure in Example 6.2, in the Newton Corporation.

EXAMPLE 7.1   *The Newton Corporation*

The Newton Corporation has tentatively allocated $40 million for capital investments after considering the financial characteristics of the following projects.

P1   Renovate the production facility for greater efficiency.

P2   License a new technology for use in production.

P3   Expand advertising by naming a stadium.

P4   Purchase land and construct a new headquarters building.

P5   Introduce a new product to complement the current line.

Project	P1	P2	P3	P4	P5
NPV	2.0	3.6	3.2	1.6	2.8
Expenditure	12	24	20	8	16

Optimization Modeling with Spreadsheets, Second Edition. Kenneth R. Baker
© 2011 John Wiley & Sons, Inc. Published 2011 by John Wiley & Sons, Inc.

After the initial analysis, which led to a total NPV of $6.8 million, some further consider-
ations have been brought up. It appears that the recommended selection of P1, P3, and P4
may not be feasible after all. The committee would still like to maximize the total NPV from
projects selected, subject to a $40-million limit on capital expenditures, but it has to recognize
the additional considerations.   ∎

The tentative representation of the problem at Newton Corporation led to the
following model.

$$\text{Maximize } z = 2.0P1 + 3.6P2 + 3.2P3 + 1.6P4 + 2.8P5$$
$$\text{subject to} \quad 12P1 + 24P2 + 20P3 + 8P4 + 16P5 \leq 40$$

Projects P2 and P5 have international dimensions, whereas the others are domestic. When the committee discussed this aspect of the projects, they decided to
select at least one project from the international arena. To represent this requirement
in the optimization model, we can add a covering constraint to the base case

$$P2 + P5 \geq 1$$

The left-hand side of this constraint *counts* the number of international
projects adopted. Of course, the addition of a new constraint may make the
objective function worse. Neither P2 nor P5 was part of the optimal set of
projects, and because there is no extra space in the budget to include P2 or P5
without removing at least one of the other projects, we should anticipate that the
inclusion of P2 or P5 could lead to a lower NPV. With the new constraint, the optimal
NPV drops to $6.4 million, obtained by accepting both projects P2 and P5. Figure 7.1
shows this solution of the revised model, with the additional constraint for international projects.

	A	B	C	D	E	F	G	H	I
1	**Capital Budgeting Model**								
2									
3	**Decision Variables**								
4	Project	P1	P2	P3	P4	P5			
5	Accept	0	1	0	0	1			
6									
7	**Objective Function**								
8	NPV	2.0	3.6	3.2	1.6	2.8	6.4		
9									
10	**Constraints**								Budget
11	Expenditures	12	24	20	8	16	40	<=	40
12		0	1	0	0	1	2	>=	1
13	International								

Figure 7.1. Solution to Example 7.1 with international constraint.

This additional constraint illustrates the fact that we can use binary variables, and standard LT, GT, or EQ constraints, to represent counting requirements of the following form.

- Select at least m of the possible projects from a given subset.
- Select at most n of the possible projects from a given subset.
- Select exactly k of the possible projects from a given subset.

To incorporate counting constraints, we must have binary variables representing each of the elements we may wish to count. At least in the capital budgeting model, that is precisely the structure we have.

7.1. SIMPLE LOGICAL CONSTRAINTS: EXCLUSIVITY AND CONTINGENCY

Relationships we normally think of as logical relationships can also be expressed with binary variables. Suppose that projects $P2$ and $P5$ are *mutually exclusive* (e.g., they could require the same staff resources). Although we might think of mutual exclusivity as a logical property belonging to a pair of variables, we can also interpret this feature as a special case of the condition for selecting at most n and write

$$P2 + P5 \leq 1$$

We know that adding a constraint will not lead to a better solution, but we can't anticipate whether the optimal NPV will actually get worse. As it happens, there is another solution that achieves an NPV of \$6.4 million without requiring both $P2$ and $P5$, as shown in Figure 7.2.

In addition, we sometimes encounter *contingency* relationships. Suppose that project $P5$ requires that $P3$ be selected. In other words, $P5$ is contingent on $P3$. To analyze

◢	A	B	C	D	E	F	G	H	I	
1	**Capital Budgeting Model**									
2										
3	**Decision Variables**									
4	Project	P1	P2	P3	P4	P5				
5	Accept	1	0	0	1	1				
6										
7	**Objective Function**									
8	NPV	2.0	3.6	3.2	1.6	2.8	6.4			
9										
10	**Constraints**								Budget	
11	Expenditures	12	24	20	8	16	36	<=	40	
12		0	1	0	0	1	1	>=	1	
13		0	1	0	0	1	1	<=	1	
14										

International / **Exclusive**

Figure 7.2. Solution to Example 7.1 with mutually-exclusive constraint.

logical requirements of this sort, consider all possible combinations for the variables $P3$ and $P5$. The following table shows that three of the four combinations are consistent with the contingency condition.

P3	P5	Consistent?
0	0	Yes
1	0	Yes
0	1	No
1	1	Yes

We can accommodate the three consistent combinations and exclude the inconsistent combination by adding the following constraint

$$P3 - P5 \geq 0$$

At this stage, we specify the model as follows.

Objective:	G8 (maximize)
Variables:	B5:F5
Constraints:	G11 ≤ I11
	G12 ≥ I12
	G13 ≤ I13
	G14 ≥ I14
	B5:F5 = binary

With the contingency constraint appended, the optimal NPV drops to $6 million, as shown in Figure 7.3.

▲	A	B	C	D	E	F	G	H	I	
1	**Capital Budgeting Model**									
2										
3	**Decision Variables**									
4	Project	P1	P2	P3	P4	P5				
5	Accept	0	0	1	0	1				
6										
7	**Objective Function**									
8	NPV	2.0	3.6	3.2	1.6	2.8	6.0			
9										
10	**Constraints**								Budget	
11	Expenditures	12	24	20	8	16	36	<=	40	
12		0	1	0	0	1	1	>=	1	
13		0	1	0	0	1	1	<=	1	
14		0	0	1	0	-1	0	>=	0	
15										
◄ ◄ ► ►		International / Exclusive / Contingency / ◄					▥		►	

Figure 7.3. Solution to Example 7.1 with mutually-exclusive constraint.

BOX 7.1	*Excel Mini-Lesson: Binary Variables and the IF Function*

Experienced users of Excel will see little difficulty in modeling a contingency constraint if they are familiar with the IF function. A logical statement of the contingency between $P3$ and $P5$ could include the recalculation $P5$ in light of $P3$. Once $P3$ and $P5$ have initial values, we could recalculate $P5$ in cell F6 according to the contingency by using the formula

$$=IF(P3=1,P5,0)$$

This formula would take the original value of $P5$ if $P3 = 1$, but it would become zero otherwise (i.e. if $P3 = 0$). The objective function can then be expressed with the formula

$$=SUMPRODUCT\ (\$B\$5:\$E\$5,B8:E8)+\$F\$6*F8$$

A similar function can represent the left-hand side of each of the constraints. However, the IF function is not a linear function. If the Nonsmooth Transformation option is set to Never and we specify the linear solver, we encounter an error message stating that the model does not satisfy the linearity conditions. To use Solver reliably for integer programming, the IF function should be avoided.

Thus, we can accommodate logical constraints among related variables within the framework of linear programming with binary variables. The Newton Corporation example illustrates how we might incorporate counting constraints, such as "at most 2," or qualitative information, such as contingency or mutual exclusivity. Such relationships usually require some specialized constraints in the model in addition to the use of binary variables. In the remainder of this chapter, we elaborate on models containing other logical constraints by examining a series of illustrative problem types.

7.2. LINKING CONSTRAINTS: THE FIXED COST PROBLEM

Linear objective functions assume strict proportionality: In particular, the cost incurred by an activity is proportional to the activity level. However, we commonly encounter situations in which an activity cost is composed of a fixed component and a variable component, where only the variable cost is proportional to the level of activity. Using a binary variable, we can represent the fixed cost as part of the objective function and still work with a linear model.

Suppose that we have already built a linear programming model, but one variable (x) has a fixed cost that we want to represent in the objective function. To incorporate a fixed cost into the model, we first separate the fixed and variable components of cost. In algebraic terms, we write total cost in the following form

Total cost = Fixed cost + Variable cost

Alternatively, using symbols, we write

$$TC = Fy + vx$$

where F represents the fixed cost and v represents the unit (variable) cost. A sketch of the total cost function is shown in Figure 7.4. The variables x and y are decision variables, where x is a normal (continuous) variable and y is a binary variable. Constraints in the linear program involve only the variable portion—that is, they involve only the variable x, not the variable y. We also want the variables x and y to work *consistently*. Specifically, we want to ensure that $y = 1$ (so that we incur the fixed cost) whenever $x > 0$, and we want to have $y = 0$ (so that we avoid fixed cost) when $x = 0$. To achieve consistency in the two variables, we add the following *linking constraint*.

$$x \leq My$$

where M represents some upper bound on the variable x.

To appreciate the linking constraint, imagine that Solver approaches the selection of variables in two stages. In the first stage, binary variables (such as y) are set to either 0 or 1; then, in the second stage, continuous variables (such as x) are determined. The two first-stage choices for the variable y provide us with the following possibilities in the linking constraint

$y = 1$ so that $x \leq My$ becomes $x \leq M$ (meaning: x can be anything)

$y = 0$ so that $x \leq My$ becomes $x \leq 0$ (meaning: x must be zero)

Thus, the variable x will be treated in a consistent way with the choice of y. In particular, it is not possible to have $y = 0$ and $x > 0$. In words, we cannot avoid the fixed cost if we wish to use x at a nonzero level.

In principle, the linking constraint does allow us to set $y = 1$ and $x = 0$. That is, the model permits us to incur the fixed cost even without using the variable x. However, Solver will not produce such a solution because it would always be less costly to set $y = 0$ and avoid the fixed cost completely.

As an example of the fixed cost structure, consider the product planning decision at the Moore Office Products Company.

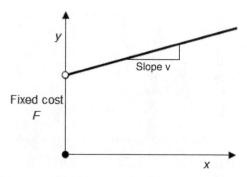

Figure 7.4. Total cost with fixed and variable components.

EXAMPLE 7.2   *Moore Office Products Company*

Moore Office Products has been producing and selling its goods in three product families ($F1$, $F2$, and $F3$) and planning for those products using a product-mix type of linear programming model. Each product family requires production hours in each of three departments. In addition, each family requires its own sales force, which must be supported no matter how large or small the sales volume happens to be. The parameters describing the situation are summarized in the following table. Moore's management is wondering whether it should continue to market all three product families.

	Hours required/1000 units family			Hours available
	$F1$	$F2$	$F3$	
Department A	3	4	8	2000
Department B	3	5	6	2000
Department C	2	3	9	2000
Profit per unit ($)	1.20	1.80	2.20	
Sales cost ($000)	60	200	100	
Demand (000s)	300	200	50	

∎

At the heart of this situation lies a decision problem analogous to the product mix example introduced in Chapter 2. The linear programming representation of the product mix problem, without the fixed costs, is shown in Figure 7.5. By defining the x-values in thousands, we have scaled the model so that the objective function is in thousands of dollars. The optimal product mix calls for producing all three families, with $F1$ and $F2$ at their demand ceilings, and $F3$ at a volume of 50,000. This product mix creates $758,000 in variable profits, as computed in cell F8. If we subtract the total fixed costs of $360,000, as computed in cell F17, we are left with a net profit of $398,000, as computed in cell F19.

The linear programming solution might represent the situation in a firm that has introduced and supported various new products over the years and now finds itself carrying out activities in three existing markets. The linear programming framework suggests how to allocate capacity, provided that all three of the product families are active. However, because fixed-cost considerations are not part of the linear programming analysis, we have no basis for determining whether any one of the families should be dropped. To make the model suitable for decisions of this kind, we must integrate the implications for fixed costs.

To formulate the full problem at Moore Office Products as an integer programming model, we make two changes in the product mix formulation. First, we write the objective function with terms for both variable profit and fixed cost, as follows

$$Net\ profit = 1.20x_1 - 60y_1 + 1.80x_2 - 200y_2 + 2.20x_3 - 100y_3$$

where x_j represents the volume for family j, in thousands, and

$$y_j = 1 \quad \text{if } x_j \text{ is positive (and the fixed cost is incurred)}$$
$$y_j = 0 \quad \text{if } x_j \text{ is zero (and the fixed cost is avoided)}$$

	A	B	C	D	E	F	G	H	
1	**Product Mix**								
2	*Linear Programming Analysis*								
3	*Decisions*								
4			F1	F2	F3				
5			300	160	50	K-units			
6									
7	*Objective*								
8		Variable profit	1.20	1.80	2.20	758			
9	*Constraints*								
10		A	3	4	8	1940	<=	2000	
11		B	3	5	6	2000	<=	2000	
12		C	2	3	9	1530	<=	2000	
13			1			300	<=	300	
14				1		160	<=	200	
15					1	50	<=	50	
16									
17		Fixed costs	60	200	100	360			
18									
19		Net Profit				398			
20									

Fixed

Figure 7.5. Solution to Example 7.2 without fixed costs.

Net profit is measured in thousands due to the scaling of the x-variables and the scaling of the fixed cost coefficients.

Next, we add linking constraints to ensure consistency between each of the x–y pairs.

$$x_1 - My_1 \leq 0$$
$$x_2 - My_2 \leq 0$$
$$x_3 - My_3 \leq 0$$

Now we need to identify a large number to play the role of M. Essentially, we need a number large enough that it will not limit the choice of these variables in any of the other (demand and supply) constraints. For example, a value of 300 (thousand) would work, since that represents the largest demand ceiling, and none of the volumes could ever be larger.

Thus, when $y_2 = 1$, the linking constraint for family $F2$ becomes $x_2 \leq 300$; and when $y_2 = 0$, the constraint becomes $x_2 \leq 0$. Similar interpretations apply to families $F1$ and $F3$. These are valid linking constraints, but we can streamline the model slightly. Instead of retaining separate constraints to represent the demand ceilings and the linking relationships, we can let the linking constraint do "double duty" if we choose a different value of M for each family and set it equal to the corresponding demand ceiling. For example, the value of M selected for the $F2$ constraint could be 200 instead of 300. Then, when $y_2 = 1$, the constraint on the production volume for family $F2$ becomes $x_2 \leq 200$, which also serves as a demand ceiling. When $y_2 = 0$, the constraint still becomes $x_2 \leq 0$, in which case the specific choice of M does not matter. The streamlined model, in its entirety, is the following

$$\text{Maximize } z = 1.20x_1 - 60y_1 + 1.80x_2 - 200y_2 + 2.20x_3 - 100y_3$$

subject to:

$$3x_1 + 4x_2 + 8x_3 \leq 2000$$
$$3x_1 + 5x_2 + 6x_3 \leq 2000$$
$$2x_1 + 3x_2 + 9x_3 \leq 2000$$
$$x_1 - 300y_1 \leq 0$$
$$x_2 - 200y_2 \leq 0$$
$$x_3 - 50y_3 \leq 0$$

There are different ways to lay this model out in a spreadsheet. We could, for instance, treat the xs and ys as six distinct variables and, in the traditional format, build the spreadsheet with six columns on the left-hand side of the constraints. Then, we could represent the constraints in the traditional format, as six rows, with the usual SUMPRODUCT functions. An alternative is to pair the xs and ys that are linked in successive rows, using just three columns (one for each product family). Then we could associate the linking constraints with variable pairs and display them in columns (one for each product family). Figure 7.6 shows the traditional layout, and Figure 7.7 shows the alternative. In the latter, formulas in cells C16:E16 compute the left-hand side of the linking constraints. For example, the formula in cell C16 reads: =C5-C15*C6.

	A	B	C	D	E	F	G	H	I	J	K
1	Product Mix with Fixed Costs										
2											
3	Decisions										
4			X1	X2	X3	Y1	Y2	Y3			
5			300	200	0	1	1	0	K-units		
6											
7	Objective										
8		Variable profit	1.20	1.80	2.20				720	K$	
9		Fixed cost				-60	-200	-100	-260	K$	
10		Net Profit							460	K$	
11											
12	Constraints										
13		A	3	4	8	0	0	0	1700	<=	2000
14		B	3	5	6	0	0	0	1900	<=	2000
15		C	2	3	9	0	0	0	1200	<=	2000
16			1			-300	0	0	0	<=	0
17				1			-200		0	<=	0
18					1			-50	0	<=	0
19											
	◄ ► ► ►	Fixed	Fixed2								

Figure 7.6. Spreadsheet layout for Example 7.2.

	A	B	C	D	E	F	G	H
1	**Product Mix with Fixed Costs**							
2								
3	**Decisions**							
4			F1	F2	F3			
5			300	200	0	K-units		
6			1	1	0	indicator		
7	**Objective**							
8		Variable profit	1.20	1.80	2.20			
9		Fixed cost	60	200	100	460	K$	
10	**Constraints**							
11		A	3	4	8	1700	<=	2000
12		B	3	5	6	1900	<=	2000
13		C	2	3	9	1200	<=	2000
14								
15		demand	300	200	50	K-units		
16		linking	0	0	0			
17								

Fixed / Fixed2 / Fixed3

Figure 7.7. Alternative layout for Example 7.2.

For the layout in Figure 7.7, we specify the model as follows.

Objective:	F9 (maximize)
Variables:	C5:E6
Constraints:	F11:F13 $\leq$ H11:H13
	C16:E16 $\leq$ 0
	C6:E6 = binary

The optimal solution achieves a net profit of $460,000, which we can obtain by setting the Integer Tolerance to zero. In order to attain this level of profits, Moore Office Products must forego production of product family $F3$ and produce families $F1$ and $F2$ up to their respective ceilings. In other words, the model detects that family $F3$ does not pay its own way and that profits would be increased by not producing or selling that family at all. By using an integer programming model that incorporates fixed costs, Moore Office Products can consider the implications of dropping a product family. Such a possibility may be influenced by factors beyond profits in the coming year, but the model helps to shape and quantify the economic considerations.

7.3. LINKING CONSTRAINTS: THE THRESHOLD LEVEL PROBLEM

Sometimes we encounter situations where, in order to do business, we are required to participate at a specified minimum level. In purchasing, for example, we might be able to qualify for a discounted price if we buy in quantity. Thus, a condition in the problem dictates that a decision variable must be either zero or at least as large as a specified threshold.

The existence of a threshold level does not require an alteration in the objective function of a model, and it can be represented in the constraints with the help of binary variables. Suppose we have a variable x that is subject to a specified minimum requirement. Let m denote the threshold value of x if it is nonzero. Then we can capture this structure in an integer programming model by including the following pair of constraints

$$x \geq my$$
$$x \leq My$$

where, as before, M is a large number that is greater than or equal to any value x could feasibly take. To see how these two requirements work, again imagine that Solver approaches the selection of variables in two stages. In the first stage, the binary variable y is set to either 1 or to 0; then, in the second stage, Solver determines x. The two first-stage choices for the variable y provide us with the following possibilities in the linking constraints.

$y = 1$ so that: $x \geq my$ becomes $x \geq m$ (meaning: x meets the threshold)
         and: $x \leq My$ becomes $x \leq M$ (meaning: x can be anything)

$y = 0$ so that: $x \geq my$ becomes $x \geq 0$ (meaning: x must be nonnegative)
         and: $x \leq My$ becomes $x \leq 0$ (meaning: x must be nonpositive)

Thus, when $y = 1$, the constraints reduce to $m \leq x \leq M$, so that x must at least meet the threshold level. When $y = 0$, the constraints reduce to $x = 0$. Thus, the pair x and y will behave consistently, and the threshold requirement will be respected.

As a brief illustration, suppose that in Example 7.2, materials for product family $F2$ can be ordered from a major supplier only if the order supports an output level of 125 (thousand) or more. The model would need two constraints, as follows

$$x_2 \geq 125y_2$$
$$x_2 \leq 200y_2$$

This pair of linking constraints ensures that if $x_2 > 0$, then it must lie between 125 and 200.

7.4. LINKING CONSTRAINTS: THE FACILITY LOCATION MODEL

In designing its distribution system, a firm wants to know how many distribution facilities it should have and where they should be located. If we think about the "how many" question, we can see a basic tradeoff. As the firm uses more and more facilities, it can place the facilities close to customer locations and thus reduce its variable distribution costs. However, larger overhead costs will occur due to operating a larger number of facilities. In the other direction, as the firm uses fewer and fewer facilities, it will encounter larger and larger variable costs, but the costs of operating the facilities will drop. Figure 7.8 shows this tradeoff graphically. The horizontal axis represents the number of facilities in the system. As this number increases, the total cost of distribution drops, while the cost of operating the facilities increases. (The graph shows this latter component as a straight line, as if each facility incurs the same operating cost, but this is only for illustration.) The total cost in the problem is the sum of distribution cost and operating cost, shown as the U-shaped function on the graph.

The graph in Figure 7.8 is only a conceptual device to illustrate the main tradeoff affected by the number of locations. Important details remain. For example, once we choose the number of facilities, we must then determine *which* facilities to use. Similarly, once we choose the facilities, we must still determine how to distribute from those facilities to the customer locations in the most desirable way. This last problem we can now recognize as a transportation problem, which we examined in Chapter 3. Thus, the graph hides two embedded problems: (1) selecting k out of the m possible locations for facilities in the network and, (2) solving the transportation problem that arises once the locations are selected.

This type of tradeoff arises in several situations, but perhaps the most familiar application relates to the location of facilities in a distribution supply chain. For this reason, the problem is known as the *facility location problem* (or sometimes, the plant location problem, or the warehouse location problem). The essential tradeoff balances the fixed costs of operating discrete sources with the variable costs of providing service from those sources. In the examples that follow, we distinguish between the capacitated and uncapacitated version of the problem. The integer programming model itself represents a variation on the incorporation of fixed costs and the use of linking constraints.

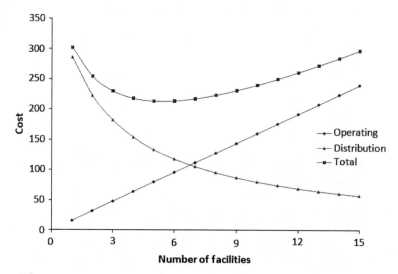

Figure 7.8. Cost Tradeoff in facility location.

7.4.1. Capacitated Version

In the classical *capacitated facility location problem*, the system contains m potential facility locations and n existing customer demand locations. For facility location i, we know the capacity (denoted C_i) and the fixed cost of operating the facility (F_i). For each customer location, we know the demand (d_j) and the unit distribution cost (c_{ij}) associated with satisfying demand at location j from capacity at facility i. In this problem statement, we typically choose a time period, such as a month or a year, as the basis for the facility costs and the demand quantities. For decision variables, we define

$$x_{ij} = \text{quantity sent from facility } i \text{ to customer location } j$$
$$y_i = 1 \quad \text{if facility } i \text{ is used in the design}$$
$$y_i = 0 \quad \text{otherwise}$$

Then the optimization problem can be formulated algebraically as follows.

$$\text{Minimize} \quad z = \sum_i F_i y_i + \sum_{ij} c_{ij} x_{ij}$$

subject to

$$\sum_i x_{ij} \geq d_j \tag{7.1}$$

$$\sum_j x_{ij} \leq C_i \tag{7.2}$$

$$x_{ij} \leq C_i y_i \tag{7.3}$$

As stated, the problem contains a transportation model, represented by constraints (7.1) and (7.2), along with the linking constraints in (7.3). The linking constraints ensure that if we distribute from facility location i (i.e., $x_{ij} > 0$ for some j), then we incur the corresponding fixed cost F_i in the objective function (by forcing y_i to be 1). Conversely, if we want to avoid the fixed cost F_i, then we must have $y_i = 0$, which prevents the use of facility location i.

The model contains mn variables x_{ij} along with m variables y_i, for a total of $m(n + 1)$ variables. There are n constraints of type (7.1), m constraints of type (7.2), and mn constraints of type (7.3), for a total of $mn + m + n$.

A more streamlined version of the same problem replaces constraints (7.2) and (7.3) with a single type of constraint

$$\text{Minimize} \quad z = \sum_i F_i y_i + \sum_{ij} c_{ij} x_{ij}$$

subject to:

$$\sum_i x_{ij} \geq d_j \tag{7.4}$$

$$\sum_j x_{ij} \leq C_i y_i \tag{7.5}$$

In this formulation, constraint (7.5) represents the linking constraint between the binary variable y_i and all of the quantities distributed from facility location i. This same inequality serves as the capacity constraint as well: when $y_i = 1$, the constraint matches (7.2) above; when $y_i = 0$, facility location i is not used, so there is no need to constrain its capacity. This more streamlined model contains $m(n + 1)$ variables, as before, but now the number of constraints is just $m + n$, quite a bit smaller than in the original model. To make the location model more concrete, we consider an example.

EXAMPLE 7.3   *Van Horne Appliance Company*

The Van Horne Appliance Company is a manufacturer of home appliances with nationwide distribution. Van Horne is designing its supply chain from scratch, having purchased some smaller companies in the last year. Its main candidates for distribution centers (DCs) are New York, Atlanta, Chicago, and Los Angeles. Each of these locations can accommodate annual volumes of up to 150,000 units, but they would require different levels of operating expense, as estimated in the table below.

DC Location	New York	Atlanta	Chicago	Los Angeles
Annual cost (000s)	$6000	$5500	$5800	$6200

One or more of these DCs will service Van Horne's four sales regions (East, South, Midwest, and West). For each combination of DC and sales region, Van Horne has estimated the average transportation cost per thousand units shipped.

(From) DC	East	South	Midwest	West	Capacity
			(To) region		
New York	$206	$225	$230	$290	150,000
Atlanta	225	206	221	270	150,000
Chicago	230	221	208	262	150,000
Los Angeles	290	270	262	215	150,000
Requirement	100,000	150,000	110,000	90,000	

The design problem facing the supply-chain manager at Van Horne is to determine which DC locations to use, based on operating expense and total distribution cost.   ■

Figure 7.9 shows a worksheet for the model. The Data section contains an array structured much like the transportation model, with rows for the potential DC locations and columns for the sales regions. For each row, the capacity (in thousands) is entered on the right-hand side of the array, in column G. For each column, the annual demand (in thousands) is entered at the bottom of the array. Annual fixed costs (in thousands)

	A	B	C	D	E	F	G	H	I	J	K	L
1	Facility Location Model		Capacitated Version									
2												
3	Data			Regions								
4	Locations	Fixed Costs	East	South	Midwest	West	Capacity					
5	New York	6000	206	225	230	290	150					
6	Atlanta	5500	225	206	221	270	150					
7	Chicago	5800	230	221	208	262	150					
8	Los Angeles	6200	290	270	262	215	150					
9		Demand	100	150	110	90						
10												
11	Decisions	In Use					Sent		Linking			
12	New York	1	100	0	0	0	100		-50	-150	-150	-150
13	Atlanta	1	0	150	0	0	150		-150	0	-150	-150
14	Chicago	1	0	0	50	0	50		-150	-150	-100	-150
15	Los Angeles	1	0	0	60	90	150		-150	-150	-90	-60
16		Received	100	150	110	90						
17												
18	Objective	Operating	23,500	Distribution	96,970	Total	120,470					
19												

Figure 7.9. Spreadsheet model for Example 7.3.

appear in column B, and the variable cost (per thousand) corresponding to each combination of DC location and customer region appears in the range C5:F8.

The Decisions section of the spreadsheet contains an array for decision variables. Column B holds the values of the y_i variables. The preliminary solution shown in the figure uses all four DC locations, so the entries in this column are all 1s. The range C12:F15 contains a solution to the transportation subproblem that constitutes the kernel of the model, although this solution may not be optimal. Finally, the array I12:L15 contains the left-hand side of the linking constraints corresponding to (7.3), expressed in the form $x_{ij} - C_iy_i$. Thus, the linking constraints are satisfied when each element in this array is less than or equal to zero.

Finally, the Objective section contains the evaluation of costs. The total operating cost in cell C18 and the total distribution cost in E18 are added to generate the total cost in G18. The model specification is as follows.

Objective:	G18 (minimize)
Variables:	B12:F15
Constraints:	G12:G15 $\leq$ G5:G8
	C16:F16 $\geq$ C9:F9
	I12:L15 $\leq$ 0
	B12:B15 = binary

Solver finds an optimal solution that achieves a cost of \$115,770 by using the New York, Atlanta, and Los Angeles DC locations, as shown in Figure 7.10. As the transportation kernel shows, the optimal solution ships from New York to both the East and Midwest and from Los Angeles to both the Midwest and West, while shipping to the South from Atlanta. By formulating and solving an integer programming model for its location problem, Van Horne can implement its national supply chain in the most cost-effective fashion.

	A	B	C	D	E	F	G	H	I	J	K	L
1	Facility Location Model		Capacitated Version									
2												
3	Data			Regions								
4	Locations	Fixed Costs	East	South	Midwest	West	Capacity					
5	New York	6000	206	225	230	290	150					
6	Atlanta	5500	225	206	221	270	150					
7	Chicago	5800	230	221	208	262	150					
8	Los Angeles	6200	290	270	262	215	150					
9		Demand	100	150	110	90						
10												
11	Decisions	In Use					Sent		Linking			
12	New York	1	100	0	50	0	150		-50	-150	-100	-150
13	Atlanta	1	0	150	0	0	150		-150	0	-150	-150
14	Chicago	0	0	0	0	0	0		0	0	0	0
15	Los Angeles	1	0	0	60	90	150		-150	-150	-90	-60
16		Received	100	150	110	90						
17												
18	Objective	Operating	17,700	Distribution	98,070	Total	115,770					
19												

Figure 7.10. Optimal solution for Example 7.3.

The streamlined version, shown in Figure 7.11, finds the same optimal solution with a model formulation that contains half as many constraints. The specification of the problem is as follows.

$$\begin{aligned}
\text{Objective:} \quad & \text{G18 (minimize)} \\
\text{Variables:} \quad & \text{B12:F15} \\
\text{Constraints:} \quad & \text{C16:F16} \geq \text{C9:F9} \\
& \text{I12:I15} \leq 0 \\
& \text{B12:B15} = \text{binary}
\end{aligned}$$

	A	B	C	D	E	F	G	H	I
1	Facility Location Model		Capacitated Version						
2									
3	Data			Regions					
4	Locations	Fixed Costs	East	South	Midwest	West	Capacity		
5	New York	6000	206	225	230	290	150		
6	Atlanta	5500	225	206	221	270	150		
7	Chicago	5800	230	221	208	262	150		
8	Los Angeles	6200	290	270	262	215	150		
9		Demand	100	150	110	90			
10									
11	Decisions	In Use					Sent		Linking
12	New York	1	100	0	50	0	150		0
13	Atlanta	1	0	150	0	0	150		0
14	Chicago	0	0	0	0	0	0		0
15	Los Angeles	1	0	0	60	90	150		0
16		Received	100	150	110	90			
17									
18	Objective	Operating	17,700	Distribution	98,070	Total	115,770		
19									

Figure 7.11. Alternative model for Example 7.3.

Two changes from the previous model are present. First, no explicit capacity constraints appear because these are combined with the linking constraints. Second, one linking constraint appears (cells I12:I15) for each potential DC location, rather than one for each combination of DC location and sales region. Its left-hand side is expressed in the form $\sum_j x_{ij} - C_i y_i$.

The facility location model can be thought of as the strategic version of the transportation problem, in the sense that the warehouse or DC locations are treated as given in the transportation problem but as choices in the facility location problem. Associated with these choices are the fixed costs of operating a facility, and these costs are incorporated into the model with the help of linking constraints.

7.4.2. Uncapacitated Version

In the classical *uncapacitated facility location problem*, no capacity constraints are associated with the potential facility locations. In a supply-chain design setting, this might be the case if capacities are completely flexible and can be determined after the facility locations are selected. The model of the capacitated case can be adapted to the uncapacitated case in different ways.

Perhaps the simplest way to represent the uncapacitated version of the model is to use the capacitated version with very large capacities. For example, the capacity at each facility location could be set equal to the sum of all demands. In symbols, this means setting

$$C_i = \sum_j d_j$$

In this formulation, capacity constraints do not inhibit the selection of facility locations based on cost, and the linking constraints ensure correct accounting for the fixed operating costs. Figure 7.12 shows the corresponding spreadsheet layout. The only change (in the streamlined version) from the formulation of the capacitated model is the value of 450, which appears in the role of capacity, in the range G5:G8. When we optimize this model, we find that the minimum cost drops to $107,510, as shown in Figure 7.12, and that the optimal configuration is to use only the Atlanta location. Without capacity constraints, we anticipate that the optimal cost should be lower than the optimal cost for the capacitated model. However, it may be surprising to find that the complete relaxation of the capacity constraints leads to modest savings. Compared to the capacitated version, the uncapacitated configuration saves $8260 ($= 115{,}770 - 107{,}510$) or about 7 percent.

An alternative modeling approach is based on an insight about the nature of optimal transportation patterns in the uncapacitated case. In the capacitated model of Figure 7.11, for example, Midwest demand is met from two sources—New York and Los Angeles. This kind of split would not occur in an optimal solution to the uncapacitated version of the problem because there is never an incentive to meet demand from two sources. In the example, it is cheaper to supply Midwest sales from New York than from Los Angeles, so there would be no reason to ship from Los Angeles to the Midwest. (In fact, if the Atlanta location is in use, there is no reason

	A	B	C	D	E	F	G	H	I
1	**Facility Location Model**	*Uncapacitated Version*							
2									
3	**Data**			*Regions*					
4	*Locations*	*Fixed Costs*	*East*	*South*	*Midwest*	*West*	*Capacity*		
5	New York	6000	206	225	230	290	450		
6	Atlanta	5500	225	206	221	270	450		
7	Chicago	5800	230	221	208	262	450		
8	Los Angeles	6200	290	270	262	215	450		
9		*Demand*	100	150	110	90			
10									
11	**Decisions**	*In Use*					*Sent*		*Linking*
12	New York	0	0	0	0	0	0		0
13	Atlanta	1	100	150	110	90	450		0
14	Chicago	0	0	0	0	0	0		0
15	Los Angeles	0	0	0	0	0	0		0
16		*Received*	100	150	110	90			
17									
18	**Objective**	*Operating*	5,500	*Distribution*	102,010	*Total*	107,510		
19									

⏮ ◀ ▶ ⏭ Loc1 Loc2 **Loc3**

Figure 7.12. Optimal solution for the unconstrained model.

to ship from New York, either.) A general property of the uncapacitated model is that an optimum exists in which each demand is met from just one source. In particular, demand should be met from the least expensive source among the facility locations in the solution. Therefore, we don't really need the x_{ij} variables. Instead, we can define

$$u_{ij} = 1 \quad \text{if facility } i \text{ serves demand } j$$
$$= 0 \quad \text{otherwise}$$

In words, u_{ij} indicates whether demand in region j is met from facility i. When $u_{ij} = 1$, we know that the corresponding distribution cost must be equal to $(c_{ij}d_j)u_{ij}$, since the entire demand quantity d_j will be met from the one source. Accordingly, the (streamlined) formulation takes the following form.

$$\text{Minimize} \qquad z = \sum_i F_i y_i + \sum_{ij} (c_{ij}d_j)u_{ij}$$

subject to

$$\sum_i u_{ij} \geq 1 \tag{7.6}$$

$$\sum_j u_{ij} \leq ny_i \tag{7.7}$$

The number (n) of demand regions appears in (7.7) because it is the largest possible value for the sum on the left-hand side. Finally, although the variables u_{ij} take on values of zero or one, we do not have to declare them as binary because the

	A	B	C	D	E	F	G	H	I	J	K	L
1	**Facility Location Model**	*Uncapacitated Version*										
2												
3	**Data**			*Regions*								
4	*Locations*	*Fixed Costs*	*East*	*South*	*Midwest*	*West*			*Total Distribution Cost*			
5	New York	6000	206	225	230	290			20,600	33,750	25,300	26,100
6	Atlanta	5500	225	206	221	270			22,500	30,900	24,310	24,300
7	Chicago	5800	230	221	208	262	*No. of*		23,000	33,150	22,880	23,580
8	Los Angeles	6200	290	270	262	215	*Locations*		29,000	40,500	28,820	19,350
9		*Demand*	100	150	110	90	4					
10												
11	**Decisions**	*In Use*					*Sent*		*Linking*			
12	New York	0	0	0	0	0	0		0			
13	Atlanta	1	1	1	1	1	4		0			
14	Chicago	0	0	0	0	0	0		0			
15	Los Angeles	0	0	0	0	0	0		0			
16		*Received*	1	1	1	1						
17												
18	**Objective**	Operating	5,500	Distribution	102,010	Total	107,510					
19												

Loc1   Loc2   Loc3   **Loc4**

Figure 7.13. Optimal solution for the alternative unconstrained model.

optimization will always lead to a 0-1 solution when the u_{ij} are treated as continuous variables. Thus, we specify the model in Figure 7.13 as follows.

> Objective: G18 (minimize)
> Variables: B12:F15
> Constraints: C16:F16 $\geq$ 1
> I12:I15 $\leq$ 0
> B12:B15 = binary

Figure 7.13 displays an optimal solution for the spreadsheet containing the alternative unconstrained model. We can confirm the optimal total cost of $107,510, and an optimal design calling for a facility in Atlanta to supply the entire set of demands. In the spreadsheet, the following changes have been made from the model in Figure 7.12.

- The "very large" capacities formerly in cells G5:G8 are no longer needed.
- The *Sent* totals now show the number of regions served from a warehouse rather than the quantity shipped.
- A typical linking constraint follows the form of (7.7). For example, the formula in cell I12 is now =G12-$G$9*$B12.
- The Total Distribution Cost array in I5:L8 holds the terms $(c_{ij}d_j)$ from the objective function. These are calculated from the original array of unit costs and demands in each region. Then, the Distribution component of total cost in cell E18 is calculated with the Excel formula =SUMPRODUCT(I5:L8,C12:F15).

The uncapacitated facility location problem is sometimes just the central portion of a larger and more complicated design problem. One reason why it is desirable to use

u_{ij} variables in the formulation is that other kinds of constraints, particularly logical conditions, may apply to the potential facility locations. For example, suppose we want to distribute to at most one customer location from New York. To achieve this requirement, add the constraint $u_{11} + u_{12} + u_{13} + u_{14} \leq 1$. As discussed earlier in the chapter, logical constraints can often be developed in linear form with the help of binary variables, or at least variables that behave as if they were binary.

We have examined two alternative modeling approaches to both the capacitated and uncapacitated problems. These alternatives are based on the streamlined linking constraint, using (7.5) in place of (7.3). One advantage of the streamlining is that there are fewer elements on the spreadsheet, so the model is easier to build and debug. However, there is a potential downside. The streamlined version may require more computational effort than the original version to locate an optimum. This difference could be important in larger models, with perhaps dozens of facility locations and hundreds of customer demands.

7.5. DISJUNCTIVE CONSTRAINTS: THE MACHINE SEQUENCING PROBLEM

Scheduling and sequencing problems are notoriously difficult to solve, but some progress is possible with the use of integer programming. In the basic machine-sequencing problem, one processor (or *machine*) is available to process several jobs. The jobs are all ready for processing at the outset (time zero), but the machine can accommodate only one job at a time. The jobs are described by a processing time (p_j for job j) and a due date (d_j).

Depending on the sequence chosen, job j will start processing at time s_j and complete its processing at time $s_j + p_j$. If a job completes after its due date, then the job is said to be *tardy*, and its tardiness is measured by $(s_j + p_j) - d_j$. On the other hand, if a job completes on or before its due date, then the job is on time, and its tardiness is zero. In other words, a job's tardiness may be zero, but it can never be negative. One way of measuring schedule performance is to sum the tardiness of all jobs, thus computing the *total tardiness* in the schedule. A common objective in scheduling is to minimize total tardiness, as a means of quantifying the effectiveness of a schedule at meeting due dates. The use of total tardiness as a performance measure prevents one job's earliness from offsetting another's lateness, thereby focusing attention on jobs that miss their due dates. Obviously, when total tardiness is zero, this means that all due dates have been met.

As an example, Miles Manufacturing faces a version of the machine sequencing problem.

EXAMPLE 7.4   *Miles Manufacturing Company*

Miles Manufacturing Company is a regionally focused production shop that fabricates metal components for auto companies. Its scheduling efforts center around a large piece of equipment that handles a variety of operations, such as drilling, shaping, polishing, and mechanical testing.

Work arrives at the machine in batches—each batch corresponding to a customer order—and the information system provides data on the size of the order, how long it will take to process, and when it is due (the due dates having been previously negotiated with customers). These due dates, which apply to completion in the shop, are adjusted for the delivery time needed to put the completed order in the customer's hands. When several orders are waiting to be processed, the supervisor looks for guidance on how the orders should be sequenced. The minimization of total tardiness is an accepted criterion for a schedule.

This morning's workload consists of six jobs, as described in the following table.

Job number	1	2	3	4	5	6
Processing time (hours)	5	7	9	11	13	15
Due date (hours from now)	28	35	24	32	30	40

The problem is to sequence the six jobs so that work can begin. With 60 total hours of work to schedule, and a latest due date of 40, it is obvious that the jobs cannot all be finished on time, and some tardiness will occur even in the best schedule. ∎

The optimization problem is to select a sequence for the jobs that minimizes total tardiness. For decision variables we can use the job start times, s_j. The key feasibility constraints reflect the fact that, for any pair of jobs j and k, either k follows j or else j follows k. In other words, either job j completes before k starts, or else job k completes before j starts. In symbols, either

$$s_j + p_j \leq s_k \quad \text{or} \quad s_k + p_k \leq s_j$$

These are called *disjunctive constraints*, meaning that one or the other—but not both—must hold for a solution to be feasible. To represent this requirement in an integer program, we use the following pair of constraints

$$s_j + p_j \leq s_k + M(1 - y_{jk})$$
$$s_k + p_k \leq s_j + My_{jk}$$

where y_{jk} is a binary variable and M represents a nonrestrictive large value, such as the sum of all the processing times. When $y_{jk} = 1$, the first constraint forces the start of job k to be at least as late as the completion of job j, and the second constraint does not restrict the choice of variables. On the other hand, when $y_{jk} = 0$, the first constraint does not restrict the choice of variables, and the second constraint forces the start of job j to be at least as late as the completion of job k. In other words

$$y_{jk} = 1 \quad \text{if job } k \text{ follows job } j, \text{ and zero otherwise.}$$
$$y_{kj} = 1 \quad \text{if job } j \text{ follows job } k, \text{ and zero otherwise.}$$

We can also rewrite the constraint pair with all variables moved to the left-hand side and parameters on the right-hand side, thus obtaining the following pair of constraints

$$s_j - s_k + My_{jk} \leq M - p_j$$
$$s_j - s_k + My_{jk} \geq p_k$$

Expressed this way, the left-hand sides of these conditions are identical, which allows for some efficiency in building the spreadsheet model. In addition to the disjunctive constraints, we need constraints that track the tardiness of job j, which is denoted by t_j. This can be accomplished by treating t_j as a nonnegative decision variable and imposing the following constraint

$$t_j \geq s_j + p_j - d_j$$

When job j is on time, the right-hand side of this constraint will be negative or zero, so the tardiness variable t_j will become zero because all variables are nonnegative by assumption. Otherwise, the constraint will be tight (because the objective is to make total tardiness as small as possible), and the tardiness variable t_j will be equal to the right-hand side. We can also write this constraint with decision variables on the left and parameters on the right, as follows

$$s_j - t_j \leq d_j - p_j$$

An algebraic statement of the entire model follows.

Minimize $z = \sum t_j$

subject to:

$$\begin{aligned}
s_j - s_k + M y_{jk} &\leq M - p_j, && \text{for all job pairs } j < k \\
s_j - s_k + M y_{jk} &\geq p_k, && \text{for all job pairs } j < k \\
s_j - t_j &\leq d_j - p_j, && \text{for all jobs } j
\end{aligned}$$

A spreadsheet model for Miles Manufacturing is shown in Figure 7.14. The first module of the spreadsheet contains the data for the problem. The next module contains the three types of decision variables: start times (s_j), tardiness values (t_j), and binary variables (y_{jk}, needed only for $j < k$). As usual, the decision variables are highlighted. The third module is a one-cell module containing the objective function, which is just the sum of the job tardiness values.

Although we need the variables y_{jk} only for $j < k$, the worksheet also shows y_{jk} for $j > k$. In the worksheet, these values are not highlighted, signifying that they are not decision variables. Instead, their values are calculated directly from the decision variables. For example, once we know the value of y_{12}, then it follows that y_{21} is its binary complement.

The last module contains the constraints of the problem. First, we see the LT inequalities $s_j - t_j \leq d_j - p_j$. These are expressed in rows 22–24, in the columns corresponding to the respective jobs. Next, we see the disjunctive constraints in rows 27–41. Each row contains a disjunctive pair, one expressed as an LT constraint and the other expressed as a GT constraint, each with the same left-hand side. The left-hand side appears in column G, while the right-hand sides appear in columns I and K.

	A	B	C	D	E	F	G	H	I	J	K
1	Sequencing Model										
2											
3	Data										
4		Job	1	2	3	4	5	6	Total		
5		Process time	5	7	9	11	13	15	60		
6		Due date	28	35	24	32	30	40			
7											
8	Decisions										
9		start	22	27	13	34	0	45			
10		tardiness	0	0	0	13	0	20			
11		binary y(j,k)	1	2	3	4	5	6	after		
12		1		1	0	1	0	1	3		
13		2	0		0	1	0	1	2		
14		3	1	1		1	0	1	4		
15		4	0	0	0		0	1	1		
16		5	1	1	1	1		1	5		
17		6	0	0	0	0	0		0		
18	Objective										
19			5	4	3	2	1	0			
20		sequence	5	3	1	2	4	6	33		
21											
22	Constrain	s - t	22	27	13	21	0	25			
23			<=	<=	<=	<=	<=	<=			
24		d - p	23	28	15	21	17	25			
25											
26		pair (j,k)	y(j,k)	s(j)	s(k)		LHS		RHS1		RHS2
27		12	1	22	27		55	>=	7	<=	55
28		13	0	22	13		9	>=	9	<=	55
29		14	1	22	34		48	>=	11	<=	55
30		15	0	22	0		22	>=	13	<=	55
31		16	1	22	45		37	>=	15	<=	55
32		23	0	27	13		14	>=	9	<=	53
33		24	1	27	34		53	>=	11	<=	53
34		25	0	27	0		27	>=	13	<=	53
35		26	1	27	45		42	>=	15	<=	53
36		34	1	13	34		39	>=	11	<=	51
37		35	0	13	0		13	>=	13	<=	51
38		36	1	13	45		28	>=	15	<=	51
39		45	0	34	0		34	>=	13	<=	49
40		46	1	34	45		49	>=	15	<=	49
41		56	1	0	45		15	>=	15	<=	47
42											

Figure 7.14. Spreadsheet model for Example 7.4.

We specify the problem as follows.

Objective: I18 (minimize)
Variables: C9:H10,D12:H12,E13:H13,F14:H14,G15:H15,H16
Constraints: C22:H22 $\leq$ C24:H24
                G27:G41 $\geq$ I27:I41
                G27:G41 $\leq$ K27:K41
                D12:H12 $=$ binary
                E13:H13 $=$ binary
                F14:H14 $=$ binary
                G15:H15 $=$ binary
                H16 $=$ binary

The worksheet in Figure 7.14 contains an optimal sequence. Although the order of the start times tells us that an optimal sequence is given by 5-3-1-2-4-6, we can also determine the sequence from the full array of y_{jk} values. In cells I12–I17, we sum the entries in the corresponding row of the array. This value tracks the number of jobs following the job in that row. For example, three jobs come after job 1, indicating that job 1 is third in sequence. We can then construct the optimal sequence in row 20 by using these numbers and the MATCH function. Thus, after downloading processing times and due dates from the central information system and then using an integer programming model, Miles Manufacturing can construct optimal sequences on the supervisor's spreadsheet.

The sequencing model is more general than Example 7.4 might suggest because it can accommodate other objective functions as well. For example, instead of minimizing the total tardiness in the schedule, we might instead want to minimize the number of tardy jobs. In other situations, there could be a contractual penalty determined by a job's delay, and the criterion could be minimization of delay penalties. Sequencing problems with a variety of criteria can fit into this framework, where disjunctive constraints enable the problem to be solved as an integer linear program.

More generally, disjunctive constraints are appropriate whenever we encounter situations in which we want at least one constraint out of a pair to apply. Suppose we have a pair of LT constraints in our model

$$\text{LHS}_1 \leq \text{RHS}_1$$
$$\text{LHS}_2 \leq \text{RHS}_2$$

Suppose also that we wish to have at least one of these two constraints satisfied. We can then represent the two constraints in our model as follows.

$$\text{LHS}_1 \leq \text{RHS}_1 + My$$
$$\text{LHS}_2 \leq \text{RHS}_2 + M(1 - y)$$

With the additional terms, the binary variable y determines which constraint will be met automatically. When $y = 1$, the right-hand side of the first constraint becomes quite large, and the constraint is satisfied for any choice of the other variables in the model. The right-hand side of the second constraint is unaffected, so the other variables must be chosen to be feasible in that constraint. When $y = 0$, the right-hand side of the second constraint becomes quite large, and the other variables must be chosen to be feasible in the first constraint.

7.6. TOUR AND SUBSET CONSTRAINTS: THE TRAVELING SALESPERSON PROBLEM

In the *traveling salesperson problem (TSP)*, a sales rep has several customers to visit, each in a separate city. The sales rep knows the distances between pairs of cities and must plan a trip that visits each of the cities once and returns home. This type of trip is called a *tour*. Specifically, the sales rep would like to plan a tour that has the minimum total distance.

The given information in the TSP is an array of distances. In the literal version of the problem, we might expect the distances to be symmetric—that is, the distance from A to B should be the same as the distance from B to A. However, there are applications where the distances need not be symmetric. For example, a paint booth may or may not need cleaning between two successive products on the production line. If two successive items use the same color of paint, then there is no cleaning required. But if the items require different colors, then there is a need to clean out the painting equipment. The time required depends on the paint color just finishing and on the paint color about to begin. The (i, j)th entry in the data array represents the time required to clean the equipment between color i and color j, and it need not be the same as the cleaning time between j and i. In a complete cycle through the products, with one batch for each color, the *painting* time is fixed, but the length of the schedule is minimized when the total *cleaning* time is minimized. Total cleaning time is in turn the total length of a tour in the array of cleaning times. As an example, consider the Douglas Electric Cart Company.

EXAMPLE 7.5   *Douglas Electric Cart Company*

The Douglas Company assembles small electric vehicles which are sold for use on golf courses, at university campuses, and in sports stadiums. In these markets, customers like to buy in a variety of colors, so Douglas offers several choices. As a result, its manufacturing operations include a sophisticated painting operation, which is separately scheduled.

Today's schedule contains six colors (C1–C6) with cleaning times as shown in the table below.

	C1	C2	C3	C4	C5	C6
C1	–	16	63	21	20	6
C2	57	–	40	46	69	42
C3	23	11	–	55	53	47
C4	71	53	58	–	47	5
C5	27	79	53	35	–	30
C6	57	47	51	17	24	–

The entry in row i and column j of the table gives the cleaning time required between product lots of color Ci and color Cj. Each production run consists of a cycle through the full set of colors, and the operations manager wishes to sequence the colors so that the total cleaning time in a cycle is minimized. ■

Returning to the traveling salesperson terminology, we refer to the colors in a production cycle as cities, and we refer to the cleaning time objective as the total distance. For example, if the painting schedule calls for the color sequence given by the cycle

$$1\text{-}2\text{-}3\text{-}4\text{-}5\text{-}6\text{-}1$$

then the total distance (cleaning time in the cycle) is $16 + 40 + 55 + 47 + 30 + 57 = 245$. We would like to know whether this is the minimum.

As a first cut at an optimization model, we define the following decision variables

$$x_{ij} = 1 \quad \text{if the city pair } (i, j) \text{ occurs on the tour.}$$
$$x_{ij} = 0 \quad \text{otherwise.}$$

We can imagine an array of x_{ij} variables in an array the same size as the table of distances, although we do not need to use the variables x_{ii} on the diagonal. Next, we can recognize that any tour must enter each city once and leave each city once. Therefore, in order for the decisions to be feasible, only one of the entries in each row of the decision array can equal 1 (one departure route from each city) and only one of the entries in each column can equal 1 (one entry route into each city.) Another way to state this requirement is that the sum along each row and the sum along each column must be equal to 1. When we impose these constraints, we are essentially formulating an assignment problem, as discussed in Chapter 3. (See Figure 3.6 for an example.) The assignment problem requires a 1 in every row and a 1 in every column, and its objective function is the SUMPRODUCT of the cost (distance) array and the decision array.

To build a spreadsheet model for the optimization problem, we first enter the given array of distances, as in Figure 7.15. To the right of the data we construct another array for the decision variables x_{ij}. For each entry in the table of cleaning times, we have a corresponding decision variable. Along the diagonal of the distance array, we have entered arbitrarily large distances, to discourage the use of decision variables x_{ii}. In the figure, we display the x-values corresponding to the cycle 1-2-3-4-5-6-1. The objective function is the SUMPRODUCT of the data array and the decision array, which for this sequence yields the value 245.

To find a solution, we specify the problem as follows.

Objective:	B12 (minimize)
Variables:	K5:P10
Constraints:	Q5:Q10 = 1
	K11:P11 = 1

	A	B	C	D	E	F	G	H	I	J	K	L	M	N	O	P	Q
1	Traveling Salesperson Problem																
2																	
3	Data				To						Decisions/Assignments						
4			1	2	3	4	5	6			1	2	3	4	5	6	sum
5		1	999	16	63	21	20	66		1	0	1	0	0	0	0	1
6		2	57	999	40	46	69	42		2	0	0	1	0	0	0	1
7	From	3	23	11	999	55	53	47		3	0	0	0	1	0	0	1
8		4	71	53	58	999	47	5		4	0	0	0	0	1	0	1
9		5	27	79	53	35	999	30		5	0	0	0	0	0	1	1
10		6	57	47	51	17	24	999		6	1	0	0	0	0	0	1
11	Objective									sum	1	1	1	1	1	1	
12		245															
13																	

Figure 7.15. Distance array and decision array for Example 7.5.

	A	B	C	D	E	F	G	H	I	J	K	L	M	N	O	P	Q
2																	
3	Data				To					Decisions/Assignments							
4			1	2	3	4	5	6			1	2	3	4	5	6	
5		1	999	16	63	21	20	66		1	0	0	0	0	1	0	1
6		2	57	999	40	46	69	42		2	0	0	1	0	0	0	1
7	From	3	23	11	999	55	53	47		3	0	1	0	0	0	0	1
8		4	71	53	58	999	47	5		4	0	0	0	0	0	1	1
9		5	27	79	53	35	999	30		5	1	0	0	0	0	0	1
10		6	57	47	51	17	24	999		6	0	0	0	1	0	0	1
11	Objective										1	1	1	1	1	1	
12		120															
13	Constraints								subtours:		1	5	1				
14											2	3	2				
15											4	6	4				
16																	

TSP TSP1

Figure 7.16. Solution to the assignment model for Example 7.5.

Figure 7.16 shows the result, which has an optimal objective function value of 120. Unfortunately, when we try to interpret the decision variables as a route for the sales rep, we do not obtain a tour. Starting at city 1, the tour goes to city 5, but then it returns to city 1. Alternatively, if we start at city 4, the tour goes to city 6 and then returns to city 4. We actually have three separate routes, called *subtours*, but no tour that visits all the cities. The subtours are listed in rows 13–15 of the spreadsheet, after Solver's run. Evidently, the assignment problem constraints, which assure an entry of 1 in every row and every column, are not sufficient to guarantee that we can interpret the result as a tour. We must impose additional constraints. Adding constraints that create a tour does not sound like it will involve linear constraints, but it is not difficult to accomplish, as we discuss next.

To proceed toward a solution, we have to add constraints that eliminate the subtours we encountered. In the solution of Figure 7.17, suppose we focus on the subtour involving cities 4 and 6. (If we can eliminate the subtour 4-6-4, that will simultaneously eliminate at least one of the other subtours. If we are fortunate, all three subtours will be eliminated.) To prohibit the tour 4-6-4, we add the following constraint

$$x_{46} + x_{64} \leq 1$$

Assuming, for the moment, that the x-values are binary variables, this constraint states that between the pair $(4, 6)$, we can have at most one link on the tour. We place the left-hand side of this constraint as a formula in cell E15 (under the heading "length"), and we place the right-hand side in cell G15 (under the heading "limit") as shown in Figure 7.17. Now we can re-run the model with the additional constraint, hoping that it will produce a tour.

Figure 7.17. Solution for Example 7.5 with one elimination constraint.

This time, we specify the problem as follows.

Objective: B12 (minimize)
Variables: K5:P10
Constraints: Q5:Q10 = 1
              K11:P11 = 1
              E15 ≤ G15

Figure 7.17 shows the solution. The objective function increases from 120 to 128, which is not surprising, given that we added a constraint to eliminate part of the previous solution. However, we still do not have a tour. Two subtours (1-4-6-5-1 and 2-3-2) appear in the solution, so we must add another elimination constraint. For convenience, we choose the smaller subtour and focus on 2-3-2. The appropriate constraint to add is the following

$$x_{23} + x_{32} \le 1$$

We place the left-hand side in cell E16 and the right-hand side in G16, and we again re-run the model, with the following specification.

Objective: B12 (minimize)
Variables: K5:P10
Constraints: Q5:Q10 = 1
              K11:P11 = 1
              E15:E16 ≤ G15:G16

This time we obtain an objective function value of 143, and subtours of 1-2-3-1 and 4-6-5-4, as shown in Figure 7.18.

	A	B	C	D	E	F	G	H	I	J	K	L	M	N	O	P	Q
1	Traveling Salesperson Problem																
2																	
3	Data				To					Decisions/Assignments							
4			1	2	3	4	5	6			1	2	3	4	5	6	
5		1	999	16	63	21	20	66		1	0	1	0	0	0	0	1
6		2	57	999	40	46	69	42		2	0	0	1	0	0	0	1
7	From	3	23	11	999	55	53	47		3	1	0	0	0	0	0	1
8		4	71	53	58	999	47	5		4	0	0	0	0	0	1	1
9		5	27	79	53	35	999	30		5	0	0	0	1	0	0	1
10		6	57	47	51	17	24	999		6	0	0	0	0	1	0	1
11	Objective										1	1	1	1	1	1	
12		143															
13	Constraints																
14			subtour		length		limit			route	1	2	3	1			
15			4,6		1	<=	1				4	6	5	4			
16			2,3		1	<=	1										
17																	

Figure 7.18. Solution for Example 7.5 with two elimination constraints.

Once more, we pursue the elimination strategy. Of the two 3-city subtours, suppose we choose to eliminate 4-6-5-4. The constraint is as follows.

$$x_{45} + x_{46} + x_{54} + x_{56} + x_{64} + x_{65} \le 2$$

This constraint prohibits the subtour 4-6-5-4, and while we're at it, the subtour 4-5-6-4. In other words, we permit at most two links on the tour from the routes involving these three cities. The left-hand side of the constraint includes all possible city pairs from the set of cities on the subtour; the right-hand side of the constraint is one less than the number of cities in the subtour. We use cells E17 and G17 for the new constraint and re-run the model. This time the objective function increases to 147.5, with a non-integer solution, as shown in Figure 7.19.

Therefore, we impose the requirement that all decision variables must be binary, specifying the problem as follows.

Objective: B12 (minimize)
Variables: K5:P10
Constraints: Q5:Q10 = 1
K11:P11 = 1
E15:E17 ≤ G15:G17
K5:P10 = binary

Now that we are solving an integer programming problem, we must remember to ensure that the Integer Tolerance is zero. Then we proceed with Solver. Figure 7.20 displays the solution, which contains two subtours and achieves an objective function of 160.

		1	2	3	4	5	6			1	2	3	4	5	6	
1	Traveling Salesperson Problem															
3	Data				*To*				Decisions/Assignments							
4			*1*	*2*	*3*	*4*	*5*	*6*			*1*	*2*	*3*	*4*	*5*	*6*	
5		1	999	16	63	21	20	66		1	0	0.5	0	0.5	0	0	1
6		2	57	999	40	46	69	42		2	0	0	0.5	0.5	0	0	1
7	From	3	23	11	999	55	53	47		3	0.5	0.5	0	0	0	0	1
8		4	71	53	58	999	47	5		4	0	0	0	0	0	1	1
9		5	27	79	53	35	999	30		5	0.5	0	0.5	0	0	0	1
10		6	57	47	51	17	24	999		6	0	0	0	0	1	0	1
11	Objective									1	1	1	1	1	1	
12	147.5															
13	Constraints															
14			subtour		length		limit									
15			4,6		1	<=	1									
16			2,3		1	<=	1									
17			4,6,5		2	<=	2									

TSP1 TSP2 TSP3 **TSP4**

Figure 7.19. Solution for Example 7.5 with three elimination constraints.

We pursue the elimination strategy one more time, eliminating the subtour 1-5-1. Having updated the model as shown in Figure 7.21, we specify the problem as follows.

Objective:	B12 (minimize)
Variables:	K5:P10
Constraints:	Q5:Q10 = 1
	K11:P11 = 1
	E15:E18 ≤ G15:G18
	K5:P10 = binary

		1	2	3	4	5	6			1	2	3	4	5	6	
3	Data				*To*				Decisions/Assignments							
4			*1*	*2*	*3*	*4*	*5*	*6*			*1*	*2*	*3*	*4*	*5*	*6*	
5		1	999	16	63	21	20	66		1	0	0	0	0	1	0	1
6		2	57	999	40	46	69	42		2	0	0	0	1	0	0	1
7	From	3	23	11	999	55	53	47		3	0	1	0	0	0	0	1
8		4	71	53	58	999	47	5		4	0	0	0	0	0	1	1
9		5	27	79	53	35	999	30		5	1	0	0	0	0	0	1
10		6	57	47	51	17	24	999		6	0	0	1	0	0	0	1
11	Objective									1	1	1	1	1	1	
12	160															
13	Constraints															
14			subtour		length		limit		route	1	5	1				
15			4,6		1	<=	1			2	4	6	3	2		
16			2,3		1	<=	1									
17			4,6,5		1	<=	2									

TSP TSP1 TSP2 TSP3 TSP4 **TSP5**

Figure 7.20. Solution for Example 7.5 with integer requirements.

	A	B	C	D	E	F	G	H	I	J	K	L	M	N	O	P	Q
1	Traveling Salesperson Problem																
2																	
3	Data				To					Decisions/Assignments							
4			1	2	3	4	5	6			1	2	3	4	5	6	
5		1	999	16	63	21	20	66		1	0	1	0	0	0	0	1
6		2	57	999	40	46	69	42		2	0	0	0	1	0	0	1
7	From	3	23	11	999	55	53	47		3	1	0	0	0	0	0	1
8		4	71	53	58	999	47	5		4	0	0	0	0	0	1	1
9		5	27	79	53	35	999	30		5	0	0	1	0	0	0	1
10		6	57	47	51	17	24	999		6	0	0	0	0	1	0	1
11	Objective										1	1	1	1	1	1	
12		167															
13	Constraints																
14			subtour		length		limit			route	1	2	4	6	5	3	1
15			4,6		1	<=	1										
16			2,3		0	<=	1										
17			4,5,6		2	<=	2										
18			1,5		0	<=	1										
19																	

TSP1 / TSP2 / TSP3 / TSP4 / TSP5 / TSP6

Figure 7.21. Optimal solution for Example 7.5.

This time, the optimal solution provides a complete tour, 1-2-4-6-5-3-1, with a length of 167, as shown in Figure 7.21. By using an integer programming approach, Douglas Electric Cart Company can find the color sequence that requires the minimum cleaning time in a production cycle, thus allowing the firm to make efficient use of its expensive painting equipment.

The solution approach described here begins with an assignment model. The optimal solution to the assignment model as a linear program is guaranteed to contain variables that are 0 or 1, as discussed in Chapter 3. However, the solution may or may not represent a tour. If it does, we are fortunate, obtaining a solution to a potentially difficult model with a single use of linear programming. More likely, we find that the solution contains subtours. In that case, we pursue the strategy of imposing what are known as *subtour elimination constraints*. One at a time, we can add a constraint that prohibits a subtour found in the previous optimal solution. The subtour constraint sums the values of all the decision variables involving the city pairs in the subtour, and requires that the sum must be less than the number of cities on the subtour.

Each time we add a subtour elimination constraint, the objective function is likely to increase, although sometimes it may stay the same. At some stage, we may have to impose the requirement that all variables must be binary, but that is not necessary until we encounter a linear programming solution containing fractions. Eventually, this iterative procedure leads to an optimal solution to the TSP.

A reasonable question to ask is why add the constraints one at a time? Of course, when we start out, we don't know which subtours we need to eliminate. However, we could add constraints that eliminate all possible subtours. The problem is that this may be a very large number of constraints. If there are n cities in the original problem, then the number of constraints that would eliminate all subtours is $2^{n-1} - n - 1$. Consider that when *n* is 12, the number of constraints is over 2000, not to mention that we would find it very tedious to enter those constraints. The empirical finding seems to be that only a very small fraction of the number of potential constraints is ever really needed to obtain an optimal solution using the iterative procedure we have illustrated. In our example, which contained six cities, we would have needed 25 constraints to guarantee an optimal solution with one model, but we found that we needed only four constraints when we implemented the one-at-a-time approach. (Most six-city problems require fewer than that.) Problems with 12, 15, or even 20 cities are usually within the reach of spreadsheet-based solution approaches because the relatively small number of elimination constraints actually needed is well within Solver's limits. The limiting factor is the time required to solve the necessary series of integer programs en route to a final solution.

Applications of the TSP occur frequently in manufacturing and logistics, and some very powerful solution methods, tailored to the TSP, have been developed for repeated use or for tackling especially large versions. The main purpose here is to illustrate a complex logical constraint (the tour requirement) and to demonstrate that it is possible to apply integer programming techniques effectively for nontrivial problem sizes. Large-scale applications require prohibitive amounts of time from Solver, and in those cases, it would be necessary to look elsewhere for a method specialized to the TSP.

SUMMARY

The ability to treat variables as integer-valued, and, in particular, the ability to designate certain variables as binary, opens up a wide variety of optimization models that can be addressed with Solver. As illustrated in Chapters 6 and 7, Solver's branch and bound capability can handle three broad types of models.

- The first type is one that resembles a linear program but with the requirement that certain variables must be integer valued. In Solver, this requirement is added as a constraint.

- The second type is one in which certain decisions exhibit an all-or-nothing structure, reflecting actions that are indivisible. This is a role for a binary variable, which is simply an integer-valued variable no less than zero and no greater than one. Such a variable allows us to model the occurrence of yes/no choices and to use Solver, provided that the structure of the model is linear in all other respects.

- The third type is one in which binary variables are used to capture certain logical constraints in linear form. We don't often think of logical constraints as being so closely related to the inequalities of linear programs, so it takes some modeling practice to appreciate how to make this connection. As the examples illustrate, binary variables are useful in representing linking constraints for fixed costs, disjunctive constraints for sequencing problems, and tour constraints for routing problems.

The categories that rely on binary variables include a number of well known *combinatorial* problems. For many of these problems, large instances can take a great deal of time to solve, whether the solution technique is based on an integer programming formulation or some other approach. In the case of sequencing problems or TSPs, instances with more than 20 elements might create a substantial computational burden for Solver, even though the sizes of the examples in this chapter do not suggest any computational difficulty. In moving to a larger scale, it may be helpful to reset the Integer Tolerance parameter to a more forgiving level, such as 5 percent, while exploring the Solver's response time. It may also be helpful to set a generous time limit (Max Time) on the Engine tab of the task pane, in case the computational burden is greater than anticipated.

EXERCISES

7.1. Moore Office Products (Revisited) Revisit the Moore Office Products example of this chapter, where there have been some revisions in the problem's data. The information is summarized below.

Family	Demand	Contribution	Fixed cost
F1	290,000	$1.20	$60,000
F2	200,000	1.80	200,000
F3	50,000	2.30	55,000

Each product requires work on three machines. The standard productivities and capacities are given below.

| | Hours per 1000 units | | | Hours |
Machine	F1	F2	F3	available
A	3.205	3.846	7.692	1900
B	2.747	4.808	6.410	1900
C	1.923	3.205	9.615	1900

(a) Determine which products should be produced, and how much of each should be produced, in order to maximize profit contribution.

(b) Suppose the demand potential for F3 is doubled. What is the maximum profit contribution? How much of each product should be produced?

7.2. Selecting R&D Projects The Northeast Communications Company (NCC) is contemplating a research and development program encompassing eight major projects. The company is constrained from embarking on all of the projects by the number of available scientists (40) and the budget available for project expenses ($300,000). The following table shows the resource requirements and the estimated profit for each project.

Project	Expense ($000)	Scientists required	Profit ($000)
1	60	7	36
2	110	9	82
3	53	8	29
4	47	4	16
5	92	7	56
6	85	6	61
7	73	8	48
8	65	5	41

(a) What is the maximum profit, and which projects should be selected?

(b) Suppose that management determines that projects 2 and 5 are mutually exclusive. What is the revised project portfolio and the revised maximum profit?

(c) Suppose that management also decides to undertake at least two of the projects involving consumer products. (These happen to be projects 5–8.) What is the revised project portfolio and the revised maximum profit?

7.3. Vendor Allocation with Price Breaks Universal Technologies, Inc. has identified two qualified vendors with the capability to supply some of its electronic components. For the coming year, Universal has estimated its volume requirements for these components and obtained price-break schedules from each vendor. (These are summarized as "all-units" price discounts in the table below.) Universal's engineers have also estimated each vendor's maximum capacity for producing these components, based on available information about equipment in use and labor policies in effect. Finally, because of its limited history with Vendor A, Universal has adopted a policy that permits no more than 60% of its total unit purchases on these components to come from Vendor A.

Product	Requirement	Vendor A Unit price	Vendor A Volume required	Vendor B Unit price	Vendor B Volume required
1	500	$225	0–250	$224	0–300
		$220	250–500	$214	300–500
2	1000	$124	0–600	$120	0–1000
		$115	600–1000		(no discount)
3	2500	$60	0–1000	$54	0–1500
		$56*	1000–2000	$52	1500–2500
		$51	2000–2500		
Total capacity (units)			2500		2000

*For example, if 1400 units are purchased from Vendor A, they cost $56 each, for a total of $78,400.

What is the minimum-cost purchase plan for Universal?

7.4. Incremental Quantity Discount   In the previous exercise, suppose that Vendor A provides a new price-discount schedule for component 3. This one is an "incremental" discount, as opposed to an "all-units" discount, as follows.

Unit price = $60 on all units up to 1000
Unit price = $56 on the next 1000 units
Unit price = $51 on the next 500 units

With the change in pricing at Vendor A, what is the minimum purchasing cost for Universal, and what is the impact on the optimal purchase plan (compared to the one in the previous exercise)?

7.5. Plant Location   The Spencer Shoe Company manufactures a line of inexpensive shoes in one plant in Pontiac and distributes to five main distribution centers (Milwaukee, Dayton, Cincinnati, Buffalo, and Atlanta) from which the shoes are shipped to retail shoe stores. Distribution costs include freight, handling, and warehousing costs. To meet increased demand, the company has decided to build at least one new plant with a capacity of 40,000 pairs per week. Surveys have narrowed the choice to three locations, Cincinnati, Dayton, and Atlanta. As expected, production costs would be low in the Atlanta plant, but distribution costs are relatively high compared to the other two locations. Other data are as follows.

To distribution centers	Distribution costs per pair from				Demand (pairs/wk)
	Pontiac	Cincinnati	Dayton	Atlanta	
Milwaukee	$0.42	$0.46	$0.44	$0.48	10,000
Dayton	0.36	0.37	0.30	0.45	15,000
Cincinnati	0.41	0.30	0.37	0.43	16,000
Buffalo	0.39	0.42	0.38	0.46	19,000
Atlanta	0.50	0.43	0.45	0.27	12,000
Capacity (pairs/wk)	32,000	40,000	40,000	40,000	
Production cost/pair	$2.70	$2.64	$2.69	$2.62	
Fixed cost/wk	$7000	$4000	$6000	$7000	

(a) Assume that Spencer Shoe Company will keep operating at Pontiac and build a plant at one of the three new alternatives. Which alternative will lead to the lowest total cost, including production, distribution, and fixed costs, and what is the minimum weekly cost?

(b) Assume that Spencer Shoe Company could start from scratch and operate any combination of the four plants. Determine the plant locations that minimize total cost. Compared to the result in part (a), how much weekly cost could be saved with the optimal system design?

7.6. Landfill Location   The Metropolis city council is examining four landfill sites as candidates for use in the city's solid waste disposal network. The monthly costs per ton have been estimated for operating at each site and for transportation to each site from the various collection areas. In addition, the amortized monthly cost for the facility at each proposed site has also been estimated. The data are shown in the table below.

From collection area	Transportation cost per ton to landfill site				Monthly tons
	L1	L2	L3	L4	
A	$14	$16	$10	$8	500
B	12	11	12	14	700
C	13	8	9	11	1500
D	10	15	14	12	1000
E	8	12	10	11	1800
F	11	10	8	6	1200
Operating cost/ton	$8	$10	$9	$11	
Fixed cost/ month	$1000	$800	$700	$900	

What is the optimal configuration and the minimum system monthly cost?

7.7. Distribution Planning   Southeastern Foods has hired you to analyze their distribution system design. The company has eleven distribution centers, with monthly volumes as listed below. Seven of these sites can support warehouses, in terms of the infrastructure available, and are designated by (W).

Center	Volume	Center	Volume
Atlanta (W)	5000	Memphis (W)	7800
Birmingham (W)	3000	Miami	4400
Columbia (W)	1400	Nashville (W)	6800
Jackson	2200	New Orleans	5800
Jacksonville	8800	Orlando (W)	2200
Louisville (W)	3000		

Information has been compiled showing the cost per carton of shipping from any potential warehouse location to any distribution center. Southeastern has standardized its warehouse design so that all such facilities can handle up to 15,000 cartons in a month. In addition, the monthly fixed cost for operating one of these warehouses is estimated at $3600. Southeastern could build warehouses at any of the designated locations, but its criterion is to minimize the total of fixed operating costs and variable shipment costs.

	Atl	Bir	Col	Jac	Jvl	Lvl	Mem	Mia	Nash	NewO	Orl
Atlanta	0.00	0.15	0.21	0.40	0.31	0.42	0.38	0.66	0.25	0.48	0.43
Birmingham	0.15	0.00	0.36	0.25	0.46	0.36	0.26	0.75	0.19	0.35	0.55
Columbia	0.21	0.36	0.00	0.60	0.30	0.50	0.62	0.64	0.44	0.69	0.44
Louisville	0.42	0.36	0.50	0.59	0.73	0.00	0.38	1.09	0.17	0.70	0.86
Memphis	0.38	0.26	0.62	0.21	0.69	0.38	0.00	1.00	0.21	0.41	0.78
Nashville	0.25	0.19	0.44	0.41	0.56	0.17	0.21	0.91	0.00	0.53	0.69
Orlando	0.43	0.55	0.44	0.70	0.14	0.86	0.78	0.23	0.69	0.65	0.00

(a) What is the total distribution cost (fixed warehouse costs plus variable distribution cost) for the optimal configuration? What is the optimal configuration of locations to use for the system?

(b) To streamline communications, management requires that each distribution center must be served by just one warehouse. When this requirement is imposed, how much does total cost increase, as compared to the cost in (a)?

7.8. Scheduling with Sequence-dependent Setups A painting operation is scheduled in blocks, where each block involves painting products with a particular color. Cleaning time is required in between each pair of blocks so that the equipment can be prepared for the new color. In each cycle there is one block of each color, and the total painting time is determined by the volume of orders. However, the actual schedule length is determined by the sequence in which the blocks are scheduled, since the cleaning time depends on the color in the previous block and the color in the next block. The table below gives the number of minutes required to clean the equipment, according to the color pair.

Cleaning times		*1*	*2*	*3*	*4*	*5*	*6*
	1	–	4	8	6	8	2
From	*2*	5	–	7	11	13	4
color	*3*	11	6	–	8	4	3
	4	5	7	2	–	2	5
	5	10	9	7	5	–	2
	6	8	4	3	6	5	–

(a) Find the block sequence that minimizes the amount of time spent in cleaning during a full cycle.

(b) What is the minimum number of minutes devoted to cleaning?

7.9. Planning a European Tour Recent graduate and amateur world traveler Alastair Bor is planning a European trip. His preferences are influenced by his curiosity about urban culture in Europe and by his extensive study of international relations while he was in school. Accordingly, he has decided to make one stop in each of 12 European capitals in the time he has available. He wants to find a sequence of the cities that involves the least total mileage. He has calculated inter-city distances using published data on latitude and longitude, and applying the geometry for arcs of great circles. These distances are shown below.

	To											
---	Ams	Ath	Ber	Brus	Cope	Dub	Lis	Lon	Lux	Mad	Par	Rom
Amsterdam	–	2166	577	175	622	712	1889	339	319	1462	430	1297
Athens	2166	–	1806	2092	2132	2817	2899	2377	1905	2313	2100	1053
Berlin	577	1806	–	653	348	1273	2345	912	598	1836	878	1184
Brussels	175	2092	653	–	768	732	1738	300	190	1293	262	1173
Copenhagen	622	2132	348	768	–	1203	2505	942	797	2046	1027	1527
From Dublin	712	2817	1273	732	1203	–	1656	440	914	1452	743	1849
Lisbon	1889	2899	2345	1738	2505	1656	–	1616	1747	600	1482	1907
London	339	2377	912	300	942	440	1616	–	475	1259	331	1419
Luxembourg	319	1905	598	190	797	914	1747	475	–	1254	293	987
Madrid	1462	2313	1836	1293	2046	1452	600	1259	1254	–	1033	1308
Paris	430	2100	878	262	1027	743	1482	331	293	1033	–	1108
Rome	1297	1053	1184	1173	1527	1849	1907	1419	987	1308	1108	–

(a) Find a minimum distance tour for Alastair, starting and ending in Brussels.

(b) What is the length of the optimal tour?

7.10. Miles Manufacturing (Revisited) Revisit the scenario of Example 7.4. Suppose we decide that it is important to distinguish among the levels of importance represented by the various jobs. In particular, we associate a *weighting factor* with each job. Now, we can take our objective to be the total weighted tardiness in the schedule, where a job's weighted tardiness is the product of its tardiness and its weight. The weights of the jobs are listed in the full table of data given below.

Job number	1	2	3	4	5	6
Processing time (hours)	5	7	9	11	13	15
Weight	8	8	6	6	4	2
Due date (hours from now)	28	35	24	32	30	40

(a) What is the total weighted tardiness for the optimal sequence (5-3-1-2-4-6) found in Example 7.4?

(b) What is the optimal value of total weighted tardiness?

7.11. Locating Emergency Service Bases The Southeast Emergency Management Agency is planning to establish a number of helicopter bases in a hurricane-prone part of the country. There are 25 sites under consideration, but the agency has funds to install only three bases. Using a specialized map, the agency has identified counties that can be served from each site in less than 15 minutes of response time. (This response time is considered the maximum desired for the purposes of servicing life-and-death emergencies that might follow a hurricane.)

The data describing the potential sites consist of a census list and an accessibility matrix. The census list gives the population of each county. The accessibility matrix contains a 1 as its (k, j)th element if county k can be serviced from a base at site j within 15 minutes.

At present, the agency has funds to install just three of the bases, and it wishes to maximize the population served by the bases. At which sites should the bases be established and what is the corresponding population served?

County	Population	1	2	3	4	5	6	7	8	9	10	11	12	13	14	15	16	17	18	19	20	21	22	23	24	25
Abbeville	93,109	0	1	1	0	0	0	1	1	0	1	0	0	0	0	0	0	0	0	1	0	0	0	0	1	0
Aiken	105,481	0	0	1	0	0	0	0	0	0	0	1	0	0	0	0	0	0	0	0	0	0	0	1	0	1
Allendale	69,358	1	1	0	0	0	0	0	0	0	0	0	1	0	0	0	1	0	0	0	0	1	0	0	0	1
Anderson	3583	1	0	0	0	0	0	0	1	1	1	0	1	0	1	0	0	0	0	0	0	0	1	0	0	0
Bamberg	135,155	0	0	0	0	0	0	0	0	1	0	1	0	0	1	0	0	0	0	0	0	0	0	0	1	0
Barnwell	134,336	0	0	0	0	0	0	1	0	1	0	0	0	0	0	0	0	0	0	0	1	0	0	0	0	0
Beaufort	55,393	0	0	0	1	0	0	0	0	0	0	0	0	0	0	0	0	0	0	0	1	0	1	0	0	0
Berkeley	91,701	0	0	1	0	0	0	0	0	0	0	1	0	0	0	0	0	0	0	0	0	0	0	0	0	0
Calhoun	26,290	0	0	0	0	0	0	0	0	0	0	0	1	0	0	0	0	0	1	0	1	0	0	0	0	0
Cherokee	58,751	1	0	0	1	0	0	0	0	0	0	0	0	0	0	1	1	0	0	0	1	0	1	0	0	0
Chester	80,815	1	1	1	1	0	1	1	0	0	0	0	0	0	0	0	0	0	0	0	0	0	0	0	0	0
Chesterfield	138,362	0	0	1	0	0	0	0	0	0	0	0	0	0	0	0	1	1	1	0	0	1	0	1	0	0
Claredon	3503	0	0	0	1	0	1	1	0	0	0	0	0	0	0	0	0	0	0	0	0	0	0	0	0	1
Colleton	28,612	0	0	0	0	1	0	0	0	0	0	1	0	0	0	0	1	0	1	0	0	0	0	0	0	0
Darlington	15,303	0	0	0	0	0	0	0	0	0	1	0	0	0	0	0	0	0	0	0	0	1	0	0	1	1
Dillon	125,505	0	0	1	0	0	0	0	0	0	1	1	0	0	0	0	0	0	0	0	0	0	0	0	0	0
Dorchester	163,144	1	0	0	0	0	0	0	0	0	0	0	0	0	0	0	0	0	0	1	0	0	0	0	0	0
Edgefield	10,692	0	0	0	0	0	0	0	0	0	0	0	0	1	0	0	0	1	0	1	1	0	0	0	0	0
Fairfield	100,910	0	0	0	0	0	1	0	0	0	0	1	0	0	0	0	0	1	0	0	0	0	0	0	1	0
Florence	71,737	1	0	0	0	0	1	1	0	0	1	1	0	0	0	0	0	0	1	0	0	0	1	0	0	0
Georgetown	96,531	0	0	0	1	0	0	0	0	0	0	1	0	0	0	1	0	0	0	0	0	1	0	0	0	0
Greenville	123,314	0	0	0	0	0	0	0	0	0	0	0	0	0	0	0	0	1	0	1	1	0	0	0	1	0
Greenwood	68,294	1	1	0	0	0	0	0	0	1	1	1	0	0	0	1	0	0	0	0	1	0	0	0	0	0
Hampton	47,899	1	0	0	0	1	0	0	1	0	0	0	0	0	0	0	1	0	1	0	1	0	1	0	0	1
Horry	11,904	0	1	1	1	1	0	1	0	0	0	0	1	1	0	1	0	0	0	0	0	0	0	0	1	0
Jasper	162,741	1	1	1	1	0	0	0	0	0	0	0	0	0	0	0	0	0	0	0	0	1	0	0	0	1
Kershaw	158,158	1	1	0	0	1	0	0	0	0	0	0	1	1	0	0	1	0	0	0	1	1	0	0	0	0
Lancaster	39,963	0	0	0	1	0	0	0	0	0	0	0	0	0	0	0	1	0	0	0	0	0	1	0	0	0
Laurens	50,358	0	0	0	0	0	0	0	1	0	0	0	0	0	0	0	0	0	0	0	0	0	0	0	0	0
Lee	159,543	0	0	0	0	1	1	1	0	1	0	0	0	0	0	0	0	0	1	0	0	0	0	0	0	0

(Continued)

County	Population	1	2	3	4	5	6	7	8	9	10	11	12	13	14	15	16	17	18	19	20	21	22	23	24	25
Lexington	77,538	0	0	0	0	1	0	0	0	0	0	0	0	1	0	0	0	0	0	1	0	0	1	0	0	1
Marion	130,967	0	1	0	0	1	0	0	0	0	0	0	0	0	0	1	0	0	0	0	0	0	0	0	0	0
Marlboro	115,343	0	1	0	0	1	0	0	0	0	0	1	0	0	1	1	0	1	1	0	0	0	0	0	0	0
McCormick	107,742	1	1	0	0	0	1	1	0	0	0	0	1	0	1	0	0	0	0	0	0	0	1	0	0	0
Newberry	131,642	0	0	0	0	0	0	0	1	0	0	0	0	0	0	1	1	0	0	0	0	1	0	0	1	0
Oconee	145,303	0	1	0	1	1	0	0	0	1	0	0	0	1	0	0	0	0	0	0	1	1	0	1	0	0
Orangeburg	15,198	0	0	1	0	0	0	1	0	0	0	0	0	1	0	0	0	0	0	0	0	0	1	0	1	0
Pickens	117,555	1	0	0	0	1	0	1	0	0	0	0	0	0	1	0	0	0	0	1	0	0	0	1	0	0
Richland	114,203	0	0	0	0	0	0	1	0	0	0	0	0	0	0	1	0	0	0	0	0	0	0	0	0	0
Saluda	56,227	0	0	0	0	0	0	0	0	0	0	1	0	0	0	0	1	0	0	1	1	0	1	0	0	0
Spartanburg	112,869	1	0	1	0	0	1	0	0	0	0	0	0	0	0	0	0	0	0	0	0	0	0	0	0	0
Sumter	43,744	1	0	0	0	0	0	0	0	1	0	0	1	1	1	1	0	0	0	0	1	0	0	0	0	0
Union	100,277	0	0	0	0	0	0	1	0	0	0	0	0	1	0	0	1	0	0	0	0	0	0	1	0	0
Williamsburg	69,503	0	0	0	0	0	0	0	0	0	0	1	0	0	0	0	0	0	0	0	0	0	0	1	0	0
York	48,458	0	1	0	0	1	0	0	0	0	0	0	0	0	0	0	0	1	0	0	0	0	0	1	0	0

Case: Hornby Products Company*

The Hornby Products Company, headquartered in Denver, Colorado, markets a broad line of handcrafted home furnishings that are produced either in its own plants or by local artisans working under contract with the company. Hornby Products has established markets throughout most of the area west of the Mississippi. Its products are distributed to these markets mainly through a series of specialized manufacturer's representatives. In a few areas, the company utilizes architectural firms and interior decorators as distributors.

The company has been so successful in western markets that management has decided to expand its market area to the east. The most recent expansion has been into a region east of the Mississippi from Illinois to western New York and as far south as Alabama and South Carolina. The company is currently serving this new region from its warehouse in Denver and a regional warehouse in St Paul. Sales in the eastern region have grown to such a level that management has decided to establish a system of distribution warehouses to serve this market. The company is now asking, how many additional warehouses are needed, and where should they be located?

History

The Hornby product line contains the full gamut of home furnishings, from heavy pieces of handcrafted furniture to delicate pottery and statues. The company's management has always insisted that the workmanship in its products meet the highest standard. Because of this insistence, the company has attained an industry-wide reputation for outstanding quality. In addition to product quality, management has also concentrated on the quality of its customer service. As its reputation for quality and service has spread, the company has begun to experience very rapid growth. With a vigorous management team, it appears possible to sustain this rapid growth rate without much difficulty.

The company has several policies that have permitted this growth without major capital additions. Subcontracting of production has reduced the necessary investment in plant and equipment. Leasing rather than buying warehouses has practically eliminated investment in this area. The company has, however, deviated from its minimum investment policy in order to maintain a high level of customer service. A full line of products is stocked at every distribution warehouse and every effort is made to provide delivery within 24 hours. The company considers this policy critical to expanding the market for its products.

Hornby Products has contracted with 22 different manufacturer's representatives and architectural firms in the expansion east of the Mississippi. As the company's product line has become established in that area, the representatives have been placing larger orders, necessitating more and more shipments from Denver rather than from St Paul. Denver shipments have been required in order not to drastically deplete the stock at St Paul. This has made it difficult to adhere to the 24-hour delivery policy. The situation has worsened to the point where management has concluded that the sales growth will be stifled unless distribution warehouses

*Adapted from Berry, W.L. and D. Clay Whybark, *Computer Augmented Cases in Operations and Logistics Management* (1972) South-Western Publishing. An edited version was graciously provided by Alan Neebe.

are set up to serve the eastern region. The final impetus to establish these warehouses was provided by the representative in Indianapolis, who complained that late delivery of samples had caused the loss of a sizable contract for the furnishings of a major hotel chain. Hornby management recognized that this would be an increasing problem if better delivery service couldn't be arranged. They went to work on establishing a new distribution system for the eastern region.

EXHIBIT 7.1   *Potential Warehouse Locations for the New Region*

Key
■ Potential warehouse locations and manufacturer's representatives.
● Manufacturer's representatives only.

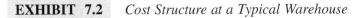

EXHIBIT 7.2   *Cost Structure at a Typical Warehouse*

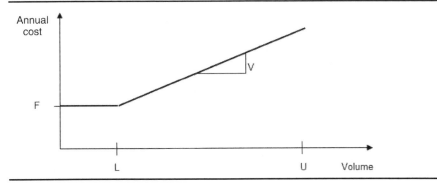

Alternatives

As a first step in establishing the system, company officers visited each of the cities in which they had manufacturing representatives. These 22 cities are shown on the map in Exhibit 7.1. (After initially drawing the map, the company officers decided that Denver should continue to serve Little Rock and Willow Springs.) Eight of these cities were judged to have sufficient transportation services and warehouse facilities for distribution warehouses. Preliminary work was done on estimating the costs and determining the availability of specific facilities. Since company policy was to lease distribution warehouses, little difficulty was encountered in finding at least some warehouse space in each of the eight possible cities.

The typical warehouse facility offers a leasing arrangement that follows the cost structure diagrammed in Exhibit 7.2. The cost structure consists of a fixed cost (F) and a variable cost (V). In addition, there is a lower limit (L) and an upper limit (U) associated with annual volume. The

EXHIBIT 7.3   *Warehouse Cost Data*

W/H	Location	Fixed cost	Variable cost	Min. (L)	Max. (U)
1	Atlanta	2700	6	200	1750
2	Buffalo	2900	8	150	1250
3	Chicago	3500	9	250	2000
4	Cincinnati	2200	7	200	1500
5	Detroit	3300	8	200	1750
6	Pittsburgh	3000	8	200	1500
7	Richmond	2000	6	150	1000
8	St. Louis	1800	5	200	1500

upper limit is a volume ceiling dictated by material handling equipment: no more than this amount of product can be moved through the warehouse. The lower limit functions as a guarantee of sorts to the leasing company. In each city, lease arrangements require a certain minimum capacity to be leased if a warehouse is established. Specifically, Hornby can choose to operate at a volume lower than L, but the fixed cost F would be charged in any event. Only volumes in excess of L incur additional costs, and here the charge is equal to the variable cost V multiplied by the excess volume. Exhibit 7.3 presents the detailed cost and capacity estimates.

For the purposes of evaluating expansion alternatives, sales levels have been forecast two years into the future. Detailed sales forecasts for each representative have been converted to hundredweights (cwt) sold annually at each location. (The term *hundredweight* refers to 100 pounds of product.) At Hornby Products Company, the use of hundredweights as a unit of measure turns out to be a relatively accurate means of aggregating demand, and it is convenient in working out transportation costs. The sales forecasts are given in Exhibit 7.4.

EXHIBIT 7.4 *Forecast for Annual Demands*

Rep. no.	Location	Volume
1	Atlanta	275
2	Birmingham	160
3	Buffalo	240
4	Charleston	260
5	Charlotte	135
6	Chattanooga	160
7	Chicago	400
8	Cincinnati	200
9	Cleveland	320
10	Columbus	220
11	Detroit	190
12	Evansville	100
13	Ft Wayne	140
14	Indianapolis	310
15	Knoxville	125
16	Louisville	340
17	Memphis	240
18	Nashville	210
19	Peoria	150
20	Pittsburgh	340
21	Richmond	300
22	St Louis	260

EXHIBIT 7.5 *Unit Costs for Distribution*

	Atlanta	Buffalo	Chicago	Cincinnati	Detroit	Pittsburgh	Richmond	St Louis
Atlanta	1	13	16	11	15	11	8	12
Birmingham	4	15	15	12	16	13	11	10
Buffalo	13	1	10	8	4	4	7	13
Charleston	7	6	11	6	8	6	4	10
Charlotte	4	10	15	10	13	8	4	14
Chattanooga	2	11	14	9	13	9	7	11
Chicago	16	10	1	9	6	9	14	7
Cincinnati	9	6	7	3	6	6	7	7
Cleveland	13	3	7	6	3	5	8	10
Columbus	10	4	8	4	5	4	7	9
Detroit	15	4	6	8	1	7	11	11
Evansville	9	10	7	6	9	8	10	4
Ft. Wayne	14	8	2	7	4	9	12	6
Indianapolis	12	9	4	6	7	8	11	4
Knoxville	4	9	12	7	11	9	6	9
Louisville	8	8	8	4	8	8	8	6
Memphis	8	14	12	10	14	12	12	6
Nashville	6	12	11	8	12	10	9	7
Peoria	16	11	2	10	8	11	15	5
Pittsburgh	11	2	9	6	5	3	5	11
Richmond	8	7	14	9	11	7	1	14
St Louis	12	13	7	9	11	11	14	1

The cost of transportation from each possible warehouse to each representative has also been determined. Exhibit 7.5 presents the warehouse-to-representative transportation costs.

Fortunately, there is no question of meeting the customer service requirements policy in the new region, because any of the warehouses being considered could deliver to any of the eastern representatives within 24 hours.

Chapter 8

Nonlinear Programming

In Chapter 1, we introduced the optimization capability of Solver with a simple revenue-maximization problem that illustrated the Generalized Reduced Gradient (GRG) algorithm, which is Excel's nonlinear solver. Then, in Chapters 2–7, we focused on linear programming models, solving them with Excel's linear solver. In this chapter, we return to the nonlinear solver and examine the types of optimization problems it can handle.

Taken literally, the term *nonlinear programming* refers to the formulation and solution of constrained optimization problems that are anything *but* linear. However, that isn't a wholly accurate assessment of the GRG algorithm's capability. Two features are important in this regard. First, in terms of finding solutions, linear programming models are actually a subset of nonlinear programming models. That is, the GRG algorithm can be used to solve linear as well as nonlinear programs. However, for linear programming, we use the linear solver because it is numerically more dependable than the GRG algorithm and provides a more extensive sensitivity analysis. The GRG algorithm provides an abbreviated sensitivity analysis, and it may also have difficulty locating a feasible solution when one exists. Still, there is nothing wrong, in principle, with using the GRG algorithm to solve a linear problem.

The second feature to keep in mind is that the GRG algorithm has limitations as a nonlinear solver. In particular, it is mainly suited to problems in which the constraints and objective function contain *smooth functions*. Informally, the definition of a smooth function would be a function without gaps or kinks. A gap means that the function is not continuous: if we were to place a pencil on a sketch of the function, we would not be able to trace the function's entire graph without lifting up the pencil at some point. A gap occurs, for example, in a price schedule with a price break, such as the first function shown on the graph in Figure 8.1. A kink in the function refers to a sharp corner, where the function comes to a point as it changes direction. A kink occurs, for example, in the relationship of output to demand, such as the second function in Figure 8.1. The presence of a nonsmooth function tends to create problems for the nonlinear solver. That said, the nonlinear solver can successfully be applied to a large variety of optimization problems, and this chapter illustrates the major categories.

Optimization Modeling with Spreadsheets, Second Edition. Kenneth R. Baker
© 2011 John Wiley & Sons, Inc. Published 2011 by John Wiley & Sons, Inc.

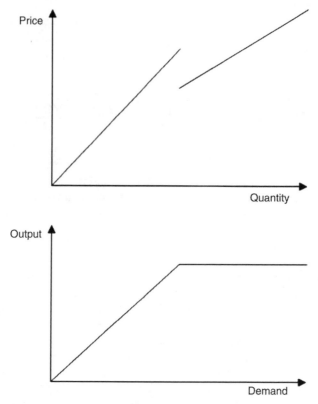

Figure 8.1. Examples of nonsmooth functions.

The nonlinear programming problems we address contain decision variables, an objective function, and usually some constraints. In this respect, they are structurally similar to linear programs except that their objective functions and/or constraint functions are not linear. We look first at problems that have no constraints, so that we can focus on the nature of a nonlinear objective function and its implications for the use of the nonlinear solver. We then look at problems with nonlinear objectives and linear constraints, and we build on some of the coverage in previous chapters. Finally, we look at the boundary of linear and nonlinear models, demonstrating how, in some very special cases, we can transform a nonlinear model into a linear one, so that we can exploit the advantages of the linear solver.

8.1. ONE-VARIABLE MODELS

By taking a brief look at models with one decision variable, we can begin to appreciate the optimization task for nonlinear problems. Conceptually, we can think about finding the maximum of a function $y = f(x)$ that we could draw on a graph. Figure 8.2 shows a graphical plot for a hypothetical nonlinear function. The function shown in

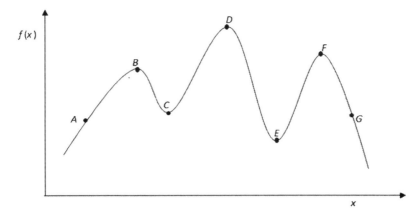

Figure 8.2. Hypothetical nonlinear objective function.

the graph is a smooth function, that is, a continuous function without breaks or corners. The nonlinear solver is well suited to this type of function. It is designed to search for the maximum value of the function and the *x*-value that achieves it.

With one-variable models, it would be possible to locate the maximum value on a spreadsheet by using Excel's Data Table tool. However, even that approach may require several repetitions, depending on the level of precision desired, and additional interventions in the spreadsheet would be required for sensitivity analysis. The use of the nonlinear solver automates the key manual steps. Nevertheless, our main reason for investigating one-variable problems here is to illustrate how the nonlinear solver works in a manageable optimization problem.

The algorithm used by Solver for nonlinear models is a *steepest ascent method*. Starting from any point on the graph, the procedure looks for the direction in which the function increases most rapidly and moves in that direction to a new point. This process repeats from the new point, ultimately stopping at a point where the function does not increase. From the graph in Figure 8.2, we can see that the stopping point may depend on the starting point. If we start the search at point *A*, the search terminates at point *B*. Likewise, if we start the search at *G*, the search terminates at *F*. Only if we start the search between points *C* and *E* will the procedure terminate at the desired point, *D*.

This example illustrates a general feature of the nonlinear solver. The steepest ascent method terminates at a *local optimum*, which is the best point within a predefined neighborhood. However, there may be a *global optimum* located some distance away. The global optimum is the best point anywhere, and that is really the solution we seek. Unfortunately, there is no guarantee that the nonlinear solver will terminate at the global optimum; all we can say is that it converges to a local optimum.

These features immediately describe a contrast between the nonlinear and linear solver. The linear solver, applied to a linear program, always finds a global optimum (assuming one exists) and does so irrespective of the values of the decision variables initially placed in the spreadsheet. The nonlinear solver, applied to a general nonlinear

program, always finds a local optimum (if one exists) but not necessarily a global optimum. Moreover, its result may depend on the initial values of the decision variables.
An example will serve to illustrate the basic optimization properties.

8.1.1. An Inventory Example

A standard inventory problem involves the tradeoff of ordering costs and carrying
costs. This tradeoff represents a common concern in managing inventories, as in the
example of Crowley Foods.

EXAMPLE 8.1   *Crowley Foods*

At grocery distributor Crowley Foods, a particular stock item has a stable demand of 5000
cartons during the year. Each time the distributor places an order for a replenishment lot, a
cost of $35 is incurred for receiving, handling, and inspection. This fixed cost is incurred less
frequently as the order quantity increases. The distributor also ties up working capital in inventory and figures its opportunity cost at 10 percent per year, assessed on the average level of
inventory. Each carton costs $30, so the carrying cost incurred annually is $3 per unit. The
annual carrying cost incurred rises as the order quantity increases. Crowley Foods wishes to
select an order quantity that minimizes the combined costs of ordering and inventory.   ∎

In Example 8.1, the order quantity is the only decision variable. If we let x represent the order quantity, then the number of orders placed per year is $5000/x$ and
the fixed cost incurred annually is $35(5000/x) = 175,000/x$.

Because Crowley Foods can order when stock has fallen essentially to zero, its
inventory level fluctuates between 0 and x, averaging $x/2$. Therefore, the carrying
cost incurred annually is $(0.10)(30)(x/2) = 1.5x$.

With demand known to be 5000 per year, the annual purchase cost of $30(5000) =$
150,000 is constant and independent of the order quantity; therefore, the purchase cost
can be ignored when determining the best order quantity. Crowley's problem is to find
the order quantity x that minimizes its annual cost of ordering and inventory, or

$$f(x) = 175,000/x + 1.5x$$

Figure 8.3 shows a spreadsheet containing the given parameters, as part of the
optimization model. The spreadsheet contains three modules: decision variables, parameters, and objective function. Cell C4 contains the arbitrary value 100, as an initial
value for the decision variable. To find the best order quantity, we specify the problem
as follows.

Objective: C16 (minimize)
Variable: C4

The model contains no explicit constraints, although it's convenient to add the
constraint $x \geq 1$ when using Solver. This modification is helpful because we could

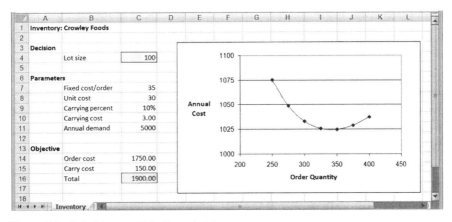

Figure 8.3. Spreadsheet model for Example 8.1.

run into problems in calculating $f(x)$ if we permit $x = 0$. When we optimize, the convergence message appears in the task pane on the Output tab

```
Solver has converged to the current
solution. All constraints are
satisfied.
```

The same message appears along the bottom of the task pane, highlighted in yellow. The convergence result means that internally Solver has not encountered the computational evidence needed to identify the solution as a local optimum. In some cases, this problem can be mitigated by choosing a better initial solution. Normally, when we encounter this result, we simply re-run the optimization starting from the newly obtained solution.

If we re-run Solver starting with the new solution, we obtain the optimality message

```
Solver found a solution. All
constraints and optimality conditions
are satisfied.
```

The same message appears along the bottom of the task pane, highlighted in green. This is the result we want from Solver, and depending on our starting solution, we may obtain this result on the very first run. It confirms that the minimum total cost is $1024.70, achieved by ordering in lots of 342.

The fact that the optimality conditions are satisfied indicates that Solver has found a local optimum. As mentioned earlier, there is no guarantee that this result is also a global optimum, at least without some additional information about the model. In other words, Solver itself has no way of determining whether the solution is a global optimum. So we might ask whether there is additional information we can bring to bear on this issue. One way is to draw a graph of the objective function. Figure 8.3 displays such a graph, which provides strong evidence that there is only one local optimum in this problem and that we have found it. However, a graph will not always provide conclusive evidence, and graphing is not a technique that generalizes easily to problems containing several variables.

In this instance, at least, Crowley Foods can minimize its annual inventory-related costs on this stock item by ordering 342 units at a time, although it wouldn't be surprising to find that the actual order size is rounded to 350 for convenience. The model can be used to verify that costs are not very sensitive to small changes in the order quantity and that, in fact, the annual cost for a quantity of 350 is virtually identical to the optimal cost.

Another approach to finding a global optimum, rather than a local optimum, is to try a variety of different starting points. In this example, we can start with several different order quantities, re-run Solver, and we will come to the same result of 342 each time. This is not a rigorous proof, but it tends to build our confidence that we have located a global optimum. In other problems, however, this approach could identify several local optima, leaving the search for a global optimum inconclusive. In other words, the technique of restarting the procedure from a different initial solution can reveal that several local optima exist, but it can never prove that there is only one local optimum. The next example helps to illustrate the behavior of local optima.

8.1.2. A Quantity Discount Example

For a second example, we continue with the inventory example and explore the implications of a price discount on the purchase of the product being stocked.

EXAMPLE 8.2   *A Purchase Discount for Crowley Foods*

Instead of the purchase cost remaining constant at $30 per carton, the following price-break schedule applies to the product that Crowley Foods has been analyzing.

Quantity purchased	Unit cost
$x \leq 100$	$30.00
$101 \leq x \leq 500$	$29.50
$501 \leq x$	$29.40

Having discovered this discount possibility, Crowley is now considering whether to alter its purchase policy of ordering in replenishment lots of 342. ■

With the possibility of a discount, we must include the annual purchase cost in the objective function, because the total annual cost depends on the order quantity. The spreadsheet in Figure 8.4 shows an extension of the first order quantity model that includes the purchase cost component and the quantity discount structure as well. The unit cost per carton, which can be $30.00, $29.50, or $29.40, gives rise to an annual purchase cost that has three different forms. The formula in cell C17 contains

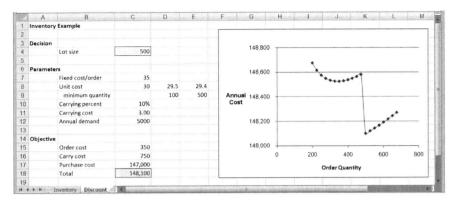

Figure 8.4. Spreadsheet model for Example 8.1.

an IF function, which chooses among the three unit costs according to whether the purchase quantity in cell C4 qualifies for a price discount, and then the formula computes the total purchase cost. In general, the IF function is nonsmooth, and a structure we prefer to avoid when using the nonlinear solver. Nevertheless, we proceed here, because this example illustrates the occurrence of a local optimum in a relatively simple, one-variable model. We can easily check our results using alternative methods.

To find the best order quantity, we specify the model as follows.

$$\text{Objective:} \quad \text{C18 (minimize)}$$
$$\text{Variable:} \quad \text{C4}$$

However, depending on the initial value, Solver converges to one of two solutions, as shown below.

Initial x	Final x	Objective
$x \le 215$	500	$148,100
$216 \le x \le 499$	342	$148,525
$500 \le x \le 2304$	500	$148,100
$2305 \le x \le 2499$	342	$148,525
$x \ge 2500$	500	$148,100

Evidently, there are two local optima, one at $x = 342$ and the other (the global optimum) at $x = 500$. (Figure 8.4 plots the objective function for a range of order quantities in the vicinity of these choices.) Starting values in the neighborhood of 342 converge to 342 as a local optimum. (Somewhat surprisingly, this is also the case for starting values near 2400.) On the other hand, starting values at or somewhat above 500 converge to the global optimum, as do relatively small initial values, below 216. However, once we find one local optimum that is not the global optimum, we can only wonder how many other local optima there might be. In this instance, the graph in Figure 8.4 indicates that only two local optima exist.

The results involving local optima also raise another issue: Are there conditions under which we can be sure that there is only one local optimum? In other words, are there situations where we can be sure that any local optimum we find is also a global optimum? The answer is that such conditions can be identified, and in many practical cases, objective functions will have just one local optimum. We examine this topic next.

8.2. LOCAL OPTIMA AND THE SEARCH FOR AN OPTIMUM

From the earlier discussion, we know that the GRG algorithm may generate local optima instead of global optima in nonlinear optimization problems. This possibility raises at least two general questions.

1. Can we identify situations in which local optima exist that are not global optima?

2. Are there situations in which the nonlinear solver guarantees that it has found a global optimum?

Some theoretical results help answer these questions, but they do not take us very far.

To provide a glimpse of the relevant theory, we first define some terms. An objective function is *convex* if a line connecting any two points on its graph lies on or above the function itself. Similarly, a function is *concave* if a line connecting any two points lies on or below the function. Informally, we can think of a convex function as having a graph that is "bowl" shaped and a concave function as having one that is an "inverted bowl." These two concepts are relatively easy to see in two dimensions, as shown in Figures 8.5 and 8.6, and they hold as well for multidimensional functions. However, functions exist that are neither convex nor concave, such as the function in Figure 8.2.

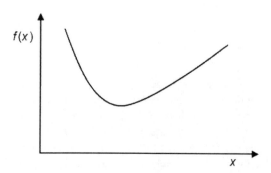

$f(x)$

x

Figure 8.5. A convex function.

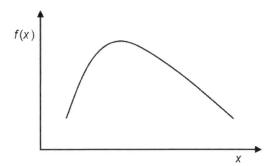

Figure 8.6. A concave function.

A set of constraints delineates a *convex feasible region* if a line connecting any two points in the region lies entirely within the region. Informally, this means that, in a convex region, any blend (weighted average) of two feasible solutions is also feasible. Figures 8.7 and 8.8 show a two-dimensional illustration of a convex region and a nonconvex region, respectively, as shaded areas. A set of linear constraints gives rise to a convex region. Nonlinear constraints may give rise to either convex or nonconvex regions.

The GRG algorithm is guaranteed to find a global optimum when the objective function is convex (when minimizing) or concave (when maximizing) if the constraints correspond to a convex region of feasible decisions. Although this property

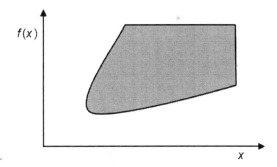

Figure 8.7. A convex region.

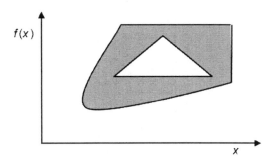

Figure 8.8. A nonconvex region.

begins to answer our question about local optima, it is not always an operational result. Unfortunately, the mathematics of identifying convexity lie beyond the scope of this book. For most practical purposes, we have a convex feasible region if we have no constraints at all or if we have a feasible set of linear constraints. In addition, we have a convex or concave objective function if it is linear or if it is made up of quadratic terms or terms involving such smooth functions as e^{ax}, $\log(ax)$, and the like, with coefficients that are all positive or all negative.

In some problems, we cannot tell whether the requisite conditions are satisfied, so we cannot be sure whether the solution generated by the GRG algorithm is a global optimum. In such cases, we may have to tolerate some ambiguity about the optimal solution. As the previous discussion has suggested, there are two ways we can try to build some evidence that Solver has located the global optimum. First, we can plot a graph of the objective function and see whether it provides a confirming picture. However, this approach is essentially limited to one- or two-variable models. A second response is to re-run Solver starting from several different initial points to see whether the same optimal solution occurs. However, there is no theory to tell us how many such runs to make, how to select the initial points advantageously, or how to guarantee that a global optimum has been found.

In a nonlinear problem, if we run Solver only once, we may have to be lucky to obtain the global optimum, unless we know something about the problem's special features. To help convince ourselves that Solver has found the global optimum, we might try rerunning from different starting points to see whether the same solution occurs. Even then, we can't be too casual about selecting those starting points; in the quantity discount example, starting points between 216 and 499 lead to the same suboptimal result. In a complicated, multidimensional problem, we might have to test many starting points to give us a reasonable chance of finding a global optimum. However, it was just this type of effort that we were trying to avoid by using Solver in the first place.

Solver contains a *MultiStart option* that automates the process of re-running with different starting values of the decision variables. This option can be found on the Engine tab of the task pane, in the Global Optimization section. (The default value for this option is False.) When using this option, it is necessary to specify upper and lower bounds for all decision variables. The nonnegativity requirement, assuming it applies, can serve as a lower bound, but the user must supply an upper bound if none is contained in the original formulation.

Thus, when we use Solver, we must consider whether the algorithm we use, applied to the optimization problem we have posed, is a *reliable algorithm*. By that, we mean the algorithm is guaranteed to find a global optimum whenever one exists. The simplex method, applied to linear programs, is always reliable. The GRG algorithm, applied to nonlinear programs, is reliable only in special circumstances.

Because the GRG algorithm is the default choice of a solver, it is tempting to use it when solving linear programming problems as well as nonlinear programming problems. A problem containing a linear objective function and linear constraints qualifies as one of the problem types in which the nonlinear solver is reliable. However, two possible shortcomings exist in solving linear problems. First, the GRG algorithm may not be able to locate a feasible solution if the initial values of the decision cells are infeasible. Sometimes, it may be difficult to construct a solution that satisfies all constraints, just for the purposes of *initiating* the steepest ascent method used in the nonlinear solver. In some cases, the nonlinear solver will report that it is unable to find a feasible solution, even when one exists. By contrast, the linear solver is always able to locate a feasible solution when one exists. A second reason for preferring the linear solver for linear problems relates to numerical aspects of the model. In some cases, the nonlinear solver may be unable to find an optimal solution without requiring the Automatic Scaling option, whereas the linear solver would not encounter such a problem.

When it comes to problems with integer constraints on some of the variables, Solver augments its basic solution algorithm with a branch-and-bound procedure, as described in Chapter 6. The branch-and-bound method involves solving a series of relaxed problems—that is, problems like the original but with integer constraints removed. When the branch-and-bound procedure is applied to a linear model, in which the simplex method is reliable, we can be sure that the search ultimately locates an optimum. However, when the branch-and-bound procedure involves a series of nonlinear models, we cannot be sure that the relaxed problems are solved to optimality. Therefore, the search may terminate with a suboptimal solution. For that reason, we should avoid using Solver on nonlinear integer programming problems, although the software permits us to use this combination.

8.3. TWO-VARIABLE MODELS

When we move from one decision variable to two, the analysis remains manageable. To check Solver's result, we can plot the outcomes of a two-dimensional grid search, based on using Excel's Data Table tool. We can also investigate the objective function behavior one variable at a time. Although such investigations are not foolproof in two dimensions, they are likely to be quite helpful. The examples that follow illustrate some of Solver's applications.

8.3.1. Curve Fitting

A common problem is to find a smooth function to fit observed data points. A more sophisticated, statistically-oriented version of this problem is known as *regression*, but here we take only the first step. Consider the Fitzpatrick Fuel Supply Company as an example.

EXAMPLE 8.3   *The Fitzpatrick Fuel Supply Company*

The Fitzpatrick Fuel Supply Company, which services residential propane gas tanks, would like to build a model that describes how gas consumption varies with outdoor temperature conditions. Knowledge of such a function would help Fitzpatrick in estimating the short-term demand for propane. A sample of 12 observations was made at customers' houses on different days, and the following observations of degree-days and gas consumption were recorded.

Day	Degree days	Gas consumption
1	10	51
2	11	63
3	13	89
4	15	123
5	19	146
6	22	157
7	24	141
8	25	169
9	25	172
10	28	163
11	30	178
12	32	176

(A degree day is one full day at a temperature 1 degree lower than the level at which heating is needed—usually 68°.) For each day in the table, the number of degree days represents an average over the day. As a first cut at the estimation problem, Fitzpatrick's operations manager would like to fit a linear model to the observed data.   ■

The proposed linear model takes the form $y = a + bx$, where y is the gas consumption in cubic feet and x is the number of degree days. The problem is to find the best values of a and b for the model. Standard practice in this type of problem is to minimize the sum of squared deviations between the model and the observations.

The curve-fitting technique proceeds by calculating, for each of the observations, the difference between the model value and the observed value. If the kth observation is represented as (x_k, y_k), then the difference between the model and the kth observation can be written as follows.

$$\text{Difference} = \text{Model value} - \text{Observed value}$$
$$d_k(a, b) = (a + bx_k) - y_k$$

A measure of how good a fit the model achieves is the sum of squared differences (between model value and observation value) or

$$f(a, b) = \sum_k [d_k(a, b)]^2$$

A small sum indicates that the fit is quite good, and our objective in this case is to minimize the sum of squared deviations. In this formulation, the model parameters a and b are the decision variables, and the objective is to minimize $f(a, b)$. Figure 8.8 displays a spreadsheet for the curve-fitting problem. The first module contains the decision variables (the model parameters a and b) in cells E3 and E4, and the second module contains a single-cell objective in E5. The third module contains the data along with

es and their differences from observed values. The
lculated from these differences using the SUMSQ

n: The SUMSQ Function

lates the sum of squared values from a list of numbers.
iments to the function, or the argument(s) can be cell
is the following

Number2, ...) or SUMSQ(*Array*)

=SUMSQ(E9 : E20) squares each of the 12 elements
ds the squares. If we were to enter the values 10 and 6
total would be 3208. Because the need to compute a
ently, Excel provides this function to streamline the

We specify the problem as follows.

Objective: E5 (minimize)
Variable: E3:E4

The solution, as displayed in Figure 8.9, is the pair (18.5, 5.5), for which the sum of
squared deviations is approximately 3053. This means that the best predictive model

	A	B	C	D	E
1	Curve Fitting				
2					
3	Decisions		*Model*	*a*	18.5
4			*Parameters*	*b*	5.5
5	Objective		*Sum of squares*		3053.00
6					
7	Data			Calculations	
8	*Number*	*Observed*	*Observed*	*Predicted*	*Difference*
9	1	10	51	73.86	22.86
10	2	11	63	79.40	16.40
11	3	13	89	90.47	1.47
12	4	15	123	101.54	-21.46
13	5	19	146	123.67	-22.33
14	6	22	157	140.28	-16.72
15	7	24	141	151.35	10.35
16	8	25	169	156.88	-12.12
17	9	25	172	156.88	-15.12
18	10	28	163	173.49	10.49
19	11	30	178	184.56	6.56
20	12	32	176	195.63	19.63
21					

Figure 8.9. Spreadsheet for Example 8.3.

for the 10 observations is the line $y = 18.5 + 5.5x$. Using this simple function, Fitzpatrick Fuel Supply can make reasonable predictions of propane consumption as the daily temperature varies. With this capability, along with short-term forecasts of daily temperatures, Fitzpatrick can predict future demand and thereby position its inventories appropriately.

The curve-fitting model can easily be extended to functions other than the linear model (or to functions with more than two parameters). For example, we might guess that a better model for consumption would be the *power model* $y = ax^b$. If we had reason to believe that this model contained better predictive power, we could revise the spreadsheet to test it. We simply have to take the linear model out of cells D9:D20 and substitute the power model. Re-running Solver with this change in the model yields a minimum sum of squared deviations equal to approximately 2743, which is a lower figure than can be achieved by any linear model. The best fit in the power family is the function $y = 11.5x^{0.81}$. Although there may well be structural reasons to prefer a model with diminishing returns (because the fuel is less efficient when used intermittently, at low x-values), the optimization criterion also leads us to the power model as a preferable choice in terms of minimizing the sum of squared deviations.

The curve-fitting model with a linear predictor and a sum-of-squares criterion has a convex objective function. This structure tells us that the optimization is straightforward, and we don't have to worry about local optima. For the sum-of-squares criterion, the local optimum found by Solver will always be the global optimum. A more challenging problem would arise if some other criterion were used. For example, had the criterion been to minimize the sum of absolute deviations, the optimization problem would have been more difficult. (We investigate this variation in Chapter 9.)

8.3.2. Two-dimensional Location

A common problem is to find a location for a facility that serves many customer sites. In Chapter 7, we encountered the discrete version of the facility location problem, which involves a specific set of possible locations. However, a first cut at a location problem might be helpful before we know the details of possible locations. In such cases we can approach the problem from a continuous perspective. Most often, the continuous location problem arises in two dimensions, as in the case of Merrill Sporting Goods.

EXAMPLE 8.4   *Merrill Sporting Goods*

Merrill Sporting Goods has decided to build a centrally located warehouse as part of its distribution system. The company manufactures several types of sports equipment, stocks them at the factory warehouse, and delivers to a variety of retail sites. Having outgrown its current warehouse and wanting to take advantage of new warehousing equipment, the firm has decided to build at a fresh location. To define a central location, their ten retail sites are first mapped on a two-dimensional grid, so that the coordinates (x_k, y_k) can be associated with each site. These values are as follows.

Site (k)	x_k	y_k
1	9	29
2	5	50
3	26	68
4	39	79
5	41	54
6	38	59
7	63	6
8	52	58
9	81	76
10	95	93

A good location is one that is "close" to all sites. To make this concept operational, Merrill's distribution manager suggests that the objective should be to minimize the sum of the distances between the warehouse and the various sites. Using this measure as a criterion, the distribution manager wishes to find the optimal location for the warehouse. ∎

To begin the analysis, we represent the location of the warehouse by the coordinates (x, y). The straight-line distance in two dimensions between the warehouse and the kth site (also known as the *Euclidean distance*) is given by

$$D_k(x, y) = \left[(x - x_k)^2 + (y - y_k)^2\right]^{1/2}$$

Based on this definition, we can express Merrill's objective function as follows

$$f(x, y) = \sum_{k=1}^{10} D_k(x, y)$$

The problem is to find the decision variables (x, y) that minimize the total distance function $f(x, y)$. The problem has no explicit constraints. Figure 8.10 shows a spreadsheet for the problem, where the coordinates of the warehouse location appear in cells E4 and E5, and the total distance objective appears in cell E8. The detailed data appear in the last module.

We specify the problem as follows

Objective: E8 (minimize)
Variable: E4:E5

The solution, as displayed in Figure 8.10, is the location (39.59, 58.43), for which the objective function reaches a minimum of approximately 301.72. The conclusion for Merrill Sporting Goods is that the map location corresponding to approximately (40, 58) represents the central location they seek.

	A	B	C	D	E
1	Location in Two Dimensions				
2					
3	Decisions				
4		*Facility*		x	39.59
5		*Location*		y	58.43
6					
7	Objective				
8		*Total Distance*			301.72
9					
10	Data	*Site*	*x location*	*y location*	*distance*
11		1	9	29	42.45
12		2	5	50	35.60
13		3	26	68	16.62
14		4	39	79	20.57
15		5	41	54	4.65
16		6	38	59	1.68
17		7	63	6	57.42
18		8	52	58	12.42
19		9	81	76	44.99
20		10	95	93	65.31
21					

Figure 8.10. Spreadsheet for Example 8.4.

We might wonder whether this figure represents a global optimum. As discussed earlier, we can re-run Solver from a variety of starting solutions. Starting with a variety of different solutions, we find that Solver always leads us to the same optimal solution of about (40, 58). Plots of the objective function as we vary x or y separately suggest a similar story. Thus, we have at least some informal evidence that our solution is a global optimum. (Because this is a two-variable optimization model, we could use the Data Table tool to confirm this result.)

8.4. NONLINEAR MODELS WITH CONSTRAINTS

In terms of building spreadsheet models, it is no more difficult to add a constraint in a nonlinear program than it is to add a constraint in a linear program. When using Solver, the steps are identical. Perhaps the only important difference lies in what we might expect as a result.

The key difference between linear and nonlinear models can be illustrated with graphs of a one-dimensional problem. Figure 8.11 shows both the linear and nonlinear cases. In the first graph, the objective is linear, in the form $f(x) = cx$. The decision variable x must satisfy the constraints $x \geq a$ and $x \leq b$. It is easy to see that the optimal value of the objective function must occur when the decision variable lies at one of the constraint boundaries. In a maximization problem, the optimum would be $x = b$; in a minimization problem, the optimum would be $x = a$. (The conclusions would be similar if the linear objective had a negative slope rather than a positive one.)

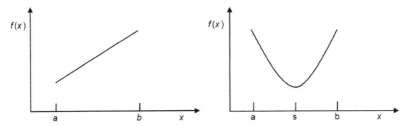

Figure 8.11. Linear and nonlinear objective functions.

In the second graph, the objective is nonlinear, in the form $f(x) = (x - s)^2$, and the same two constraints apply. Assuming that the parameter s lies between a and b, the minimum value of $f(x)$ occurs at $x = s$, and neither of the constraints is binding. On the other hand, the maximum value of $f(x)$ does lie at one of the constraint boundaries.

This graphical example shows that we should always expect at least one constraint to be binding for a linear objective, but that may not be so for a nonlinear objective. In the nonlinear case, the mathematical behavior of the objective function may lead to an optimal decision for which no constraints are binding.

8.4.1. A Pricing Example

When a problem contains both price and quantity decisions, it is likely that a nonlinear programming model will result. The nonlinearity derives from the fact that profit on a given product is equal to (*Price* − *Cost*) × *Volume*, and *Price* depends on *Volume*. Consider the situation at Nells Furniture Company.

EXAMPLE 8.5   *Nells Furniture Company*

Nells Furniture Company (NFC) sells two main products, sofas and dining tables. Based on the last few years of experience in the sales region, the marketing department has estimated demand curves relating the price and demand volume for each product. For sofas, the relationship is

$$p_1 = 220 - 0.4x_1$$

where p_1 and x_1 are the price and volume, respectively. For tables, the price–volume relationship is

$$p_2 = 180 - 0.2x_2$$

The variable costs are \$60 per unit for the sofas and \$45 per unit for the tables. Each item is assembled on site and then inspected carefully. The inspection usually involves some rework and touch-up. There are 800 hours available in the assembly department and 500 in the inspection department. Sofas require 2 hours assembly time and 2 hours inspection time. Tables require 3 hours assembly time and 1 hour inspection time. The management at NFC wants to maximize profit under these conditions.   ■

Taking the volumes x_1 and x_2 as decision variables, we first write the objective function in terms of these variables by substituting for p_1 and p_2

$$\text{Profit} = (p_1 - 60)x_1 + (p_2 - 45)x_2$$
$$= (160 - 0.4x_1)x_1 + (135 - 0.2x_2)x_2$$

The constraints in the problem are linear constraints

$$2x_1 + 3x_2 \le 800 \text{ (assembly)}$$
$$2x_1 + x_2 \le 500 \text{ (inspection)}$$

The problem becomes one of maximizing the nonlinear profit function, subject to two linear constraints on production resources.

Figure 8.12 shows a spreadsheet model for the problem. The three modules in the spreadsheet correspond to decision variables, objective function, and constraints. In the objective function module, we list the unit price, unit cost, and unit profit explicitly. The unit price of sofas in cell C6 is given by the formula relating sofa price and sofa volume, and similarly for the unit price of tables in cell D6. This layout allows us to express the total profit using a SUMPRODUCT formula, although it is not a linear function. Finally, the constraints are linear, so their structure follows the form we have seen in earlier chapters for linear programs.

We specify the problem as follows

Objective:	E8 (maximize)
Variables:	C4:D4
Constraints:	E11:E12 $\le$ G11:G12

Solver returns the optimal decisions as approximately 144 sofas and 170 tables. The corresponding prices are $162.27 and $145.91, and the optimal profit is about $31,960. Although we formulated the model using volumes as decision variables, it

	A	B	C	D	E	F	G
1	Furniture Company						
2							
3	Decisions		Sofas	Tables			
4		Volume	175.0	100.0			
5							
6	Objective	Price	150.00	160.00			
7		Cost	60	45			
8		Profit	90.00	115.00	27,250.00		
9							
10	Constraints						
11		Assembly	2	3	650.0	<=	780
12		Inspection	2	1	450.0	<=	500
13							

Figure 8.12. Spreadsheet for Example 8.5.

would probably be the case in this type of a setting that the focus would be on prices. As the model indicates, optimal prices are approximately \$162 and \$146 for sofas and tables, respectively. By solving this optimization problem, NFC has an idea how to set prices in the face of a price-sensitive customer market.

8.4.2. Sensitivity Analysis for Nonlinear Programs

In Chapter 4, we described two software-based procedures for sensitivity analysis, Parameter Sensitivity and the Sensitivity Report. For nonlinear programs, the use of the Parameter Sensitivity tool is essentially the same as it is for linear programs. However, the Sensitivity Report is a little different, and we describe it here.

Returning to the example of the previous section, suppose we optimize the NFC example and then create the Sensitivity Report. Solver provides the report shown in Figure 8.13. As in the case of linear programs, there are three parts to the report, relating to objective function, decision variables, and constraints. For decision variables, the report lists the optimal value for each variable (which, of course, repeats information on the worksheet itself) along with the *reduced gradient*. This value, like the reduced cost in linear programs, is zero if the variable does not lie at its bound.

For constraints, the report lists the optimal value for each left-hand side (again, duplicating information in the spreadsheet) along with the *Lagrange multiplier*. This value is essentially a shadow price. When the constraint is not binding, the shadow price is zero; otherwise, the Lagrange multiplier provides us with the instantaneous rate of change in the objective function as the constraint constant changes.

	A	B	C	D	E	
1	Microsoft Excel 12.0 Sensitivity Report					
2						
3	Objective Cell (Max)					
4		Cell	Name	Final Value		
5		$E$8	Profit	31960.23		
6						
7	Decision Variable Cells					
8				Final	Reduced	
9		Cell	Name	Value	Gradient	
10		$C$4	Volume Sofas	144.32	0.00	
11		$D$4	Volume Tables	170.45	0.00	
12						
13	Constraints					
14				Final	Lagrange	
15		Cell	Name	Value	Multiplier	
16		$E$11	Assembly	800.00	22.27	
17		$E$12	Inspection	459.09	0.00	
18						

⋈ ◂ ▸ ⋈   **Sensitivity Report 1** Pricing

Figure 8.13. Sensitivity report for Example 8.5.

For example, suppose we vary the number of assembly hours in the NFC model and reoptimize. The table below, obtained from the Parameter Sensitivity tool, summarizes the results for values above and below the given value of 800 hours.

Assembly hours	Optimal profit	Rate of change
750	30,801	–
760	31,040	23.91
770	31,276	23.55
780	31,508	23.18
790	31,736	22.82
800	31,960	22.45
810	32,181	22.09
820	32,398	21.73

Thus, when the number of assembly hours changes from 770 to 780, the optimal profit improves by $231.82 (= 31,507.50 − 31,275.68), or $23.18 per additional assembly hour over this interval. From the table, we can see that the value of an additional hour of assembly time varies depending on the number of assembly hours in the model, dropping from nearly $24 to under $22 over the range shown. The rate of change in the table is calculated from changes in the optimal profit on a grid of size 10. If we reduced the grid to size five or size one, we would see that rate change more gradually, row to row. The entry for 800 assembly hours would change from $22.45 on the size 10 grid to $22.36 on the size five grid, and to $22.29 on the size one grid. We can imagine continuing this process to ever finer grids. As we do so, the incremental value of assembly hours declines, and the rate of change at 800 gets ever closer to a limiting value of $22.27. This limiting value corresponds to the Lagrange multiplier.

The Sensitivity Report provides the shadow price for linear programs and the Lagrange multiplier for nonlinear programs. Their values are zero when the constraint is not binding; and when the constraint is binding, their values give the incremental value of the scarce resource. In the typical linear program, however, this incremental value stays constant for some amount of increase or decrease in the constraint constant. In the typical nonlinear program, as illustrated here, this incremental value is always changing with the constraint constant. The Lagrange multiplier represents only the instantaneous rate of change. For that reason, no ranging information, such as the allowable increase or decrease reported in the linear model, would be appropriate.

8.4.3. The Portfolio Optimization Model

A *portfolio* is a collection of assets. In a stock portfolio, the investor chooses the stocks, and the dollar value of each, to hold in the portfolio at the start of an investment period. Over this period, the values of the stocks may change. At the end of the period, performance can be measured by the total value of the portfolio. For a given size (or dollar value) of the portfolio, the key decision is how to allocate the portfolio among its constituent stocks.

A stock portfolio has two important projected measures: return and risk. *Return* is the percentage growth in the value of the portfolio. *Risk* is the variability associated with the returns on the stocks in the portfolio. The information on which stocks are evaluated is a series of historical returns, typically compiled on a monthly basis. This history provides an empirical distribution of a stock's return performance. For stock k in the portfolio, this return distribution can be summarized by a mean (r_k) and a standard deviation (s_k).

EXAMPLE 8.6 *Counseling Ms Downey*

Suppose we are providing investment advice to Ms Downey, who has a nest egg to invest and some very clear ideas about her preferred stocks. In fact, she has identified stocks in five different industries that she believes would constitute a good portfolio. The performance of the five stocks in two recent years is summarized by the following data.

Stock	Mean	St. dev.
National Computer	0.0209	0.0981
National Chemical	0.0121	0.0603
National Power	0.0069	0.0364
National Auto	0.0226	0.0830
National Electronics	0.0134	0.0499

Ms Downey does not, however, know how to allocate her investment among these five stocks. National Computer Company and National Auto Company stocks have achieved the best average returns in the two-year period, but they also have relatively high volatility, as measured by their standard deviations. National Power Company is the least volatile, but it also has the lowest average return. Ms Downey wishes to navigate between these different extremes. Our task is to organize this quantitative information so that we can help her make the allocation decision. ■

Figure 8.14 shows a worksheet containing the monthly returns for Ms Downey's five stocks over the last two years. The data can be found in columns I through N. The mean returns are calculated using the AVERAGE function in cells B4:F4, and the standard deviations are calculated using the STDEV function in cells B5:F5.

Next, the task is to combine the individual stock behaviors into a summary for the portfolio as a whole—that is, a calculation of the mean and variance. For the portfolio mean, we use a weighted average of individual stock returns. Thus, if we allocate a proportion p_k of our portfolio to stock k, then the return on the portfolio is the weighted average

$$R = \sum_k p_k r_k$$

	A	B	C	D	E	F	G	H	I	J	K	L	M	N
1	Portfolio Model													
2									Data					
3	Data Summary	Computer	Chemical	Power	Auto	Electronic			Month	Computer	Chemical	Power	Auto	Electronic
4	Avg Return	0.0209	0.0121	0.0069	0.0226	0.0134			1	0.22616	-0.07205	0.01730	0.22266	0.06202
5	St Deviation	0.0981	0.0603	0.0364	0.0830	0.0499			2	0.09134	0.02588	0.05646	0.01278	-0.03499
6									3	-0.01288	-0.04771	0.02280	0.00379	0.01662
7	Covariances						Proportions		4	-0.17196	0.06342	0.00000	0.04101	-0.07496
8	Computer	0.0092	-0.0006	0.0003	0.0026	0.0012	0.132		5	0.16557	0.03670	0.00510	0.07576	-0.00810
9	Chemical	-0.0006	0.0035	0.0000	-0.0006	0.0003	0.304		6	-0.00789	0.01372	0.02244	0.06817	0.05446
10	Power	0.0003	0.0000	0.0013	0.0006	-0.0001	0.158		7	-0.04909	0.05960	0.06583	-0.07143	-0.06607
11	Auto	0.0026	-0.0006	0.0006	0.0066	0.0017	0.225		8	0.22967	-0.02083	0.00812	-0.02564	0.01712
12	Electronic	0.0012	0.0003	-0.0001	0.0017	0.0024	0.181		9	0.10117	0.00681	0.02360	0.12632	-0.00510
13									10	-0.10530	-0.05128	0.00865	0.16406	0.08376
14	Proportions								11	-0.02767	0.04730	-0.02926	-0.05593	0.04890
15		0.132	0.304	0.158	0.225	0.181	1.000		12	0.00813	-0.01247	0.00893	0.01327	0.08498
16									13	0.05323	0.11894	-0.00885	0.15493	0.09790
17	Calculations								14	0.05364	0.00197	-0.06917	-0.07317	-0.00382
18		0.000161	-0.000025	0.000006	0.000077	0.000028			15	-0.01818	-0.04479	-0.06473	-0.08640	-0.01546
19		-0.000025	0.000322	-0.000002	-0.000038	0.000016			16	-0.09556	0.04366	0.01384	-0.07952	0.03534
20		0.000006	-0.000002	0.000032	0.000020	-0.000004			17	0.02459	0.08765	0.00259	0.03665	0.02402
21		0.000077	-0.000038	0.000020	0.000333	0.000070			18	-0.06400	-0.03260	-0.01379	-0.03535	-0.02736
22		0.000028	0.000016	-0.000004	0.000070	0.000078			19	0.01393	0.05736	0.06993	0.01316	0.04604
23									20	0.10971	0.08680	0.02588	-0.00260	0.05501
24	Portfolio Variance	Risk	0.00122						21	-0.06464	0.05025	0.00645	-0.05990	-0.00350
25									22	0.01114	-0.06070	0.01603	0.08357	-0.03981
26	Weighted Average	Return	0.0150		Floor	0.015			23	0.01610	-0.12925	0.04076	-0.00257	-0.03415
27									24	0.01188	0.06094	-0.06442	0.01856	0.00763
28														

H ◄ ► H   Portfolio

Figure 8.14. Spreadsheet model for Example 8.6.

This calculation lends itself to the SUMPRODUCT formula and appears in the worksheet in cell C26. The proportions themselves, highlighted as decision variables, appear in cells B15:F15, with their sum in cell G15.

For the portfolio variance, we use a standard statistical formula for the variance of a sum. For this purpose, we must know the covariance σ_{kj} between every pair of stocks (k, j). The covariance values are calculated from the historical data with Excel's COVAR function. These figures appear in the spreadsheet in cells B8:F12.

BOX 8.2   *Excel Mini-Lesson: The COVAR Function*

The COVAR function in Excel calculates the covariance between two equal-sized sets of numbers representing observations of two variables. The covariance measures the extent to which one variable tends to rise or fall with increases and decreases in the other variable. If the two variables rise and fall in unison, their covariance is large and positive. If the two variables move in opposite directions, their covariance is negative. If the two variables move independently, their covariance is close to zero. The basic form of the function is

COVAR(Array1, Array2)

- *Array1* references the observations of the first variable.
- *Array2* references the observations of the second variable.

The arrays must be of the same size.

In cell C11 of Figure 8.14, the function =COVAR($M4:$M27,$K4:$K27) finds the covariance between the returns of National Chemical Company and those of National Auto Company. In this case, the function generates the value −0.0006. The fact that it is a small number in absolute value indicates that the two sets of returns are nearly independent; the fact that it is negative indicates that there is a slight tendency for National Auto's returns to go up when National Chemical's returns go down, and vice versa.

The formula for the portfolio variance is

$$V = \sum_k \sum_j p_k \sigma_{kj} p_j$$

This formula sometimes appears in statistics books in a different but equivalent form. From this form, however, it is not difficult to make the calculation in Excel. The value of $p_k \sigma_{kj} p_j$ is computed as the (k, j)th element of the array in cells B18:F22. (For this purpose, it is convenient to replicate the proportions from row 15 in cells G8:G12.) Then the elements of this array are summed in cell C24. As a result, the risk measure V appears in cell C24, and the return measure R appears in C26.

The portfolio optimization problem is to choose the investment proportions to minimize risk subject to a floor (lower bound) on the return. That is, we want to minimize V subject to a minimum value of R, with the p-values as the decision variables. A value for the lower bound appears in cell F26. We specify the model as follows.

> Objective: C24 (minimize)
> Variables: B15:F15
> Constraints: C26 ≥ F26
>   G15 = 1

For a return floor of 1.5 percent, Solver returns the solution shown in Figure 8.14. All five stocks appear in the optimal portfolio, with allocations ranging from 30 percent of the portfolio in National Chemical to 13 percent of the portfolio in National Computer.

For this model, the spreadsheet layout is a little different from the others we have examined, mainly due to the close relationship between the historical data and the elements of the analysis. The spreadsheet, as constructed, could easily be adapted to the optimization of any five-stock portfolio. All that is needed is the set of returns data, to be placed in the data section of the spreadsheet. For a data collection period of longer than 24 periods, the formulas for average, standard deviation, and covariance would have to be adjusted. The Calculations section separates the decision variables from the objective function, but the logic of the computations flows from Proportions to Calculations to Risk and Return.

In principle, two modeling approaches are possible in portfolio optimization.

Minimize portfolio risk, subject to a floor on the return

or

Maximize portfolio return, subject to a ceiling on the level of risk

The former structure is usually adopted, because it involves a convex objective and linear constraints, a case for which the GRG algorithm is reliable.

Beyond a single optimization of the portfolio model, investors are usually interested in the tradeoff between risk and return. If we minimize risk subject to a floor on the return, we can repeat the optimization for several values of the floor. This process traces out points along the so-called *efficient frontier*, which plots the best risk achievable for any desired level of return. A complementary approach is available if we maximize return subject to a ceiling on risk. Results from the Optimization Sensitivity tool

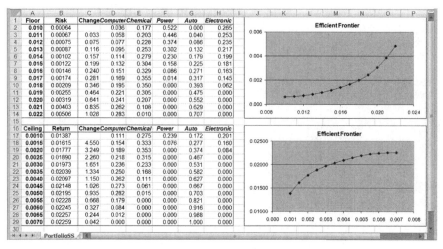

	Floor	Risk	Change	Computer	Chemical	Power	Auto	Electronic
1	Floor	Risk	Change	Computer	Chemical	Power	Auto	Electronic
2	0.010	0.00064		0.036	0.177	0.522	0.000	0.265
3	0.011	0.00067	0.033	0.058	0.203	0.446	0.040	0.253
4	0.012	0.00075	0.075	0.077	0.228	0.374	0.086	0.235
5	0.013	0.00087	0.116	0.095	0.253	0.302	0.132	0.217
6	0.014	0.00102	0.157	0.114	0.279	0.230	0.179	0.199
7	0.015	0.00122	0.199	0.132	0.304	0.158	0.225	0.181
8	0.016	0.00146	0.240	0.151	0.329	0.086	0.271	0.163
9	0.017	0.00174	0.281	0.169	0.355	0.014	0.317	0.145
10	0.018	0.00209	0.346	0.195	0.350	0.000	0.393	0.062
11	0.019	0.00255	0.464	0.221	0.305	0.000	0.475	0.000
12	0.020	0.00319	0.641	0.241	0.207	0.000	0.552	0.000
13	0.021	0.00403	0.835	0.262	0.108	0.000	0.629	0.000
14	0.022	0.00506	1.028	0.283	0.010	0.000	0.707	0.000
15								
16	Ceiling	Return	Change	Computer	Chemical	Power	Auto	Electronic
17	0.0010	0.01387		0.111	0.275	0.239	0.172	0.201
18	0.0015	0.01615	4.550	0.154	0.333	0.076	0.277	0.160
19	0.0020	0.01777	3.249	0.189	0.353	0.000	0.374	0.084
20	0.0025	0.01890	2.260	0.218	0.315	0.000	0.467	0.000
21	0.0030	0.01973	1.651	0.236	0.233	0.000	0.531	0.000
22	0.0035	0.02039	1.334	0.250	0.168	0.000	0.582	0.000
23	0.0040	0.02097	1.150	0.262	0.111	0.000	0.627	0.000
24	0.0045	0.02148	1.026	0.273	0.061	0.000	0.667	0.000
25	0.0050	0.02195	0.935	0.282	0.015	0.000	0.703	0.000
26	0.0055	0.02228	0.668	0.179	0.000	0.000	0.821	0.000
27	0.0060	0.02245	0.327	0.084	0.000	0.000	0.916	0.000
28	0.0065	0.02257	0.244	0.012	0.000	0.000	0.988	0.000
29	0.0070	0.02259	0.042	0.000	0.000	0.000	1.000	0.000

Figure 8.15. The efficient frontier in Example 8.6.

for these two approaches, along with summary plots, are shown in Figure 8.15. Both plots describe the same risk-return trade-off; they just happen to take slightly different forms. By exploring Ms. Downey's preferences as they play out in these graphs, we can make a more persuasive recommendation on how her investment funds should be allocated.

8.5. LINEARIZATIONS

As discussed earlier, the linear solver is a reliable procedure when we apply it to solve a linear programming problem, but the GRG algorithm is not reliable in general for a nonlinear programming problem. For that reason, and especially when our model contains integer variables, we always prefer to solve a linear model rather than a nonlinear model. Some problems that are formulated naturally with nonlinear functions can be reformulated as linear programs. Two examples of these transformations, or *linearizations*, are presented in this section.

Our purpose here is to show how to convert certain nonlinear forms to linear forms permitting us to construct a linear model before invoking Solver. It's important to know that RSP contains an option that can automate these linearizations, but with very little transparency. As a first step, it is helpful to turn off these automated procedures, and to do so, we set the Nonsmooth Model Transformation option to Never on the Platform tab of the task pane. The default option is Automatic, but we will assume the user has selected Never instead.

8.5.1. Linearizing the Maximum

Suppose our objective function is the maximum of several expressions involving decision variables, such as $\max_k\{\sum_j a_{kj} x_j\}$. Presumably, we would encounter this kind of objective in a minimization problem. The natural way to represent this criterion in a spreadsheet model would be to use Excel's MAX function in the objective, or in cells referenced in the objective. If we were to invoke the linear solver, we may encounter an error message stating that our model does not satisfy its linearity requirements (because the MAX function is not linear). If we invoke the nonlinear solver, we may get a solution, but we cannot be sure that it is a global optimum.

To improve our results, we can convert to a linear form by introducing a variable y that plays the role of the maximum. Then we add definitional constraints of the form

$$y \geq \sum_j a_{kj} x_j \qquad (8.1)$$

With the variable y as the objective function to be minimized, we have a linear model, so we can use the linear solver. As an example, consider the situation at the Armstrong Advertising Agency.

EXAMPLE 8.7 *Armstrong Advertising Agency*

The Armstrong Advertising Agency has several publishing projects that are ready for production. Four departments are capable of implementing these projects, and the agency wants to distribute the work among departments as evenly as possible.

Each of the projects will take a certain number of days. The following table shows the workload in each project, as estimated by the sales manager.

Project	1	2	3	4	5	6	7	8
Days	10	21	32	53	65	77	89	100

Distributing work "as evenly as possible" is not a precise description of an objective function; it tells us only what an ideal solution would look like. In this problem, with 447 days' worth of work, an ideal solution would allocate 111.75 days to each department. However, because individual projects cannot be split, we know that an ideal solution is impossible. The substantive question for determining an objective function is how to measure a nonideal solution. At Armstrong, the notion of distributing work evenly derives from a goal of fairness. Therefore, the consensus is that the best solution is one that minimizes the largest amount of work assigned to any of the departments. ■

A natural algebraic formulation of the problem is straightforward. Let a_j represent the time for project j, and define the following binary decision variables.

$$x_{kj} = 1, \quad \text{if project } j \text{ is assigned to department } k$$
$$= 0, \quad \text{otherwise}$$

With this notation, the optimization model is as follows

$$\text{Minimize } z = \max_k \left\{ \sum_j a_j x_{kj} \right\}$$

subject to

$$\sum_k x_{kj} = 1 \quad \text{for } j = 1, 2, \ldots, 8$$

A spreadsheet model for assigning the projects to the four departments is shown in Figure 8.16. The times required for the projects are entered in cells B5:I5. Binary variables assigning each project to a department are displayed in the array B7:I10. The row below this array contains the sum of the decision variables in each column—the sum over all departments. The column to the right of this array shows the total number of days assigned to each department, and the maximum of these values, computed in cell J4 with the formula =MAX(J7:J10), serves as the objective function.

We specify the problem as follows

Objective:	J4 (minimize)
Variables:	B7:I10
Constraints:	B11:I11 = 1
	B7:I10 = binary

Normally, the linear solver does not run on this model because of the presence of the MAX function, which is technically a nonsmooth function. In the output window of the task pane, Solver's error message appears when an attempt is made to use the linear solver.

```
The linearity conditions required by
this Solver engine are not satisfied.
```

In contrast, the nonlinear solver does run, but it may not find an optimal solution because the model contains binary variables as well as nonlinearity. However, a linearization is possible. We can introduce a new variable y to represent the largest of the departmental workloads, as in (8.1). This variable is displayed in cell J4 and treated like the other decision variable cells, as shown in Figure 8.17. But this cell is special, because it is also the value of the objective function. In addition to the constraints already formulated, we need to add constraints requiring y to be at least as large as the total number of days assigned to each department.

	A	B	C	D	E	F	G	H	I	J
1	Loading									
2										
3	Data									Max Time
4		Proj. 1	Proj. 2	Proj. 3	Proj. 4	Proj. 5	Proj. 6	Proj. 7	Proj. 8	153
5	Time	10	21	32	53	65	77	89	100	
6	Decisions									Total Time
7	Dept1	1	0	0	0	1	0	0	0	75
8	Dept2	0	1	0	0	0	1	0	0	98
9	Dept3	0	0	1	0	0	0	1	0	121
10	Dept4	0	0	0	1	0	0	0	1	153
11		1	1	1	1	1	1	1	1	
12										

Figure 8.16. Spreadsheet model for Example 8.7.

We specify the problem as follows

Objective:	J4 (minimize)
Variables:	B7:I10
	J4
Constraints:	B11:I11 = 1
	B7:I10 = binary
	J7:J10 ≤ J4

The last set of constraints is unconventional because the right-hand side appears to be just one cell, while the left-hand side references an array of four cells. However, Solver interprets the meaning correctly. Alternatively, the constraint could be expressed in a more standard fashion.

The linear solver returns the solution shown in Figure 8.17 quickly and reliably. The workloads at Armstrong will be 109, 110, 110, and 118 days, so that the entire set of projects will take 118 days to complete. By using the linearized model, Armstrong can be sure that the work is distributed in the fairest way, at least when fairness is defined to mean minimizing the maximum workload.

As this example demonstrates, the transformation of the MAX function to a linear form is not difficult, but Solver offers the capability of making the transformation automatically. This transformation would be initiated if we set the Nonsmooth Model Transformation option to Automatic (or to Always) on the Platform tab in the task pane. This option is convenient because we can set up the model in an intuitive fashion, even if it does not satisfy the linearity requirement, and Solver can compensate by performing the necessary transformation. However, the transformation actually implemented by Solver is not visible to the user, so it's not possible to know precisely how the model is transformed. For example, in the case of Example 8.7, the original model contains 32 variables and 8 constraints. Our transformation, shown in Figure 8.17, uses 33 variables and 12 constraints. Solver's automatic transformation

	A	B	C	D	E	F	G	H	I	J
1	Loading	(Linear)								
2										
3	Data									Max Time
4		Proj. 1	Proj. 2	Proj. 3	Proj. 4	Proj. 5	Proj. 6	Proj. 7	Proj. 8	118
5	Time	10	21	32	53	65	77	89	100	
6	Decisions									Total Time
7	Dept1	0	1	0	0	0	0	1	0	110
8	Dept2	0	0	1	0	0	1	0	0	109
9	Dept3	0	0	0	1	1	0	0	0	118
10	Dept4	1	0	0	0	0	0	0	1	110
11		1	1	1	1	1	1	1	1	
12										

Loading **Loading2**

Figure 8.17. Optimal solution for Example 8.7.

uses 38 variables and 21 constraints, as reported in the Current Problem section of the Engine tab. (Solver's summary counts the objective function as a separate constraint.) Thus, the details of the automatic transformation may be a bit different than the manual transformation, but the details of the automatic transformation are not made available to the user.

8.5.2. Linearizing the Absolute Value

Suppose our objective function contains terms involving absolute value expressions, such as $|\sum_j a_{kj} x_j|$. The natural way to build a spreadsheet model would be to use Excel's ABS function in the objective function, or in cells referenced by the objective function. If we were to invoke the linear solver, we may see an error message, either stating that our model does not satisfy the linearity requirements (because the ABS function is nonsmooth) or stating that the model is unbounded. If we invoke the nonlinear solver, we may get a solution, but we cannot be sure that it is a global optimum.

To tackle this problem, we can define a pair of *auxiliary variables*, u_k and v_k, to account for the difference between $\sum_j a_{kj} x_j$ and zero. Then we include constraints of the following form

$$\sum_j a_{kj} x_j + u_k - v_k = 0 \qquad (8.2)$$

In this linear formulation, two cases arise.

If $\sum_j a_{kj} x_j \leq 0$, then $v_k = 0$ and u_k measures the negative difference (if any).

If $\sum_j a_{kj} x_j \geq 0$, then $u_k = 0$ and v_k measures the positive difference (if any).

In either case, the value of $(u_k + v_k)$ measures the absolute value of the difference between $\sum_j a_{kj} x_j$ and zero. In the objective function, we can then use $(u_k + v_k)$ in place of the original absolute value expression.

As an example, we return to the situation at the Armstrong Advertising Agency in Example 8.7 and revisit the question of measuring a nonideal distribution of work. We might be skeptical of using a maximum value in the objective function because in the final solution, only one of the departments (Department 3) contributes directly to the objective. Departments 1, 2, and 4 have loads far less than 118, and they don't seem to affect the objective.

We can construct a more comprehensive objective. For convenience, let

$$L_k = \sum_j a_{kj} x_j \qquad (8.3)$$

In words, L_k represents the workload assigned to Department k. Next, consider the department workloads and focus on their pairwise differences: $(L_1 - L_2)$, $(L_1 - L_3)$, $(L_1 - L_4)$, $(L_2 - L_3)$, $(L_2 - L_4)$, and $(L_3 - L_4)$. Take the absolute value of these differences and calculate their sum. That total serves as the objective. With this notation, we can state the optimization problem algebraically as follows.

$$\text{Minimize } z = \sum_{i<j} |L_i - L_j|$$

subject to

$$\sum_k x_{kj} = 1 \qquad \text{for } j = 1, 2, \ldots, 8$$

$$L_k - \sum_j a_{kj}x_j = 0 \qquad \text{for } k = 1, \ldots, 4$$

A spreadsheet model for assigning the projects to the four departments is shown in Figure 8.18. The difference between this worksheet and the one shown in Figure 8.16 lies only in the objective function. The decision variables in rows 7–10 play the same role as in the previous model. Below the decision variables, in column B, we list the six department pairs, and in column C we record for each pair the difference in their workloads. The absolute values of these differences appear in column E, and the total of these absolute differences serves as the objective function in cell J14 with the formula =SUM(E14:E19).

We specify the problem as follows.

Objective:	J14 (minimize)
Variable:	B7:I10
Constraints:	B11:I11 = 1
	B7:I10 = binary

	A	B	C	D	E	F	G	H	I	J
1	Loading									
2										
3	Data									
4		Proj. 1	Proj. 2	Proj. 3	Proj. 4	Proj. 5	Proj. 6	Proj. 7	Proj. 8	
5	Time	10	21	32	53	65	77	89	100	
6	Decisions									Total Time
7	Dept1	1	0	0	0	1	0	0	0	75
8	Dept2	0	1	0	0	0	1	0	0	98
9	Dept3	0	0	1	0	0	0	1	0	121
10	Dept4	0	0	0	1	0	0	0	1	153
11		1	1	1	1	1	1	1	1	
12										
13		Pairs	Delta (Δ)		ABS					Total Delta
14		1,2	-23		23					257
15		1,3	-46		46					
16		1,4	-78		78					
17		2,3	-23		23					
18		2,4	-55		55					
19		3,4	-32		32					
20										

Figure 8.18. Spreadsheet for Example 8.7 with absolute value objective.

Normally, the linear solver does not run on this model because of the presence of the ABS function, which is nonsmooth. In the output window of the task pane, Solver's error message appears when an attempt is made to use the linear solver.

> The linearity conditions required by
> this Solver engine are not satisfied.

If we invoke the nonlinear solver, the GRG algorithm appears to run, but we can't tell whether its solution is a global optimum. In fact, if we use the solution in Figure 8.18 as the starting solution, the nonlinear solver generates the convergence message, but the solution remains unchanged.

The linearized model requires pairs of auxiliary variables, u_k and v_k, corresponding to each absolute value calculation. Those variables are defined by a constraint in the form of equation (8.2).

$$\text{Minimize } z = \sum_k (u_k - v_k)$$

subject to

$$\sum_k x_{kj} = 1 \qquad \text{for } j = 1, 2, \ldots, 8$$

$$\sum_j a_{kj} x_j + u_k - v_k = 0 \qquad \text{for } k = 1, \ldots, 4$$

This is a linear program containing six pairs of auxiliary variables as well as the binary variables.

A worksheet for the linearized problem is shown in Figure 8.19. In the Objective module, the auxiliary variables appear in cells E14:F19. The objective function appears in cell J14 with the formula =SUM(E14:F19).

	A	B	C	D	E	F	G	H	I	J
1	Loading	(Linear)								
2										
3	Data									
4		Proj. 1	Proj. 2	Proj. 3	Proj. 4	Proj. 5	Proj. 6	Proj. 7	Proj. 8	
5	Time	10	21	32	53	65	77	89	100	
6	Decisions									Total Time
7	Dept1	0	1	0	0	0	0	1	0	110
8	Dept2	1	0	0	0	0	0	0	1	110
9	Dept3	0	0	0	1	1	0	0	0	118
10	Dept4	0	0	1	0	0	1	0	0	109
11		1	1	1	1	1	1	1	1	
12	Objective									
13		Pairs	Delta (Δ)		u-value	v-value	Δ-u+v			Total Δ
14		1,2	0		0	0	0			27
15		1,3	-8		0	8	0			
16		1,4	1		1	0	0			
17		2,3	-8		0	8	0			
18		2,4	1		1	0	0			
19		3,4	9		9	0	0			
20										

Figure 8.19. Spreadsheet for Example 8.7 with absolute value objective.

We specify the problem as follows.

Objective:	J14 (minimize)
Variable:	B7:I10
	E14:F19
Constraints:	B11:I11 = 1
	G14:G19 = 0
	B7:I10 = binary

The linear solver produces a solution, which is shown in Figure 8.19, that achieves an optimal value of 27. Although the objective is quite different than the minimax value used earlier, the assignment of departments to projects is similar, and the maximum workload remains minimal at 118. By linearizing the model, Armstrong can be sure that it has found the optimal solution to its revised formulation.

Solver offers the capability of transforming the use of the ABS function automatically. This transformation would be initiated if we set the Nonsmooth Model Transformation option to Automatic (or to Always) on the Platform tab in the task pane. This option is convenient because we can set up the model in an intuitive fashion, even if it does not satisfy the linearity requirement, and Solver can compensate by performing the necessary transformation. However, the transformation actually implemented by Solver is not visible to the user, so it's not possible to know precisely how the model is transformed. For example, in the case of Example 8.7, the original model contains 32 variables and 8 constraints. Our transformation, shown in Figure 8.19, uses 44 variables and 14 constraints. Solver's automatic transformation uses 44 variables (38 of which are integer variables) and 44 constraints (not including the objective function), as reported in the Current Problem section of the Engine tab. Thus, the details of the automatic transformation may be a bit different than the manual transformation, but the details of the automatic transformation are not made available to the user.

SUMMARY

The default choice for a solution algorithm in Solver is the nonlinear solver, also known as the GRG Nonlinear Engine. The nonlinear solver uses a steepest ascent strategy to search for an optimal set of decision variables, and it can be invoked for any nonlinear or linear programming problem. For linear programming problems, however, the linear solver is preferred because it is numerically stable and produces a comprehensive sensitivity report. For nonlinear problems that have smooth objective functions, the GRG algorithm is the best choice. Table 8.1 summarizes the features of the two solution algorithms.

Although it is capable of solving both linear and nonlinear problems, the nonlinear solver does have its limitations. In general, the GRG algorithm guarantees only that it will find a local optimum. This solution may or may not be a global optimum. If the objective function is concave or convex, and if the constraints form a convex set, then we can be sure that the nonlinear solver produces a global optimum. Otherwise, we can try alternative starting points as a way of marshalling evidence about optimality, but there is no foolproof scheme for identifying the

Table 8.1. Comparison of the Linear and Nonlinear Algorithms

Linear solver	Nonlinear solver
Suitable for linear models	Suitable for nonlinear models; can also solve most linear models.
Finds a global optimum each time	Finds a local optimum each time. No guarantee of global optimum, except in special circumstances.
Ignores initial decision variables	Uses initial decision variables in search; result may depend on starting values.
Finds a feasible solution if one exists	May not be able to find a feasible solution when one exists.
Always leads to an optimum, unless problem is infeasible or unbounded	May generate "convergence" message; a re-run may be necessary.
Comprehensive sensitivity information from the Sensitivity Report	Sensitivity Report does not include allowable ranges.

global optimum in general. Solver's MultiStart option is often a powerful feature in trying to solve problems with several local optima, but it does not provide any guarantees, either.

Another limitation concerns integer-valued variables. The presence of integer constraints in an otherwise nonlinear model generally leaves us in a situation where the nonlinear solver may fail to find a global optimum, even to a relaxed problem that is encountered during Solver's implementation of branch and bound. This feature renders the GRG algorithm unreliable (in the sense of producing a guaranteed global optimum), and the implication is that we should avoid trying to solve integer nonlinear programming problems with Solver. Fortunately, in some practical cases, we can transform the most natural formulation into a linear model. With the transformation, an integer-valued problem can be solved reliably with the linear solver augmented by the branch and bound procedure. For models that contain Excel's MAX, ABS, or IF functions, Solver's Nonsmooth Model Transformation option can often provide the linear equivalent of a nonsmooth formulation, although the details of the model it builds remain opaque.

Finally, because the nonlinear solver is applicable to such a wide variety of optimization problems (and therefore must accommodate exponents, products, and special functions) we know of no standard layout that conveniently captures the necessary calculations in the context of spreadsheets. This feature stands in contrast to the use of the linear solver, where one standard layout could, in principle, always be used. (Nevertheless, as we have seen in Chapters 3–6, there are sometimes good reasons for using a few non-standard variations.) The most useful guideline, as with all spreadsheet models, still seems to be to modularize the spreadsheet and thereby separate objective function, decision variables, and constraints.

EXERCISES

8.1. Merrill Sporting Goods (Revisited)   Revisit Example 8.4, in which the criterion gives equal weight to each of the retail sites. But in practice, there will be different levels of traffic between the warehouse and the various sites. One way to incorporate this consideration is to estimate the number of trips between the warehouse and each retail site and then weight the distances by the trip volumes. Thus, the original data set has been augmented with volume data (v_k), as listed in the table below.

Site (k)	x_k	y_k	v_k
1	9	29	12
2	5	50	15
3	26	68	20
4	39	79	12
5	41	54	8
6	38	59	16
7	63	6	18
8	52	58	20
9	81	76	12
10	95	93	24

Now we can use as a criterion the weighted sum of distances between the warehouse and the retail sites.

(a) What location is optimal for the weighted version of the criterion?

(b) How much of an improvement is achieved by the solution in (a) over the optimal location for the unweighted version (39.59, 58.43)?

8.2. **Curve Fitting for Revenues** A large food chain owns a number of pharmacies that operate in a variety of settings. Some are situated in small towns and are open for only eight hours a day, five days per week. Others are located in shopping malls and are open for longer hours. The analysts on the corporate staff would like to develop a model to show how a store's revenues depend on the number of hours that it is open. They have collected the following information from a sample of stores.

Hours of operation	Average revenue
40	$5958
44	6662
48	6004
48	6011
60	7250
70	8632
72	6964
90	11,097
100	9107
168	11,498

(a) Use a linear function to represent the relationship between revenue and operating hours and find the values of the parameters that provide the best fit to the given data. What revenue does your model predict for 120 hours?

(b) Suggest a two-parameter nonlinear model for the same relationship and find the parameters that provide the best fit. What revenue does your model predict for 120 hours? Which of the models in **(a)** and **(b)** do you prefer and why?

8.3. Curve Fitting for Costs   Newton Manufacturing Company has reached a stable volume in the last couple of years and is interested in developing a planning model for its production levels, based on aggregate units of output. One element will be a cost model that describes the relationship of unit cost to production volume. Newton's capacity is thought to be around 2500 aggregate units at current equipment and labor force levels, and it is well known that unit costs tend to rise when output volumes are significantly above or below this figure. For volumes above this figure, costs rise due to overtime premiums and to high congestion levels in the plant. For volumes below the nominal figure, costs rise due to inefficiencies in production. Analysts at Newton have therefore decided that some type of quadratic function would be a suitable model for unit costs, and they have proposed the form $ax^2 + bx + c$, where x represents the aggregate number of output units, and the parameters a, b, and c remain to be determined. For this purpose, the model will be fit as closely as possible to the last 12 months of observed data, as reproduced in the table below.

Month	Aggregate output	Unit cost
1	2350	$53.35
2	2200	54.60
3	2450	49.62
4	2600	53.62
5	2550	49.69
6	2400	51.18
7	2300	53.25
8	2650	51.91
9	2700	54.23
10	2750	50.06
11	2500	49.08
12	2250	54.46

(a) What values of the three parameters provide the best fit to the data, as measured by the minimum sum of squared differences?

(b) What does the model in **(a)** predict as the unit cost for an output of 2500?

8.4. Economic Order Quantity (EOQ)   A distributor of small appliances wishes to calculate the optimal order quantity for replenishing its stock of a particular washing machine. Demand for the $200 machine is stable throughout the year and averages about 1000 units annually. Each order involves the cost of transportation, receiving and inspection, accounting for expenses of $500 per order. Holding costs are figured at 20 percent per year.

(a) What order quantity minimizes the annual replenishment cost?

(b) How does the optimal cost break down into holding and carrying components?

8.5. EOQ for Multiple Products   In another location, the distributor of the previous problem stocks four different items in common warehouse space. Each item is described by an annual demand rate, a fixed cost per order, a holding cost per year, a unit purchase cost and a space requirement. The data in the following table describe the four products.

Item	1	2	3	4
Demand	5000	10,000	30,000	300
Fixed cost	400	700	100	250
Holding cost	50	25	8	100
Purchase cost	500	250	80	1000
Space (sq. ft)	12	25	5	10

(a) Considering each product separately, as if it were independent from the others, what are the respective economic order quantities? What is the total annual cost of ordering, holding, and purchasing across the four products at these order quantities?

(b) What is the minimum total annual cost for the four products if the average space taken up must be no more than 12,000 square feet?

(c) What is the minimum total annual cost for the four products if the average space taken up must be no more than 12,000 square feet and the number of orders per year must be no more than 65?

(d) In part (b), with a square-foot limit on storage space, what is the economic value of more space?

(e) In part (c), what is the economic value of more space?

8.6. Pricing with Dependent Demands Covington Motors is a car dealership that specializes in the sales of sport utility vehicles and station wagons. Due to its reputation for quality and service, Covington has a strong position in the regional market, but demand is somewhat sensitive to price. After examining the new models, Covington's marketing consultant has come up with the following demand curves.

$$\text{Truck demand} = 400 - 0.014 \text{ (truck price)}$$
$$\text{Wagon demand} = 425 - 0.018 \text{ (wagon price)}$$

The dealership's unit costs are $17,000 for SUVs and $14,000 for wagons. Each SUV requires 2 hours of prep labor, and each wagon requires 3 hours of prep labor. The current staff can supply 320 hours of labor.

(a) Determine the profit-maximizing prices for SUVs and Wagons. (Round off any fractional demands.)

(b) What demand levels will result from the prices in (a)?

(c) What is the marginal value of dealer prep labor?

8.7. Pricing with Interdependent Demands Covington Motors sells sport utility vehicles and station wagons in a price-sensitive market. Its marketing consultant has rethought the simple demand curves first proposed (in the previous exercise) and now wants to recognize the interaction of the two markets. This gives rise to a revised pair of demand curves for SUVs and wagons, as shown below.

$$\text{SUV demand} = 300 - 0.014 \text{ (SUV price)} + 0.003 \text{ (wagon price)}$$
$$\text{Wagon demand} = 325 - 0.018 \text{ (wagon price)} + 0.005 \text{ (SUV price)}$$

The dealership's unit costs are $17,000 and $14,000 per unit, respectively. Each SUV requires 2 hours of prep labor, and each Wagon requires 3 hours of prep labor. The current staff can supply 320 hours of labor. Covington Motors wants to maximize its profits from the SUVs and Wagons that it acquires for its stock.

(a) Determine the profit-maximizing prices for SUVs and Wagons. (Ignore the fact that these prices may induce fractional demands.)

(b) What sales levels will result from the prices in (a)?

(c) What is the marginal value of dealer prep labor?

8.8. Allocating an Advertising Budget A regional beer distributor has $125,000 to spend on advertising in four markets, where each market responds differently to advertising. Based on observations of the market's response to several advertising initiatives, the distributor has estimated the sales response by fitting a curve of the form $R = ax^b$, where R represents sales revenue and x represents advertising dollars, both measured in thousands. The estimated demand curves are shown in the table below.

Market	Sales revenue
Domestic	$66x^{0.55}$
Premium	$77x^{0.44}$
Light	$88x^{0.33}$
Microbrew	$99x^{0.22}$

(a) How should the funds be allocated among the four markets so that the revenue to the company as a whole will be maximized?

(b) How much would it be worth (in terms of incremental revenue) to raise the amount available for advertising by $1000?

8.9. Supply Chain Design Muslin Office Furniture manufactures a popular line of filing cabinets and has a very strong competitive position in its market. The company sells its product to a number of wholesale distributors who, in turn, sell to retail customers. In this environment, the company faces a demand curve of the following form

$$Q_1 = 20 - 0.6P_1$$

where P_1 denotes its selling price and Q_1 denotes the volume (in thousands) sold at that price. Muslin also experiences increasing marginal costs of the form $0.8Q_1$. (This means that its total cost is $0.8(Q_1)^2/2$.) Increasing marginal costs occur because of quality losses and congestion on the shop floor as volume rises.

One of Muslin's distributors is a subsidiary known as New England Supply. They represent Muslin's exclusive distributor in the northeast, and the parent company allows them to operate as an independent entity, focused on distribution. They buy filing cabinets from Muslin and sell them to retail customers in the northeast. In that market, New England Supply faces its own demand curve as follows

$$Q_2 = 10 - 0.2P_2$$

where P_2 denotes the retail selling price and Q_2 denotes the volume (in thousands) sold in the northeast at that price. New England Supply incurs its own operating costs, in addition to the cost of purchasing the product from Muslin, so that its marginal cost function takes the form $P_1 + 0.4Q_2$. This means that its total cost is $P_1Q_2 + 0.4(Q_2)^2/2$.

(a) Suppose that Muslin Office Furniture and New England Supply each analyze their own pricing strategies separately. That is, Muslin finds its profit-maximizing price. Then New England Supply, whose cost is influenced by Muslin's price, maximizes its own profits. What is each firm's optimal price and how much profit is earned between the two companies?

(b) Suppose instead that the two firms make coordinated decisions. In other words, they choose a pair of prices, one wholesale and one retail, aimed at maximizing the total profit between the two firms. What is each firm's optimal price in this coordinated environment? How much profit is earned between the two companies?

8.10. Estimating Beta   In finance it is important to be able to predict the return on a stock from the return on the market, that is, on a market index such as the S&P 500 index. It is often hypothesized that a particular prediction equation exists

$$y = \alpha + \beta x$$

where y is the return on a stock during a time period, x is the return on the market index during the same time period, and α and β are constants that must be estimated. The value of β is of particular interest, because it indicates how closely the returns on a particular stock tend to follow the returns on the market as a whole.

If our knowledge of the parameters α and β were perfect, then we could predict individual stock returns accurately from the behavior of the market. Typically, such knowledge does not exist, and our values of α and β are imperfect. In other words, when we use them, we encounter errors in our predictions. The best we can do is to choose the estimates α and β in order to make prediction errors close to zero.

Find data on returns for Coca-Cola stock on a monthly basis for the period January 2, 2001 to December 1, 2006, and returns for the S&P 500 index for the same 72 months. Fit the linear prediction equation to this set of data. Use as a criterion the minimum sum of squared differences between the actual stock returns and their predicted values. For the historical data, estimate the parameters of the prediction equation for Coca-Cola stock.

(a) What is the estimated value of β, for Coca-Cola stock?

(b) Repeat the estimation process for Microsoft stock. What do you expect to find in terms of the relationship between the β for Microsoft and the β for Coke?

8.11. Portfolio Model   The information on which stocks are evaluated is a series of historical returns, typically compiled on a monthly basis. This history provides an empirical distribution of a stock's return performance. For stock k in the portfolio, the table below summarizes the monthly returns for five stocks over a two-year period in the late 1990's.

Stock	Mean
National Computer (NCO)	0.0371
National Chemical (NCH)	0.0145
National Power (NPW)	0.0118
National Auto (NAU)	0.0185
National Electronics (NEL)	0.0217

In addition, the covariance values for the five stocks are displayed in the following table.

	NCO	NCH	NPW	NAU	NEL
NCO	0.0110	−0.0004	0.0000	0.0019	0.0013
NCH	−0.0004	0.0032	−0.0002	0.0002	0.0003
NPW	0.0000	−0.0002	0.0015	0.0007	−0.0002
NAU	0.0019	0.0002	0.0007	0.0051	0.0008
NEL	0.0013	0.0003	−0.0002	0.0008	0.0044

(a) Determine the portfolio allocation that minimizes risk (i.e., portfolio variance) for a portfolio consisting of these five stocks, subject to maintaining an average return of at least two percent. What is the minimum variance?

(b) Determine the portfolio allocation that maximizes return for a portfolio consisting of these five stocks, subject to maintaining a variance of at most 0.002. What is the optimal return?

(c) Suppose an investor prefers an objective function that combines return and risk, as in the following

$$\text{Objective} = \text{Return} - 2(\text{Risk})$$

(d) What is the optimal allocation for this measure of performance?

8.12. Production Smoothing   A supplier of raw material has made plans to provide monthly deliveries to a customer. The customer's requirements are shown in the following table.

Month	1	2	3	4	5	6	7	8
Units	100	200	300	400	100	100	500	300

The raw material can be processed and prepared for delivery in any volume because part-time labor can be used, and the labor pool is quite large. However, changes in month-to-month production volumes can be costly. When production levels increase, costs must be incurred in acquiring and training new workers. When production levels decrease, costs are incurred due to layoff policies.

Based on historical data, the cost estimate for increasing production from one month to the next is $1.50 per unit increase in capacity. In the other direction, reducing production from one month to the next incurs a cost of $1.00 per unit reduction in capacity. The other relevant cost is the cost of inventory: each unit held in stock incurs a cost of $2.00 per month held.

Entering month 1, the starting inventory is 80 units, and the production level has been steady at 100 units. To make sure the plans can be extended into the future, inventory is required to be at least 50 units at the end of the eighth month, and the planned production level for month 9 is 200.

What is a minimum-cost production plan for the supplier?

8.13. Political Redistricting   Based on the new census information, it is time to redraw the boundaries of the political districts in the state of Idazona. Each district will have one representative in the next Congress, and Idazona has been allocated four representatives based on its share of the national population. The state is made up of nine counties, with populations (in thousands) shown in the table. (See the state map in Figure 8.20.)

The main requirement in the formation of districts is that they produce equal populations, or as close to equal as possible. Furthermore, the districts must be composed of

County	1	2	3	4	5	6	7	8	9
Population	25	23	29	20	22	37	34	21	34

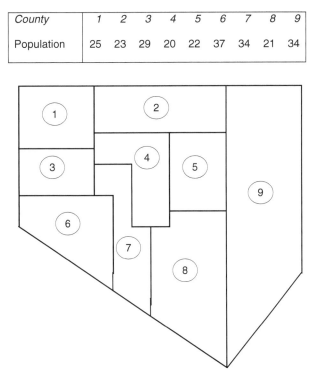

Figure 8.20. State map of ldazona.

adjacent counties without splitting any county between two or more districts. Officials in Idazona interpret the requirement to mean that if a district is created from two counties, then those two counties must share a border. Furthermore, if a district is created from three counties, then at least one of the counties must be adjacent to the other two. No district is permitted to have exactly one county or more than three counties.

Mathematically, officials are seeking a districting plan for which the maximum deviation between a district population and the average district population will be as small as possible.

What assignment of counties to districts will satisfy the desired conditions?

Case: Delhi Foods

Manisha Patel recently completed her first week of work as a summer intern at Delhi Foods. Earlier this morning, Manisha's boss, the Director of Marketing, asked her to come up with a recommendation on the level of marketing expenses (advertising and promotion expenditures) for a line of frozen Indian dinners as it enters its seventh year in the marketplace. Exhibit 8.1, which Manisha received from her boss, contains an accounting summary of essential product costs and revenues in the first six years, during which there has been some trial-and-error experimentation with marketing policies. For year seven, the table shows projections for the coming

EXHIBIT 8.1	*Summary of Product Costs and Revenues*						
Year	1	2	3	4	5	6	7
Demand (cartons)	3200	3400	3500	3600	3800	4400	4700
Revenue $(000)	62,000	63,000	66,000	75,000	86,000	98,000	105,000
Production							
Materials	27,000	29,000	30,000	35,000	39,000	33,000	35,000
Other variable	1700	2200	2800	3500	2400	10,800	11,600
Fixed	4500	4700	4900	5000	5300	5600	5900
Marketing							
Advertising	10,300	11,700	15,000	16,200	17,800	22,000	24,000
Promotion	9000	6000	4000	11,000	12,000	13,000	14,000
Overhead	6000	6000	5000	5000	5000	5000	6000
Operating margin	3500	3400	4300	(700)	4500	8600	8500

year based on a continuation of last year's policy. This includes a new high of $38,000 in marketing expense, but Manisha's boss intimated that this might be excessive.

Late last week, Manisha read an internal marketing study that had been completed at Delhi Foods. The study concluded that it is possible to represent the influence of marketing expenses on demand by means of the equation

$$D = aM^b$$

where D and M represent demand and marketing expenses, respectively, and where a is called the *scale factor* and b the *elasticity* of marketing expenses. Manisha knows from courses she has taken that this model belongs to a family of demand equations commonly used in market analysis. To determine values for the parameters a and b that apply to this product, she will have to match this model to the observations as closely as possible.

Manisha ponders the information in the table. Costs for the coming year appear to be known; therefore, variable costs have already been estimated. Overhead and fixed production costs do not appear to be variable costs, so they don't enter into a calculation of gross margin. Instead, the gross margin is based on revenue, materials costs, and other variable costs. Using the projected figures for the coming year, Manisha expects that she will be able to compute the gross margin per unit. From there, Manisha believes she can represent profit for the line of dinners by using the gross margin per unit along with an estimate of demand to predict this year's gross margin. Then she can subtract marketing expenses and fixed costs to arrive at a profit figure. She sees that marketing expenses show up in her profit calculation, but they also affect her demand estimate. If she can sort out all the relationships in a spreadsheet model, Manisha believes that she can find the optimal level to spend on marketing.

Chapter 9

Heuristic Solutions with the Evolutionary Solver

In previous chapters, we have encountered three powerful optimization procedures—the linear solver, the branch-and-bound procedure, and the nonlinear solver. For linear models, we use the linear solver. This algorithm is reliable: It always finds a global optimum when the model does not contain an unbounded objective function or conflicting constraints. For linear programming models with integer constraints, we also rely on the linear solver. The integer constraints are added in the problem formulation, informing the linear solver to use its branch-and-bound procedure in the search for an optimal solution. The branch-and-bound procedure relies on solving a series of linear programs, so if Solver does not run out of time, this is a reliable procedure, too. However, when the model does not satisfy the conditions of linearity, the linear solver is of no use.

For nonlinear programming problems, we use the nonlinear solver. This algorithm is not as reliable as the linear solver because it may stop its hill climbing at a local optimum and it is unable to determine whether it has found a global optimum or stopped short of one. We can at least improve our chances of finding a global optimum by re-running the nonlinear solver from a variety of different starting points, a process we can automate with the MultiStart option. However, when the problem is not composed of smooth functions, the nonlinear solver often fails to help.

The fourth solution procedure in RSP is the evolutionary solver, which is the subject of this chapter. This procedure is particularly useful for tackling optimization models containing *nonsmooth functions*. As suggested in Chapter 8, a nonsmooth function is one that exhibits gaps or kinks. The presence of a nonsmooth function undermines the performance of the linear and nonlinear solvers. However, the availability of a solution procedure suitable for nonsmooth functions allows us to build models with more flexibility than under the restrictions of the linear and nonlinear solvers. In particular, we can take advantage of several Excel functions in the model. We can include the IF function, which allows us to represent some simple logical choices. We can include several other familiar mathematical functions, such as ABS, MIN, MAX, CEILING, FLOOR, ROUND, and INT. (Although it is sometimes

Optimization Modeling with Spreadsheets, Second Edition. Kenneth R. Baker
© 2011 John Wiley & Sons, Inc. Published 2011 by John Wiley & Sons, Inc.

possible to avoid using these functions directly, doing so may require the use of binary variables or auxiliary variables in cumbersome or unusual ways.) We can also include spreadsheet-oriented functions such as CHOOSE, COUNTIF, INDEX, and LOOKUP, which may provide convenience in spreadsheet calculations even though they are seldom used in other circumstances. Thus, another way of interpreting *non-smooth* is any computation that uses one of these dozen functions or one of the other specialized functions in Excel.

The modeling flexibility comes at a price. Because the evolutionary solver makes virtually no assumptions about the nature of the objective function, it has a limited ability to identify an optimal solution. Essentially, it conducts a search, compares the solutions encountered as it proceeds with the search, and stops when it senses that it is making very little progress at finding improvements. The solution it generates may not even be a local optimum, such as the solution the hill-climbing procedure delivers, yet in many kinds of problems, the evolutionary solver delivers a good solution, if not an optimal one. This type of procedure is called a *heuristic procedure*, meaning that it is a systematic procedure for seeking good solutions, but it cannot guarantee optimality.

9.1. FEATURES OF THE EVOLUTIONARY SOLVER

A few features of the evolutionary solver are helpful to know. First, it is important to realize that the procedure contains some randomized steps. As a consequence, we may get different solutions when we run the evolutionary solver twice on exactly the same model.

The evolutionary solver works with a population of solutions. At intermediate stages of the solution procedure, it keeps track of several solutions rather than maintaining just the one, best solution found so far. This population of solutions develops, or *evolves*, in steps that mimic naturally occurring evolutionary processes. From the population of solutions that it builds and maintains, the procedure can generate new solutions, following the principle that an *offspring solution* should combine traits from each of two *parent solutions*. In addition, there are occasional *mutations*, which are offspring solutions with some random characteristics that do not come from their parents. Over the course of the procedure, the population is governed by a *fitness criterion* (based on the objective function) that removes the poorer solutions and keeps the better ones. This process of *selection* drives the population toward better levels of fitness (better values of the objective function). If there is evidence that the population is no longer improving, or if one of the user-designated stopping conditions is met, then the procedure stops. When it stops, Solver displays the best member of the final population as the solution.

The inner workings of the evolutionary solver do not concern us at this stage. However, in the next section, we provide an example that will help explain conceptually how the procedure works. The main point is that the evolutionary solver is not handicapped by the presence of nonsmooth functions, as would be the case for the linear and nonlinear solvers. It is also helpful to set some user-controlled options when running the evolutionary solver. However, in the end, the evolutionary solver cannot guarantee that it has found a global optimum, so some judgment is required—even more than with the nonlinear solver—when applying it to a particular optimization problem.

In this chapter, we examine a series of examples that contain nonsmooth functions, to illustrate how the evolutionary solver works. In some cases, we revisit problems that we tackled with other solution procedures in earlier chapters, mainly to provide a contrast in optimization approaches. The variety of examples should provide a working knowledge of the evolutionary solver, but, more than the other solvers we have covered, this one requires practice and experience in order to use it effectively.

9.2. AN ILLUSTRATIVE EXAMPLE: NONLINEAR REGRESSION

As our first example, we look at a curve-fitting problem in which the relationship between two variables is nonlinear and in which the criterion is the sum of absolute deviations. As discussed in Chapter 8, the most appropriate tool for curve-fitting problems is the nonlinear solver when the criterion is the sum of squared deviations. But when the criterion is the sum of absolute deviations, several local optima may exist, and the nonlinear solver may not find the best fit. The evolutionary solver is often well suited to such problems.

Our purpose here is to describe, in an approximate way, how the evolutionary solver works. This is not meant to be a precise description of the algorithm, but rather a suggestive description of the evolutionary approach and the elements it contains. For a specific example, we revisit the data from Fitzpatrick Fuel Supply (Example 8.3), where we wanted to predict gas consumption on the basis of degree days.

Data from Example 8.3

A sample of 12 observations was made at customers' houses on different days and the following observations of degree days and gas consumption were recorded.

Day	Degree days	Gas consumption
1	10	51
2	11	63
3	13	89
4	15	123
5	19	146
6	22	157
7	24	141
8	25	169
9	25	172
10	28	163
11	30	178
12	32	176

As a first cut at the estimation problem, Fitzpatrick's operations manager would like to fit a linear model to the observed data.

Fitzpatrick's operations manager believes that the power curve, $y = ax^b$ is a good model. As a criterion, suppose that we want to minimize the sum of absolute deviations (instead of squared deviations) between model and observations. This is a less common criterion than the sum-of-squares measure that was used in Chapter 8, but it is just as plausible for optimization purposes. Whereas the sum-of-squares measure penalizes large deviations more severely than small ones, that is not the case for the absolute-deviation measure.

Figure 9.1 displays a worksheet for this problem. The given data, consisting of 12 observations, can be found in the first three columns. The parameters a and b, which serve as the decision variables, are located in cells E3 and E4. Specifying these two parameters allows us to generate the values found in the column labeled *Predicted* in column D, and the differences between model and observation are calculated in column E. The absolute value of this difference appears in the next column, under the heading *Deviation*. The sum of these absolute deviations, which is the objective function to be minimized, appears in cell F5.

Knowing a little about the range of observations, we can make an educated guess that the best value of a lies between 0 and 50, while the best value of b lies between 0 and 1. These are coarse limits, but they are sufficient to get us started. We generate an

	A	B	C	D	E	F	
1	Curve Fitting			Power Model: y = ax^b			
2							
3	Parameters			a	30.00		
4				b	0.50		
5	Objective					209.07	
6							
7	Data	Degree Days	Consumption				
8	Number	Observed	Observed	Predicted	Difference	Deviation	
9	1	10	51	94.87	43.87	43.87	
10	2	11	63	99.50	36.50	36.50	
11	3	13	89	108.17	19.17	19.17	
12	4	15	123	116.19	-6.81	6.81	
13	5	19	146	130.77	-15.23	15.23	
14	6	22	157	140.71	-16.29	16.29	
15	7	24	141	146.97	5.97	5.97	
16	8	25	169	150.00	-19.00	19.00	
17	9	25	172	150.00	-22.00	22.00	
18	10	28	163	158.75	-4.25	4.25	
19	11	30	178	164.32	-13.68	13.68	
20	12	32	176	169.71	-6.29	6.29	
21							

Fitting

Figure 9.1. Spreadsheet model for Example 8.3.

Table 9.1. Initial population

a	b	Fitness
30.8	0.19	975
19.7	0.55	440
47.2	0.82	5230
30.0	0.59	519
43.8	0.66	2257
7.6	0.72	817

initial set of pairs (a, b) by sampling randomly from these two ranges. Let's suppose this process generates the values shown in Table 9.1. In each case, the fitness number is the objective function that corresponds to the values of a and b, and this value can be calculated directly by using the worksheet. Here, we have constructed a population of size 6. The best fitness is 440, and the average fitness is about 1706.

Next, we create new members of the population by the *crossover method*. In particular, we take the first two solutions and swap their a values. That way, the a value of the first solution is paired with the b value of the second solution, and vice versa. In other words, the two new solutions are (30.8, 0.55) and (19.7, 0.19). We can think of these two solutions as being "offspring" of the original two solutions, with values of a and b (interpreted as genes) that are inherited from their "parents."

Suppose that the next new member of the population is created by the mutation method. For the third solution, we keep the second gene (b) and randomly generate the first gene (a), obtaining (20.0, 0.82)

Next, we'll perform the crossover step on solutions 4 and 5, and then generate another mutation from the sixth solution by keeping the first gene and randomly generating the second. The six new members are shown in Table 9.2.

We can think of this list as newcomers to the population in one generation or cycle. We'll combine these members with the existing members and apply the fitness criterion. This means that we'll select a second generation of size 6, keeping just the six best fitness values. The list becomes Table 9.3.

The best fitness in the new population has dropped from 440 to 322, and the average fitness has dropped from 1706 to 684.

Table 9.2. First generation of offspring

a	b	Fitness
30.8	0.55	322
19.7	0.19	1210
20.0	0.82	1278
30.0	0.66	1033
43.8	0.59	1506
7.6	0.45	1273

Table 9.3. Population updated for fitness

a	b	Fitness
30.8	0.19	975
30.0	0.59	519
30.8	0.55	322
19.7	0.55	440
7.6	0.72	817
30.0	0.66	1033

To create the third generation, we follow a similar procedure. We use the first two solutions as parents to generate two offspring by the crossover operation. We use the third solution to generate a mutation by randomly replacing the a value. Then we repeat the process, applying the crossover operation to the fourth and fifth solutions, and generating another mutation by randomly replacing the b value in the sixth solution. The six new members of the populations are shown in Table 9.4.

Combining this list with the previous one, we use the fitness criterion to remove the least-fit members of the population, thus selecting the six best solutions as the third generation (Table 9.5).

Now, the best solution in the population has improved to 217, and the average has dropped to about 417. Another generation leaves the best solution unchanged but the average drops to about 352.

Table 9.4. Second generation of offspring

a	b	Fitness
30.8	0.59	576
30.0	0.19	992
17.8	0.55	533
19.7	0.72	474
7.6	0.55	1147
30.0	0.54	217

Table 9.5. Second updated population

a	b	Fitness
30.0	0.54	217
30.8	0.55	322
19.7	0.55	440
19.7	0.72	474
30.0	0.59	519
17.8	0.55	533

As these first few iterations suggest, the crossover and mutation procedures, along with the fitness criterion, tend to generate populations with improving fitness values. Clearly, a generation of solutions always has a best value and an average value that are no worse than those of the previous generation. As we continue the process, which Solver can do at great speed, we tend to find additional improvements.

The evolutionary solver does not follow the precise details of the generation-building process we have outlined here, although it does rely on the crossover and mutation procedures. The details of the actual implementation are not important in order to understand how to implement the evolutionary solver, but here are some relevant observations.

- For the purposes of implementing the crossover operation, the specific form of a gene depends on the model and is determined within the evolutionary solver.
- The frequency with which mutations appear is an option set by the user. The genetic form of a mutation, however, is determined within the evolutionary solver.
- The procedure contains some randomness, so two successive runs from the same starting point can produce different solutions.
- There can be no guarantees of optimality; the procedure may stop short of finding an optimum.

To understand how the procedure stops, let's look at the various options available when we implement the evolutionary solver on a particular model.

In the task pane, we select the Standard Evolutionary Engine from the drop-down menu on the Engine tab. Some elements that appear in the task pane are tailored to the evolutionary solver, whereas others are common to the linear solver and the nonlinear solver as well. For example, the *Max Time parameter* limits the amount of time Solver uses trying to find a good solution before stopping. Normally, we use this option as a kind of last resort. It should be set long enough that other options have an opportunity to take effect, and it should reflect the amount of time we are willing to allow the procedure to run without intervening. For large and complicated problems, this could mean a long wait, but we often choose a short time limit so that we can get feedback quickly. When debugging a model, or just trying to get a feel for performance on a given model, we might set this option to 20 or 30 seconds.

The user can also set the *Population Size parameter*. The purpose here is to make sure that the population is sufficiently diverse. We used a population of size six in our curve-fitting example, but that would be small for the automated implementation used by Solver. In the course of solving a particular problem, we might start with a value as small as 25 and later try a larger value for greater diversity. The evolutionary solver will stop (with a convergence message) when 99 percent or more of the population has fitness values whose relative differences are less than the *Convergence parameter* shown in the task pane. A population size no more than 200 is required, but 50 might often be adequate for even very difficult problems.

The *Mutation Rate parameter* affects the level of randomness in generating new members of the population. A low rate would create few mutations, whereas a high rate offers greater diversity. The default value is 7.5 percent. We might raise this value if we find evidence that the evolutionary solver stalls due to lack of diversity. As in our example, the population may gravitate toward a set of similar solutions. When that type of population convergence begins to take place, we may be located near a global optimum, and our chances of locating that optimum become high. Raising the mutation rate in such a case is unlikely to produce much improvement. On the other hand, when convergence occurs at some distance away from a global optimum, the process is analogous to finding a local optimum with the nonlinear solver. In that case, we'd want to increase the diversity in the population, and it would be desirable to raise the mutation rate. Normally, we do not know whether we are close to a global optimum, but the effect of raising the mutation rate may provide a clue.

Another option is the *Require Bounds option*, asking whether to require upper and lower bounds on the decision variables. This option should set to True, meaning that the model must contain at least simple bounds entered as constraints. One of the bounds may be dictated by a nonnegativity requirement, which is most conveniently implemented by setting the *Assume Non-Negative option* to True. The evolutionary solver tends to work more efficiently when the decision variables are bounded.

Finally, in the Limit section of the task pane, we encounter additional parameters. The first two options in this section are the *Max Subproblems parameter* and the *Max Feasible Solutions parameter*, both of which can limit the amount of effort Solver devotes to a problem before stopping. However, these parameters can be left blank as long as the Max Time parameter is set.

The next pair of options in the Limits section work together. They specify that the search should stop if an improvement of at least the *Tolerance* has not been found in the last *Max Time without Improvement*. It's usually convenient to keep the Tolerance at 0 percent but to vary the time without improvement according to previous outcomes.

The list in Box 9.1 describes particular settings that would be appropriate in the initial stages of using the evolutionary solver. Some of the values are Solver default values, while others are entered by the user, in some cases overriding the default values. In addition, the *Nonsmooth Model Transformation option*, which appears on the Platform tab of the task pane, should be set to Never. (Otherwise, Solver may add some variables and constraints to the model that undermine the effectiveness of the evolutionary solver.)

Returning to our example of nonlinear regression, suppose we set the initial values of the decision variables to $a = 30.0$ and $b = 0.50$ and set the Assume

---

BOX 9.1 | *Initial Values for Parameters in the Evolutionary Solver*

Max time: 30 sec	Population Size: 25
Convergence: 0.0001	Mutation rate: 7.5%
Tolerance: 0	Max time w/o improvement: 15 sec

Non-negative option to True (so that we have lower bounds on both decision variables). We specify the problem as follows.

Objective:	F5 (minimize)
Variables:	E3:E4
Constraints:	E3 $\leq$ 50
	E4 $\leq$ 1

For the sake of comparison, we might initially run the nonlinear solver. It produces a solution with a total absolute deviation of 173.41. We turn now to the evolutionary solver.

Due to randomness, we may not find that any two runs of the evolutionary solver match exactly, but in this case, the results are similar. Suppose we initialize the model with the decision variables shown in cells E3 and E4 of Figure 9.1. Two runs stop with an objective function value of 160.10 and the following message in the Output window.

```
Solver cannot improve the current solution.
All constraints are satisfied.
```

This "improvement" message means that no improvements were encountered in the last 15 seconds of searching. This stopping condition occurred within the 30-second Max Time limit.

The third run reaches the 30-second Max Time limit and produces a window with the message: The maximum time limit was reached; continue anyway? At this stage, the user can choose whether to continue or stop. When we press the Stop button, the run terminates. The solution happens to again be 160.10 and the following message appears in the Output window.

```
Stop chosen when the maximum time limit was reached.
```

From these results, it is difficult to determine how close we might be to an optimal solution. Because the time-limit parameters limited the search, we might re-run the evolutionary solver with a Max Time parameter of 60 seconds and a Max Time without Improvement parameter of 30 seconds. If we find no improvements, we might try a larger population size or a larger mutation rate, but in this case no improvements occur. Although we have no guarantee, the evidence suggests that further searching will not turn up an objective function value lower than 160.10. Figure 9.2 shows the best solution found during the last run of the evolutionary solver.

Our example of nonlinear regression served two purposes. First, it allowed us to use a manual method to describe the main workings of the evolutionary solver—crossovers, mutations, and selection by a fitness criterion. Second, it illustrated a straightforward optimization problem in which the nonlinear solver may not work as well as the evolutionary solver. This is partly due to the existence of many local optima in the example, but it's also true that evolutionary methods have proven particularly effective on complex regression problems. In the examples that follow, we focus more on the model than on the refinements needed in the options to produce a good solution.

	A	B	C	D	E	F
1	Curve Fitting			Power Model: y = ax^b		
2						
3	Parameters			a	10.62	
4				b	0.83	
5	Objective					160.10
6						
7	Data	Degree Days	Consumption			
8	Number	Observed	Observed	Predicted	Difference	Deviation
9	1	10	51	71.61	20.61	20.61
10	2	11	63	77.49	14.49	14.49
11	3	13	89	89.00	0.00	0.00
12	4	15	123	100.21	-22.79	22.79
13	5	19	146	121.90	-24.10	24.10
14	6	22	157	137.65	-19.35	19.35
15	7	24	141	147.94	6.94	6.94
16	8	25	169	153.03	-15.97	15.97
17	9	25	172	153.03	-18.97	18.97
18	10	28	163	168.11	5.11	5.11
19	11	30	178	178.00	0.00	0.00
20	12	32	176	187.78	11.78	11.78
21						

H ◀ ▶ H   Fitting   **Fitting2**

Figure 9.2. Best solution found for Example 8.3.

9.3. THE MACHINE-SEQUENCING PROBLEM REVISITED

In the machine-sequencing problem, a set of jobs is waiting to be processed. The machine can work on only one job at a time, so the jobs must be processed in a sequence. The problem is to find the best sequence for a given objective function. In Chapter 7, we saw how to build an integer programming model for this problem. That model requires a number of disjunctive constraints to accommodate the conditions of feasibility. An alternative approach is available if we use the evolutionary solver.

We revisit the Miles Manufacturing Company (Example 7.4), in which we have six jobs waiting to be scheduled. Each job will be either on time or late, depending on the sequence chosen. If a job is late, the amount of time by which it misses its due date is called its *tardiness*. Tardiness is zero when a job completes prior to its due date. The objective is to minimize the total tardiness in the schedule.

Data from Example 7.4

This morning's workload consists of six jobs, as described in the following table.

Job number	1	2	3	4	5	6
Processing time (hours)	5	7	9	11	13	15
Due date (hours from now)	28	35	24	32	30	40

The problem is to sequence the six jobs so that work can begin.

Figure 9.3 displays a model for this problem. The first module contains the tabulated data describing the specific problem to be solved. The next module contains a row of decision variables corresponding to the job sequence. Each position in sequence is assigned a job number (from 1 to 6). Since the sequence does not necessarily match the numbered sequence in which the data appear, we use the INDEX function to access the processing times and due dates that match the job in each sequence position. For example, the formula in cell C11, for the processing time of the first job, is =INDEX($C$4:$H$6,2,C$10). The INDEX function references the element in the second row of the data in the column corresponding to the number in C10. A similar function in cell C13 references the third row of the data, with the formula =INDEX($C$4:$H$6,3,C$10).

The processing times and due dates thus appear in rows 11 and 13. From the processing times, we can compute the completion times directly, as shown in row 12. In row 14, we compute tardiness values, working from the completion time and due date in the two rows directly above and using the formula =MAX(0,C12-C13) in cell C14, and then copying the formula to the right. We sum the tardiness values in cell C16; this total represents the value of the objective function.

	A	B	C	D	E	F	G	H	I
1	**Sequencing Model**								
2		*Single-Machine Tardiness*							
3	**Data**								
4		Job	1	2	3	4	5	6	Total
5		Process time	5	7	9	11	13	15	60
6		Due date	28	35	24	32	30	40	
7									
8	**Decisions**								
9		Position	1	2	3	4	5	6	
10		Job	6	5	4	3	2	1	
11		Process time	15	13	11	9	7	5	
12		Completion	15	28	39	48	55	60	
13		Due date	40	30	32	24	35	28	
14		Tardiness	0	0	7	24	20	32	
15	**Objective**								
16		Total Tardiness	83						
17									

Tardiness

Figure 9.3. Spreadsheet for Example 7.4.

In the cells corresponding to decision variables, we want to choose integers between 1 and 6. Therefore, our first instinct might be to add constraints that restrict the decision variables to integers no less than 1 and no greater than 6. However, those constraints permit the choice of some jobs more than once. We would have to add a module that tests for duplication and penalizes solutions that choose any job multiple times. Wouldn't it be nice if we could avoid the intricacies of this inefficient filtering device and generate only solutions for which the integers in the decision cells contain no duplicates?

The capability we seek is usually called an *alldifferent constraint*: It ensures that the values of the decision variables form a set of integers with no duplicates. To implement the alldifferent constraint, we enter the cell range as the left-hand side and then use the drop-down menu of constraint types to select *dif*, as shown in Figure 9.4. The alldifferent constraint fills the designated range of cells with the integers from 1 to n in some order, where n is the number of cells in the range.

A comparison with the integer programming model of Figure 7.14 shows that the evolutionary solver model is more compact and easier to understand. Its layout on the worksheet resembles the calculations we might make if we were verifying the value of total tardiness with pencil-and-paper calculations. However, because the objective function relies on the INDEX function and on the MAX function, it is a nonsmooth model and cannot be solved using the linear solver.

We specify the problem as follows.

Objective: C16 (minimize)
Variables: C10:H10
Constraints: C10:H10 = alldifferent

We run the evolutionary solver, starting arbitrarily with the solution 6-5-4-3-2-1 and using the default options. The procedure may examine several thousand solutions, or it may terminate due to the Convergence criterion. When we run the model again, starting with the sequence generated by the previous run, we may get a better solution. This cycle can be repeated if improvements are found. If not, we can try modifying the initial sequence and re-running Solver. After a few trials of this sort, Solver is likely to produce the solution shown in Figure 9.5, with a value of 33. We recognize this as the optimal value, from our work in Chapter 7. There is no guarantee, however, that another run of the very same model will terminate with this solution.

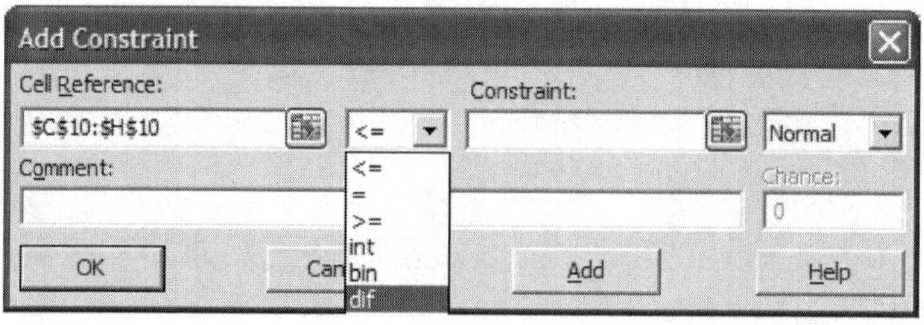

Figure 9.4. Specifying the alldifferent constraint.

	A	B	C	D	E	F	G	H	I
1	Sequencing Model								
2		*Single-Machine Tardiness*							
3	Data								
4		Job	1	2	3	4	5	6	Total
5		Process time	5	7	9	11	13	15	60
6		Due date	28	35	24	32	30	40	
7									
8	Decisions								
9		Position	1	2	3	4	5	6	
10		Job	3	1	5	2	4	6	
11		Process time	9	5	13	7	11	15	
12		Completion	9	14	27	34	45	60	
13		Due date	24	28	30	35	32	40	
14		Tardiness	0	0	0	0	13	20	
15	Objective								
16		Total Tardiness	33						
17									

Tardiness / Tardiness2

Figure 9.5. Final solution for Example 7.4.

9.4. THE TRAVELING SALESPERSON PROBLEM REVISITED

We encountered the traveling salesperson problem in Chapter 7, and we saw how to find optimal solutions by starting with an assignment model and appending subtour elimination constraints as needed. This approach required the solution of a series of integer programs with an unpredictable number of constraints. For large problems, the manual task of keeping track of the appended constraints could be daunting even if the resulting integer programming problems could be solved in a reasonable amount of time. As an alternative, we look at a solution approach that relies on the evolutionary solver, revisiting the Douglas Electric Cart Company (Example 7.5).

Data from Example 7.5

In today's schedule, there are six colors (C1–C6) with cleaning times as shown in the table below.

	C1	C2	C3	C4	C5	C6
C1	–	16	63	21	20	6
C2	57	–	40	46	69	42
C3	23	11	–	55	53	47
C4	71	53	58	–	47	5
C5	27	79	53	35	–	30
C6	57	47	51	17	24	–

The entry in row i and column j of the table gives the cleaning time required between product batches of color Ci and color Cj. Each production run consists of a cycle through the full set of colors, and the operations manager wishes to sequence the colors so that the total cleaning time in a cycle is minimized.

Using the evolutionary solver, our formulation can be much more compact and readable than the integer programming model. Figure 9.6 displays a spreadsheet model for Example 7.5. The first module contains the distance array, which serves as the given data for the problem. Then, in the second module, the decision variables are listed in row 13, comprising the sequence of cities in the tour. For an n-city problem, this simply means a single row listing the integers from 1 to n, in some order. By definition, a tour must return to its starting point, so we repeat the starting city in cell I13. (This cell is not a decision variable; it is simply a reference to cell C13.)

Directly below the cells of the tour, we capture the distances between pairs of cities on the tour, as shown in Figure 9.6. Again, we can use the INDEX function for this purpose. For example, the distance corresponding to the pair in cells C13 and D13 is isolated in cell D14 with the formula =INDEX($C$5: $H$10,C13,D13), which is copied to the right. In the third module, consisting of cell D17, we compute the sum of the pairwise distances calculated in row 14. This sum represents the total tour length.

The inputs and the outputs of this calculation are more natural than in the case of an integer programming formulation. In addition, the spreadsheet is easier to

	A	B	C	D	E	F	G	H	I	
1	Traveling Salesperson Problem									
2										
3	Data				To					
4			1	2	3	4	5	6		
5		1	999	16	63	21	20	66		
6		2	57	999	40	46	69	42		
7	From	3	23	11	999	55	53	47		
8		4	71	53	58	999	47	5		
9		5	27	79	53	35	999	30		
10		6	57	47	51	17	24	999		
11										
12	Decisions									
13		Tour	6	5	4	3	2	1	6	
14		Distances		24	35	58	11	57	66	
15										
16	Objective									
17		Tour length		251						
18										

Figure 9.6. Spreadsheet model for Example 7.5.

understand on its face. However, because we use the INDEX function as a component in the objective function, this is a nonsmooth model, and it is not appropriate for either the linear solver or the nonlinear solver.

We specify the problem as follows.

Objective:	D17 (minimize)
Variables:	C13:H13
Constraints:	C13:H13 = alldifferent

Even with the default settings, we are likely to obtain a solution of 167, as shown in Figure 9.7. (In Chapter 7, we found that this value was optimal.) The evolutionary solver rather quickly finds the tour 6-5-3-1-2-4, which matches the optimal tour found in Chapter 7. (Starting the tour at city 1 corresponds to the solution 1-2-4-6-5-3-1.)

Is the evolutionary solver always capable of finding an optimum with such limited effort? Unfortunately, it's not. It is difficult to generalize about the effectiveness of the evolutionary solver on sequencing problems, but some experience suggests that problems of finding the best sequence can be solved to optimality with modest effort if the sequence length is 10 or sometimes 15. In the traveling salesperson problem, as in the machine sequencing problem, the model is simpler and the solution is obtained more quickly using the evolutionary solver than with an integer programming approach. However, the evolutionary solver cannot guarantee optimality. Next, we turn to problems that we have not previously solved, so that we will not know the optimum when we set out to find a solution.

	A	B	C	D	E	F	G	H	I
1	Traveling Salesperson Problem								
2									
3	Data				To				
4			1	2	3	4	5	6	
5		1	999	16	63	21	20	66	
6		2	57	999	40	46	69	42	
7	From	3	23	11	999	55	53	47	
8		4	71	53	58	999	47	5	
9		5	27	79	53	35	999	30	
10		6	57	47	51	17	24	999	
11									
12	Decisions								
13		Tour	6	5	3	1	2	4	6
14		Distances		24	53	23	16	46	5
15									
16	Objective								
17		Tour length		167					
18									

TSP   TSP2

Figure 9.7. Final solution for Example 7.5.

9.5. TWO-DIMENSIONAL LOCATION

In many location decisions, costs are mainly determined by geographic distances, and it is possible to gain some insight into location possibilities by building models based on the geometry of physical location. Consider the location problem facing Drezner Chemical Company.

EXAMPLE 9.1   *Drezner Chemical Company*

Drezner Chemical Company delivers its products to 10 firms in the wholesale chemicals business and will continue to do so when its new plant comes on line and replaces current production. The actual customers who use Drezner's products can be classified into clusters, with each cluster serviced by a single wholesaler. From Drezner's point of view, however, each cluster represents one demand source because each wholesaler handles the logistics for all of the customers in its cluster. The transportation cost for the new plant will be related to the distances between the plant and each of the clusters. Since the wholesalers are responsible for the logistics within each cluster, Drezner delivers to the nearest member of the cluster. Truck capacity will not be a factor in the foreseeable future.

The customer base is spread out over the state, which to good approximation can be viewed as a square, 100 miles on each side. Each customer within each cluster has a location in that square, denoted by the (x, y) pair on a graph that has a lower left-hand point at the origin and an upper right hand point at $(100,100)$. There are 10 customers in each cluster.

Drezner makes one round-trip delivery to each cluster every week. The distance for a round trip is twice the distance from the plant to the nearest point in the cluster. The Euclidean distance metric applies: if (x_k, y_k) denotes the location of cluster k, then the distance to cluster k from the plant at (x, y) is given by

$$D_k(x, y) = [(x - x_k)^2 + (y - y_k)^2]^{1/2}$$

Based on this geometric model, Drezner wishes to find the optimal location for its plant. ■

A model for the problem is shown in Figure 9.8, with some columns omitted. The first module contains the customer location data—100 pairs of (x, y) values describing each customer's location, organized into 10 sets for each of 10 clusters. The second module contains the decision about the plant's location, represented by x- and y-coordinates in cells B20:C20. This module also contains the objective function. The Results module contains distances from the plant to each of the 100 customers, again organized in 10 sets of 10. At the bottom of the Results module, we calculate the minimum distance in the cluster, and the objective function (cell E20) sums the lengths of the 10 distances and multiplies by two to account for round trips.

We specify the model as follows.

Objective:	E20 (minimize)
Variables:	B20:C20
Constraints:	B20:C20 ≤ 100
	B20:C20 ≥ 0

	A	B	C	D	E	F	G	R	S	T	U
1	Drezner Chemical Co.										
2											
3	Data										
4		Location Table									
5		Cluster	1	Cluster	2	Cluster	3	Cluster	9	Cluster	10
6		x	y	x	y	x	y	x	y	x	y
7		79	89	65	16	99	23	28	30	89	4
8		29	74	16	45	4	99	64	0	46	46
9		42	50	73	77	47	26	21	62	62	95
10		19	53	1	0	21	97	80	82	34	30
11		47	93	31	74	87	33	60	54	62	97
12		31	84	97	68	29	95	55	86	49	47
13		15	1	93	62	74	3	3	41	29	44
14		11	56	49	39	51	89	94	55	91	41
15		15	72	80	4	48	64	24	86	2	1
16		69	71	90	40	23	53	4	2	98	18
17	Decision										
18		Plant Location			Total Distance						
19		x	y								
20		50.00	50.00		251.88						
21	Results										
22	1	48.60		37.16		55.95		29.73		60.31	
23	2	31.89		34.37		67.21		51.92		5.66	
24	3	8.00		35.47		24.19		31.38		46.57	
25	4	31.14		70.01		55.23		43.86		25.61	
26	5	43.10		30.61		40.72		10.77		48.51	
27	6	38.95		50.33		49.66		36.35		3.16	
28	7	60.22		44.64		52.77		47.85		21.84	
29	8	39.46		11.05		39.01		44.28		41.98	
30	9	41.34		54.92		14.14		44.41		68.59	
31	10	28.32		41.23		27.17		66.48		57.69	
32	min	8.00		11.05		14.14		10.77		3.16	

⏮ ◄ ► ⏭	Drezner						

Figure 9.8. Spreadsheet model for Example 9.1.

The last of these constraints can be omitted if we check the option for Assume Non-Negative instead. But in any case, this model is ready for the evolutionary solver.

It is instructive to attack this problem with the nonlinear solver. Although the reliance on the square-root formula for distances might suggest that the nonlinear solver should work effectively, it turns out that the solution is sensitive to the starting point, and several local minima exist. The table below lists five cases, showing the starting point, the solution produced by the nonlinear solver, and the corresponding value of the objective function.

Starting solution	Local optimum	Solution value
(40, 60)	(23.00, 53.00)	266.12
(45, 55)	(48.32, 48.75)	250.60
(50, 50)	(49.09, 49.92)	251.32
(55, 45)	(48.32, 48.75)	250.60
(60, 40)	(48.32, 48.75)	250.60

We might be inclined to conclude that the optimal location is in the vicinity of (50, 50), with an objective function value close to 250. However, we discover a different story when we use the evolutionary solver.

When we switch to the evolutionary solver, we are very likely to find improvements. Recall that there is some built-in randomness and the evolutionary solver does not necessarily stop with the same solution each time. In addition, the developers of the evolutionary solver offer the following advice for producing solutions.

- Restart the evolutionary solver, using the solution it produced on the first run, to see if an improvement can be found.
- Restart the evolutionary solver with changes in the Convergence value (tighter) or the Tolerance value (tighter, if it's not already zero).
- Restart with a larger Population Size parameter and/or a larger Mutation Rate parameter. These changes will result in longer runs, and they tend to examine a larger number of candidate solutions.
- Switch to the nonlinear solver and see whether it can produce an improvement.

Finally, some insight may come from examining Solver's Population Report. Stability in the Best Values and relatively small Standard Deviations are signs to look for. Those signs suggest little room for improvement.

Using just the first of the listed suggestions, and restarting Solver a few times, we are likely to encounter a solution that is significantly better than those found with the nonlinear solver. For example, the evolutionary solver may find the objective function value of 217.61 at a plant location of (87.33, 53.43). By using the evolutionary solver, Drezner can find a location that improves on the solution generated by the nonlinear solver. If the distance metric is a good proxy for annual distribution expenses, Drezner will be able to reduce its expenses more than 13 percent by using the evolutionary solver, as compared to the decisions it would have reached using the nonlinear solver.

9.6. LINE BALANCING

The *line-balancing* problem arises in the design of a new production process for assembled products. Examples might include home appliances (refrigerators), electronics (televisions), light vehicles (lawn mowers), and automobiles. At the end of the product design phase, the product and its components are well known, and so are the specific tasks that must be carried out to make the product. The next step is to design the production line on which the product will be assembled.

The first type of information is the time required for each task. Required times might be based on previous experience with the same task in other lines or estimated by experts in work measurement techniques. The second type of information is precedence information. In other words, we need to know which tasks must be completed before some other task can begin. We say, "task j *precedes* task k" to mean that k cannot begin until j is completed. Precedence information can be expressed in a list or in a diagram.

The production line typically has a target output rate—so many units per hour. The *cycle time* is the inverse of the output rate. For example, if we specify a target of five units per hour, the cycle time is $1/5$ of an hour, or 12 minutes.

The physical production line consists of several work stations, typically numbered according to their position along the line. At each station, a single operator carries out a set of tasks. The problem is to assign the various tasks to stations. The criterion is to use as few stations as possible, since the number of stations dictates the number of operators, and therefore the labor cost per unit. There are essentially two types of constraints. First, the amount of work assigned to any individual station may not exceed the cycle time; otherwise, the target production rate cannot be met. Second, no task can appear earlier in the line (i.e., at a lower-numbered station) than any of its predecessor tasks. An example arises at Munoz Manufacturing Company, in the assembly of microwave ovens.

EXAMPLE 9.2   *Munoz Manufacturing Company*

Along with the design of a new countertop oven, the manufacturing engineers at Munoz Manufacturing Company have determined the 12 distinct tasks that comprise the assembly process. They have summarized this information in a table showing the time for each task and its logical predecessors—that is, the tasks that must be done earlier in the process. Predicted volume targets have been translated into a desired cycle time of 15 minutes. The following table shows the relevant information.

Task	Time	Predecessors	
1	12	–	
2	6	1	
3	6	2	
4	2	2	
5	2	2	
6	12	2	
7	7	3	4
8	5	7	
9	1	5	
10	4	6	9
11	6	8	10
12	7	11	

To complete the design of the production process, the individual tasks must be assigned to stations, respecting the desired cycle time and minimizing the number of stations required. ∎

The precedence relations among activities in a line-balancing problem present a significant challenge in formulating and implementing an optimization model. Moreover, optimization models usually require a large number of variables for a design of realistic scale. For those reasons, line-balancing problems are often solved by heuristic methods. Here, we describe an approach to solving the line-balancing problem that relies on the evolutionary solver.

Figure 9.9 shows a spreadsheet model, with the given information reproduced in columns A–D. The optimization model occupies columns F–L. Row 3 contains the desired cycle time, a penalty, and the objective function. The penalty, shown in this example as the value 999, must be a large number, adjusted to the scale of the data in the problem.

The range F7:F18 contains the decision variables of the model. These are the station numbers assigned to the tasks. These variables must be integers starting at 1 and increasing to the number of stations in the solution. Although we don't know that number in advance, we can make a conservative guess and use this guess as an upper bound when we specify the problem. The solution in column F of Figure 9.9 arbitrarily assigns two tasks to each station, proceeding roughly in order of the tasks. Columns G and H reference the predecessors in columns C and D and look up their stations using the INDEX function. The two columns allocated to the predecessor list in the given data (columns C and D) and the two columns allocated to the predecessor-station list in the model (columns G and H) are used because no task in the problem has more than two predecessors. Obviously, this layout would have to be modified for problems with more than two predecessors for some tasks.

Column I contains a feasibility check to see whether each task is assigned a station number at least as large as that of its predecessors. If not, the penalty from cell E2 is assigned. In the solution of Figure 9.9, task 10 is assigned to station 6 and task 11 to station 5. But task 10 is a predecessor to task 11, so those assignments are out of precedence order. Hence the penalty in cell I17.

Columns J, K, and L represent a table that examines the solution station by station. (This table may actually not need the same number of rows as the rest of the model, but extra rows can simply be assigned zeros.) Column K shows the total time assigned to each station, using the SUMIF (see Box 9.2) function. Finally, column L contains

	A	B	C	D	E	F	G	H	I	J	K	L
1	Line-Balancing Model											
2												
3		*Cycle Time*	15	*Penalty*	999	*Stations*	2004					
4												
5	Data					Model						
6	Task	Time	Predecessors			Station	Predecessor Station		Penalty	Station	Time	Penalty2
7	1	12	0	0		1	0	0	0	1	18	999
8	2	6	1	0		1	1	0	0	2	8	0
9	3	6	2	0		2	1	0	0	3	14	0
10	4	2	2	0		2	1	0	0	4	12	0
11	5	2	2	0		3	1	0	0	5	13	0
12	6	12	2	0		3	1	0	0	6	5	0
13	7	7	3	4		4	2	2	0	7	0	0
14	8	5	7	0		4	4	0	0	8	0	0
15	9	1	5	0		6	3	0	0	9	0	0
16	10	4	6	9		6	3	6	0	10	0	0
17	11	6	8	10		5	4	6	999	11	0	0
18	12	7	11	0		5	5	0	0	12	0	0
19												
20						*Bound*	5					
21												

LineBal

Figure 9.9. Spreadsheet model for Example 9.2.

BOX 9.2   *Excel Mini-Lesson: The SUMIF Function*

The familiar SUM function in Excel computes the total value in the cells of a specified range. The SUMIF function is similar, in that it totals the values in a range of cells (called the *sum range*), but it includes only those items in the range for which a specified *criterion* is met. To satisfy the criterion, a specified condition must be met in a *specified range*. The form of the function is the following.

$$= \text{SUMIF}(\textit{Specified range, Criterion, Sum range})$$

In Example 9.2, we have

Specified range: F7:F18 (the list of station assignments)

Criterion: a reference to a cell in column J (that is, a station number)

Sum range: B7:B18 (the list of task times).

Thus, in cell K10 we have the formula =SUMIF($F$7:$F$18,J10,$B$7:$B$18). This function scans the list in column F to see if any entries match the contents of cell J10 (which is station number 4), and if so, the corresponding entry in column B is included in the sum. When the entire list has been scanned, the function returns the sum of the task times assigned to station 4, which in this case is 12.

another feasibility check and assigns a penalty to any station assigned a total time that exceeds the desired cycle time in cell C3.

Finally, cell G3 is the objective function. It contains the maximum value among the decision variables (the assigned station numbers), augmented by the total of the penalties. The use of penalties thus substitutes for explicit feasibility constraints. The only constraints that need to be specified for Solver are the upper and lower limits on the station assignments. As mentioned earlier, the lower limit is obviously one, but the upper limit requires an educated guess. In the worst case, each task would be assigned its own station, so we can always use the number of tasks as an upper limit. We specify the problem as follows.

Objective:	G3 (minimize)
Variables:	F7:F18
Constraints:	F7:F18 $\leq$ 12
	F7:F18 $\geq$ 1
	F7:F18 = integer

One last step is helpful in the line-balancing model. As we use the evolutionary solver to search among solutions, it is helpful to know a lower bound on the minimum possible number of stations. This lower bound can be calculated by taking the sum of the task times, dividing by the desired cycle time, and rounding up to the next larger

	A	B	C	D	E	F	G	H	I	J	K	L
1	Line-Balancing Model											
2												
3		Cycle Time	15	Penalty		999	Stations	6				
4												
5	Data					Model						
6	Task	Time	Predecessors			Station	Predecessor	Station	Penalty	Station	Time	Penalty2
7	1	12	0	0		1	0	0	0	1	12	0
8	2	6	1	0		2	1	0	0	2	14	0
9	3	6	2	0		2	2	0	0	3	14	0
10	4	2	2	0		2	2	0	0	4	12	0
11	5	2	2	0		3	2	0	0	5	5	0
12	6	12	2	0		3	2	0	0	6	13	0
13	7	7	3	4		4	2	2	0	7	0	0
14	8	5	7	0		4	4	0	0	8	0	0
15	9	1	5	0		5	3	0	0	9	0	0
16	10	4	6	9		5	3	5	0	10	0	0
17	11	6	8	10		6	4	5	0	11	0	0
18	12	7	11	0		6	6	0	0	12	0	0
19												
20						Bound	5					
21												

Figure 9.10. Final solution for Example 9.2.

integer. This bound follows from the observation that if the tasks were packed into stations with perfect efficiency, the sum of the task times at each station would equal the desired cycle time, and the total sum of the task times divided by the cycle time would give the number of stations. In Example 9.2, the sum of the task times divided by the desired cycle time yields the value 4.67, which rounds up to 5. This calculation appears in cell G20. It allows us to stop searching if we see that the evolutionary solver has located a solution with this value. However, it is important to keep in mind that the lower bound may not be achievable; the optimal solution may lie above the lower bound, so we will not always be able to tell whether our searching should be terminated. In Example 9.2, the evolutionary solver leads us repeatedly to a solution with 6 stations, but we cannot be sure whether an improvement to five is possible. Figure 9.10 shows one of those solutions. In this solution, task 1 alone is assigned to station 1; tasks 2–4 are assigned to station 2; and then tasks are assigned in numerical order, two to a station. From this solution, however, we cannot know whether a five-station solution exists, but Munoz still has a reasonably efficient set of station assignments for its assembly line.

9.7. GROUP ASSIGNMENT

In several different application areas, a common problem involves the organization of items or people into groups. Often, the goal is to place similar items in the same group, as in cellular manufacturing (where we try to group similar parts together) or in positioning analysis (where we try to group similar products together). Sometimes, the goal is the opposite: to place different items in the same group. A familiar example in educational programs involves the formation of diverse student teams (where we try to form groups of students with dissimilar backgrounds for the purposes of carrying out a particular group task). Business applications of the same type of model arise when consultants are assigned to different project teams or trainees are assigned to discussion groups. An example of forming student groups arises in a typical course project.

EXAMPLE 9.3   *Oxbridge College's Accounting Department*

Each term, the Accounting Department at Oxbridge assigns students to teams for the purposes of a simulated audit engagement. In this problem, we are given a description of each student on various dimensions, expressed with a set of zeros and ones. In particular, the Department has recorded the following information for each student.

- Majored in accounting as an undergraduate (1 = yes, 0 = no).
- Previously worked for an accounting firm (1 = yes, 0 = no).
- Gender (1= male, 0 = female).
- International background (1 = yes, 0 = no).

This term, 20 students will be participating in the exercise, and there will be five 4-person teams. For the purposes of this exercise, the Department's goal is to achieve diversity in its assignment of students to teams. ∎

In Example 9.3, each student is described by a string of four binary digits. For example, a male student from the US who had not majored in accounting but had worked for an accounting firm would be represented by the string {0, 1, 1, 0}. A natural definition of decision variables for this problem is the following

$x_{jk} = 1$ if student j is assigned to group k, and 0 otherwise.

Suppose now that we want to form five teams of four students each. We can express the essential constraints in the problem as follows

$$\sum_j x_{jk} = 4 \quad \text{for } k = 1 \text{ to } 5$$

$$\sum_k x_{jk} = 1 \quad \text{for } j = 1 \text{ to } 20$$

The first set of these constraints fixes the size of each group; the second set ensures that each student is assigned to a unique group. If we model the decisions this way, the problem contains 25 constraints and 100 variables. This is too large a pair of numbers to expect the evolutionary solver to perform effectively.

The usual approach to an objective function builds on a metric that, for each attribute, calculates the sum of squared differences from the population average. Suppose, for example, that there are 10 accounting majors in the group of 20. Then the average number per group is two. Suppose that the number of accounting majors assigned to the respective groups follows the profile $\{1, 2, 2, 3, 2\}$. Then the calculation of the performance measure is as follows.

$$(1 - 2)^2 + (2 - 2)^2 + (2 - 2)^2 + (3 - 2)^2 + (2 - 2)^2 = 2$$

If the profile is $\{1, 0, 2, 3, 4\}$, then the metric is 10. Clearly, the ideal distribution of accounting majors among the groups would generate a metric of zero. For an objective function, we usually calculate the metric for each attribute and then sum over the attributes. This objective function can thus be expressed as a nonlinear function of the decision variables x_{jk}.

Although this is a natural formulation of the problem, it creates difficulties for two types of solution approaches. First, a direct formulation as an optimization problem leads to a nonlinear programming model with integer variables. As we pointed out in Chapter 8, this class of problems is poorly suited to the nonlinear solver. Instead, it makes sense to tackle the problem with the evolutionary solver. However, the natural formulation is also poorly suited to the evolutionary solver because it has many constraints and variables.

An alternative formulation of the problem can take advantage of the alldifferent constraint. Here, we let

$$y_i = \text{student number assigned to position } i$$

where there are 20 positions: four corresponding to the first group, four for the second group, and so on. The assignment of students to positions is equivalent to an assignment of students to groups. In our example, the y_i values need to satisfy the alldifferent constraint for the integers from 1 to 20. From that definition, we can build a spreadsheet model well suited to the evolutionary solver. Figure 9.11 shows the model. The problem data occupy columns A–E, with a four-element string for each student. The solution is described in columns I–K, where the shaded decision cells give the assignment of student numbers to groups and positions. The squared differences between each group's attribute count and the population mean are calculated in columns P–S, and their sum appears in cell G5 as the objective function. Although this may seem to be a complicated way of computing the objective, it is nevertheless suitable for the evolutionary solver.

We specify the problem as follows.

> Objective: G5 (minimize)
> Variables: K5:K24
> Constraints: K5:K24 = alldifferent

Again, the alldifferent constraint is sufficient to capture the constraints of the model. Starting with different assignments, the evolutionary solver takes us in most cases to a solution with a metric of 4 quite quickly (see Figure 9.12), suggesting, perhaps, that this is likely to be the optimal value. Alternative starting points and modifications of the options do not seem to produce any improvement. Again, this is stronger evidence that we might have found the optimum, although the evidence is not conclusive.

	A	B	C	D	E	F	G	H	I	J	K	L	M	N	O	P	Q	R	S
1	Team Formation																		
2																			
3	Data						Objective				Decisions						Calculations		
4	Student	Major	Firm	Gender	Int		Metric		Team	Position	Student	Major	Firm	Gender	Int	Maj	Firm	Gen	Int
5	1	0	0	0	0		8		1	1	1	0	0	0	0				
6	2	0	1	1	0				1	2	2	0	1	1	0				
7	3	1	0	1	1				1	3	3	1	0	1	1				
8	4	1	0	0	0				1	4	4	1	0	0	0	0.04	0.16	0.04	0.36
9	5	0	1	1	0				2	1	5	0	1	1	0				
10	6	1	0	1	1				2	2	6	1	0	1	1				
11	7	1	0	0	1				2	3	7	1	0	0	1				
12	8	0	0	1	1				2	4	8	0	0	1	1	0.04	0.16	0.64	1.96
13	9	0	1	0	1				3	1	9	0	1	0	1				
14	10	1	1	0	0				3	2	10	1	1	0	0				
15	11	0	0	1	1				3	3	11	0	0	1	1				
16	12	1	0	0	0				3	4	12	1	0	0	0	0.04	0.36	1.44	0.16
17	13	0	0	1	0				4	1	13	0	0	1	0				
18	14	0	0	1	1				4	2	14	0	0	1	1				
19	15	0	1	0	0				4	3	15	0	1	0	0				
20	16	1	1	1	0				4	4	16	1	1	1	0	0.64	0.36	0.64	0.36
21	17	0	0	1	0				5	1	17	0	0	1	0				
22	18	1	0	0	1				5	2	18	1	0	0	1				
23	19	1	0	1	0		Groups		5	3	19	1	0	1	0				
24	20	0	1	0	0		5		5	4	20	0	1	0	0	0.04	0.16	0.04	0.36
25	Total	9	7	11	8														
26	Avg.	1.80	1.40	2.20	1.60														
27																			

H ◀ ▶ H Teams

Figure 9.11. Spreadsheet model for Example 9.3.

By using the evolutionary solver, administrators at the Accounting Department can achieve their assignment goals where other methods, such as nonlinear integer programming, would likely have failed.

The group assignment problem illustrates the fact that there may be creative ways of formulating models to take advantage of the alldifferent constraint. This means that we may want to think beyond the typical structures of linear and nonlinear programming models, but no standard templates have been developed in this regard.

	A	B	C	D	E	F	G	H	I	J	K	L	M	N	O	P	Q	R	S
1	Team Formation																		
2																			
3	Data						Objective				Decisions						Calculations		
4	Student	Major	Firm	Gender	Int		Metric		Team	Position	Student	Major	Firm	Gender	Int	Maj	Firm	Gen	Int
5	1	0	0	0	0		4		1	1	6	1	0	1	0				
6	2	0	1	1	0				1	2	10	1	1	0	0				
7	3	1	0	1	1				1	3	1	0	0	0	0				
8	4	1	0	0	0				1	4	8	0	0	1	1	0.04	0.16	0.04	0.16
9	5	0	1	1	0				2	1	15	0	1	0	0				
10	6	1	0	1	1				2	2	4	1	0	0	0				
11	7	1	0	0	1				2	3	11	0	0	1	1				
12	8	0	0	1	1				2	4	16	1	1	1	1	0.04	0.36	0.04	0.36
13	9	0	1	0	1				3	1	7	1	0	0	1				
14	10	1	1	0	0				3	2	2	0	1	1	0				
15	11	0	0	1	1				3	3	12	1	0	0	0				
16	12	1	0	0	0				3	4	13	0	0	1	0	0.04	0.16	0.04	0.36
17	13	0	0	1	0				4	1	19	1	0	1	0				
18	14	0	0	1	1				4	2	14	0	0	1	1				
19	15	0	1	0	0				4	3	20	0	1	0	0				
20	16	1	1	1	0				4	4	3	1	0	1	1	0.04	0.16	0.64	0.16
21	17	0	0	1	0				5	1	9	0	1	0	1				
22	18	1	0	0	1				5	2	5	0	1	1	0				
23	19	1	0	1	0		Groups		5	3	17	0	0	1	0				
24	20	0	1	0	0		5		5	4	18	1	0	0	1	0.64	0.36	0.04	0.16
25	Total	9	7	11	8														
26	Avg.	1.80	1.40	2.20	1.60														
27																			

H ◀ ▶ H Teams Teams2

Figure 9.12. Final solution for Example 9.3.

SUMMARY

The evolutionary solver contains an algorithm that complements the linear solver, the nonlinear solver, and the branch-and-bound procedure. Unlike those algorithms, however, it does not explicitly seek a local optimum or a global optimum. Nevertheless, it can often find optimal solutions to very difficult problems, and it may be the only effective procedure we can apply when a nonsmooth function exists in the model.

The considerations influencing the building of models for the evolutionary solver are different from those for linear and nonlinear programs. Because nonsmooth functions are permitted, we have great flexibility in drawing on Excel's various built-in functions if we wish to calculate complex results in convenient ways. Also, experience suggests that the evolutionary solver performs best if the number of variables and the number of constraints is not large. To avoid constraints, we can often impose a numerical penalty when a condition is violated and include the penalty in the objective function instead of entering the constraint explicitly. Having built a model this way, it is helpful if we can start with an initial solution that satisfies all constraints—that is, a solution without penalties. Otherwise, the evolutionary solver may not be effective at finding feasible solutions (those without penalties) in models that contain penalty terms in the objective.

The evolutionary solver is not likely to be trapped by local optima, as is the case with the nonlinear solver. This feature is advantageous in searching for good solutions to problems containing nonsmooth functions, especially nonlinear problems with integer variables. On the other hand, we must realize that the search procedure is both random (subject to probabilistic variation) and heuristic (not guaranteed to find an optimum). For that reason, we usually reserve the use of the evolutionary solver for only the most difficult problems.

The evolutionary solver works with a set of specialized parameters. Although we offered default settings, these settings are merely a starting point. Different choices might be suitable for different problem types. In addition, we may want to use one set of choices at the start and then other settings in subsequent runs, while we look for improvements. As compared to arbitrary settings, the intelligent selection of these parameters can enhance the performance of the evolutionary solver considerably. Aside from the guidelines given here, practice and experience using the evolutionary solver are the key ingredients in effective parameter selection.

EXERCISES

9.1. Sequencing Jobs   A fundamental model in scheduling contains a set of jobs that are waiting to be processed by a machine or processor. The machine is capable of handling only one job at a time, so the jobs must be processed in sequence. The problem is to find the best sequence for a given objective function.

For example, the processor might be an integrated machining center that performs a number of metal-cutting operations on components for complex assemblies. Ten different components have reached the center and are awaiting processing. These jobs and their processing times (expressed in hours) are described in the following table. In addition, each job has a corresponding due date that has been calculated by the production control system. As a result of the sequence chosen, each job will either be on time or late. If it is late, the amount of time by which it misses its due date is called its *tardiness*. The objective is to minimize the total tardiness in the schedule.

Job	1	2	3	4	5	6	7	8	9	10
Processing time	6	1	2	5	9	8	12	3	9	7
Due date	17	5	25	15	20	8	44	24	50	20

What is the minimum total tardiness and the sequence that achieves it?

9.2. Scheduling a Shop Midwest Parts Supply (MPS) is a fabricator of small steel parts that are sold as components to manufacturers of electronic appliances and medical equipment. In the MPS fabrication department, steel sheets are subjected to a series of three main operations—cutting, trimming, and polishing. Each job must have the operations completed in this order, and each machine sees the same job order, so it is sufficient to specify a single job sequence in order to describe a schedule. No machine can process more than one job at a time.

This morning, 10 jobs have been released to the shop by the ERP system, and the production manager is interested in minimizing the time it takes to complete the entire schedule, usually referred to as the schedule *makespan*. The following table gives the number of hours required for each operation.

Job	1	2	3	4	5	6	7	8	9	10
Cutting time	1	5	3	7	9	7	8	8	3	6
Trimming time	2	9	2	10	7	6	9	9	1	1
Polishing time	9	7	3	4	7	8	9	4	1	3

What sequence achieves the minimum makespan and what is the minimum length of a schedule?

9.3. Planning a Tour Recent graduate and amateur world traveler Alastair Bor is planning a European trip. His preferences are influenced by his curiosity about urban culture in Europe and by his extensive study of international relations while he was in school. Accordingly, he has decided to make one stop in each of 12 European capitals in the time he has available. He wants to find a sequence of the cities that involves the least total mileage. He has calculated inter-city distances using published data on latitude and longitude, and applying the geometry for arcs of great circles. These distances are shown below.

	Ams.	Ath.	Ber.	Brus.	Cope.	Dub.	Lis.	Lon.	Lux.	Mad.	Par.	Rom.
Amsterdam	–	2166	577	175	622	712	1889	339	319	1462	430	1297
Athens	2166	–	1806	2092	2132	2817	2899	2377	1905	2313	2100	1053
Berlin	577	1806	–	653	348	1273	2345	912	598	1836	878	1184
Brussels	175	2092	653	–	768	732	1738	300	190	1293	262	1173
Copenhagen	622	2132	348	768	–	1203	2505	942	797	2046	1027	1527
Dublin	712	2817	1273	732	1203	–	1656	440	914	1452	743	1849
Lisbon	1889	2899	2345	1738	2505	1656	–	1616	1747	600	1482	1907
London	339	2377	912	300	942	440	1616	–	475	1259	331	1419
Luxembourg	319	1905	598	190	797	914	1747	475	–	1254	293	987
Madrid	1462	2313	1836	1293	2046	1452	600	1259	1254	–	1033	1308
Paris	430	2100	78	262	1027	743	1482	331	293	1033	–	1108
Rome	1297	1053	1184	1173	1527	1849	1907	1419	987	1308	1108	–

From (label at left of table)

What sequence achieves a minimum-distance tour for Alastair, starting in Brussels, and what is the minimum tour length?

9.4. Cutting Stock Poly Products sells packaging tape to industrial customers. All tape is sold in 100-foot rolls that are cut in various widths from a master roll, which is 15 inches wide. The product line consists of the following widths: 2″, 3″, 5″, 7″, and 11″. These can be cut in different combinations from a 15-inch master roll. For example, one combination might consist of three cuts of 5″ each. Another combination might consist of two 2″ cuts and an 11″ cut. Both of these combinations use the entire 15-inch roll without any waste, but other combinations are also possible. For example, another combination might consist of two 7″ cuts. This combination creates one inch of waste for every roll cut this way.

Each week, Poly Products collects demands from its customers and distributors and must figure out how to configure the cuts in its master rolls. To do so, the production manager lists all possible combinations of cuts and tries to fit them together so that waste is minimized while demand is met. (In particular, demand must be met exactly, because Poly Products does not keep inventories of its tape.) This week's demands are shown in the table.

Size	2″	3″	5″	7″	11″
Demand	60	50	40	30	20

(a) How many combinations can be cut from a 15-inch master roll so that there is less than two inches of waste (i.e. the smallest quantity that can be sold) left on the roll?

(b) Find a set of combinations that meets demand exactly and generates the minimum amount of waste. (Stated another way, the requirement is to meet or exceed demand for each size, but any excess must be counted as waste.) What is the optimal set of combinations and the minimum amount of waste?

9.5. Locating Warehouses Southeastern Foods has hired you to analyze their distribution system design. The company has 11 distribution centers, with monthly volumes as listed below. Seven of these sites can support warehouses, in terms of the infrastructure available, and are designated by (W).

Center	Volume	Center	Volume
Atlanta (W)	5000	Memphis (W)	7800
Birmingham (W)	3000	Miami	4400
Columbia (W)	1400	Nashville (W)	6800
Jackson	2200	New Orleans	5800
Jacksonville	8800	Orlando (W)	2200
Louisville (W)	3000		

The monthly fixed cost for operating one of these warehouses is estimated at $3600, although there is no capacity limit in their design. Southeastern could build warehouses at any of the designated locations, but its criterion is to minimize the total of fixed operating costs and variable shipment costs. Information has been compiled showing the cost per carton of shipping from any potential warehouse location to any distribution center.

	Atl	Bir	Col	Jac	Jvl	Lvl	Mem	Mia	Nash	NewO	Orl
Atlanta	0.00	0.15	0.21	0.40	0.31	0.42	0.38	0.66	0.25	0.48	0.43
Birmingham	0.15	0.00	0.36	0.25	0.46	0.36	0.26	0.75	0.19	0.35	0.55
Columbia	0.21	0.36	0.00	0.60	0.30	0.50	0.62	0.64	0.44	0.69	0.44
Louisville	0.42	0.36	0.50	0.59	0.73	0.00	0.38	1.09	0.17	0.70	0.86
Memphis	0.38	0.26	0.62	0.21	0.69	0.38	0.00	1.00	0.21	0.41	0.78
Nashville	0.25	0.19	0.44	0.41	0.56	0.17	0.21	0.91	0.00	0.53	0.69
Orlando	0.43	0.55	0.44	0.70	0.14	0.86	0.78	0.23	0.69	0.65	0.00

(a) What is the minimum total cost?

(b) To achieve the cost in (a), which warehouse locations should be used?

9.6. **Locating Emergency Centers** After the damage caused in Florida by a series of severe hurricanes, the governor ordered the Florida Emergency Management Agency (FLEMA) to design a systematic plan for emergency services following severe weather events. The state has 11 emergency offices, and it would be possible to build a warehouse next to each of the offices to store emergency equipment. As a consultant to FLEMA, you were asked to determine how many centers would be needed to ensure that there would be a warehouse within 50 miles of any emergency office. After studying your recommendation, however, FLEMA's Director decided that the cost of the plan would be prohibitive, so a revised formulation was developed. This one requires building just four warehouses.

With this standard in mind, you have obtained the distances between the eleven offices (identified by their cities).

	DB	Ft L	Ft M	Gain	Mia	Nap	Orl	St P	Sara	Talla	Tam
Daytona Beach	0	229	207	98	251	241	54	159	186	234	139
Ft Lauderdale	229	0	133	312	22	105	209	234	202	444	234
Ft Myers	207	133	0	230	141	34	153	110	71	356	123
Gainesville	98	312	230	0	331	264	109	143	179	144	128
Miami	251	22	141	331	0	107	228	251	214	463	245
Naples	241	105	34	264	107	0	187	143	107	389	156
Orlando	54	209	153	109	228	187	0	105	132	242	85
St Petersburg	159	234	110	143	251	143	105	0	39	250	20
Sarasota	186	202	71	179	214	107	132	39	0	286	53
Tallahassee	234	444	356	144	463	389	242	250	286	0	239
Tampa	139	234	123	128	245	156	85	20	53	239	0

FLEMA would like to ensure that there will be a warehouse center within x miles of any office. What is the minimum value of x that can be achieved when there are four warehouses in the system?

9.7. **Touring the Agents** Professor Moonlight runs a fund of funds in order to supplement his academic salary. Every winter, he pays a visit to each of the fund managers with whom he works. These visits are all made in one trip, during which he visits investment agents in nine cities. Prof. Moonlight doesn't mind flying, but he dislikes long flights. For this trip, he wants to find a route through the various cities starting and ending in San Antonio, and he wants the longest leg of the trip (measured in miles) to be as short as possible. The pairwise distances in miles are shown below.

	San Antonio	Phoenix	Los Angeles	Seattle	Detroit	Atlanta	New York	Boston	Philadelphia
San Antonio	0	602	1376	1780	1262	935	1848	2000	1668
Phoenix	602	0	851	1193	1321	1290	2065	2201	1891
Los Angeles	1376	851	0	971	2088	2140	2870	2995	2702
Seattle	1780	1193	971	0	1834	2178	2620	2707	2486
Detroit	1262	1321	2088	1834	0	655	801	912	654
Atlanta	935	1290	2140	2178	655	0	940	1096	765
New York	1848	2065	2870	2620	801	940	0	156	180
Boston	2000	2201	2995	2707	912	1096	156	0	333
Philadelphia	1668	1891	2702	2486	654	765	180	333	0

(a) What is the minimum value of the trip's longest leg?

(b) What is the optimal tour?

9.8. Optimizing Capacity Pelham Power Company (PPC) uses a system of boilers and turbines to produce power. PPC owns five boilers. If a given boiler is operated, it can produce steam within an output range given in the following table. Quantities are shown in tons. The cost per ton of producing steam is also shown in the table.

Boiler	1	2	3	4	5
Min.	300	325	350	355	375 tons of steam
Max.	800	820	840	920	960 tons of steam
Cost	2.20	2.35	2.50	2.65	2.80 dollars per ton of steam

Steam from the boilers is used by the turbines to produce power. PPC owns four turbines. If a given turbine is operated, it can produce power from steam at the rate given in the following table. The amount of steam each turbine can accommodate is also shown in the table, along with the maximum and minimum of its input range (in tons of steam). The cost of producing power is also shown in the table.

Turbine	1	2	3	4
Rate	4.00	4.50	5.00	5.50 kwh per ton of steam
Min.	420	450	480	510 tons of steam
Max.	825	875	925	975 tons of steam
Cost	2.15	2.50	2.75	2.95 dollars per ton of steam

What is the minimum cost of deploying boilers and turbines to produce 10,000 kwh of power at PPC?

9.9. Balancing Workloads Over the next six weeks, an insurance company needs to send more than 1.75 million pieces of marketing literature to customers in 16 states. In order to coordinate with other marketing efforts, all the mailings for a given state must go out the same week (i.e., if mailings for Georgia are sent in week 2, then all 136,562 pieces of mail for Georgia must be sent that week). The operations manager would like to minimize the largest amount of mail processed in any given week during the four-week campaign. The required volumes are shown below.

State	Volume
AZ	82,380
CA	212,954
CT	63,796
GA	136,562
IL	296,479
MA	99,070
ME	38,848
MN	86,207
MT	33,309
NC	170,997
NJ	104,974
NV	29,608
OH	260,858
OR	63,605
TX	214,076
VA	134,692

(a) Determine which states should be assigned for processing each week in order to achieve the desired objective.

(b) What is the largest amount of mail processed in any given week?

9.10. Scheduling Power Plants   During the next 8 months, Metropolis Power Company forecasts the demands shown below (measured in thousands of kwh).

Month	1	2	3	4	5	6	7	8
Demand	96	154	148	77	84	92	119	126

The power will be supplied from the four generating facilities, GF1–GF4. The facilities are each characterized by a generating capacity, a monthly operating cost, a startup cost, and a shutdown cost. These are each shown in thousands of dollars in the table below. When a generator is in operation, it provides service at its full capacity, even if that exceeds demand. No operating cost is saved by partial (rather than full) use of a generator's capacity. At the beginning of each month, it is possible to shut down any of the facilities that have been operating or to start up any of the facilities that have been idle, with the cost implications indicated in the table.

Facility	Capacity	Cost	Startup	Shutdown
GF1	70	8	4	3
GF2	60	7	3	2
GF3	50	6	3	2
GF4	40	5	2	3

At the start of month 1, facilities GF1 and GF2 are in operation.
What is the minimum total cost of providing the power demanded?

9.11. Team Assignment   A new class of 15 students has been admitted to the graduate Film Studies program at the State University. During much of the first year, these students will be working on teams, producing short films. The program director wants to assign students to teams so that the teams are as diverse as possible. There will be three teams of five students each.

Diversity is measured based on four characteristics or *factors*: undergraduate film major (1 if yes, 0 if no), previous employment in the film industry (1 if yes, 0 if no), interest in documentaries (1 if so, 0 otherwise), and gender (1 if female, 0 if male). Thus, each student is represented by four factor ratings.

Student	UG	Emp	Int	Feml
1	0	0	0	0
2	0	1	1	0
3	1	0	1	1
4	1	0	0	0
5	0	1	1	0
6	0	0	1	1
7	1	0	0	0
8	0	0	1	0
9	0	0	1	1
10	0	1	0	0
11	1	1	1	0
12	0	0	1	0
13	1	0	0	1
14	1	0	1	0
15	0	1	0	0
Total	6	5	9	4
Average	2.00	1.67	3.00	1.33

For a given factor j, team i has a factor rating ($c_{i,j}$ for factor j) equal to the total number of 1s among its team members. The challenge is to convert a profile of factor ratings into a quantitative measure of diversity. A specific diversity measure has been adopted, based on the principle that if the teams "resemble" each other, then the makeup of the teams must be diverse. The calculation is made as follows. Find the average factor rating per team. (This figure can be computed from the raw data, as shown in the table.) For each group, calculate the absolute deviation between its rating and the average factor rating on the same factor. Sum the four deviations to get the group value. Sum the three group values to get a total. Minimize the total. This measure would have a value of zero if the teams resembled each other perfectly. In symbols, the diversity measure is

$$z = \sum_{i=1}^{3} \sum_{j=1}^{4} |c_{i,j} - \bar{c}_j|$$

Find the assignment of students to teams that minimizes the diversity measure z.

9.12. Making Car Assignments   You are organizing rides for a group of campers going on an all-day, off-site trip. You have lined up some drivers, and your problem, essentially, is to assign campers to drivers. The drivers, and the capacities of their cars, are provided in the following table.

Driver	Capacity
Saul	5
Chris	4
Rob	3
Erick	5
Anna	6
Jim	5

The campers represent different age groups. Each age group is to be delivered to a different location. Thus, if a car holds campers of different ages, then the driver will have to drive to different destinations. An ideal solution would require each driver to go to just one location. However, such a solution is unattainable. The campers and their age groups are listed in the table below.

Group	Camper	Group	Camper
Age 7	George	**Age 9**	Eric
	Marcia		Scott
	Steve		Sarah
	Andrew		Gretchen
	Brian		Jamie
	Suzanne		Liz
Age 8	Lisa	**Age 10**	Patty
	Ben		Francesca
	Tommy		Adrian
	Vanessa		Ali
	Alberto		Cliff
	Jason		Mickey
	Sean		Matt

Although we know what an "ideal" solution would look like, we need a metric for evaluating less-than-ideal solutions. One suitable metric is the total number of delivery stops. Find the minimal number of stops and the assignment of campers to cars that achieves it.

Case: Colgate Wave (Abridged)*

Introduction

In 1996, Colgate-Palmolive was trying to maintain its market presence in the tooth-brush category, with three strong brands spanning the price spectrum. Colgate *Classic* was the company's low-priced brand, Colgate *Plus* was a mid-priced, pre-mium brand, and Colgate *Total* represented the company's most recent entry (three years earlier) into the super-premium segment. There were several competitors in each of these three market segments, but Colgate had been the market leader, with a total share of about 24 percent in 1995, followed by Gillette (Oral B) and Procter & Gamble (Crest) with 18 percent and 16 percent, respectively. By 1996, however, Colgate's market share was slipping in the face of dual pressures: low prices from private-label brands and new entries from competitors in the premium/super-premium sector.

The company was closely monitoring its market share in the super-premium and premium segments. These segments not only provided higher dollar margins than the lower segment, but they were also expected to expand as consumers became more conscious of oral hygiene. Therefore, Colgate had been planning to introduce a new super-premium toothbrush named *Wave*. Exhibit 9.1 provides a concept description of the *Wave* toothbrush. Colgate had conducted a concept test for the product, and the results had been quite promising.

The company also felt it was important to preserve its product portfolio share in the premium and super-premium segments. Informally, Colgate's rule of thumb was that the market share of each brand in these two segments had to exceed 4 percent because experience showed that distribution drops off exponentially at lower market shares.

At the same time, Colgate was concerned about an anticipated 18 percent price rollback on Procter & Gamble's Crest *Complete*. Colgate wanted to assess the impact of the possible price cut on existing market shares and to decide on a suitable response, in terms of both its pricing of existing products and its introduction of the new product.

The Study

The company had designed and conducted a conjoint study to assist in its product line pricing decision. Data for the national study were gathered through personal inter-views with 510 adults who were the primary shoppers for their households and who had purchased a non-electric toothbrush in the previous six months. Complete, usable responses were obtained from 484 of these respondents in a three-part question-naire. The first part asked people about their preferred toothbrushes and obtained infor-mation about their shopping behavior. The second part was a conjoint exercise that

---

*This is an abridged version of an original case written by Professor Kusum Ailawadi of Dartmouth College and is used with permission.

EXHIBIT 9.1　*Wave Concept Statement*

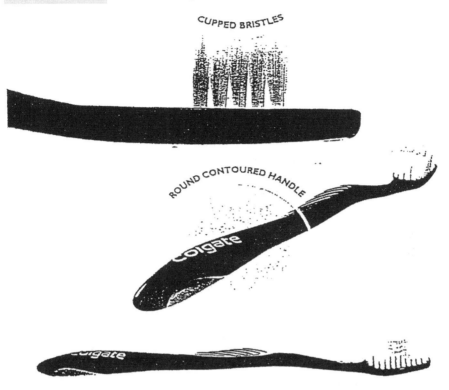

CUPPED BRISTLES

ROUND CONTOURED HANDLE

Better Control
Means Better Clean!

Brushing your teeth may not require great skill, but to do it well, requires a certain degree of control.

New Colgate Wave is the only toothbrush where the handle and the bristles are <u>both</u> naturally contoured to work <u>together</u> to provide the control you need to do a better job brushing your teeth.

The multi-level "cupped" bristles surround each tooth to clean both the sides as well as in between. The round, contoured handle allows you to turn your brush more easily so you can pivot the bristles to exactly the angle you need. The result is more effective cleaning, even in the most difficult spots.

New Colgate Wave. Better Control. Better Clean.

AVAILABLE IN: Extra Soft Full Head • Soft Full Head • Soft Compact Head • Medium Full Head • Medium Compact Head
Price: $2.99

formed the core of the study. The final section contained some basic demographic questions.

In the conjoint exercise, consumers were shown a simulated display containing 11 existing toothbrush brands that accounted for approximately 70 percent of the market, along with the new Colgate *Wave*. The display was configured to resemble shelf displays in actual stores and the toothbrushes were shown in their normal packaging, with prices clearly marked. (At the beginning of the interview, respondents were asked what kind of store they usually purchased toothbrushes at—such as discount stores/mass merchandisers, drug/grocery stores, etc. The prices they were subsequently shown were consistent with the outlets they shopped at—lower prices for those shopping at discount and mass merchandisers and higher prices for those shopping at drug/grocery stores.) Respondents were free to pick up and examine each product if they wished. Respondents were initially shown this display with prices for each toothbrush set at 24 percent below market level and were asked to select the brand that they would buy. Once the respondent made a choice, the price of the chosen item was raised by 6 percent while prices of all others remained constant. Then, the respondent was asked to make a choice again. Prices for each brand were varied from 24 percent below market level to 24 percent above market level, in 6 percent increments. The choice process was repeated until the respondent had gone through all brands at all the price levels, or would not buy any brand at the prices shown, or refused to continue with the exercise. The result was a matrix of choices made for brands at up to nine different price levels. Not all respondents had the same number of choices because they could opt out earlier saying, "All prices are too high."

These choices were used as inputs to a proprietary model that estimated each respondent's part-worth utilities (on a scale of 1000) for each brand and price level. These utilities, along with demographic information for each respondent, made up the input data for the model. Given a price scenario, the model calculated market shares from the data on utilities. The case appendix provides a description of the Excel workbook containing the model.

The actual market prices and market shares of the 11 existing brands in the study, along with the market price being planned for Colgate *Wave*, are listed in the table below. In this table, market shares have been re-scaled from their original values for the entire US market so that they add up to 100 percent for the 11 brands included in the study. These 11 brands accounted for anticipated sales of roughly 300 million toothbrushes in 1996.

Brand	Price	Share: %
Colgate Wave	2.99	
Colgate Plus	2.14	18.10
Colgate Classic	0.99	2.90
Colgate Total	2.69	6.79
Crest Complete	2.54	12.70
Oral-B Advantage	2.99	10.81
Oral-B Indicator	2.39	12.09
Store brands (Rite Aid)	1.09	17.31
Mentadent	2.99	7.40
Aquafresh Flex Direct	2.59	2.90
Reach Plaque Sweeper	2.89	0.70
Reach Regular	2.14	8.30

At these prices, the contribution and net profit margins for the four Colgate brands were as follows.

	Classic	Plus	Total	Wave
Unit price	0.99	2.14	2.69	2.99
Variable cost	0.59	1.18	1.34	1.35
Contribution margin	0.40	0.96	1.35	1.64

Case Appendix: Market Share Simulation Model (Colgate.xls)

The workbook consists of three sheets: (1) data, (2) calculations, and (3) simulation. As the names of the sheets imply, the data sheet contains raw input data for the model, the calculations sheet performs all the necessary calculations, and the simulation sheet determines the final market shares for each simulation. The contents of the three sheets are described below. A copy of the model can be downloaded from the book's website: http://mba.tuck.dartmouth.edu/opt/

Data

Column A contains the respondent ID for each of the 484 respondents. Columns B through M contain the estimated utilities for each of the 12 brands in the study. Columns O through W contain the utilities for each of the nine price levels in the study. Column Y contains *Kendall's Tau* (a measure of model fit) for each respondent. Columns AA through AE contain some basic demographic data for the respondents. Finally, column AF contains data on the number of toothbrushes purchased per year by each respondent. The information on toothbrushes purchased is ultimately used to compute the "share of toothbrushes" in the other sheets.

Calculations

Columns A through H convert actual dollar prices entered in the simulation sheet into price levels (e.g., 24 percent below or 12 percent above market price) for which utilities are available. Columns F, G, and H assign an integer to each of the nine price levels (e.g., 24 percent below equals 14 and 24 percent above equals 22). Column E lists the current market prices of each brand. (The market price for Wave is the super-premium price of $2.99 used in its concept test.) Column B converts the price entered in the simulation sheet to the closest (lower) integer between 14 and 22, corresponding to the scale in column G. It also truncates prices at both ends. Thus, if a price is more than 24 percent below (or above) market price in the Simulation sheet, it will be truncated to 24 percent below (or above). Column C calculates the price difference as a percentage. This information is used to interpolate price utilities between the nine discrete levels used in the study.

Column J lists the respondent IDs. Columns K through V compute the total utilities of each brand in the simulation, given the prices entered in the simulation sheet. These columns pick the utilities of the appropriate brand and the appropriate integer price level from the data sheet, and include any necessary interpolation of price utility.

Column X lists the maximum utility across the 12 brands. If a price of 100 is entered for *Wave* in the simulation sheet, *Wave* is left out of the calculation in Column Y. Columns Z through AK compute 0/1 variables indexing the brand with the maximum utility (i.e., the brand that will be chosen). These columns are summed in row 487 to provide the total number of times that each brand is chosen in the sample of 484 respondents. The choices are weighted by each respondent's number of toothbrushes purchased per year (from the data sheet) to get the total number of toothbrushes of each brand in row 488.

Simulation

Current ("Original") market prices of each brand are listed in C9:C20. New prices for each simulation should be entered in the yellow area (B9:B20). The resultant percentage change in price is computed in D9:D20. Prices must not fall beyond the permissible range (24 percent below market price to 24 percent above market price). The limits of the permissible ranges are shown in cells F9:G20. Although the worksheet allows prices beyond this range in the simulation sheet, the actual prices used to calculate utilities will be appropriately truncated in the calculation sheet. To run a simulation without *Wave* in the market, enter a price of 100 for *Wave*. This value will cause it to be disregarded in the prediction of choice and share.

Each brand's predicted share of choices by the 484 respondents is computed in B24:B35. The corresponding share of toothbrushes (choices weighted by number of toothbrushes purchased per year) is computed in C24:C35. Cells D24:D35 contain adjustment factors for these results. Finally, predicted shares of toothbrushes, adjusted by these factors, appear in cells E24:E35.

The adjustment factors in cells D24:D35 bring predicted share of toothbrushes in the base case (current prices in current market) in line with actual market shares. That is, when current prices are placed in cells B10:B20, the adjustment factors produce the market shares listed in the case. In order to make this calculation, the model is run once for the base case and its predictions are saved. Then the base case shares listed in the case are entered. The adjustment factors are calculated directly from these figures.

Appendix 1

Optimization Software and Supplemental Files

A1.1. RISK SOLVER PLATFORM

Purchasers of this book may download a powerful software package called Risk Solver Platform (RSP) that was developed by the same team that created Excel's Solver, and that accommodates all Excel Solver models. This book uses Risk Solver Platform for Education (RSPE), which has all the functionality of the commercial product RSP but with lower limits on the size of optimization problems and "educational use" watermarks on charts. All the examples and exercises in this book can be solved within the limits of RSPE.

If you've purchased this book and you are a student enrolled in a university course, you can download and install the software and use RSPE for a full semester (140 days) at no charge. To do this, visit www.solver.com/student, fill out the form on this page, and click the button to register and download. To complete the form, you'll need two pieces of information: a **Textbook Code**, which is **BOMS2**, and a **Course Code**, which your instructor can obtain from Frontline Systems, the software developers, and give to you.[1]

If you've purchased this book for self-study but you're not enrolled in a university course, you have two options: (1) Visit www.solver.com and register on the forms presented there, download and install the software, and use RSP (the full commercial product with much higher size limits) on a free trial, which is currently limited to 15 days; or (2) Contact Frontline Systems at 775-831-0300 or info@solver.com and request a Course Code that will allow you to use RSPE for 140 days. As long as you're using the software for learning rather than production use, the company's current policy is to routinely grant these licenses.

The software works with Excel 2003, Excel 2007 and Excel 2010, but if you are using the 64-bit version of Excel 2010, be sure to download and run the Setup program

---

[1]For longer-term licenses, course instructors should contact Frontline Systems at 775-831-0300 or info@solver.com

Optimization Modeling with Spreadsheets, *Second Edition*. Kenneth R. Baker
© 2011 John Wiley & Sons, Inc. Published 2011 by John Wiley & Sons, Inc.

for 64-bit Risk Solver Platform, named RSPSetup64.exe. In all other cases, you'll download and run RSPSetup.exe. Running the Setup program is straightforward, but you'll need to pay attention to three prompts.

1. You'll be asked for an installation password. This will be emailed to you, at the email address you give when you fill out the registration form.

2. You'll be asked for a license activation code. This appears in the same email as the installation password; it determines whether you'll be using full RSP for 15 days, RSPE for 140 days, or something else.

3. You'll be asked whether you want to run initially as full Risk Solver Platform, or a subset product. There are several choices, but for use with this book, the recommended selection is *Premium Solver Platform*. (You can change this selection later, using Help—About on the RSP/PSP Ribbon.)

To uninstall the software, you can either re-run RSPSetup.exe, or use the Windows Add/Remove Programs feature.

A1.2. SUPPLEMENTAL EXCEL FILES

This book is supported by a website that contains supplementary files. The URL for the website is http://mba.tuck.dartmouth.edu/opt/. Specifically, the website contains a collection of Excel files corresponding to all of the spreadsheet exhibits in the book. This collection is not intended merely for backup purposes: you are encouraged to open these files while reading the text and to explore them carefully. This exploration provides a hands-on feel for the examples in the text and potentially serves as a template for other, similar problems.

A second collection of Excel files contains data sets for selected end-of-chapter exercises and cases. The data sets are provided for situations in which it would be tedious to enter all the data into an Excel file for the purpose of working on the exercise.

Some of the cases contain references to an existing spreadsheet model. The website also contains Excel files for these models.

Appendix 2

Graphical Methods in Linear Programming

We can use graphical methods to solve linear optimization problems involving two variables. When there are two variables in the problem, we can refer to them as x_1 and x_2, and we can do most of the analysis on a two-dimensional graph. Although the graphical approach does not generalize to a large number of variables, the basic concepts of linear programming can all be demonstrated in the two-variable context. When we run into questions about more complicated problems, we can ask, what would this mean for the two-variable problem? Then, we can look for answers in the two-variable case, using graphs.

Another advantage of the graphical approach is its visual nature. Graphical methods provide us with a picture to go with the algebra of linear programming, and the picture can anchor our understanding of basic definitions and possibilities. For these reasons, the graphical approach provides useful background for working with linear programming concepts.

A2.1. AN EXAMPLE

Consider the planning and scheduling problem facing a manufacturer of microwave ovens with two models in its line—the standard and the deluxe. Each oven is assembled from component parts and subassemblies that are produced in the mechanical and electronics departments. The following table shows the number of production hours per oven required in each department and the capacities of the three production departments, in monthly hours.

	Standard (h/oven)	Deluxe (h/oven)	Capacity (h/mo)
Assembly Department	4	4	560
Mechanical Department	3	2	400
Electronics Department	2	4	400

Optimization Modeling with Spreadsheets, *Second Edition*. Kenneth R. Baker
© 2011 John Wiley & Sons, Inc. Published 2011 by John Wiley & Sons, Inc.

The sales department believes that there will be demand for as many ovens as the company can produce. The accounting department has determined that the variable profit contributions are $50 for each standard and $40 for each deluxe. The problem is to determine a production plan to maximize monthly profit contribution.

Our first step in analyzing this problem is to express it algebraically. The problem of devising an output plan boils down to finding the best number of standard ovens and deluxe ovens for the firm to produce in the coming month. Thus, we let

$$x_1 = \text{number of standard ovens}$$
$$x_2 = \text{number of deluxe ovens}$$

Once we determine the values of x_1 and x_2, the problem will be solved. Furthermore, the criterion is to maximize the profit contribution generated by our plan. In particular, we can write our objective function as

$$\text{Maximize } z = 50x_1 + 40x_2$$

where z represents the value of the objective function.

Having specified decision variables and an objective function, we turn our attention to the constraints of the problem, the limited capacities in the assembly, mechanical, and electronics departments. In assembly, the number of hours consumed by a production schedule cannot exceed the 560 hours available. We can write this requirement algebraically as

$$4x_1 + 4x_2 \leq 560$$

Similarly, for the mechanical and electronics departments, we require

$$3x_1 + 2x_2 \leq 400$$
$$2x_1 + 4x_2 \leq 400$$

In standard form, an algebraic statement of our full model is

$$
\begin{aligned}
\text{Maximize} \quad & z = 50x_1 + 40x_2 \\
\text{subject to} \quad & 4x_1 + 4x_2 \leq 560 & (A)\\
& 3x_1 + 2x_2 \leq 400 & (M)\\
& 2x_1 + 4x_2 \leq 400 & (E)
\end{aligned}
$$

Finally, implicit in our definition of the two decision variables is the requirement that they must both remain nonnegative ($x_1 \geq 0$ and $x_2 \geq 0$).

We begin the graphical analysis with the constraints. For a graphical approach, we can work with equations more readily than inequalities, so we consider the equations corresponding to each of the constraints in turn. For the assembly department constraint (A), the line $4x_1 + 4x_2 = 560$ defines the locus of all points at which the department is fully utilized. That is, the line represents the set of product mix combinations

(x_1, x_2) that consume all 560 available hours in assembly. To plot the line, note that the x_1 intercept is 140 (obtained by setting $x_2 = 0$ and solving the equation for x_1). Similarly, the x_2 intercept is 140. Plotting the two intercepts, (140, 0) and (0, 140) on a graph, and connecting the two points with a straight line, we construct the plot shown in Figure A2.1, where the label A on the graph is used to associate this line with the assembly hours constraint.

The line plotted in Figure A2.1 represents all combinations (x_1, x_2) that consume exactly 560 hours of assembly time. Our model, however, looks for combinations that consume no more than 560 hours. Combinations that consume fewer that 560 hours are also admissible, and these correspond to points (x_1, x_2) that lie below the line. In fact, if we consider only the points that are admissible in the assembly constraint and that also meet the nonnegativity requirements, then we are left with the shaded triangle shown in Figure A2.1.

Next, we plot a line corresponding to mechanical department hours, or $3x_1 + 2x_2 = 400$, as shown in Figure A2.2 with the label M. Points on this line represent combinations of standard and deluxe ovens that consume exactly 400 hours of mechanical time, and points below the line consume fewer than 400 hours. The line corresponding to the mechanical department has a slope of $-3/2$, in comparison to the assembly department line, which has a slope of -1. Only points that lie below both constraint lines (and in the nonnegative region) are admissible decisions, as indicated by the shading.

Finally, we plot a line corresponding to the electronic department limit, $2x_1 + 4x_2 = 400$, shown in Figure A2.3 with the label E. This line has a slope of $-1/2$, and again we shade the region that lies below all three of the lines, as shown in figure. The shaded region now represents the set of all points that are admissible decisions: They satisfy all of the constraints in our problem.

The shaded area in Figure A2.3 is called the *feasible region*. It is a five-sided polygon containing, along its boundary or inside, all of the points that correspond to

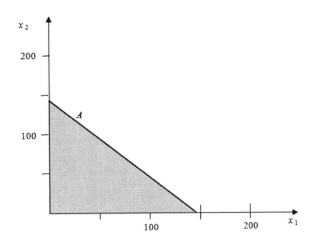

Figure A2.1. Sketch of first constraint.

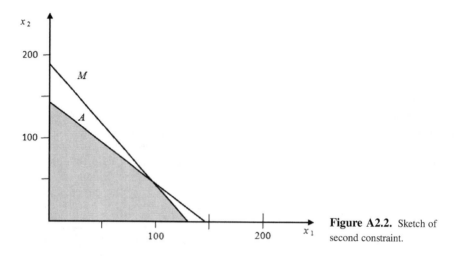

Figure A2.2. Sketch of second constraint.

feasible decisions in our model. Our next step is to find the best value of the objective function that can be achieved by a point in this feasible region.

To pursue this search, consider what happens when we set the objective function (z) equal to a fixed value. For example, suppose $z = 2000$. Then all points (x_1, x_2) that achieve a value of 2000 in the objective function lie on the line $50x_1 + 40x_2 = 2000$. Furthermore, all points that achieve a value of 2000 and that are feasible in the constraints lie along this line and within the feasible region. Consider a second line corresponding to $z = 4000$. Like the first objective function line, this one has a slope of $-5/4$, so it is parallel to the first. However, it has different intercepts and lies above and to the right of the first line, as shown in Figure A2.4. From these two lines, we can imagine an entire family of lines, each with a slope of $-5/4$ and each corresponding

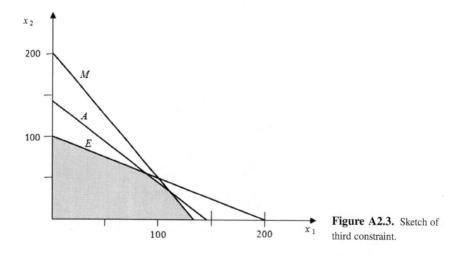

Figure A2.3. Sketch of third constraint.

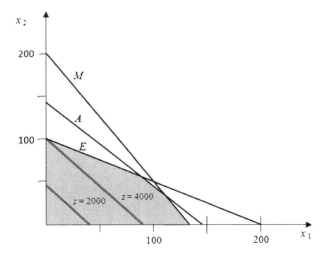

Figure A2.4. Sketch of
objective function lines.

to a particular value of z. Relatively larger values of z correspond to lines in this family
that lie farther above and to the right. We wish to find the largest value of z attainable in
this family and within the feasible region. A look at the figure indicates that this value
occurs at the intersection of the assembly and mechanical constraints.

We can make this result more precise by solving for the point at which the
assembly and mechanical constraints intersect. This point is (120, 20), as shown in
Figure A2.5, corresponding to a product mix of 120 standard ovens and 20 deluxe
ovens. The corresponding profit total is $6800, corresponding to the objective function
line for $z = 6800$, labeled OF in the figure. Using graphical methods, we have found
the best value of the objective function and the decisions that generate it.

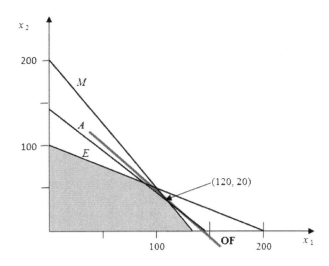

Figure A2.5. Sketch of
optimal point.

A2.2. GENERALITIES

The oven-manufacturing problem was merely an example, but it does illustrate the principles of graphical solution methods for optimization. In the example, all constraints are of the LT (less-than) variety. This means that points on the graph are feasible if they lie on or below the corresponding constraint line. On the other hand, had we encountered GT (greater-than) constraints, the feasible points would have been found on or above the corresponding constraint line. The other possibility, EQ (equal-to) constraints, would force us to consider only points lying directly on the constraint line.

In our example, the criterion was to maximize the objective function. By sketching the implications for two lines, each corresponding to a particular value of the objective function (sometimes called an *iso-value* line), we can begin to see a family of related objective function lines, leading to a maximum feasible value at one corner of the feasible region. Our objective function contained all positive coefficients, so the process of maximization led us to lines ever higher and to the right on our graph. Had we been interested in minimization (of a function with all positive coefficients), we would have been led to lines lower and to the left of a given starting point. For other combinations involving negative coefficients, the idea is to plot the graph of two or three iso-value lines, in order to see where on the graph the optimum will ultimately be found.

An examination of iso-value lines could reveal that there is no limit, in some direction, to the value of the objective function. This would be the case if we were analyzing an *unbounded* problem. In other circumstances, attempting to delineate the feasible region itself will reveal an *infeasible* problem, in which the constraints are mutually contradictory. These two exceptional cases can therefore be identified while carrying out the graphical analysis.

The graphical method is valuable because it produces a picture of the optimization process. That picture may make it easier to interpret what occurs during an optimization procedure. However, the graphical method is more difficult when there are three dimensions and impossible when there are more than three dimensions, so we can use it only for relatively simple cases. Nevertheless, two-dimensional examples illustrate most of the principles of linear programming.

As an example, suppose we consider well-posed linear programs in which the feasible region exists and in which the objective function is not unbounded. The theory tells us that an optimum can be found at one of the corners of the feasible region. This property is very useful, because it means that we don't have to search for an optimal point in the interior of the region (an area that contains an infinite number of points.) Instead, we can limit our search to the boundary, and just to the corner points on that boundary, which are finite in number. This is what most linear programming codes do: They search systematically among the corner points on the boundary of the feasible region, stopping only when an optimum has been located.

A second theoretical result tells us that we can identify an optimal corner point by showing that its objective function value is better than those of its neighboring corner points. Each of the corner points in our graph has two neighbors, and either of these can be reached by moving along one of the boundaries of the feasible region. When we start our search at one of the corner points, only two things can happen. Either the objective function is better than at both neighboring corners (in which case, we have found the optimum), or one of the neighbors has a better value. In the latter case, we move to that point and then evaluate the neighboring possibilities from the new location. In linear programming problems, we are essentially guaranteed that this search procedure ultimately leads to the optimum. Indeed, this approach lies at the heart of the *simplex algorithm*, which is the most popular method in use today for finding solutions to linear programming problems. (For an algebraic glimpse of the simplex method, see Appendix 3.)

Appendix 3

The Simplex Method

The simplex method is the algorithm most frequently used in computer programs for solving linear programming problems. The linear solver in Excel is an implementation of the simplex method, and the simplex method constitutes part of virtually every successful commercial software package for optimization. In this appendix, we use an example to illustrate the simplex method, and we comment on how the algorithm can be adapted to special situations that arise.

A3.1. AN EXAMPLE

We use a variation of Example 2.1 to illustrate how the simplex method works. For this purpose, we drop the wood constraint and address the following optimization problem.

$$
\begin{aligned}
\text{Maximize } z = 16C \quad +20D \quad +14T & \\
\text{subject to} & \\
4C \quad +6D \quad +2T \quad &\leq \quad 2000 \\
3C \quad +8D \quad +6T \quad &\leq \quad 2000 \\
9C \quad +6D \quad +4T \quad &\leq \quad 1440
\end{aligned}
$$

The simplex method works not with inequalities but rather with equalities, so our first step is to recast the constraints of the model as equations. To do so, we introduce three additional variables that account for unused amounts of the three resources. In other words, these variables represent the difference between the right-hand side (RHS) and left-hand side (LHS) of the constraints, as they are posed above. The constraints may be written as follows.

$$
\begin{array}{llll}
\textbf{Set 1:} & 4C + 6D + 2T \quad +u & = 2000 & \text{(A3.1)} \\
& 3C + 8D + 6T \qquad +v & = 2000 & \text{(A3.2)} \\
& 9C + 6D + 4T \qquad\qquad +w & = 1440 & \text{(A3.3)}
\end{array}
$$

The variables u, v, and w are called *slack variables*: they measure the amount of slack, or unused resource, in each constraint. These three variables, like the three original

Optimization Modeling with Spreadsheets, Second Edition. Kenneth R. Baker
© 2011 John Wiley & Sons, Inc. Published 2011 by John Wiley & Sons, Inc.

decision variables C, D, and T, are all considered to be nonnegative. (We assume throughout that all variables are nonnegative.)

We also express the objective function in a parallel form, with variables on the LHS and a number on the RHS. We include the slack variables in the following expression, but thereafter we leave out variables with zero coefficients.

$$z - 16C - 20D - 14T + 0u + 0v + 0w = 0$$

In their rewritten form, the model's constraints and objective function have two important features. First, the constraints are expressed as equations. Equations are easier to manipulate than inequalities, and we can apply procedures for solving systems of equations. In other words, we'll rely on the ability to solve three equations in three unknowns. (If we had m constraints, we'd want to solve m equations in m unknowns.)

The second feature of our constraints, with the slack variables added, is that the constraint equations appear in *canonical form*. This means that each constraint equation contains one variable with a coefficient of 1 that does not appear in the other equations. These variables are called *basic variables*; the other variables are called *nonbasic*. Canonical form includes the objective function, which we express in terms of the nonbasic variables. Put another way, the basic variables have zero coefficients in the objective function when we display canonical form of the problem.

When the problem is displayed in canonical form, we can find a solution to the system of equations by inspection. We simply set the nonbasic variables to zero and read the solution from what remains. In our example, the solution is as follows.

$$u = 2000$$
$$v = 2000$$
$$w = 1440$$

In terms of our original decision variables, this solution corresponds to the values $C = 0$, $D = 0$, and $T = 0$, for which $z = 0$. Thus, in our initial canonical form, the slack variables are the basic variables and the decision variables are nonbasic and zero. A set of basic variables is said to constitute a *basic feasible solution* whenever the values of all variables are nonnegative.

To test whether this basic feasible solution is optimal, we examine the objective function equation, written here with all of the variables

$$z - 16C - 20D - 14T = 0 \qquad\qquad (A3.1)$$

The value on the right-hand side represents the current value of the objective function, which is consistent with the solution $C = 0$, $D = 0$, and $T = 0$.

Next, we ask whether making any of the nonbasic variables positive would improve the value of the objective function. All else equal, if we could increase C, D, or T, then the value of the objective function would increase. When we are faced with a choice of this sort, we select the variable for which the objective function will increase the fastest, on a per-unit basis. Here, that means choosing D.

The variable D is called the *entering variable*, referring to the fact that it is about to enter the set of basic variables. As D enters, the value of z increases by 20 for each unit of D; thus we wish to make D as large as possible. To determine how large D can become, we return to the three equations of the first canonical form (Set 1) and trace the implications for the other positive variables.

Consider equation (A3.1), and ignore the nonbasic variables because they are zero. We obtain the following relationship between u and D.

$$u = 2000 - 6D$$

This relationship implies that u decreases as D increases and that the ceiling on D is $2000/6 = 333.3$. Values of D greater than 333.3 would drive u negative. Now, consider equation (A3.2)

$$v = 2000 - 8D \tag{A3.2}$$

This equation implies a ceiling on D of $2000/8 = 250$. Equation (A3.3) is

$$w = 1440 - 6D \tag{A3.3}$$

This equation implies a ceiling of $1440/6 = 240$.

The idea is to make D as large as possible without driving *any* of the existing variables negative, which means that D can increase to 240, the minimum of the ratios. At that point, the variable w drops to zero and becomes a nonbasic variable. Thus, there has been a change in the set of basic variables, from the set $\{u, v, w\}$ to the set $\{u, v, D\}$. The entering variable D was selected because it had the most negative coefficient in the objective function equation. The leaving variable w was then chosen because it was the first variable driven to zero by increasing D. The choice of w and the entering value of D can be determined by calculating the ratios of RHS constants to coefficients of the entering variable in each row and identifying the smallest ratio. The minimum ratio corresponds to the equation in which the leaving variable appears, referred to as the *pivot equation*.

To reconstruct canonical form with respect to the new set of basic variables, we must rewrite the equations so that the basic variables each appear in just one equation, and appear with a coefficient of 1. This means that the variable D must appear in the third equation, because u and v already appear in the other two equations. Moreover, D must appear with a coefficient of zero in those two equations. To rewrite the equations, we perform *elementary row operations*.

There are two types of elementary row operations. First, we can multiply an equation by a constant. Multiplication by a constant does not affect the set of values that satisfy the equation. In effect, it makes only a cosmetic change in the equation, altering its appearance but not its information content. Second, we can add to any equation some multiple of another equation. Addition of another equation also does not affect the set of values that satisfy the equations.

Thus, the first step is to divide equation (A3.3) by six. (This value, the coefficient of the entering variable in the pivot equation, is called the *pivot value.*) This division gives D a coefficient of 1

$$\frac{3}{2}C + D + \frac{2}{3}T + \frac{1}{6}w = 240 \tag{A3.3b}$$

Next, we subtract six times this equation from equation (A3.1), thus eliminating D from the equation. Similarly, we subtract eight times this equation from equation (A3.2). Finally, for the objective function, we add 20 times this equation. In summary, the elementary row operations are

$$(A3.3b) = (A3.3)/6$$
$$(A3.1b) = (A3.1) - 6(A3.3b)$$
$$(A3.2b) = (A3.2) - 8(A3.3b)$$
$$(A3.0b) = (A3.0) + 20(A3.3b)$$

The second set of equations, indicated by a (b), then takes the following form.

Set 2:						
$-5C$		$-2T$	$+u$		$-1w$	$= 560$	(A3.1b)
$-9C$		$+\frac{2}{3}T$		$+v$	$-\frac{4}{3}w$	$= 80$	(A3.2b)
$\frac{3}{2}C$	$+D$	$+\frac{2}{3}T$			$+\frac{1}{6}w$	$= 240$	(A3.3b)
$z + 14C$		$-\frac{2}{3}T$			$+\frac{10}{3}w$	$= 4800$	(A3.0b)

From equations (A3.1b)–(A3.3b) we can immediately read the values of the basic variables ($u = 560$, $v = 80$, and $D = 240$.) From equation (A3.0b) we can read the new value of the objective function ($z = 4800$), and as a check, we can confirm that this value corresponds to the set of decision variables ($C = 0$, $D = 240$, and $T = 0$.) Finally, we can see that there is potential for improvement in the objective function, as signified by the negative coefficient for T. If we increase T from this point, we will increase the value of z.

The next iteration follows the procedure outlined above. Given that there is room for improvement, we must identify an entering variable and a leaving variable, and then update the canonical equations accordingly. The steps in the procedure are outlined in Box A3.1.

In Step 1, we observe that not all coefficients in equation (A3.0b) are positive, and in Step 2, we note the negative coefficient of T. This value indicates that an improvement is possible and that the improvement can come from increasing the value of T, which is currently nonbasic. Because no other variable has a negative coefficient in equation (A3.0b), T becomes the entering variable.

In Step 3, we compute two ratios, skipping equation (A3.1b) because its coefficient for T is negative. The ratios are $80/0.667 = 120$ in equation (A3.2b) and $240/0.667 = 360$ in equation (A3.3b). The minimum thus occurs for equation (A3.2b),

---

BOX A3.1. *Outline of the Simplex Method*

Basic Steps in Maximization (starting from a basic feasible solution).

1. *Test the current solution for optimality.* If all coefficients in the objective function are nonnegative, then stop; the solution is optimal.

2. *Select the entering variable.* Identify the most negative objective function coefficient, breaking ties arbitrarily. The corresponding variable is the entering variable.

3. *Select the leaving variable.* For each equation, calculate the ratio of right-hand side constant to coefficient of the leaving variable, performing this calculation only for coefficients that are positive. Identify the equation for which this ratio is minimal, breaking ties arbitrarily. This is the pivot equation. The coefficient of the entering variable in this equation is the pivot value.

4. *Update the canonical equations.* First, update the equation corresponding to the leaving variable. Divide it through by the pivot value. Next, eliminate the entering variable from each other equation. To do so, subtract a multiple of the new pivot equation equal to the coefficient of the entering variable.

5. *Return to Step 1.*

---

which becomes the pivot equation. This calculation indicates that T can become as large as 120 without driving any of the current basic variables negative.

In Step 4, we create the new canonical equations with the following elementary row operations.

$$(A3.2c) = (A3.2b)/(2/3)$$
$$(A3.1c) = (A3.1) + 2(A3.2c)$$
$$(A3.3c) = (A3.3) - (2/3)(A3.2c)$$
$$(A3.0c) = (A3.0) + (2/3)(A3.2c)$$

These calculations yield the third set of canonical equations.

Set 3:
$$-32C \qquad\qquad +u \quad +3v \quad -5w \;=\; 800 \qquad (A3.1c)$$
$$-\frac{27}{2}C \qquad +T \qquad +\frac{3}{2}v \;-2w \;=\; 120 \qquad (A3.2c)$$
$$\frac{21}{2}C \;+D \qquad\qquad\qquad -2w \;=\; 160 \qquad (A3.3c)$$
$$z+5C \qquad\qquad\qquad +1v \;+2w \;=\; 4880 \qquad (A3.0c)$$

When we return to Step 1, we find that the optimality conditions hold: No negative coefficients appear in equation (A3.0c). The set of basic variables at this stage is $\{u, D, T\}$, and the solution corresponds to $D = 160$ and $T = 120$. We can also read the value of the slack variable, $u = 800$. This value is consistent with the solution of $C = 0, D = 160$, and $T = 120$, which uses only 1200 of the 2000 available hours in the fabrication

	A	B	C	D	E	F	G	H	I	J	
1	Simplex Tableau										
2											
3			C	D	T	u	v	w	RHS		Ratios
4	(A3.0)	-16	-20	-14	0	0	0	0		0	
5	(A3.1)	4	6	2	1				2000		333.3
6	(A3.2)	3	8	6		1			2000		250.0
7	(A3.3)	9	6	4			1		1440	*	240.0
8											
9											
10	(A3.0*)	14	0	-0.66667	0	0	3.333333		4800		
11	(A3.1*)	-5	0	-2	1	0	-1		560		-
12	(A3.2*)	-9	0	0.666667	0	1	-1.33333		80	*	120.0
13	(A3.3*)	1.5	1	0.666667	0	0	0.166667		240		360.0
14											
15											
16	(A3.0**)	5	0	0	0	1	2		4880		
17	(A3.1**)	-32	0	0	1	3	-5		800		
18	(A3.2**)	-13.5	0	1	0	1.5	-2		120		
19	(A3.3**)	10.5	1	0	0	-1	1.5		160		
20											

Tableau

Figure A3.1. Simplex tableau.

department. Thus, the algorithm terminates with an optimal solution, which attains an objective function value of $4880.

The calculations required by the simplex method are normally organized in tabular form, as illustrated in Figure A3.1 for our example. This layout is known as a *simplex tableau*, and in our example, the tableau consists of four rows for each iteration, each row corresponding to an equation of canonical form. The columns of the tableau correspond to the decision variables, the slack variables, and the RHS constants. The body of the tableau contains the coefficients of the equations used in the algorithm. To the right of the tableau, in column J, we display the ratio calculations of Step 3, with the minimum ratio flagged in column I. The figure shows all three iterations of the procedure as an alternative representation of the three canonical equation sets: set 1, set 2, and set 3.

A3.2. VARIATIONS OF THE ALGORITHM

The simplex method as illustrated here works for maximization problems, given that we start with a basic feasible solution. From the starting solution, the procedure moves inexorably toward an optimal solution because each basic feasible solution encountered is better than the previous one. The relevant theory confirms that an optimum can be found by examining only basic feasible solutions and that improvement (suitably defined) occurs at each iteration. The details of the theory, however, are beyond the scope of this appendix (1,2).

For minimization problems, the steps would be the same, except that the optimality condition would require that all coefficients in the objective function must be nonpositive. The selection of the entry variable relates to the direction of optimization: Negative coefficients signal the potential for improvement in a maximization problem, and positive coefficients signal the potential for improvement in a minimization problem. The selection of the leaving variable relates only to feasibility: The minimum ratio identifies the equation containing the leaving variable, thereby assuring that the new set of basic variables remains nonnegative. Therefore, the selection criterion is the same for minimization and maximization. One additional feature is worth noting. When no positive coefficients appear in the column for the entering variable (that is, when there are no ratios to be formed), this pattern indicates that the solution is unbounded. In other words, by making the entering variable positive—and as large as we wish—we generate a value of the objective function as large as we wish. Therefore, the objective is unbounded. If Solver encounters no positive coefficients in the column for the entering variable, it reports that the objective function is unbounded.

As described in Box A3.1, the simplex method produces an optimal solution, provided that we can initiate it with a basic feasible solution. This is not a difficult task when all the constraints are LT constraints and their right-hand sides are positive, as demonstrated in the example. A slack variable is added to each constraint in order to convert the inequality to an equation, and then all variables other than the slack variables are set equal to zero. The slack variables appear one in each constraint, and each with a coefficient of 1, so they form a natural starting basic feasible solution. But what happens when the problem does not come with LT constraints?

Suppose instead we have a linear programming problem in which all constraints are equations in the original model, and in which all constraint constants are nonnegative. Now we add one variable to each equation with a coefficient of 1. These are called *artificial variables*. They resemble slack variables in that they allow us to form an initial basic feasible solution. They differ from slack variables in one important way: Whereas slack variables may remain positive throughout the various iterations of the simplex algorithm, and even in the optimal solution, artificial variables must all be driven to zero to feasibly satisfy the original constraints. This feature allows the simplex method to be implemented in two phases. In phase I, as it is called, the objective is to minimize the sum of the artificial variables. At the end of this phase, the solution on hand must be a basic feasible solution for the original problem. From that solution, we enter phase II, returning to the original objective function and following the steps outlined in Box A3.1 in order to reach an optimum.

The so-called two-phase simplex method has another feature. If phase I cannot reach an objective function with value zero—that is, if it is impossible to drive all artificial variables to zero, then we know that no feasible solution exists. Thus, a failure of phase I prompts Solver to display the message that it could not find a feasible solution; it is a systematic procedure for detecting inconsistency among the constraints of a model.

Having addressed EQ constraints, suppose now we have a problem in which all constraints are GT constraints with RHS constants that are nonnegative. We handle GT constraints by converting them to equations and inserting two variables, an artificial variable and a surplus variable. Just as a slack variable converts an LT constraint to an equality by measuring the amount by which right-hand side exceeds left-hand side, a surplus variable converts a GT constraint to an equality by measuring the amount by which left-hand side exceeds right-hand side. In phase I of the algorithm, we start by using the artificial variables to make up a basic feasible solution, and we attempt to drive them all to zero. Assuming we succeed, we may find that we have surplus variables at positive amounts throughout phase II, wherever GT constraints are not binding.

For example, suppose our original model contains the following GT constraints.

$$A1 + B1 + C1 + D1 + E1 + F1 \geq 1$$
$$A2 + B2 + C2 + D2 + E2 + F2 \geq 1$$
$$A3 + B3 + C3 + D3 + E3 + F3 \geq 1$$
$$A4 + B4 + C4 + D4 + E4 + F4 \geq 1$$
$$A5 + B5 + C5 + D5 + E5 + F5 \geq 1$$
$$A6 + B6 + C6 + D6 + E6 + F6 \geq 1$$

Because there are six GT constraints, we must insert six artificial variables ($a_1 - a_6$) and six surplus variables ($s_1 - s_6$). The equations take the following form.

$$A1 + B1 + C1 + D1 + E1 + F1 + a_1 - s_1 = 1$$
$$A2 + B2 + C2 + D2 + E2 + F2 + a_2 - s_2 = 1$$
$$A3 + B3 + C3 + D3 + E3 + F3 + a_3 - s_3 = 1$$
$$A4 + B4 + C4 + D4 + E4 + F4 + a_4 - s_4 = 1$$
$$A5 + B5 + C5 + D5 + E5 + F5 + a_5 - s_5 = 1$$
$$A6 + B6 + C6 + D6 + E6 + F6 + a_6 - s_6 = 1$$

The first basic feasible solution contains all of the artificial variables $a_1 = a_2 = \cdots = a_6 = 1$. This solution is sufficient to initiate phase I. From that point on, we can use iterations of the simplex method, as outlined in Box A3.1, to find an optimum if one exists, or to prove that there is no feasible solution.

Although we have discussed cases in which all constraints were LT or all were EQ or all were GT, the principles apply to the constraints individually. Thus, in any linear programming model, we convert the constraints to equations suitable for the simplex method by

- inserting a slack variable into each LT constraint,
- inserting an artificial variable into each EQ constraint,
- inserting an artificial variable and a surplus variable into each GT constraint.

Before doing so, we want to make sure that each constraint has a RHS value that is nonnegative. Thus, if any constraint in the original model has a negative RHS value, we first multiply through by -1 (and if it is an inequality, change the direction of the inequality) before converting it to an equation.

In summary, the variations within the simplex algorithm allow for systematic treatment of all linear programming models. Phase I can detect infeasible sets of constraints, and phase II can detect unbounded objective functions. If those conditions fail, the algorithm proceeds to an optimal solution.

REFERENCES

1. WINSTON, W.L. and VENKATARAMANAN, M. *Introduction to Mathematical Programming*. Brooks/Cole, Pacific Grove, CA, 2003.
2. RARDIN, R. *Optimization in Operations Research*. Prentice-Hall, Upper Saddle River, NJ, 1998.

Appendix 4

Stochastic Programming

For the most part, the optimization problems covered in this book are deterministic. In other words, parameters are assumed known, and nothing about the problem is subject to uncertainty. In practice, problems may come to us with uncertain elements, but we often suppress the randomness when we build an optimization model. Quite often, this simplification is justified because the random elements in the model are not as critical as the main optimization structure. However, it is important to know that the techniques we develop are not limited to deterministic applications. Here, we show how to extend the concepts of linear programming to decision problems that are inherently probabilistic. This class of problems is generally called *stochastic programming*.

A4.1. ONE-STAGE DECISIONS WITH UNCERTAINTY

We can think of stochastic programming models as generalizations of the deterministic case. To demonstrate the relevant concepts, we examine probabilistic variations of a simple allocation problem.

EXAMPLE A4.1   *General Appliance Company*

General Appliance Company (GAC) manufactures two refrigerator models. Each refrigerator requires a specified amount of work to be done in three departments, and each department has limited capacity. The Standard refrigerator model is sold nationwide to several retailers who place their orders each month. In a given month, demand for the Standard model is subject to random variation. Demand for the Deluxe model comes from a single, large retail chain which requires delivery of 25 units each month but is willing to take more refrigerators if more can be delivered. At current prices, the unit profit contribution is $50 for each Standard model and $30 for each Deluxe model. The data shown below summarize the parameters of the problem.

Optimization Modeling with Spreadsheets, *Second Edition*. Kenneth R. Baker
© 2011 John Wiley & Sons, Inc. Published 2011 by John Wiley & Sons, Inc.

	Requirements per unit		
	STD	*DLX*	Hours available
Department 1 (hrs)	4	4	600
Department 2 (hrs)	3	2	400
Department 3 (hrs)	2	4	500
Profit per unit	$50	$40	

The Operations Manager at General Appliance would like to maximize profit contribution for the month by choosing production quantities for the two models.   ■

To formulate an optimization model for this scenario, let variables *STD* and *DLX* represent the number of Standard and Deluxe models produced (and sold). If we represent the demand for the Standard model by *X*, we can formulate the optimization problem for GAC as follows.

$$\text{Maximize } z = 50\,STD + 30\,DLX$$

subject to

$$4\,STD + 4\,DLX \leq 600$$
$$3\,STD + 2\,DLX \leq 400$$
$$2\,STD + 4\,DLX \leq 500$$
$$STD \quad\quad \leq\ X$$
$$DLX \geq\ 25$$

Thus, for any value of *X*, we can solve the optimization problem and determine the optimal production quantities of *STD* and *DLX*.

In probability language, the possible demand scenarios are called *states of nature* (or simply *states*), to indicate that the conditions are beyond our control. A *probability distribution* lists the possible states and associates a probability with each state. (For convenience, we'll number the states.) In our example, we might have some market intelligence that leads us to adopt the following probability distribution.

State	1	2	3
Demand	80	104	160
Probability	0.2	0.5	0.3

Our optimization model takes three forms, depending on which state occurs. For state 1, the optimal output mix is 80 Standard models and 70 Deluxe models. For state 2, the optimal output mix is 104 Standard models and 44 Deluxe models. Finally, for state 3, the optimal output mix is 116.7 Standard models and 25 Deluxe models.

If we could learn the demand state in advance, we could determine the optimal production quantity by solving the linear program with the appropriate demand parameter. The crux of the problem, however, is that the production decision must be determined *before* demand is known. Because we decide on production before demand is resolved, there may be a difference between the quantity produced and the quantity sold to retailers. (In the deterministic model, this difference does not arise because feasible production quantities are sure to be sold.) The probabilistic scenario forces us to consider what happens when production and sales don't match.

For the purposes of our example, suppose that GAC can sell its excess inventory through a discount channel and earn a profit contribution of $15. Now, we must distinguish between the number of items produced and the number sold in each channel, since those can differ when demand is stochastic. Thus, we introduce the variable $SS1$ to represent the number of Standard models sold to retailers in state 1 and $SX1$ to represent the number of excess Standard models (sold to the discounter) in state 1. Then, our model requires two constraints.

$$SS1 \leq 80$$
$$STD - SS1 - SX1 = 0$$

If production exceeds the demand of 80, then the first constraint limits retail sales to demand, while the second constraint sets the excess equal to the difference between production and retail sales. On the other hand, if demand exceeds production, then the second constraint limits sales to production. (The excess quantity will then be zero, because retail sales are more profitable than discount sales.) We do not need to track the excess Deluxe models because all units of the Deluxe will be sold.

A similar set of constraint pairs is required for the other states.

State 2
$$SS2 \leq 104$$
$$STD - SS2 - SX2 = 0$$

State 3
$$SS3 \leq 160$$
$$STD - SS3 - SX3 = 0$$

Finally, we must account for the profits in a consistent manner, recognizing that sales levels depend on which state occurs. For state 1, the objective function can be expressed as follows.

$$Z1 = 50SS1 + 15SX1 + 30DLX$$

Rearranging terms

$$50SS1 + 15SX1 + 30DLX - Z1 = 0$$

We next add this equality constraint to the model, as a means of defining Z1 internally. For the other two states, we insert similar equalities.

$$50SS2 + 15SX2 + 30DLX - Z2 = 0$$
$$50SS3 + 15SX3 + 30DLX - Z3 = 0$$

Guided by the theory of decision making under uncertainty, our objective is to maximize the expected value of profit. Having accounted separately for the profit in each state, we can compute this expected value as a probability-weighted average, using the following formula.

$$z = 0.2Z1 + 0.5Z2 + 0.3Z3$$

This expression is linear, as are all of the additional constraints, so when we include them in our model, we still have a linear programming problem. The full spreadsheet model is displayed in Figure A4.1. The constraints have been organized into four sets. The first set of (three) constraints carries over from the original model and includes the production decisions, which must be determined before the uncertainty about demand gets resolved. The next set of four constraints corresponds to state 1, the following set of four constraints corresponds to state 2 and the final set of four constraints corresponds to state 3. The expected value of profit appears in the objective function.

Recall that the original deterministic model contained five constraints and two variables. This new model contains 15 constraints and 11 variables, somewhat more than in the original model. But these values depend directly on the number of outcomes in our probability model. Had we represented demand with ten outcomes instead of three, the model would contain 43 constraints and 25 variables.

Although we can reduce the problem size slightly by substituting for the profit variables *Z*1, *Z*2, and *Z*3, the model is more transparent if the profit measure is tracked separately for each state and then simply weighted in the objective function to show the expected value calculation clearly. This is one of our design principles for stochastic programming models.

	A	B	C	D	E	F	G	H	I	J	K	L	M	N	O
1	**Production Decisions under Uncertainty**														
2															
3	**Decisions**	STD	DLX	SS1	SX1	SS2	SX2	SS3	SX3	Z1	Z2	Z3			
4		100	50	80	20	100	0	100	0	5800	6500	6500			
5															
6	**Objective**									0.2	0.5	0.3	6360		
7															
8	**Constraints**	4	4										600.0	<=	600
9		3	2										400.0	<=	400
10		2	4										400.0	<=	500
11	State 1			1									80.0	<=	80
12			1										50.0	>=	25
13		1		-1	-1								0.0	=	0
14			30	50	15					-1			0.0	=	0
15	State 2					1							100.0	<=	104
16			1										50.0	>=	25
17		1				-1	-1						0.0	=	0
18			30			50	15				-1		0.0	=	0
19	State 3							1					100.0	<=	160
20			1										50.0	>=	25
21		1						-1	-1				0.0	=	0
22			30					50	15			-1	0.0	=	0
23															

ProbModel

Figure A4.1. Stochastic program for Example A4.1.

A second principle is to modularize the linear programming formulation by gathering together the constraints that correspond to a given state. In our example, that meant appending three constraint modules to the basic production-hours constraints. Because the problem is stochastic, targets that might be met in one state may lead to surplus or shortage in another state, so we must introduce additional variables to track the consequences.

Finally, a third principle illustrated by our example spreadsheet is that the initial decision variables reappear in each of the modules. In particular, the production decision variables *STD* and *DLX* occur in the relevant demand constraints within each of the three modules.

The optimal solution to the model, which achieves an expected profit of $6360, is displayed in Figure A4.1. The optimal production mix is 100 Standard models and 50 Deluxe models, which corresponds to none of the output mixes produced by the model for the individual scenarios.

The production of 100 Standard models and 50 Deluxe models represents a policy that recognizes the risks due to uncertain demand. Under state 1, we have excess Standard models and must accept the lower profit in the discount channel for some of our output. On the other hand, under state 3, and to some extent under state 2, we have a shortage of Standard models and must accept the lower profit from selling Deluxe models instead. It would be feasible to produce a larger number of Deluxe models, and those additional models would be certain to sell. But the profit available from this strategy would not offset the expected losses that would occur from producing fewer Standard models because of limited resources. The need to balance the risks arises because we have only one decision period. A two-period scenario is discussed next.

A4.2. TWO-STAGE DECISIONS WITH UNCERTAINTY

In the one-stage model, a decision is made, and then the uncertain state is revealed. At that point, all conditions are determined, and the economic consequences can be computed. A more general structure is a two-stage model, which contains some opportunity to react to the uncertainty. The technical term for this structure is *stochastic programming with recourse*. Again, we illustrate the principles with a modification of Example A4.2.

EXAMPLE A4.2   *General Appliance Company (continued)*

Although monthly demand at GAC is uncertain, the uncertainty is resolved about half way through the month. At that point, it is still possible to alter production plans slightly. In particular, GAC can reschedule during the last week of the month, enough to raise the available hours in each department by 12 percent. Now, the Operations Manager faces a decision involving possible rescheduling as well as determining the output mix. ∎

The addition to monthly capacity can be implemented after the demand state has been resolved. Thus, 72 additional hours can be brought on line in department 1, 48 additional hours in department 2, and 56 more in department 3. (The production capability might come, for example, from an opportunity to schedule some unplanned overtime or simply by reassigning personnel.) How does this new opportunity affect the decision?

As before, an initial production decision must be made before the demand state is known. Should the level of demand be higher than expected, however, there is still an opportunity to produce additional items, perhaps to fill the gap between the initial production and the newly determined demand, or else to take advantage of the additional capacity. In this second round of production decisions no uncertainty exists, and we can proceed as if we were in a deterministic environment.

The analysis builds on the previous example. One new feature is an additional set of production decisions corresponding to the second-stage. Thus, we define $STD1$ and $DLX1$ as the Standard and Deluxe production quantities made with the additional hours in the case of state 1. Similarly, $STD2$ and $DLX2$ represent the additional production quantities for state 2, and $STD3$ and $DLX3$ represent the additional production quantities for state 3.

Suppose that state 1 occurs after initial production decisions have been made. The second-stage decision problem calls for choosing $STD1$ and $DLX1$ subject to three resource constraints and the need to track any surplus that might occur. The module of resource constraints takes the following form.

$$4\,STD1 + 4\,DLX1 \leq 72$$
$$3\,STD1 + 2\,DLX1 \leq 48$$
$$2\,STD1 + 4\,DLX1 \leq 56$$

Next, with the second-stage production variables defined, we can modify the definitional constraints of the one-stage example and add the following equations for the state 1.

$$
\begin{aligned}
STD + STD1 - SX1 - SS1 &= 0 \\
SS1 &\leq 80 \\
DLX + DLX1 &\geq 25
\end{aligned}
$$

Similar constraints apply to the other states.

State 2
$$
\begin{aligned}
STD + STD2 - SX2 - SS2 &= 0 \\
SS2 &\leq 104 \\
DLX + DLX2 &\geq 25
\end{aligned}
$$

State 3
$$
\begin{aligned}
STD + STD3 - SX3 - SS3 &= 0 \\
SS3 &\leq 160 \\
DLX + DLX3 &\geq 25
\end{aligned}
$$

Finally, as in the previous example, we can capture the profits in auxiliary variables.

$$50SS1 + 15SX1 + 30DLX + 30DLX1 - Z1 = 0$$
$$50SS2 + 15SX2 + 30DLX + 30DLX2 - Z2 = 0$$
$$50SS3 + 15SX3 + 30DLX + 30DLX3 - Z3 = 0$$

The entire model is shown in the spreadsheet of Figure A4.2. Here, again, the model contains four modules, three of which correspond to the three demand states. However, these are larger modules than in the one-stage example because of the second production opportunity. For the two-stage model, we have 24 constraints and 17 decision variables. Again, the model's size depends on the number of states; with ten states, our model would have 73 constraints and 45 decision variables.

Before we discuss the solution to the problem, we reiterate the three design features shown in Figure A4.2.

- A constraint module corresponds to each state.
- The first-stage decisions appear in each of the modules corresponding to states.
- Separate accounting is done for each of the objective function components that correspond to states.
- The objective function components are weighted by probabilities to construct the overall expected value for the objective.

The solution displayed in Figure A4.2 has a complicated but logical pattern. The initial production quantities are 98 Standard models and 52 Deluxe models. If state 1 occurs, the number of Standard models is already larger than demand, so additional capacity will be devoted exclusively to 15 Deluxe models, bringing the total output levels to 98 and 67. If state 2 occurs, the additional capacity will be used to bring the number of Standard models up to retail demand and to add to the number of Deluxe models, bringing the total output levels to 104 and 64. If state 3 occurs, the additional capacity will be devoted exclusively to Standard models to the extent available hours permit, bringing the totals to 114 and 52.

Thus, the initial production quantities leave several options open, and the optimal plan takes one of three directions depending on the demand state. The expected profit under the optimal plan is about $6994. By comparison, suppose we were to expand the model in Figure A4.1 to reflect the full 112 percent capacity levels. The optimal solution to that model (which has no recourse structure) achieves an expected profit of only $6,952. Therefore, the ability to tailor our second-stage reactions to the stochastic outcome allows us to achieve the greater profit level.

For another comparison, imagine that we could learn the demand state first and then respond with a single production plan that had access to the incremental 12 percent capacity. For that situation, the expected profit (based on probabilities of 0.2, 0.5, and 0.3 for the three states, respectively) turns out to be $7103. It would always be preferable to resolve uncertainty before making a production decision,

Production Decisions under Uncertainty (with recourse)

	STD	DLX	STD1	DLX1	STD2	DLX2	STD3	DLX3	SS1	SX1	SS2	SX2	SS3	SX3	Z1	Z2	Z3			
Decisions	98	52	0	15	6	12	16	0	80	18	104	0	114	0	6280	7120	7260			
Objective															0.2	0.5	0.3	6994		
Constraints	4	4																600	<=	600
	3	2																398	<=	400
	2	4																404	<=	500
			4	4														60	<=	72
			3	2														30	<=	48
			2	4														60	<=	60
	1		1						-1	-1								0	=	0
									1									80	<=	80
		1		1														67	>=	25
		30		30					50	15					-1			0	=	0
					4	4												72	<=	72
					3	2												42	<=	48
					2	4												60	<=	60
	1				1						-1	-1						0	=	0
											1							104	<=	104
		1				1												64	>=	25
		30				30					50	15				-1		0	=	0
							4	4										64	<=	72
							3	2										48	<=	48
							2	4										32	<=	60
	1						1						-1	-1				0	=	0
													1					114	<=	160
		1						1										52	>=	25
		30						30					50	15			-1	0	=	0

Recourse

Figure A4.2. Stochastic program with recourse for Example A4.2.

but in this case, there is sufficient flexibility in the two-stage structure that the expected profit is only about $109 lower for having to make the major decisions without knowing demand for sure. This low figure depends, of course, on the parameters of the example, but it does suggest that the two-stage structure affords considerable flexibility. Stochastic programming enables us to quantify this kind of flexibility.

A4.3. USING SOLVER

As described in Section A4.2, the optimization model for stochastic programming with recourse can be viewed as an expanded linear program, with explicit treatment of each random state. The expanded linear program can be developed and optimized by running Solver. But keep in mind that our example contained essentially just five constraints and two variables, only one of which was subject to uncertainty. Moreover, that uncertainty was expressed in the form of a discrete probability distribution with just three outcomes. For that small problem, the stochastic program was 24 by 17. Stochastic programming models can become quite large, and constructing them can be tedious and error-prone. We might wonder whether some of the modeling task can be automated.

Risk Solver Platform has specialized capabilities for solving stochastic programs, but to describe those capabilities, we must first examine its representation of probabilistic outcomes. RSP is an integrated software tool that uses probability distributions in simulation models. A design feature in RSP is that only one simulation model can be supported in a given workbook. Therefore, in building a stochastic programming model, or any simulation model, we should make sure that if our workbook contains other worksheets, they do not contain probability distributions. (By contrast, RSP supports one optimization model per worksheet.)

Suppose, for example, that we wish to construct a cell that behaves like demand for Standard models in Example A4.1. The relevant type of distribution in Solver is the Discrete distribution, which we can access from the RSP ribbon via the Simulation Model group of commands. Choose a cell to contain the demand model and select Distributions ► Custom ► Discrete. The Discrete distribution window offers the opportunity to specify *values* and *weights*, which are equivalent to outcomes and relative probabilities. For our example of demand for Standard refrigerators, the values would be {80, 104, 160} and the weights would be {0.2, 0.5, 0.3}. Entering these values produces the display shown in Figure A4.3.

By specifying the probability distribution for demand, we allow Solver to draw samples from this distribution for the purposes of simulation. In general, a simulation sample may not necessarily represent the relative probabilities in a distribution faithfully. In our example, if we draw 10 samples, we expect to obtain the value 80 about a fifth of the time, which means twice. But in Monte Carlo sampling, we may draw the

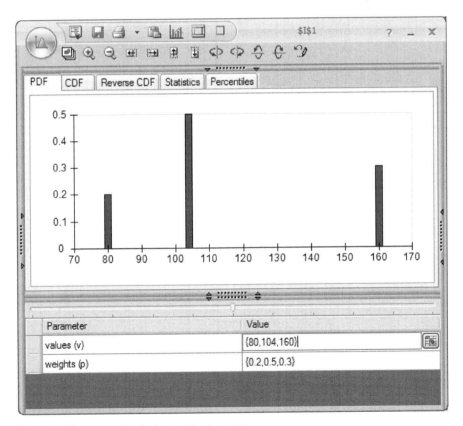

Figure A4.3. Discrete distribution in risk solver platform.

	A	B	C	D	E	F	G	H	I	J
1	Production									
2										
3	Decisions	STD	DLX	S2	D2	SS	SX			
4		98	52	0	15	80	18			
5										
6	Objective	0	30	0	30	50	15	6280		
7										
8	Constraints	4	4					600	<=	600
9		3	2					398	<=	400
10		2	4					404	<=	500
11	Stage 2			4	4			60	<=	72
12				3	2			30	<=	48
13				2	4			60	<=	60
14						1		80	<=	80
15			1		1			67	>=	25
16		1		1		-1	-1	0	=	0
17										

DetEq

Figure A4.4. Solver model for the stochastic program of Example A4.2.

value 80 just once, or perhaps three times. Only in a large sample can we depend on drawing the value 80 about 20 percent of the time. However, we can make the outcomes conform much more closely to the given distribution by invoking Latin Hypercube sampling. (This option can be selected by from the drop-down menu for Options: select All Options and then select the Latin Hypercube radio button under Sampling Method. In the same window, select All Trials as the Value to Display, and set Trials per Simulation equal to 10.) Under Latin Hypercube sampling, a sample of ten draws from the distribution will contain 80 twice, 104 five times, and 160 three times, conforming precisely to the frequencies in the given probability model.

Because Solver has the capability of representing discrete probability models as simulated outcomes, the stochastic program can be represented efficiently on a spreadsheet. The recourse variables need only be represented once in the model. The spreadsheet model for Example A4.2 is shown in Figure A4.4.

In the spreadsheet model, the original variables are *STD* and *DLX*, as before. The second stage decision variables are *S2* and *D2*, representing the quantities produced using the 12 percent resource capability at the second stage, and *SS* and *SX*, as before, represent the number of Standard models sold to retailers and the number of excess Standard models (sold to discounters). These last four decision variables are designated Recourse variables in specifying the model elements in the task pane. In addition, the demand distribution is imbedded in cell J14.

The worksheet has only one explicit representation of the second stage, but Solver can sample (10 times) for the value in cell J14, following the probability distribution.[1] Thus, Solver actually solves the problem two times with the demand outcome of 80 in

---

[1] To obtain the optimal solution, we must set the Stochastic Transformation option on the Platform tab of the task pane either to Deterministic Equivalent or to Automatic.

cell J14, five times with 104, and three times with 160. The corresponding optimal solutions are stored and can be retrieved by clicking on the arrows in the Tools group on the ribbon. When the number showing between the arrows is 1, the optimal solution corresponding to the first simulation sample is displayed. When the number showing is 2, the second sample is displayed, and so on. By clicking through the 10 outcomes, we can verify that three sets of decisions appear, according to the demand outcome. These sets of decisions, taken from row 4 of the worksheet, are summarized in the table below.

Demand	STD	DLX	S2	D2	SS	SX
80	98	52	0	15	80	18
104	98	52	6	12	104	0
160	98	52	16	0	114	0

These results match those in Figure A4.2. However, the table layout makes it clearer that the first-stage production quantities are 98 Standard models and 52 Deluxe models, but the second-stage quantities depend on the demand outcome.

Finally, the expected-value objective function is not explicit in the worksheet for Solver. However, to find the optimal value of the objective function, we can go to the drop-down menu between the two arrows in the Tools group and select Sample Mean. In place of the simulation trial number, the letter μ appears. In addition the objective function cell and the decision variable cells also display averages over the sample outcomes. In the case of the objective function, the mean value corresponds to the optimal value of the transformed model, in this case, $6994.

Stochastic programming can be a powerful form of analysis. It allows us to address issues of uncertainty instead of making deterministic simplifications. And in the case of stochastic programming models with recourse, the solution helps us tailor our responses to uncertain outcomes. However, there is a modeling cost for this capability. Whereas a deterministic description allows us to meet targets exactly, it is not possible to be as specific in a probabilistic setting. Instead, we may have to invent variables to measure the surplus and shortage outcomes that occur when uncertain factors are present. These new variables become part of a more complicated view of the problem than we captured in the original, deterministic model. In addition, we have to come up with a reasonable probability model for the uncertain elements of the problem. In our example, we illustrated the use of a simple discrete distribution with only three outcomes. In many cases, three outcomes might not be sufficient to provide a meaningful description of the uncertainty. However, as we add outcomes to the probability model, we expand the size of the model by requiring additional sets of variables and constraints. Thus, accommodating even one source of uncertainty can lead to an order of magnitude expansion in the size of the model. Modeling multiple sources compounds this complexity. For these reasons, stochastic programming models are still not widely used, but now that Solver can provide solutions, that situation may change.

Index

Optimization Modeling with Spreadsheets, *Second Edition*. Kenneth R. Baker
© 2011 John Wiley & Sons, Inc. Published 2011 by John Wiley & Sons, Inc.